Negotiating Censorship in Modern Japan

Censorship in Japan has seen many changes over the last 150 years and each successive system of rule has possessed its own censorship laws, regulations and methods of enforcement. Yet what has remained constant through these many upheavals has been the process of negotiation between censor and artist that can be seen across the cultural media of modern society.

By exploring censorship in a number of different Japanese art forms – from popular music and kabuki performance through to fiction, poetry and film – across a range of historical periods, this book provides a striking picture of the pervasiveness and strength of Japanese censorship across a range of media; the similar tactics used by artists of different media to negotiate censorship boundaries; and how censors from different systems and time periods face many of the same problems and questions in their work. The essays in this collection highlight the complexities of the censorship process by investigating the responsibilities and choices of artists, censors, audience and ideologues, in a wide range of case studies. The contributors shift the focus away from top-down suppression, towards the more complex negotiations involved in the many stages of an artistic work, all of which involve movement within boundaries, as well as testing of those boundaries, on the part of both artist and censor. Taken together, the essays in this book demonstrate that censorship at every stage involves an act of human judgment, in a context determined by political, economic and ideological factors.

This book and its case studies provide a fascinating insight into the dynamics of censorship and how these operate on both people and texts. As such, it will be of great interest to students and scholars interested in Japanese studies, Japanese culture, society and history, and media studies more generally.

Rachael Hutchinson is an Associate Professor in Japanese Studies at the University of Delaware, USA.

Routledge contemporary Japan series

1 **A Japanese Company in Crisis**
Ideology, strategy, and narrative
Fiona Graham

2 **Japan's Foreign Aid**
Old continuities and new
directions
Edited by David Arase

3 **Japanese Apologies for World
War II**
A rhetorical study
Jane W. Yamazaki

4 **Linguistic Stereotyping and
Minority Groups in Japan**
Nanette Gottlieb

5 **Shinkansen**
From bullet train to symbol of
modern Japan
Christopher P. Hood

6 **Small Firms and Innovation
Policy in Japan**
Edited by Cornelia Storz

7 **Cities, Autonomy and
Decentralization in Japan**
*Edited by Carola Hein and
Philippe Pelletier*

8 **The Changing Japanese Family**
*Edited by Marcus Rebick and
Ayumi Takenaka*

9 **Adoption in Japan**
Comparing policies for children in
need
Peter Hayes and Toshie Habu

10 **The Ethics of Aesthetics in
Japanese Cinema and Literature**
Polygraphic desire
Nina Cornyetz

11 **Institutional and Technological
Change in Japan's Economy**
Past and present
*Edited by Janet Hunter and
Cornelia Storz*

12 **Political Reform in Japan**
Leadership Looming Large
Alisa Gaunder

13 **Civil Society and the Internet in
Japan**
Isa Ducke

14 **Japan's Contested War
Memories**
The 'memory rifts' in historical
consciousness of World War II
Philip A. Seaton

15 **Japanese Love Hotels**
A cultural history
Sarah Chaplin

16 **Population Decline and Ageing in Japan – The Social Consequences**
Florian Coulmas

17 ***Zainichi* Korean Identity and Ethnicity**
David Chapman

18 **A Japanese Joint Venture in the Pacific**
Foreign bodies in tinned tuna
Kate Barclay

19 **Japanese–Russian Relations, 1907–2007**
Joseph P. Ferguson

20 **War Memory, Nationalism and Education in Post-War Japan, 1945–2007**
The Japanese history textbook controversy and Ienaga Saburo's court challenges
Yoshiko Nozaki

21 **A New Japan for the Twenty-First Century**
An inside overview of current fundamental changes and problems
Edited by Rien T. Segers

22 **A Life Adrift**
Soeda Azembo, popular song and modern mass culture in Japan
Translated by Michael Lewis

23 **The Novels of Oe Kenzaburo**
Yasuko Claremont

24 **Perversion in Modern Japan**
Psychoanalysis, literature, culture
Edited by Nina Cornyetz and J. Keith Vincent

25 **Homosexuality and Manliness in Postwar Japan**
Jonathan D. Mackintosh

26 **Marriage in Contemporary Japan**
Yoko Tokuhiro

27 **Japanese Aid and the Construction of Global Development**
Inescapable solutions
Edited by David Leheny and Carol Warren

28 **The Rise of Japanese NGOs**
Activism from above
Kim D. Reimann

29 **Postwar History Education in Japan and the Germanys**
Guilty lessons
Julian Dierkes

30 **Japan-Bashing**
Anti-Japanism since the 1980s
Narelle Morris

31 **Legacies of the Asia-Pacific War**
The Yakeato generation
Edited by Roman Rosenbaum and Yasuko Claremont

32 **Challenges of Human Resource Management in Japan**
Edited by Ralf Bebenroth and Toshihiro Kanai

33 **Translation in Modern Japan**
Edited by Indra Levy

34 **Language Life in Japan**
Transformations and prospects
Edited by Patrick Heinrich and Christian Galan

35 **The Quest for Japan's New Constitution**
An analysis of visions and constitutional reform proposals 1980–2009
Christian G. Winkler

36 **Japan in the Age of Globalization**
Edited by Carin Holroyd and Ken Coates

37 **Social Networks and Japanese Democracy**
The beneficial impact of interpersonal communication in East Asia
Ken'ichi Ikeda and Sean Richey

38 **Dealing with Disaster in Japan**
Responses to the Flight JL123 crash
Christopher P. Hood

39 **The Ethics of Japan's Global Environmental Policy**
The conflict between principles and practice
Midori Kagawa-Fox

40 **Superhuman Japan**
Knowledge, nation and culture in US–Japan relations
Marie Thorsten

41 **Nationalism, Realism and Democracy in Japan**
The thought of Masao Maruyama
Fumiko Sasaki

42 **Japan's Local Newspapers**
Chihōshi and revitalization journalism
Anthony S. Rausch

43 **Mental Health Care in Japan**
Edited by Ruth Taplin and Sandra J. Lawman

44 **Manga and the Representation of Japanese History**
Edited by Roman Rosenbaum

45 **Negotiating Censorship in Modern Japan**
Edited by Rachael Hutchinson

Negotiating Censorship in Modern Japan

Edited by Rachael Hutchinson

LONDON AND NEW YORK

First published 2013
by Routledge
2 Park Square, Milton Park, Abingdon, Oxfordshire OX14 4RN

Simultaneously published in the USA and Canada
by Routledge
711 Third Avenue, New York, NY 10017

First issued in paperback 2015

Routledge is an imprint of the Taylor & Francis Group, an informa business

© 2013 selection and editorial material, Rachael Hutchinson; individual
chapters, the contributors

The right of Rachael Hutchinson to be identified as the author of the
editorial material, and of the authors for their individual chapters, has been
asserted in accordance with sections 77 and 78 of the Copyright, Designs
and Patents Act 1988.

All rights reserved. No part of this book may be reprinted or reproduced or
utilized in any form or by any electronic, mechanical, or other means, now
known or hereafter invented, including photocopying and recording, or in
any information storage or retrieval system, without permission in writing
from the publishers.

Trademark notice: Product or corporate names may be trademarks or
registered trademarks, and are used only for identification and explanation
without intent to infringe.

British Library Cataloguing in Publication Data
A catalogue record for this book is available from the British Library

Library of Congress Cataloging in Publication Data
    p. cm. – (Routledge contemporary Japan series)
    Includes bibliographical references and index.
    1. Censorship–Japan–History–20th century. 2. Japanese literature–20th
    century–History and criticism. 3. Prohibited books–Japan–History–20th
    century. 4. Literature and state–Japan–History–20th century. 5.
    Freedom of information–Japan. I. Hutchinson, Rachael.
    Z658.J3N46 2013
    363.310952'0904–dc23   2012038149

ISBN13: 978-1-138-93471-9 (pbk)
ISBN13: 978-0-415-52078-2 (hbk)

Typeset in Times New Roman
by Wearset Ltd, Boldon, Tyne and Wear

Contents

List of figures		ix
Notes on contributors		x
Acknowledgments		xiii

1 **Introduction: negotiating censorship in modern Japan**   1
RACHAEL HUTCHINSON

2 **Censorship and patronage in Meiji kabuki theater**   13
RACHEL PAYNE

3 **Seditious obscenity/obscene seditions: the radical eroticism**
of Umehara Hokumei   35
JONATHAN ABEL

4 **The censor as critic: Ogawa Chikagorō and popular music**
censorship in imperial Japan   58
HIROMU NAGAHARA

5 **Kawabata's wartime message in *Beautiful Voyage***
(*Utsukushii tabi*)   74
HIROMI TSUCHIYA DOLLASE

6 **Banned books in the hands of Japanese librarians: from**
Meiji to postwar   93
SHARON H. DOMIER

7 **Self-censorship: the case of wartime Japanese poetry**   112
LEITH MORTON

viii *Contents*

8 Kurosawa Akira's *One Wonderful Sunday*: censorship, context and counter-discursive film 133
RACHAEL HUTCHINSON

9 Censoring Tamura Taijirō's *Biography of a Prostitute* (*Shunpuden*) 153
ELEANOR KERKHAM

10 Censoring imperial honorifics: a linguistic analysis of Occupation censorship in newspapers and literature 176
NORIKO AKIMOTO SUGIMORI

11 'Art' il-legally defined? A legal and art historical analysis of Akasegawa Genpei's Model Thousand-yen Note Incident 195
YAYOI SHIONOIRI

12 Parodying the censor and censoring parody in modern Japan 211
KIRSTEN CATHER

Index 231

Figures

3.1 A cover of *Arts Market*, mapping the tortuous path a publication must follow through the censorship process   41
5.1 Comparison of Nakahara Jun'ichi's illustration for *Beautiful Voyage* and Hatsuyama Shigeru's illustration from the next issue   81
5.2 *Beautiful Voyage* illustrated by Fukiya Kōji, showing a 'composition delegation' formed by ten children of different ethnic backgrounds   87
6.1 The cover of a catalog of books put into protective custody by the Fukagawa Public Library   100
6.2 The sticker on the *Collected Works of Stalin* (*Sutārin chosakushū*) showing that it was added to the Prohibited from Sales or Distribution List   106
6.3 The card from the staff catalog for *Outlook of Monopoly Capitalism in Japan* held by Hitotsubashi University Library   107
6.4 A card from the staff catalog of Sankō Library (the former Ōhashi Library)   107
9.1 Suppressed *Shunpuden*, opening pages with Prologue and Ihara illustration   154
9.2 PPB examiners at work: Japanese nationals in print censorship scanning Japanese galleys, 1945   156
9.3 Nakajima report with second examiner's overlaid comments   160
11.1 Akasegawa Genpei, The Morphology of Revenge (Look Well Before You Kill) (*Fukushū no Keitaigaku* (*Korosu mae ni aite o yoku miru*)), 1963   197
11.2 Akasegawa Genpei, Collection of Currency Knock-offs (*Shihei Ruiji Korekushon*), 1966   199
12.1 The Big Bad Censor versus the Beleaguered Artist in *University of Laughs*   221

Contributors

Jonathan Abel is an Assistant Professor in the Department of Comparative Literature at Penn State University. He has held Postdoctoral Fellowships in the Expanding East Asian Studies Program at Columbia's Weatherhead East Asian Institute and at the Reischauer Institute of Japanese Studies at Harvard University. His essay on postwar desire appears in *Perversion and Modern Japan: Psychoanalysis, Literature, Culture* (Routledge, 2009). His work on translation appears in *Nation, Language, and the Ethics of Translation* (Princeton, 2005) and other articles have appeared in *Comparative Literature Studies*, *Japan Forum* and *Asian Cinema*. He co-translated Azuma Hiroki's *Otaku: Japan's Database Animals* (University of Minnesota Press, 2009) and authored *Redacted: The Archives of Censorship in Transwar Japan* (University of California Press, 2012).

Kirsten Cather, Associate Professor of Japanese literature and film at the University of Texas at Austin, earned her B.A. from Connecticut College, and her M.A. and Ph.D. from the University of California, Berkeley in Japanese literature with a secondary specialization in film. Her book, *The Art of Censorship in Postwar Japan* (University of Hawai'i Press, 2012) addresses the landmark obscenity trials of literature, film and manga in postwar Japan – from that of the translation of *Lady Chatterley's Lover* in the 1950s to the unprecedented judicial proceedings against manga in the twenty-first century. Her next monograph, *Scripting Suicide in Modern Japan*, considers the representation of suicide in contemporary Japanese art and society, looking especially at artists and intellectuals who scripted their own (or others') suicides in their art.

Hiromi Tsuchiya Dollase is Associate Professor of Japanese at Vassar College. Her research interest is Japanese girls' magazines from the early twentieth century. Her work includes: 'Shōjo on the Homefront: An Examination of *Shōjo no tomo* 1938–1945' (*Asian Studies Review* 32.3, 2008); 'Ribbons Undone: The *Shōjo* Story Debates in Prewar Japan', in *Girl Reading Girl in Japan* (ed. Tomoko Aoyama and Barbara Hartley, Routledge, 2009); and '*Shōfujin* (*Little Women*): Recreating Jo for the Girls of Meiji Japan' (*Japanese Studies* 30.2, 2010). She co-edited a special issue of *US–Japan Women's Journal* featuring shōjo manga (2010), and a book entitled *Shōjo Manga Wonderland* (Meiji Shoin, 2012).

Contributors   xi

Sharon H. Domier has been the East Asian Studies librarian for the University of Massachusetts at Amherst, Amherst College and Smith College since 1996. She has a B.A. in East Asian Studies from the University of Alberta, a Master's degree from the University of Library and Information Science in Tsukuba, Japan and an M.L.I.S. from the University of Alberta. She has presented papers on Japanese library history at the International Convention of Asian Scholars (Berlin), the Asian Studies Conference Japan (Tokyo) and the Library History Seminar XI (Illinois). Her article 'From Reading Guidance to Thought Control: Wartime Japanese Libraries' was published in *Library Trends* (55.3, 2007). She currently serves on the editorial board of the *Journal of College and University Libraries in Japan* and is a member of the Japan Association of Library and Information History.

Rachael Hutchinson is Associate Professor in Japanese Studies at the University of Delaware. She received her D.Phil. from the University of Oxford in 2000, and her research addresses representations of Japanese identity in literature, film, manga and videogames. She co-edited *Representing the Other in Modern Japanese Literature: A Critical Approach* (Routledge, 2007) and authored *Nagai Kafū's Occidentalism: Defining the Japanese Self* (SUNY Press, 2011). Her work on Tezuka Osamu appears in Stephen Tabachnik's *Teaching the Graphic Novel* (MLA, 2009) and Roman Rosenbaum's *Manga and the Representation of Japanese History* (Routledge, 2012), while her essays on Kurosawa Akira are included in *Remapping World Cinema* (ed. Song-Hwee Lim and Stephanie Dennison, Wallflower, 2006) and *World Cinema's 'Dialogues' with Hollywood* (ed. Paul Cooke, Palgrave Macmillan, 2007). She has published in *Japan Forum*, *Monumenta Nipponica* and *Games and Culture*.

Eleanor Kerkham, Associate Professor of Japanese Literature at the University of Maryland (retired), specializes in classical and early modern Japanese literature and has taught at Colby College and Tenri University in Japan. She teaches pre-modern and modern Japanese language and literature and has published in English and Japanese on the prose, comic linked verse and literary career of Matsuo Bashō, on Japanese women writers and on the 'theory of the body' and Korean 'comfort women' stories of Tamura Taijirō. Current research includes a study of Matsuo Bashō's early apprenticeships and linked verse, and a translation and critical study of Tamura Taijirō's World War II fiction. She co-edited and contributed to the collection of essays *War, Occupation, and Creativity, Japan and East Asia 1920–1960* (University of Hawai'i Press, 2001), and edited and contributed to the collection *Matsuo Bashō's Poetic Spaces: Exploring Haikai Intersections* (Palgrave Macmillan, 2006).

Leith Morton is a professor at the Tokyo Institute of Technology, Japan. His books include: *Divided Self: A Biography of Arishima Takeo* (Allen & Unwin, 1988); Editor/Translator, *Seven Stories of Modern Japan* (Wild Peony Press, 1991); Editor/Translator, *Mt Fuji: Selected Poems 1943–1986* by Kusano Shinpei (Katydid Press, 1991); Editor/Translator, *An Anthology of*

xii *Contributors*

Contemporary Japanese Poetry (Garland Publishing, 1993); *Modern Japanese Culture: The Insider View* (Oxford University Press, 2003); *Modernism in Practice: An Introduction to Postwar Japanese Poetry* (Hawai'i University Press, 2004); poetry co-editor, *The Columbia Anthology of Modern Japanese Literature, Volume 1* (Columbia University Press, 2005); and *The Alien Within: Representations of the Exotic in Twentieth-century Japanese Literature* (Hawai'i University Press, 2009).

Hiromu Nagahara is Assistant Professor of History at MIT. He earned his Ph.D. in History from Harvard University. His research interests include the history of popular culture, mass entertainment and censorship in modern Japan. He is currently preparing a book manuscript on the rise of popular songs as a form of mass entertainment in twentieth-century Japan and the simultaneous emergence of mass culture critique in public discourse.

Rachel Payne received her D.Phil. from the University of Oxford with the thesis *Early Meiji Drama Reforms at the Shintomi-chō Theatre*. She is currently Senior Lecturer in Japanese in the School of Languages, Cultures and Linguistics at the University of Canterbury, New Zealand. Her main research interests are Meiji era reform, Nō masks and their collections in Japan and the West and the duality of kabuki actors' identities as on-stage fictional characters and living superstars, as celebrated in ukiyo-e actor prints and kabuki's public ceremonies.

Yayoi Shionoiri serves as Assistant General Counsel to the Guggenheim Museum. Previously she served as Legal Advisor to Japanese contemporary artist Takashi Murakami. With research focusing on modern and contemporary Japanese art, she is interested in the effects of legal paradigms on artistic production, examining the efficacy of the current copyright and intellectual property framework for the protection of artists' rights. She has an A.B. from Harvard University, a J.D. from Cornell Law School and an M.A. in Modern Art: Critical Studies from Columbia University. Publications include an analysis of Hosoe Eikoh's photographs of Mishima Yukio in *Barakei* appearing in *Beyond Boundaries: East and West Cross-Cultural Encounters* (Cambridge Scholars Publishing, 2011).

Noriko Akimoto Sugimori is Assistant Professor of Japanese at Kalamazoo College. Her research interests include sociolinguistics, linguistic anthropology, critical discourse analysis, bilingualism and second language acquisition. She attained her Ph.D. from Boston University in the Program of Applied Linguistics, with the dissertation *Imperial Honorifics as an Index of Social Change in Modern Japan, 1972–2008*. She has published articles on the use of imperial honorifics in Japanese newspapers, in *The Japan Journal of Sociolinguistic Sciences* (11.1, 2008) and *Intelligence* (11, 2010), as well as a chapter in Ray T. Donahue's *Exploring Japaneseness: On Japanese Enactments of Culture and Consciousness* (Ablex, 2002). She is currently working on a book focusing on discourse approaches to imperial honorifics.

Acknowledgments

This volume grew out of a special issue of *Japan Forum* titled *Censorship in the Japanese Arts* (19.3), which I edited in 2007. From that issue, essays by Jonathan Abel, Rachel Payne, Leith Morton and myself were revised for the current volume. New essays by Kirsten Cather, Hiromi Tsuchiya Dollase, Sharon H. Domier, Eleanor Kerkham, Hiromu Nagahara, Yayoi Shionoiri and Noriko Akimoto Sugimori were written for this book. I must thank all the contributors for their hard work and patience, and for teaching me so much about censorship in Japan. The original idea for the edited collection came about as the result of discussion following a panel on Japanese censorship at the Mid-Atlantic Region Association for Asian Studies conference (as always an excellent venue for sharing ideas and fostering collaborative projects), and was developed further at the Association for Asian Studies annual conference in Philadelphia in 2010. I am grateful to Marlene Mayo for acting as discussant for our panel in Philadelphia, particularly for her insightful comments on the relationship between censorship and thought control.

Special thanks go to Stephanie Rogers at Routledge for her enthusiastic support of the project from its very early days, and to Leanne Hinves, Ed Needle and Hannah Mack for ushering it through the publication process. I am grateful to the anonymous reviewer for the detailed comments and reading suggestions which enriched the final product immeasurably. Any errors which remain in the final manuscript I acknowledge as my own.

For funding which enabled me to attend and present at the MAR/AAS and AAS conferences, I thank the University of Delaware Department of Foreign Languages and Literatures and the College of Arts and Sciences. I am grateful to Julie Nelson Davis and Cappy Hurst of the University of Pennsylvania Center for East Asian Studies for hosting me as Visiting Researcher in 2006–2007, which is when I stumbled upon the SCAP journals in the Franklin Library while looking for something completely different. I am extremely grateful to the Toshiba International Foundation and the British Association for Japanese Studies, for awarding my original essay on Kurosawa the Toshiba International Foundation Prize for 2007, and for bringing me to Manchester to give the Toshiba Address at the annual conference in 2008. I will never forget the experience of speaking about Occupation censorship in front of an audience including

xiv *Acknowledgments*

British ex-servicemen who had been stationed in Kure. Their positive comments following the presentation inspired the vision of the book project as a whole.

My essay on Kurosawa was written on a sabbatical supported by a Picker Research Fellowship granted by the Colgate University Research Council, while the book manuscript was completed on sabbatical from the University of Delaware. I sincerely thank my colleagues for their support, particularly Mark Miller for running the Japanese program in my absence.

Finally I thank my family, particularly my wonderful husband Chris for his support every day. I thank my daughter Natalie for the applause and cheering, and baby Sophie for her arrival.

1 Introduction

Negotiating censorship in modern Japan

Rachael Hutchinson

Censorship in Japan has seen many changes over the last 150 years, from the time of the late Tokugawa period to the present. Administrative regimes have ranged from the feudal *bakufu* of the Tokugawa era (1603–1867), through the imperial institutions of the Meiji (1868–1912), Taishō (1912–26) and early Shōwa periods, transitioning to military rule in the 1930s, followed by the Allied Occupation (1945–52) and reversion to a demilitarized Japanese government. Each system of rule possessed its own censorship laws and regulations, as well as methods of enforcement. But what has remained constant through these many upheavals has been the process of negotiation between censor and artist that may be seen in all the cultural media of modern society, including popular songs, dramatic performance, journalism, literature, fine arts and film. The purpose of this volume is to focus more closely on that process of negotiation, in order to cast light on the human subjectivity inherent in any censorship system, and to better understand the dynamics of censorship and power as they play out in real-world case studies.

While there are many models to work with in understanding censorship, we may loosely define censorship as an act of suppression, deletion, omission or revision performed upon an artistic work or medium by the artist or an external body, which limits the work's publication or dissemination to some extent. The enactment and enforcement of censorship is often seen in negative terms as a suppression of 'free speech' or of the artist's creative expression. Censorship regulations from 'above' may apply to a single speech act or to a whole medium, while self-censorship from 'below' may be motivated by positive or negative factors – to gain reward or to avoid punishment, for example. In what Miklós Haraszti (1987) calls the 'classical' model of censorship, one may see the process from the perspective of the state's exercise of power in putting forward one main discourse which must be protected from corrupting influences, answered by the artist's compliance with or resistance to that discourse (perhaps in the act of creating a 'counter-discursive' utterance from the margins). But, as Haraszti explains, to think of state censorship only in terms of suppression, silencing or changing the artist's voice is to recognize power only in one sector of society, making that power completely negative in aspect and its application homogeneous and objective. One could argue that censorship is common to

2   R. Hutchinson

every society, being a struggle between the expressive statement and its suppression. But Haraszti reveals this oppositional dichotomy of state versus artist, struggling over artistic freedom, as no more than a 'rumor', because we must take into account the fact that very often both the state and the artist are complicit in one another's enterprise.

Most research on Japanese censorship to date – including the work of Richard Mitchell, Jay Rubin, Gregory Kasza, and most recently Tomi Suzuki and her colleagues – has taken the classical approach, focusing on top-down suppression and surveillance as well as regulations, laws and methods of enforcement. However, it is interesting to note that most scholars also acknowledge a certain degree of subjectivity inherent in the censorship systems of imperial, wartime and Occupation Japan. Kasza goes so far as to say that the most important legacy of Meiji policy was 'the wide discretion granted to administrators in making and implementing the law' (1988: 7). In this volume, we focus more closely on that subjectivity and discretion to see the censorship process in more holistic and human terms.

In contrast to the classical model, an alternative way to approach censorship is through the choices that must be made by people at every stage of the censorship process, in the three main spheres of artist, state and audience. On the part of the artist, Nagai Kafū (1879–1959) pointed out that writing itself is a matter of careful selection and editing. The artist must choose at every stage of the work what to include and what to leave out (Nagai 1920). But at what point does 'selection and editing' become 'self-censorship'? Much depends on the artist's expectation of how the work will be received, which in turn may depend on knowledge of state regulations and demands of the target audience. On the part of the state, the choice must be made as to which materials to censor and how to apply that censorship. Is it possible to police the output of every part of the media, and when does this become too large a task to manage in terms of employee numbers and work hours? Finally, for the audience, Henry David Thoreau (1817–62) claimed that it is the responsibility of every person to keep their own mind clear of polluting influences, by carefully choosing to view only those materials which will educate the mind and enlighten the soul (Thoreau 1997 [1854]). But how are audiences to make informed choices? At what age can audiences decide for themselves what to listen to, read or watch? For those deemed too young to make choices for themselves, is it the right of parents, guardians, schools, the church or the state to govern and police their media consumption? As this brief selection of questions makes clear, the artist, state and audience face the issue of choice at all stages of the censorship process.

Complicating the matter, these choices are further informed by the advice and suggestions of various regulatory entities, often seen as 'middlemen' in the process: independent ratings boards and pressure groups, publishers, editors, and heads of film studios and radio stations. Cultural critics, politicians and journalists all add to the public discourse on censorship, opining on what should and should not be available for consumption. The questions of who has the right to censor a work, and whether it is the responsibility of the artist, the state, the

Introduction 3

audience, or someone else to consider such matters, lie at the heart of the censorship process, with rights and responsibilities providing the site of contention for dissident artists, underage consumers, pundits and government committees alike. The essays in this volume highlight the complexities of the censorship process by investigating the responsibilities and choices of all four groups – artists, censors, audience and ideologues – in a range of case studies from the Japanese arts.

Historically, censorship in Japan has been marked by both complicity and complexity, with formal imperial or governmental edicts accompanied in equal measure by extralegal and informal methods of censorship. Despite the many changes in rule, it is clear from a brief chronological overview that top-down censorship regulations have been continuously balanced by systems of negotiation. Although the legacy of the Tokugawa administration has most often been analyzed in terms of suppression and control (see for example Mitchell 1983: 3–12; Suzuki *et al.* 2012: 8–9), I will focus here on those aspects of the feudal censorship system which laid the basis for negotiation and subjectivity in subsequent periods.

When commercial publishing started in the Tokugawa period, the first official censorship regulations were passed against Christian books, particularly Chinese translations of works by European missionaries. Official edicts passed in 1657 and 1673 defined categories of objectionable material, but the popularity and prevalence of erotic books in the marketplace suggest that these edicts were ineffective. In 1721 and 1722, however, the *bakufu* of shogun Tokugawa Yoshimune (1684–1751) required all new books to be inspected before reaching the marketplace, and to bear a stamp showing the true names of both author and publisher for the first time. While authors could get around these rules by disseminating work underground or by keeping their work in manuscript form (Kornicki 1998), printed material was to be regulated by a new system. The 1721 edict ordered publishers to form guilds, while the 1722 edict required those guilds to take responsibility for inspecting books and enforcing the regulations. Faced with the brunt of financial losses if objectionable material was released on the marketplace, the publishers' guilds soon worked out that loss could be avoided with a pre-publication system of censorship rather than waiting for post-publication inspection. By placing responsibility for censorship on the publishing guilds, the *bakufu* had fostered a system of pre-publication self-censorship – a system that would reappear often in Japan's history.

Censorship on ideological grounds was also common in the Edo period, repeated in successive eras as each ruling ideology naturally sought to suppress opposition. Laws attempting to foster political and ideological homogeneity were passed in 1790, in the Kansei Reforms of Matsudaira Sadanobu (1759–1829). The Prohibition of Heterodoxy edict reinforced earlier laws and put new bans in place to control political satires and scandals. Punishments could be harsh, including prison, fines or being placed in manacles for a number of days. The next major edicts of 1823 and 1842 aimed to slow the spread of Western ideas, controlling works of science, astronomy and 'Dutch learning' as well as Western medicine.

4   R. Hutchinson

An interesting result of the 1842 laws was the dissolution of the publishers' guilds, to be replaced by a *bakufu* institution requiring all new books to undergo the same standard practice of pre-publication censorship. However, the sheer volume of work involved in such an enterprise proved overwhelming, leading to many categories of undesirable books being considered exempt for practical purposes. In this case we see the physical limitations that can be placed on a bureaucracy by overly stringent or ambitious regulations. The relationship between artist, censor and state in the Tokugawa period thus emerges not as a simple 'top-down' equation but as a reflection of the human side of the censorship process as a whole. Three main features of the system may be seen as continuous with the eras to come: the state's use of a middleman as censor, fostering an atmosphere of self-censorship; shifts in censorship policy on ideological grounds; and the limitations of policy subject to logistical restraints.

Censorship of the Meiji period is often represented as the ultimate in top-down state suppression and control, with Mitchell (1983) and Kasza (1988) in particular painting the Meiji years as the source of all that was severe and grim in the institutional running of imperial Japan. In the first year of the new regime, books could only be published with government permission. New media such as newspapers and magazines came under tight supervision and many were banned, especially those critical of the new government. Certainly, from the perspective of state suppression, Meiji censorship seems far more powerful and effective than the Tokugawa system. However, looking at censorship as a complex and dynamic process, many elements are seen to be continuous with both the earlier Tokugawa system and later periods. For example, the 1869 regulations required two copies of all books and periodicals to be presented for post-publication censorship. Having already expended a great deal of effort, time and money to produce the materials, publishers and authors faced huge losses if the product failed inspection, leading to stricter in-house rules regarding what should be published and what should not. Editors and publishers thus safeguarded the fortunes of the publishing house in a similar way to the guilds of the Tokugawa period, while authors could also take it upon themselves to edit their own material in the hope of a favorable result.

From 1875 censorship became the responsibility of the Home Ministry, which passed strict libel and press regulations. Editors were now held criminally responsible for the content of what they printed and for any troubles arising in public order as a result of what they printed. Bans of sale could be applied to new and old books, meaning that a system of re-inspecting old works had to be instituted. This kind of retrospective censorship would be a major feature of censorship in wartime as well as the Occupation. Laws were strictly enforced, to the extent that some newspapers began to use 'prison editors', where people already imprisoned would append their names to editorials and bear the blame for the content while the real day-to-day running of the paper was carried out by someone else. In answer to this tactic, the government could implement indefinite suspension of publication from the 1880s, when censorship laws were tightened yet again. The 1883 Press Regulations, expanded and promulgated by imperial decree as the Press and Publication

Introduction 5

Regulations of 1887, strengthened the power of the Home Ministry and brought back pre-publication censorship. The Home Ministry was empowered to charge anyone for activities that 'disturbed the peace', including political meetings as well as publications. With the new constitution of 1890 came the inclusion of Article 29, stating that 'Japanese subjects shall, *within the limits of the law*, enjoy the liberty of speech, writing, publication, public meetings and association' (Rubin 1984: 6). The emphasis that Rubin adds to the phrasing highlights the practical application of the Home Ministry's regulations, which were open to no appeal and which would be enforced by the Home Ministry's own Police Bureau Censorship Division (see Rubin 1984: 15–27).

Extralegal methods of censorship evolved further through the years of imperial rule: the Home Ministry could issue pre-publication embargoes to certain publishers, letting them know in advance what subjects were likely to be banned; similarly, publishers could be let off with a warning, post-publication, to avoid publishing such dangerous material in the future. Some works were allowed to be published contingent on deletions of passages or the insertion of *fuseji*, Xs and Os that substituted for characters on the printed page. *Fuseji* were inserted not by the authors or the police, but by the publishers and editors. In emphasizing the continuity between Tokugawa and Meiji extralegal methods of censorship negotiation, Rubin (1984: 28–9) provides an alternative perspective to the suppressive state model in the imperial years.

This kind of cooperation between publishers and censors may be called 'complicity' in Haraszti's model, but may also be seen as a practical approach to working within the boundaries of censorship regulation. Such practical complicity is clear in Rachel Payne's essay on early Meiji kabuki censorship, in which both state reformers and kabuki artists of the 1870s and 1880s are shown to be heavily interdependent, with a very fine line between the private realm, where reform was encouraged through individual relationships, and the public realm, where strict regulations were printed and patronage was offered by the state. Payne reminds us that artists can sometimes agree with censorship reforms and regulations, often benefiting from state scholarships, prizes and rewards even under a totalitarian government.

Just as Meiji censorship needed to deal with a burgeoning press, censorship in the Taishō period (1912–26) had to address the new media of film. The Motion Picture Exhibition Regulations of 1917 required pre-screening of films for the censors, licensing of all *benshi* narrators and a system of ratings to indicate appropriate age ranges for the audience. This law applied only to Tokyo, the first national law being the 1925 Motion Picture Film Inspection Regulations, issued by the Home Ministry. Now each film had to be stamped by the censor before exhibition, on the criteria that it not be 'harmful' to the public. The broad criteria generally applied to violence, sexuality or criticism of the imperial system, although left-leaning works came under great scrutiny at this time (Anderson and Richie 1982: 69). The Proletarian Film League in particular attracted a great deal of attention, and was finally closed down in 1925 under the Peace Preservation Law. This law, banning any kind of speech act that advocated abolishing

6   R. Hutchinson

private property or doing away with the imperial system, was primarily directed against Socialists and Communists, although publications of all kinds came under greater scrutiny. One of the most serious crimes was to publish criticism of the *kokutai* or 'nation state', officially established in law for the first time (Mitchell 1983: 190–7). The Justice Ministry created a Thought Section in 1926 to deal with subversive ideology, and 'thought guidance' took a dual approach to the problem, clarifying the meaning of *kokutai* on the one hand while condemning leftist ideology on the other (Mitchell 1976: 150). The role of the Education Ministry became more important in these years, inculcating a love for the emperor and family nation-state.

Although imprisonment, interrogation and even torture were employed to encourage ideological offenders to recant, Jonathan Abel demonstrates that proletarian literature, as well as erotic literature, flourished under the heavy censorship of interwar Japan. Abel shows how writers, publishers and editors manipulated censorship through personal relationships and other strategies, making money and cultivating marginal genres in the process. Through the career of Umehara Hokumei (1901–46), Abel explores the potential for both complicity and subversion in the act of publication in mainstream discourse. The question of how to be both radical and involved in the mainstream highlights the paradoxical relationship between radicalism and complicity, and the balancing act needed by the artist to negotiate boundaries successfully.

The Shōwa period (1926–89) began with a massive publishing boom, which quickly showed the limitations of the Taishō censorship system. Strained to the limits of work hours, the Police Bureau Censorship Division of the Home Ministry was forced to end its informal consultations with individual publishers and editors (Rubin 1984: 247–8). From the 1930s, war with China demanded a stronger program of positive propaganda, to be carried out by the Cabinet Information Committee founded in 1936. The need for propaganda and the significance placed upon it may be seen in the upgrading of this Committee to Division in 1937 (when the Nanking massacre demanded increased information control) and to Bureau in 1940 (when news reports of the failing war demanded increasingly strict regulation). By 1940, the new Bureau was in direct competition with the Home Ministry's Police Bureau for authority over censorship and information. When the new office prevailed, censorship was no longer regulated by a ministry according to law, but by army and navy personnel according to military policy and decisions (Rubin 1984: 256–7).

One of the most interesting issues of wartime censorship is the visibility of the censorship process as a whole, seen in the different treatments of *fuseji* under different regimes. While the Home Ministry officially prohibited the use of *fuseji* in 1885, this prohibition was not enforced until the 1930s, as it was too useful a tool in encouraging self-censorship. The Home Ministry Police Bureau's Censorship Division finally told editors to phase out *fuseji* from 1936, and in 1941 military law forbade it altogether. While the physical, visible effect of censorship on the page in peacetime had encouraged citizens to regulate their words and recognize the hand of authority, *fuseji* in wartime would suggest that authors

Introduction 7

had spoken critically of imperial policy or the *kokutai*, the great nation of Japan. In order to present a united ideological front, it was necessary to elide all evidence of opposition.

The dual nature of Japanese censorship is perhaps clearest in the war years (1931–45), when the state took a more active role in both censoring offensive material and promoting military ideology. We see this process in the growing tendency towards propaganda in literature, film and popular songs, linked closely to ideas of 'educating the people'. As Mitchell (1976, 1983) and Kasza (1988) have demonstrated, thought control in the media came not only from government directives but also from members of society who took it upon themselves to act as guardians or gatekeepers for others. These ideologues informed and shaped public discourse in ways that government directives and laws could not. Although it is convenient to treat them as a group, it is well to keep in mind that different individuals may have had very different roles, occupying different kinds of positions within the censorship process. Hiromu Nagahara's essay on Ogawa Chikagorō (b.1896) shows him as record censor, music critic and consumer of popular culture, analyzing the blurred boundaries of state and civil society, censorship and cultural critique that continued through the war years and well into the postwar period. Hiromi Tsuchiya Dollase's essay on wartime writing by Kawabata Yasunari (1899–1972) similarly shows the blurred boundaries between government education and the promotion of children's literature in the composition movement (*tzuzurikata undō*) in mainland Asia. Charting the transformation of the magazine *Girls' Friend* (*Shōjo no tomo*) in the war years, Dollase shows its increasingly nationalistic bent, exploring how Kawabata struggled to fulfill his own artistic goals in such an environment by clinging to the ideals of 'children's sentiment' and 'girls' culture'.

Recognizing cinema's potential for propaganda, a Committee on Film Control was set up in 1934 to involve the state more closely in film production, leading to the establishment of the Great Japan Film Association in 1935. Japanese films bound for export came under close scrutiny, to ensure that a good image of Japan was projected overseas. Home Ministry recommendations were published in 1937 and 1938 concerning film content, exhibition and distribution (Anderson and Richie 1982: 128–9), while the comprehensive 1939 Film Law restricted the number of foreign films coming into Japan and required licenses for all film industry personnel. As well as post-production inspections which could result in bans, cuts or forced revisions, scripts were also censored prior to production, a move welcomed by some producers as an effective way to minimize losses (Davis 1996: 64–9). By 1943, the major film companies had been compressed into just three organizations: Daiei, Tōhō and Shōchiku, streamlining the censorship process. Although pre-production censorship had its difficulties and freedom of expression was limited in wartime, it seems that most filmmakers were content to work within the guidelines to produce the best films possible. My essay on the film *One Wonderful Sunday* (*Subarashiki Nichiyōbi*, 1947) by Kurosawa Akira (1910–98) shows the director benefiting from prizes and state recognition while learning his trade under the military regime. Kurosawa's

8   R. Hutchinson

career under the imperial and Occupation systems of censorship bears out Haraszti's point that compromise and creativity are not mutually exclusive, and that the voluntary internalization of regulations can make creativity possible within even the tightest restrictions.

When considering artistic production in wartime, one question that arises is what happens to militaristic works after the war is over. Sharon H. Domier and Leith Morton investigate censorship from the side of the librarians and editors who must decide what to do with works deemed ideologically subversive, both during the period of censorship enforcement and afterwards. Domier examines Japanese libraries from late Meiji through to the immediate postwar period, focusing on the ingenuity of library directors in dealing with the police, the Home Ministry and the Education Ministry, negotiating as best they could to keep Socialist and Communist books in their possession – hidden in cabinets, boxes and basement shelving, some to be later reinstated and some to remain invisible. Morton's essay on self-censorship in wartime Japanese poetry examines why writers such as Miyoshi Tatsuji (1900–64) and Tsuboi Shigeji (1897–1975) revised their patriotic poetry for postwar publication or excised it from their collected works altogether. Addressing the role of the writers, their publishers and later editors, Morton analyzes the moral debate surrounding self-censorship and war guilt in postwar Japan. Is it ethical for poets to conceal their wartime patriotism and omit those poems inspired by fascist ideology from their collected works, or is this hypocrisy of the worst kind? This debate reminds us of Haraszti's 'rumor' of artistic freedom, assuming that only the whole original artwork represents some higher truth, while a censored or revised version of that artwork is somehow false.

Censorship during the Allied Occupation (1945–52) was similar in its mission to that of the Japanese military system, with the double aim of encouraging one ideology while suppressing another. In this case, the Civil Information and Education (CI&E) Section of General Headquarters aimed to promote films displaying democratic qualities, while suppressing those with feudal or militaristic themes. Once again retrospective censorship came into effect, as hundreds of pre-1945 films were banned. From January 1946 to June 1949 films were subject to double inspection – once by CI&E and once by the Civil Censorship Detachment (CCD), which was responsible for applying censorship regulations and enforcing any bans, cuts or revisions required (see Mayo 1991: 135–8). The two elements of the censorship process here – the promotion of ideology and the policing of infractions – were thus codified into two separate departments, making concrete and visible the dual role of the censor which had been in effect through much of Japanese history.

Occupation censorship may be seen at its most secretive and oppressive in the censorship of material dealing with the atomic bombing of Hiroshima and Nagasaki, designated as taboo subjects soon after the fact (Braw 1991). However, formal censorship gradually lessened in degree from 1947, when kabuki, bunraku and Nō were removed from pre-performance censorship and radio scripts no longer required pre-broadcast inspection. Books and periodicals also

Introduction 9

shifted from pre- to post-publication censorship, and in 1949 the CCD was dissolved, ending official censorship but opening the way to more subjective and informal means of control (Dower 1999: 432). Although the Film Ethics Regulation Control Committee (usually referred to as Eirin) was established in 1949 as a self-regulating body to replace external censorship, CI&E continued to monitor films in post-production from 1949 to 1952 (Anderson and Richie 1982: 424). In the last years of the Occupation we see continuity with earlier regimes, as the general shift to post-publication censorship made publishers and authors nervous and more likely to self-censor in the hope of avoiding costly mistakes (Dower 1999: 432–3).

Critics are divided as to how liberal the atmosphere of Occupation publishing really was – Etō Jun (1989) and Dower (1999) emphasizing the restrictive nature of SCAP censorship and Rubin (1985) arguing for the flowering of ideas in the new regime (see Mayo 1991). The debate is fueled by the paradox that the Occupation was established to impose democratic order and to free Japan from militaristic imperial rule, yet as an occupying force, SCAP had to employ means such as censorship and purges more suited to the authoritarian regime they had just replaced. Nowhere is this paradox more evident than in what we might call the 'invisibility rule' of Occupation censorship, as no mention was to be made of the censorship process itself in any published media.

Another problem of Occupation censorship appeared in the figure of the emperor – a symbol of outmoded feudal and military values in 1945, but of national unity in the face of Communist threat by 1950. Such a shift in ideology led to the banning of Kamei Fumio's *The Japanese Tragedy* (*Nihon no higeki*, 1946) for its criticism of the emperor. That the film was withdrawn from distribution after having already gone through the censorship process and been approved was astounding, and the financial costs to the film studio, Nichiei, were heavy (Dower 1999: 429). In this volume, Eleanor Kerkham and Noriko Sugimori both analyze the ways in which ideological change affected the Occupation censorship process. Kerkham examines the 1947 novel *Biography of a Prostitute* (*Shunpuden*) by Tamura Taijirō (1911–83), following the text through various levels of the CCD and detailing the many comments and suggested revisions at each stage of re-examination. The unusual decision to suppress the text in its entirety rather than allow publication in a revised form shows the degree to which the Occupation authorities feared the exposure of racist Japanese attitudes towards Koreans – but, as Kerkham argues, it also shows a much deeper desire to avoid the subject of military 'comfort women' becoming part of the postwar public discourse. Sugimori traces the linguistic changes in print media in representing the figure of the emperor and imperial family, analyzing the use of 'imperial honorifics' in the *Asahi* newspaper. While critics generally attribute the postwar simplification of imperial honorifics to Occupation censorship practice, Sugimori demonstrates that changes came rather from the independent decisions of journalists and their editors.

The enactment of censorship is thus a complex process, with many motivating factors. But it is also important to consider the significance of 'non-censorship' – the reasons why a work may escape revisions or suppression, and the degree to which context determines the reception and censorship of any given text. This is seen in the reception of Kurosawa Akira's *No Regrets for Our Youth* (*Waga seishun ni kuinashi*) as a 'democratization film' in 1946, making it more likely that his following films would not be seen as problematic. While it is readily acknowledged that banned artists will be subject to closer scrutiny with their next works, the converse of this process is equally important: if artists create works very much in line with government directives (whether purposefully or not), then they will enjoy greater freedom with their next efforts. The process of 'non-censorship' receives less attention than enacted censorship, but the question of why some works might evade censorship is significant, providing insight into how artists can manage their reputation and calculate the effects of their work. Yayoi Shionoiri's essay on Akasegawa Genpei (1937–) shows how the artist used his legal trial to stage an artistic 'happening' in the courtroom, garnering attention and notoriety in the 'Model Thousand-yen Note Incident' of 1964. Shionoiri explores the intersections between Japanese constitutional law and contemporary artistic practice, arguing that non-censorship in Akasegawa's case may be seen as a form of Direct Action.

One facet of the censorship process in Japan that differs to that of other countries is the lack of appeal to the court system until after 1945. Tokugawa and imperial courts were used mainly to decide punishments for censorship offenders, rather than as a forum for artists to defend their works. In the 1950s, the courts took on a new role, acting for the first time as a forum for public debate regarding the rights and responsibilities of citizens and the state in the case of artistic expression. The famous trial of Itō Sei (1905–69) and Oyama Hisajirō (1905–84), respectively the translator and publisher of the Japanese version of D.H. Lawrence's *Lady Chatterley's Lover*, was the first Japanese censorship trial to debate openly the respective responsibilities of audience, artist, publisher and the state in determining what should be allowed to enter mainstream discourse (Sherif 2007). Opening the way for a slew of court trials in the postwar era, the *Lady Chatterley's Lover* trials of 1951–2 demonstrate that a vital and dynamic public sphere was possible even as Japan was shifting from occupied territory to sovereign nation, carrying on the tradition of public dissent and critique in the face of authoritarian regimes before 1945 (Berry 1998).

Kirsten Cather's essay at the end of the volume provides a fitting conclusion to our study of censorship in modern Japan, giving an overview of how censors themselves have been represented in literature and film over the course of the twentieth century. Cather examines parodic stories from 1921 and 1987 to show how the figure of the censor changed over time, illustrating the difference between classical models of censorship and newer forms of negotiation. Her study of the 2004 film *University of Laughs* (*Warai no daigaku*) shows the censor as a liminal figure, contributing to the artistic process and becoming to some extent an artist himself. That this accords well with Nagahara's portrait of Ogawa Chikagorō underscores the continuity of blurred boundaries in the Japanese censorship process.

In exploring the relationship between artists, the state, regulatory bodies and the audience in the creation and censorship of artistic works, we hope to build

Introduction   11

upon existing research as well as broaden the disciplinary focus in regard to censorship studies as a whole. We aim to shift the focus away from top-down suppression towards the more complex negotiations involved in the many stages of an artistic work, from the inception and original creation, to editing, drafting and revising (sometimes according to suggestions from a government agency), the many cuts and omissions, or additions such as *fuseji*, the bans of sale, police collections of prints, the destruction of works or their final release in a revised form, or even the much later release of a work in a form more in accord with the artist's original vision. All these steps involve movement within boundaries, as well as testing of those boundaries, on the part of both artist and censor. Any part of the process may be either public or private, in turn affecting sales, public perception, critical reception and academic treatment of the work. Taken together, the essays in this book show ample evidence that censorship at every stage involves an act of human judgment, in a context determined by political, economic and ideological factors. By exploring censorship in a number of different art forms we attempt to gain a clearer picture of a number of issues, including the pervasiveness and strength of Japanese censorship across a range of media; the similar tactics used by artists of different media to negotiate censorship boundaries; and how censors from different systems and time periods face many of the same problems and questions in their work. Overall, we seek a greater understanding of the dynamics of censorship and how these operate on both people and texts. Reading through the case studies, it becomes clear that enacted censorship and non-censorship are equally worthy of study, illuminating the power dynamics at work in a process that affects each of our own societies to some extent. We hope that the present volume will be of both historical interest and contemporary relevance.

References

Anderson, Joseph L. and Richie, Donald (1982) *The Japanese Film: Art and Industry*, Princeton: Princeton University Press.

Berry, Mary Elizabeth (1998) 'Public Life in Authoritarian Japan', *Daedalus* 127(3): 133–65.

Braw, Monica (1991) *The Atomic Bomb Suppressed: American Censorship in Occupied Japan*, Armonk, NY: M.E. Sharpe.

Davis, Darrell William (1996) *Picturing Japaneseness: Monumental Style, National Identity, Japanese Film*, New York: Columbia University Press.

Dower, John (1999) *Embracing Defeat: Japan in the Wake of World War II*, New York and London: Norton.

Etō, Jun (1989) *Tozasareta gengo kūkan: senryōgun no ken'etsu to sengo Nihon* (The Sealed Linguistic Space: Occupation censorship and postwar Japan), Tokyo: Bungei Shunjū.

Haraszti, Miklós (1987) *The Velvet Prison*, trans. Katalin and Stephen Landesmann and Steve Wasserman. New York: Basic Books.

Kasza, Gregory J. (1988) *The State and Mass Media in Japan, 1918–1945*, Berkeley, Los Angeles and London: University of California Press.

12 *R. Hutchinson*

Kornicki, Peter (1988) *The Book in Japan: A Cultural History from the Beginnings to the Nineteenth Century*, Leiden: Brill.

Mayo, Marlene (1991) 'Literary Reorientation in Occupied Japan: Incidents of Civil Censorship', in Ernestine Schlant and J. Thomas Rimer (eds.), *Legacies and Ambiguities: Postwar Fiction and Culture in West Germany and Japan*, Washington: Woodrow Wilson Center Press; Baltimore and London: Johns Hopkins University Press, 135–61.

Mitchell, Richard H. (1976) *Thought Control in Prewar Japan*, Ithaca and London: Cornell University Press.

Mitchell, Richard H. (1983) *Censorship in Imperial Japan*, Princeton: Princeton University Press.

Nagai, Kafū (1920) *Shōsetsu sakuhō* (How to Write a Novel), in *Kafū zenshū*, 28 vols., Tokyo: Iwanami Shoten, 1962–1974, vol. 14, 395–408.

Rubin, Jay (1984) *Injurious to Public Morals: Writers and the Meiji State*, Seattle and London: University of Washington Press.

Rubin, Jay (1985) 'From Wholesomeness to Decadence: The Censorship of Literature Under the Allied Occupation', *Journal of Japanese Studies* 11(1): 71–103.

Sherif, Ann (2007) 'Foreign Sex, Native Politics: *Lady Chatterley's Lover* in Post- Occupation Japan', in Rachael Hutchinson and Mark Williams (eds.), *Representing the Other in Modern Japanese Literature: A Critical Approach*, New York and London: Routledge, 183–210.

Suzuki, Tomi, Toeda Hirokazu, Hori Hikari and Munakata Kazushige (eds.) (2012) *Censorship, Media, and Literary Culture in Japan: From Edo to Postwar*, Tokyo: Shin'yōsha.

Thoreau, Henry David (1997) [1854] *Walden*, with introduction and annotations by Bill McKibben, Boston: Beacon Press.

2 Censorship and patronage in Meiji kabuki theater

Rachel Payne

Introduction

Kabuki is recognized today as one of the finest examples of Japan's rich cultural heritage, and government-sponsored international tours promote the country's image overseas. However, this universal approbation is in sharp contrast to the official disdain with which kabuki was regarded for the first two and a half centuries of its existence. This chapter examines the changes in official attitudes toward, and control of, kabuki after the Meiji Restoration of 1868. Particular attention will be paid to the major shift in censorial policy during the early Meiji era, when kabuki became the focus of the first efforts to harness its power as a civilizing agent for the modernizing nation. Meiji kabuki censorship has received little attention from Western historians of Meiji society and theater, but this topic sheds light on the relationship between art and the state in Meiji Japan and contributes to our understanding of a highly formative era in the development of kabuki as we know it today.

Unlike the censorship of literature or film, examined in later chapters of this book, theatrical censorship addresses much more than textual elements of the artistic work. A performance communicates meaning not only through the spoken word, but also through elements such as movement, costumes, scenery, props and music. Moreover, as an event of several hours involving an audience assembled at a venue providing other additional services, theater has the potential to excite, disturb or incite many people in a relatively short time. Official control of Japan's kabuki theater has therefore historically necessitated a broad range of regulations covering any factors of the theater-going experience that the authorities considered potentially offensive and contrary to the 'proper' mindset. While the following discussion will concentrate on textual censorship, these regulations are best understood within the context of measures to police the whole theater-going experience.

Kabuki at the end of the Edo era

From its origins as a side-show for prostitutes in the early seventeenth century, kabuki flourished during the Edo era (1603–1867) to become one of the mainstays of urban popular culture. For the *chōnin* townsmen, who were greatly

14   *R. Payne*

limited by the Edo class hierarchy, theaters and the pleasure quarters provided welcome fun and fantasy, and occasional visits there by samurai were also usually reluctantly permitted by the authorities. However, restrictions were applied when the corrupting influence of these so-called *akusho* (wicked places) grew too strong. Takahashi (1995: 141–2) describes *akusho* as 'sites of negotiation between the subordinate classes seeking freedom and the ruling classes trying to impose control'. Popular theater was accepted as a necessary evil, but the price it paid for governmental tolerance was a strict set of regulations covering all aspects of the professional and private lives of actors. These were intended to force them to behave in a manner appropriate to their low social rank. For, although officially despised as *hinin* (non-human), successful actors earned huge salaries and enjoyed star status among fans.

Theater regulations were also part of the Tokugawa *bakufu* regime's efforts to preserve the peace and prevent the hedonistic tendencies of *chōnin* from contaminating the Confucian frugality espoused by the samurai elite. Licentiousness, lavishness and seditious staged portrayals of *bakufu* policies and named officials, as well as rousing depictions of topical events, were all curbed by a steady stream of directives. Salacious publications, art, gambling and prostitution were similarly curbed. However, the indomitable nature of the *chōnin* spirit ensured that, once official vigilance relaxed, the kabuki world once again started pushing the boundaries of the acceptable. Playwrights and actors became most skilful and daring in their interpretation of the rules. *Sewamono* (domestic pieces), depicting the quotidian affairs of the urban middle classes, avoided censure by either detailing matters of little interest to the censors or creating false identities and settings for recent scandals. Likewise, it became an accepted convention for the semi-fictional *jidaimono* (period pieces) to circumvent censorship by repositioning contemporary incidents in the past and altering the names of samurai characters. Officials generally tolerated these infringements, so long as there was no direct criticism of the regime (Shively 1982: 23–4).

The Bunka-Bunsei era (1804–30) was the last of three periods within the Edo era identified as times of relative cultural freedom, individualism and experimentation (see Metzler 1994). In the subsequent Tempō era (1830–44), however, rampant inflation, lawlessness and official corruption, compounded with failed harvests, brought widespread rural famine and social unrest (Bolitho 1993: 118–33). Kabuki reflected this social malaise in a new genre called *kizewamono* (raw domestic pieces), in which lust, vengeance, deceit and murder were depicted with grotesque realism. Its antiheroes were prostitutes, blackmailers and gangsters: people 'struggling to survive and find their paths – even if by criminal acts' while feudal society crumbled (Brandon and Leiter 2002: 1). The *bakufu*'s belated Tempō reforms of 1841–3 were an unmitigated disaster (Metzler 1994: 69, 101). Although ostensibly issued to reduce economic hardship, in reality they concentrated on stemming the nation's moral decline by re-imposing Confucian discipline. Prostitution, pornography, drinking and gambling were all censured.[1] Kabuki was again reprimanded for its depravity, and harsh restrictions harried actors into adopting austerity in their personal and professional lives.[2] The future Ichikawa Danjūrō VII was banished from Edo for leading a lifestyle 'rather imperfectly attuned to economy and frugality' (Bolitho 1993: 145).[3]

The Tempō theater reforms culminated in 1842 with the banishment of the *sanza* (Edo's three authorized kabuki theaters) from their downtown locations to Saruwaka-machi, a remote northern area. The motive was to limit the damage kabuki posed to Edoites through both fires and moral corruption.[4] Keene (1976: 469) notes how kabuki was only saved from extinction when a proposed complete ban on it was overruled by the city magistrate. In exchange for continued official tolerance, limits were imposed on the size and design of the new theaters, and demands again came for plays extolling *kanzen chōaku* (promoting virtue and rejecting vice). This Confucian concept had long been a key criteria in censorship codes covering both theater and literature, but late Edo writers and dramatists had been particularly guilty of employing it to justify lurid depictions of evil, provided retributive justice was eventually achieved (Rubin 1984: 18–19).

Although the Tempō reforms ended in 1843, kabuki's banishment was not rescinded. Other restrictions, however, were gradually loosened, to the extent that 1851 saw the premiere of Edo kabuki's most radical protest play, *The Tale of Sakura the Martyr* (*Higashiyama Sakura zōshi*) by Segawa Jokō III (1806–81), depicting a peasant revolt against an oppressive and corrupt feudal regime.[5] The final theater edict of the *bakufu* regime was the one issued in 1866 forbidding excessive realism in the depiction of evil characters because this was counter to the tenets of *kanzen chōaku*.

Meiji society in transition

From the 1850s increased international contact brought Japan face to face with Western nations whose military, industrial and social institutions seemed to the Japanese to be inherently superior to their own. The ensuing political turmoil precipitated the Meiji Restoration of 1868, after which a new imperial government embarked on a 'forced march toward modernization' (Mitchell 1983: 15). The new directive elite included the former low-ranking provincial samurai Itō Hirobumi (1841–1909), Inoue Kaoru (1836–1915), Ōkuma Shigenobu (1838–1922) and Shibusawa Eiichi (1841–1931), in addition to able imperial courtiers like Iwakura Tomomi (1825–83). All applied their progressive ideals to the urgent task of reforming the nation along Western lines. Throughout Japan traditional systems were compared to overseas counterparts, and those considered outdated or uncivilized were modified to suit the new age.

The need was soon recognized for a redefinition of the nation's goals and self-identity. This was achieved by the samurai-bureaucrats' manipulation of public opinion through renewed censorship and propaganda measures (Mitchell 1983: 14–15). A Shintō-Confucian-inspired national doctrine which encouraged reverence for the deities and obedience to the Imperial Will was rigorously propagated. To this end, the Office of Shintō Worship (Jingi-kan), established in

16 *R. Payne*

1868, developed a propaganda network whose *senkyōshi* (preachers) were to disseminate this ideology to the masses.

There were, however, numerous ideological contradictions within the ruling elite. We can see evidence of both progressive and conservative attitudes in their dealings with kabuki (Brandon and Leiter 2003: 33), which they considered vulgar but wished to reform into a refined entertainment for the new age. Two early Meiji edicts deserve attention here: first, in September 1868 the *sanza*'s banishment to Saruwaka-machi was repealed, and second, in 1871 both *hinin* actors and *eta* outcasts were made *shin-heimin* (new commoners). Various motives can be suggested for these measures. They coincided with the launch of a new fiscal system, and, as full members of society, these groups were now subject to full taxation. Furthermore, the Charter Path of Five Articles issued on 6 April 1868 heralded the start of a more inclusive society (Mitchell 1983: 18). It is also possible that the Meiji statesmen had already envisaged a new function for kabuki which necessitated its full social status and separation from the neighbouring pleasure quarters. Certainly, a clear break between theater and prostitution was vital if kabuki were to enter good society.

Meanwhile, the demographics of kabuki's audience base were changing. The repeal of the *bakufu*'s segregation policy meant that enjoyment of kabuki was now open to all. The rural migrants who poured into Tokyo seeking the benefits of the new 'enlightened' era had a liberalizing effect on kabuki's predominantly conservative middle-class fan base (Bach 1995: 265, 277). More worrying to the authorities were the increasing numbers of Westerners attending the theater. The political elite were particularly sensitive to criticism from Westerners concerning perceived uncivilized elements of their culture, and they soon realized the need to prevent kabuki from shaming the nation (Shively 1976: 81).

But what did the early Meiji statesmen know about kabuki? Moreover, what did they know about Westerners' opinions of kabuki? Few, if any, had seen kabuki before the Meiji Restoration. However, many of the samurai-bureaucrats had undertaken some Western studies before the Meiji Restoration, and by 1870 most had visited the West in search of the building blocks of the new society. Owing to the gravity of their task, they gave little thought to frivolous entertainments like theater. One by-product of their Western travels, however, was an awareness that Western civilized society attended opera, ballet and various types of sophisticated theater (Powell 2005: 105–6). From this the Japanese elite formed their own opinion of what Western spectators might think of kabuki, and censured those aspects that such 'hypothetical' Westerners might find unacceptable (Takahashi 1995: 142).

Some Westerners, including Britain's highest ranking diplomat Rutherford Alcock (1863, vol. 2: 113) and the American academic Edward Morse (1990, vol. 1: 404) were indeed shocked by both the brutality and vulgarity of early Meiji kabuki and the audience's unconcerned reaction to it.[6] Such views were balanced, however, by others like the American teacher and future congregational minister William Elliot Griffis, who noted in his diary of 1871 with amused detachment the somewhat gory plot and fine acting (1876: 514–15).

Censorship in Meiji kabuki theater 17

Powell (2005: 104) notes that there were many other Western visitors who expressed their wonder and admiration for kabuki's animated nature. It must be remembered that much Western theater at this time, for example the musical hall variety shows popular in Victorian cities, was similarly ribald. The American journalist Edward House noted this fact in a *Cornhill Magazine* article of September 1872, together with his frank appreciation of kabuki's artistry (Yokoyama 1987: 102).

The 1872 kabuki edicts

Because the Meiji statesmen could not ban kabuki outright, they had no alternative but to accept its existence and concentrate on limiting its damage to the sensitivities of polite society and the nation's international prestige. These became key themes of their kabuki control measures, which were issued from 1872. Certain Tokyo newspapers reported the new edicts verbatim, adding their own positive editorials justifying their implementation. The acceptance of these papers of their role as governmental propaganda machines is hardly surprising when one considers that Meiji statesmen were their greatest patrons and financial backers (Mitchell 1983: 40–1).[7]

The first edict, dated February 1872, was reported as follows:[8]

> At the end of February, the managers and dramatists of the Saruwaka-machi *sanza* were summoned by the Tokyo Prefectural Authorities and informed that because members of good society and foreigners were now attending plays, theaters were forbidden to show anything inciting lewdness which parents and children could not watch together, but they should rather show wholesome plays which could be considered educational.
>
> (*Tokyo Nichinichi shinbun*, 22 February 1872)

The editorial comment read as follows:

> Generally speaking, it is through the eyes that the heart is touched. All feelings, be they pleasure, anger, compassion or joy, arise from what we see. The theater is a means of delighting the eyes and gladdening the heart, but its main aim must be to educate. Light amusement is acceptable in moderation: however, there are many licentious things that must not appear on stage, things that, if we watched with our families, would make us hide our faces in our sleeves. If foreigners saw such shows, they would surely think that these are part of our national customs and that we indulge in them ourselves. Naturally they would come to despise us because of it. This is a problem that must concern cultured people, and it is precisely for this reason that vulgar customs must change and that we must progress towards civilization. This is why the government has issued this warning.
>
> (*Tokyo Nichinichi shinbun*, 22 February 1872)

18   *R. Payne*

From these texts we can isolate the two key issues of the new policy as education and refinement. We can also sense a shift in the official attitude towards kabuki in the positive recognition of its potential to be both useful and enjoyable. These points were reiterated on 5 April 1872 when kabuki representatives were summoned to another meeting at the Tokyo Number One Ward Office (Matsumoto 1974: 36), the purport of which was as follows:

> It is taken for granted that kabuki should spread moral teachings. Attention should be given to ridding plays of meaningless decorations, so Hashiba Hideyoshi must not be presented as Mashiba Hisayoshi, for this might confuse the young into thinking that Hideyoshi's name was Hisayoshi, or Oda Nobunaga's name was Harunaga. Everything should be true to the facts. However, it should not be assumed that everything dry is good, and everything amusing is bad, for even levity can be used for instruction. All these points should be noted and transmitted to other theaters and dramatists.[9]
>
> (*Shinbun zasshi* 40, April 1872)

This decree introduces another pillar of the new control policy: namely to end the custom of disguising historical figures behind false names. The reasoning behind this point was explained as follows:

> In terms of *bunmei kaika* (civilization and enlightenment),[10] theaters are a sort of junior school, but instead of [teaching] instructions of the saints and sages, they teach nothing but retribution for crimes.... An actor is an instructor. If education is his profession, there should not be elements which are indiscreet. Regarding play content, one should not be setting them in the Kamakura era and changing names to the Ashikaga line.... These improvements will rid kabuki of its baseness, which will benefit not only theaters, for the public should also be grateful.
>
> (*Tokyo Nichinichi shinbun*, 7 April 1872)

These two edicts can be considered as moral guidelines for kabuki rather than censorship codes, for neither came with notices of punishments for noncompliance (Kawatake 1993: 140). However, such measures were added two months later, when the newly established Department of Religious Affairs (Kyōbushō) announced that henceforth kabuki theaters were required to present scripts for censoring and to register the content of each season's schedule.[11] Noncompliance would result in the suspension of the theater's licence. In this version of control, guidance was enforced by censors who also had authority to ban.

Most Meiji theater histories list the Three Guidance Edicts, issued by the Department of Religious Affairs on 14 March 1872, as the second major theater censorship edict of that year. However, at this time kabuki had not yet formally entered the jurisdiction of that Department. Furthermore, these edicts applied only to the *senkyōshi* (preachers) who had already been officially appointed to spread the State's moral teachings (Kobitsu 1988: 781). Whereas the Three Guidance Edicts did set the tone of the Department's later dealings with kabuki, they were not applied to kabuki until August 1872, when they were re-worded to fit the theater's particular situation in the Three Regulations of Musical and Theatrical Entertainments, which read as follows:

> Since nō, kyōgen and other forms of music and dance influence people's emotions and manners, they must adhere to the following rules:
>
> - All disrespectful and blasphemous references to the Emperor are forbidden.
> - Plays extolling *kanzen chōaku* (rewarding good and chastising evil) are encouraged and excessive lewdness and wickedness harmful to public morals must be avoided.
> - Theaters should revise the customs and practices employed when actors were considered as being outside society, for they must now act in a way appropriate to their new social status.
>
> (*Tokyo Nichinichi shinbun*, 25 August 1872)

Then, on 20 September 1872, all kabuki theaters were informed that they were required to apply for a performance license and pay tax on their earnings. This constituted a new form of control over theater business, which had hitherto been considered outside civilized society and therefore exempt from tax. Although this tax reduced kabuki's revenues, it stood as an important symbol of its acceptance into mainstream society: a prerequisite for any further rise in status.[12]

Objectives of the 1872 edicts

At the time of these regulations, prominent Meiji statesmen like Itō, Iwakura, Inoue, Shibusawa and Ōchi were on the last and most extensive fact-finding mission to the West: the Iwakura Mission of 1871–3. Meanwhile, the caretaker government, including Saigō Takamori, Ōkuma Shigenobu and Itagaki Taisuke, conducted major reforms including the abolition of *daimyō* domains, and education and military reforms were also under review (Soviak 1976: 8). None of these statesmen had been overseas, and their approach to theater reform reflected little of the Western inspiration behind later official dealings with theater. In January 1868 the new Meiji government had announced its intention to leave good aspects of the *bakufu* regime unchanged (Mitchell 1983: 20). Scholars use the similarities between the 1872 theater edicts and the late Edo censorship policy to illustrate this point in relation to kabuki. Matsumoto Shinko regards the edicts predominantly as a reapplication of the pre-existing feudal regulations (1974: 35), while Kawatake Toshio concludes that although the reforms included 'new ingredients', the 'basic cooking style' (1993: 144) remained unchanged.

The first directive of the Three Regulations of Musical and Theatrical Entertainments simply repeated Edo restrictions on depictions of the Head of State: all

20   R. Payne

that had changed was his identity. The *bakufu* had forbidden literary and dramatic portrayals of the Shogun, but permitted even quite uncharitable depictions of the Emperor and court, provided that they were set in the past (Mitchell 1983: 8). However, reverence for the Meiji Emperor was a key pillar of the new *kokutai* or national identity, so depictions of him were tightly controlled. Regarding the second article of the Three Regulations, this simply reapplied the familiar Edo code of retributive justice in order to stamp out salacious and wicked elements.

Alongside the replication of earlier regulations, however, we can also detect a new approach to drama control. Chief among its new responsibilities was to become educationally and ideologically sound. Kabuki was expected to employ *kanzen chōaku* principles as a means to civilize, inspire and instruct the nation, rather than merely as a plot mechanism. Moreover, for the first time in its long history, kabuki was encouraged to ensure that the facts in its historical plays were correct, so that impressionable women and children would not be misled.[13] This constituted a remarkable change in official attitude from disdain and fear to a positive, if somewhat utilitarian, effort to give kabuki a nobler social function.

Rather than banishing kabuki to the periphery of society, the directive elite now expected it to interact with mainstream society. To achieve this kabuki was expected to revise its traditional practices and behave in a manner more appropriate to its new social status. This concept has received little attention from scholars, but I regard it as the most important pillar of the new control policy. The Meiji government wanted kabuki to end its defiance of authority, and instead co-operate in ensuring that potentially offensive elements never even reached the public arena. In other words, kabuki was supposed to develop its own code of self-censorship. This applied not just to scripts, but to every element of the performance that deviated from the spirit of *bunmei kaika*. The 1872 edicts supplied few guidelines on those areas of kabuki that needed reform, but newspapers printed many editorials and letters criticizing uncivilized elements.[14]

After entering the jurisdiction of the Department of Religious Affairs in 1872, actors were granted permission to become *yūshi*, or trainee *kyōdōshoku* (lay preachers) (Kobitsu 1988: 993). However, only one reference can be found to a kabuki actor actually preaching morality to the people (Matsumoto 1974: 49). One kabuki magazine reported that the star actor Ichikawa Danjūrō IX (1839–1903) did achieve the title of *kyōdōshoku*, but only much later, in 1884 (*Kabuki shinpō* 440, 17 July 1884). This leads one to conclude that this was just another expression of the government's covert pressure on actors to behave respectably: their mere connection with that title would have considerably altered actors' perception of their social duty to depict examples of noble virtues on stage, and set good examples in their private lives. I would argue that this constitutes covert pressure on actors to extend self-censorship to all elements of their off-stage lives and on-stage performances by adopting a *kōshō* (refined) tone.

The 1875 kabuki edict

By early 1873 dissatisfaction was mounting over the new government's failure to produce a national assembly and constitution (Mitchell 1983: 44–5). This dissent coalesced into the Freedom and Popular Rights Movement (Jiyū Minken Undō), which the government sought to quell by increasingly authoritarian means. In November 1873 the Home Ministry was formed under Ōkubo Toshimichi (1830–78) as the centralized police power, which in June 1875 issued the Press Law prohibiting press criticism of the authorities (de Lange 1988: 44), and the Libel Law, prohibiting injury of a person's honor or reputation (Mitchell 1983: 48–9). Three months later, the Publication Law brought book censorship under Home Ministry jurisdiction. Its fourth article prohibited publication of anything threatening public peace or morals (Mitchell 1983: 50). Furthermore, in July 1876 more laws gave the Home Ministry powers to suspend the license of any newspaper that threatened national security. This drastic restriction of freedom of expression illustrates the severity with which the government regarded the threat from subversive ideas (de Lange 1988: 47).

Kabuki also felt the force of this new approach in an edict issued on 7 September 1875, issued three months after the Home Ministry took over theater jurisdiction. The fact that this edict started by repeating the objectives of the earlier decrees suggests that sufficient moral rectitude and historical authenticity had not yet been incorporated into plays. More importantly, however, both scripts and the theaters' adherence to them now came under direct Home Ministry surveillance. As in the publishing and press worlds, deviation from the agreed format would bring an instant ban. Clearly, actors' own self-censorship measures were not yet considered sufficiently reliable to prevent lapses in decorum. The following extract from the 1875 edict, as relayed in the press, reveals another modification of the official standpoint:

> We have noticed that there are plays based on nonsense novels about families whose relatives are still alive. It is unbearable when their retainers and dependants hear these matters, especially when fictional elements are also added. If this is true, these plays should be eradicated, for this is a bad state of affairs. Do not disregard this rule.
>
> (*Tokyo Nichinichi shinbun*, 8 September 1875)

While earlier edicts encouraged kabuki to revert to correct names in the service of historical accuracy, this regulation echoed the recent Libel Law in preventing kabuki from offending characters' descendants through uncomplimentary exposure of their ancestors' deeds. Although there were no punitive measures for inaccurate historical facts, theaters now risked punishment for correct but libellous references to real people.

Western models of refined theater

As with other Meiji reforms, questions arise over the extent to which they were inspired by Western models. As noted, most Meiji statesmen had at least some first-hand Western experience. Moreover, upon their return home, many other *ryūgakusei* (Japanese overseas students) had taken influential positions in the new bureaucracy, education, journalism and publishing industries (Cobbing 2005: 53). References to performing arts in these returnees' travel accounts are disappointingly scarce and brief. This is presumably because they would not have wanted to give the impression that they wasted time on idle pleasures. However, as noted, many Japanese visitors did at least appreciate the fact that theaters were splendid buildings located in good sectors of the city and attended by both men and women of high society, in an atmosphere of intelligent appreciation (Mine 1996: 69). Shibusawa Eiichi, for example, noted in his diary of 1867 that although he could not follow the plot, he was entranced by the performance he saw at the Paris Opéra – the dances of both sexes and the dazzling visual spectacle (Craig 1994: 158). Images such as these contributed to the widespread perception in Japan that Western theater was a refined entertainment that eschewed vulgarity.

These impressions were confirmed by the Iwakura Mission. Its three-fold aims were to build diplomatic links with the West, discuss the repeal of the Unequal Treaties[15] and to collect information for Japan's own modernization process. As part of their official reception in British cities, the high-ranking delegates also attended at least six staged performances, and they were similarly entertained in continental Europe (Anthony and Healey 1996: 21–8). As expected, the Mission's official account provides detailed observations of many aspects of Western life and society, as well as its industrial and military systems, but little mention is made of theater.[16] However, practical concepts that were adopted into later theater reform plans, including the idea of state support, architectural grandeur, gas lighting, fire safety and hygienic sanitation, were all first noted around this time (Kobitsu 1988: 116–17). Moreover, the statesmen who were influential in later theater reforms, namely Fukuchi Gen'ichirō (Ōchi), Inoue and Itō, now had extensive experience of the type of theater that they later called on kabuki to emulate.

Kabuki's response to the early Meiji edicts

In October 1868 the capital's Morita-za and Nakamura-za theaters presented a joint season entitled *Dedication of Loyalty to the Eastern Capital* (*Azuma no miyako chūshin yurai*), where 'Azuma' was another reading for 'Tokyo', the capital's new name (Brandon and Leiter 2003: 3). However, little else in kabuki at this time reflected the great events that were reshaping the nation. Although the creators of the 1872 and 1875 theater edicts had no real idea of their practical implications, the kabuki community knew that compliance required either the composition of new texts or the rewriting of old texts, in addition to the search for accurate historical sources. But why bother when the traditional format might be accepted, if grudgingly, by the authorities? Kabuki soon discovered that it could continue undisturbed with performances that were similar, if not identical, to those that had pleased audiences for generations.

Some efforts were made to incorporate token progressive elements, however. It is believed that the 1870 Ichimura-za play *Pioneer Photograph Pictures of Actors* (*Sakigakete shashin no yakusha-e*), featuring Japan's first photo shop, was the first to depict Meiji society (Brandon and Leiter 2003: 18). In 1872, two Kyoto theaters performed adaptations of a popular translation of the book *Self Help* by Samuel Smiles (1812–1904).[17] Their European settings and depictions of both Victorian ethics of self-development and Confucian filial piety were praised by the Kyoto Assembly and the press for their modernity and morality (Matsumoto 1974: 58).[18] Moreover, November 1873 saw the Morita-za premiere of *Tokyo Daily Newspaper* (*Tokyo Nichinichi shinbun*), which dealt with contemporary events – a murder mystery featuring a modern journalist (Toita 1956: 215).

Sporadic attempts were also made to introduce greater textual accuracy, but resistance from conservative actors obstructed any systematic application of genuine names to kabuki's semi-legendary heroes. The difficulties encountered are demonstrated in early Meiji performances of the popular classic *Treasury of the Loyal Retainers* (*Kanadehon chūshingura*), which dramatized the true events of the Akō vendetta undertaken in 1703 by forty-seven *rōnin* (masterless samurai) against their former lord's enemy. Before the Morita-za performance of May 1872 it was rumored that the main hero's fictional name (Ōishi Kuranosuke) would be replaced by his real name (Ōboshi Yuranosuke). However, problems surrounding the modifications delayed the play's premiere, and the plan was eventually abandoned (Ihara *et al.* 1973: 178). The November 1873 Murayama-za version entitled *Alphabetical Listing of the Loyal Retainers* (*Chūshin iroha jikki*) did include the true names of the *rōnin*, but all those characters portrayed negatively retained their fictional names (Tamura 1922: 148–9). The use of real names did not spread to other theaters, and conventional fictional names were retained for the Sawamura-za performance of 1874 and most subsequent performances.

Similarly, little progress was made in the incorporation of correct names and data into plays set in the recent past. A new play of 1874 at the Yokohama Minato-za entitled *A New Year's Dream of Enlightenment* (*Minato norifune kaika no hatsuyume*), concerning Commodore Perry's landing in Japan in 1854, disappointed those expecting a new approach to recent historical material. Concessions to modern relevance were found in the inclusion of Western vocabulary, costumes and hairstyles, but the plot was closer to a kabuki fantasy than an account of the incident, and all names were altered: so Tokugawa became Okugawa and Itō became Yūi (Matsumoto 1974: 111–13).

Unlike newspapers, which were severely policed, there are few incidents of kabuki being punished for its subversive content. Offensive items were either avoided completely, or were sufficiently hidden so that the censors were not

24 R. Payne

alerted. It appears that the former option is more applicable here. Kabuki plays were traditionally composed for specific actors, and rather than burning with political agendas, most star actors were loath to endanger their new-found official approbation by staging subversive pieces. According to Keene (1976: 473), Meiji's leading dramatist Kawatake Mokuami (1816–93)[19] had 'no social principles he wanted to incorporate in plays – he did not wish to mock or criticize society'. One of the few examples of direct censorial intervention concerned the play *Mito Komon and the Destruction of the Atakemaru* (*Komon-ki osana kōshaku*) performed at the Shintomi-za (successor of the Morita-za) in 1877. Mokuami had intentionally included historically accurate facts, but performances were temporarily halted when a distant relative of Mito Komon used the 1875 Libel Law to prevent the theater sullying his ancestor's memory. Performance permission was only granted once the offending sections had been rewritten (Kimura 1943: 502).[20]

Reforms at the Shintomi-za

One could wonder at the extent to which the Meiji statesmen expected their theater edicts to be followed. The creation of a refined theater required modifications not only of plays, but also performance space and audience behavior. Implementation of such large-scale changes required the co-operation of like-minded dramatists, actors and managers and a large financial investment, but in the 1870s most theaters had neither the financial security nor the inclination to consider such reforms. However, connections had been growing between certain kabuki individuals and members of the political elite since the dawn of the Meiji era. Through this network the Meiji elite became aware that reform was welcomed in at least some quarters of kabuki.

Morita Kan'ya XII (1846–97) was the ambitious and astute young manager of the Morita-za, who courted any opportunity to mix with Tokyo's new elite. Kan'ya's money-lender introduced him to a relative named Matsumoto Jun (1832–1907), who went on to become Japan's first Army Chief Medical Officer. Around 1871 Matsumoto introduced Kan'ya to Ōkubo Toshimichi, who, according to Kimura, sent letters to Kan'ya from abroad describing Western theaters (1943: 259, 269). Just before embarking on the Iwakura Mission, Ōkubo introduced Kan'ya to the statesman and journalist Fukuchi Ōchi, who was already transmitting his considerable overseas experience and opinions on kabuki reform to the future star Danjūrō IX. It was Ōkubo who assisted Kan'ya in obtaining the first of the new theater licenses, and encouraged him to leave the Saruwaka-machi theater district (Kawatake 1993: 146).

In November 1872 the Morita-za reopened in Shintomi-chō in central Tokyo in significantly grander and more modern premises. In response to changes in the expectations of Tokyo audiences, toilets and Western chairs were installed for the first time, and many of kabuki's chaotic conventions concerning ticket and refreshment acquisition were modified. Further, the theater employed none of kabuki's traditional *tomeba* (security guards), showing that Morita-za

Censorship in Meiji kabuki theater   25

audiences were expected to behave in a civilized manner. Henceforth, disturbances would be dealt with by the Tokyo Metropolitan Police. Both these changes, and the improved fire safety standards, were undertaken to prove that this theater could be incorporated into society rather than shunned as a hazard to public safety and morality (Payne 2003: 7–14).

Renamed as the Shintomi-za from 1875, the theater pioneered a new genre of *sewamono* known as *zangirimono* (cropped hair plays), which were written by Mokuami primarily for the great actor Onoe Kikugorō V (1844–1903). Mirroring contemporary conceptual and material changes, *zangirimono* featured trains, telegraphs, top hats and short hairstyles (from which the genre got its name) and other imported paraphernalia. The plots adhered more closely to the true spirit of *kanzen chōaku* by focusing on the process leading to the villains' punishment and repentance. Thus, the bandit-hero of the 1881 play *Senta and Shimazō* (*Shima chidori tsuki no shiranami*) not only gave up his criminal activities, but even called for his example to be a lesson for others, and the heroine of the 1877 play *Woman Student* (*Fujibitai Tsukuba no shigeyama*) disguised herself as a man in order to study at university.[21] Only one early Meiji play presented a negative picture of the Edo era. *Sogoro the Fishmonger* (*Sakanaya Sōgorō*), performed at the Shintomi-za in 1883, portrayed the arrogance and corruption of the *bakufu* regime in a manner which would have not have been permitted twenty years earlier.[22]

Other artistic reforms reflecting the spirit of the official edicts were pioneered primarily at the Shintomi-za in a genre called *katsurekigeki* (living history plays) that were written by Mokuami for Danjūrō IX. From his early childhood Danjūrō had been interested in historical accuracy, and he strived to reinvigorate performances with refinement, intellect and moral probity by eliminating dramatic conventions that belittled noble characters. Danjūrō's performance in 1875 of the new play *Tales of Minister Kibi's Mission to China* (*Kibi Daijin Shina monogatari*), concerning Japan's recent diplomatic negotiations with China, was welcomed for its contemporary relevance and intellectual content (Kawatake 1993: 151), though traditional fans criticized his highbrow style. He continued his reforms when he joined the Shintomi-za the next year, where premieres of *Newspaper Journal of the Amakusa Incident* (*Amakusa nisshi kabuki shinbun*) (1876) and *The Glorious Pine* (*Matsu sakae Chiyoda no shintoku*) (1878) were praised for their factual authenticity (Ihara 1933: 246–7). To support his endeavours he founded the Historical Research Society (Kojitsu-kai) in 1877 and the Antiquarian Society (Kyūko-kai) in 1883. These boasted eminent scholars among their members, including Yoda Gakkai (1833–1909), an important figure in Meiji literary and art circles, and Matsuda Michiyuki (1839–82), who became Home Ministry Chief Secretary in 1877.

When the new Shintomi-za theater building opened in 1878, the theater's cast included the majority of kabuki's progressive actors and dramatists. With gas lighting, modified auditorium and restrained decorations, the new building reflected more closely the ideal of a sophisticated institution suitable for Japanese and Western genteel society (Payne 2003: 14–20). It far outshone its rivals, most of which were still located in Saruwaka-machi and limited by their

26   R. Payne

conservative artistic outlook and financial insecurity. Prime Minister Sanjō Sanemori was among the elite audience at the opening ceremony, at which Danjūrō read a speech composed by Ōchi, who was now Chairman of the Tokyo Assembly. The most famous part of this speech reads as follows:

> Recently the theater has been drinking the dregs of the world and breathing in the stench of baseness. It has lost sight of the marvellous principle of *kanzen chōaku*, and has fallen instead into the wanton pursuit of novel mannerisms, sliding ever further downhill. This trend is at its worst now. I, Danjūrō, am profoundly disturbed by this, and earnestly intend to co-operate with others to clean away these evil practices.
>
> (Kawatake 1959: 776–7)

This shows the depth to which notions of kabuki's new social responsibility had permeated the top echelon of the kabuki community.[23]

Throughout the late 1870s and 1880s the Shintomi-za excelled in the production of the progressive genres championed by Kikugorō and Danjūrō. One new play of particular interest was the 1878 premiere of *The Seinan War* (*Okige no kumo harau asagochi*), Japan's first onstage reportage of the recent civil war in Kyushu. Their search for original documents, eyewitness accounts and weaponry brought Shintomi-za members in contact with statesmen who had been directly involved in the incident. These included Kōmyōji Saburō (1849–93), a recent returnee from France, who was also happy to provide the Shintomi-za reformers with his impressions of Western theater (Takahashi 1995: 143). Kōmyōji is credited as having first mentioned to Kan'ya the possibility that his adherence to the government's reform guidelines might lead to state funding, following the Parisian model (Kimura 1943: 512–13).

Impressed with this theater's reform zeal, Meiji statesmen demonstrated their support by arranging high-profile events there to which both Japanese and Western dignitaries were invited. These included Prince Heinrich of Prussia and two members of the imperial household, who attended a welcome gala there in 1879. Also that year Kan'ya premiered *Humanity and the World of Money* (*Ningen banji kane yononaka*), an adaptation of Bulwer-Lytton's 1840 play *Money*. As with several other Western-inspired Shintomi-za plays, linguistic and stylistic assistance was provided by Fukuchi Ōchi. The grandest of these events was held in honor of the visit by former US President Ulysses Grant in June 1879, for which no expense was spared. Under Ōchi's direction, Mokuami composed a new play in Grant's honor, followed by a dance by over seventy geisha clad in kimonos of red, white and blue (Chang 1969).

Reform or self-censorship?

How much of the Shintomi-za's style at this time can be regarded as evidence of actors practising self-censorship rather than developing reforms? The line between the two is hard to define. Self-censorship is the active decision by an artist to avoid bringing controversial materials into the public arena. This decision is made in response to pressure from the social and political environment, driven primarily by fear of reprisals. In contrast, reform is an inwardly driven artistically creative force inspired by the dynamics of the era and the artistic milieu. It is an expression of progressive ideals developed in an atmosphere of creative freedom and experimentation.

Aspects of the Shintomi-za's adopted style, including Kikugorō's emphasis on contemporary settings and morally uplifting plots, Danjūrō's focus on intellectual probity and Kan'ya's gentrification of the auditorium, could be interpreted simply as acts of self-censorship, for they closely followed the early Meiji edicts. However, I would argue that rather than being the product of political manipulation, they were conceived by artists as a continuation of kabuki's tradition of reflecting contemporary trends and public preoccupations. *Zangirimono*, despite their heavy moral tone, were little more than a *sewamono* reflecting Meiji material and social culture. Moreover, Danjūrō's interest in historical accuracy predated Meiji censorship edicts by a decade (Ihara 1933: 114–15). Although encouraged by the educated elite, he nevertheless incorporated their ideas into reforms motivated primarily by his own artistic vision. His reforms were not shaped by fear of censors, but rather by a desire to make kabuki more dignified. Likewise, Kan'ya was ambitious for his theater's advance into the glamour of high society and the security of state funding. His close relationship with his sponsors would have been ruined if his theater's plays, audience or venue had embarrassed them and their Western guests with a show of vulgarity.

Censorship or patronage? A mutually beneficial relationship

It was in this way that early Meiji official dealings with kabuki split between broad censorial controls and friendly support for the Shintomi-za. The catalyst for this was the realization that, so long as the uncivilized elements of mainstream kabuki were effectively curbed by edicts, refined entertainment could best be achieved by nurturing one co-operative theater, rather than reforming them all. It was only natural that official attention turned to the Shintomi-za, which had already demonstrated its willingness and ability to reform.

This was the background to the meeting in April 1878 at the house of Matsuda Michiyuki, now Governor of Tokyo (and keen *katsurekigeki* supporter), between Shintomi-za actors and statesmen including Itō Hirobumi, senior councillor in the Council of State (Dajōkan) and soon to become Head of the Home Ministry. Yoda Gakkai (another member of the Historical Research Society) recorded in his diary how Itō praised the grandeur, sophistication and restraint of Western theater. He suggested that Japanese actors could also enjoy the respect afforded to Western actors if their performances reflected the spirit of *bunmei kaika*. He called for reform in areas ranging from architecture to heroic speeches and costumes. Here again, requests for historical rectitude and moral probity were balanced with warnings to avoid slandering named individuals (Gakkai Jiroku Kenkyū-kai 1992, vol. 4: 119–20).

28   *R. Payne*

During the decade from 1878 the relationship between politicians and the Shintomi-za grew ever closer as they strove to maintain the theater's progressive stance. Both Kikugorō and Danjūrō continued to develop their new artistic genres, and the theater's repertory and tone reflected greater refinement.[24] Large-scale gala events were staged there for visiting dignitaries, and actors were invited to perform selected programs at elite private gatherings. The influential entrepreneur Shibusawa Eiichi and Fukuchi Ōchi (now leader of the Tokyo Chamber of Commerce) both actively promoted the Shintomi-za's services for official engagements (Toita 1956: 192). These efforts culminated in 1883 with the opening of the Rokumeikan: an imitation European manor 'devoted to the dissemination of Western manners and customs' (Barr 1968: 10). Eminent Tokyo figures invited Shintomi-za actors to perform at private parties which were attended by the same journalists, businessmen, diplomats and Western guests who patronized Rokumeikan events.

Should we regard the Meiji elite's relationship with the Shintomi-za as censorship or patronage? Again, the boundary is difficult to define. Itō's reform guidelines of 1878 resembled censorship in that their content echoed earlier edicts, and had political and diplomatic motives. However, they differed from pure censorship in two ways: first, non-compliance would not entail punishment, and second, they were transmitted to Shintomi-za reformers alone in a private setting, rather than as an official announcement to all theaters. If we define patronage as a private relationship between politically or socially powerful individuals and selected artists who enjoy benefits including financial support, privileged use and protection, then the symbiotic relationship between the Shintomi-za and Meiji statesmen displays many of these characteristics. In this particular case, however, full financial support never materialized, so the relationship cannot be considered as true patronage. We can conclude that it lies part way along the continuum between patronage and censorial manipulation.

The kabuki edicts of 1882

Throughout the 1870s, political dissent from the Freedom and Popular Rights Movement threatened to destabilize the Meiji regime. In an effort to counter this, the Public Gatherings Ordinance of April 1880 gave the police power to dissolve meetings that threatened the public peace (Mitchell 1983: 67). Since 1876 Tokyo kabuki theaters had been submitting their scripts to the new Police Department (Keishichō) (Kimura 1943: 469), and in 1882 this office issued strict new regulations known as the Regulations for Control of Theater. These established the protocol for random theater inspections and the immediate ban on performances deviating from agreed scripts or threatening to disturb the peace. Auditorium seats were to be reserved at all times for inspectors, and at least two policemen were to attend each performance (Ihara 1933: 451). High standards of fire safety and hygiene were also compulsory. These regulations had little impact on the Shintomi-za, however, which already met the stipulated requirements.

Censorship in Meiji kabuki theater 29

It is important to note that there are no recorded incidents of kabuki performance being banned under these regulations. Its classic plays were set in a bygone
age and its new plays did not incorporate contemporary materials subversive
enough to attract censorial attention. Kabuki actors could no longer regard themselves as representatives of an oppressed social class: Edo social hierarchies had
been abolished, and the theater now had a wider audience base. The political
elite no longer saw themselves as being pitted against kabuki's pernicious social
influence: they had recognized its potential as both pedagogic tool and cultural
showpiece.

The end to politically motivated reform pressure

The close co-operation between politics and kabuki culminated in the establishment of the Drama Reform Society (Engeki Kairyō-kai) in 1886. Its leader was
Suematsu Kenchō (1855–1920) who, during the 1870s, had been Itō's informant
at the Japanese legation in London while studying at Cambridge. There are few
surviving reports of the plays Suematsu attended, but his letters home provided
insightful impressions of Western theater (Mehl 1993: 181). Mason (1979:
18–19) notes that a reform article he published in 1884 was based on a genuine
desire to reinvigorate Japan's traditional arts by incorporating Western concepts.
After returning home in 1879, Suematsu formulated a radical plan to modernize
kabuki along Western lines. The list of the Society's members reads like a *Who's
Who* of Meiji Japan, and it is thought that Inoue and Shibusawa helped Suematsu
compose the Society's manifesto (Tomita 1994: 61). Its main aims can be sum-
marized as follows:

1 reforming earlier bad practices in drama in order to encourage the development of good theater;
2 making play-writing a respected profession;
3 establishing a modern playhouse.

Of these proposals, the first had been promoted by the government since 1872,
and the second had been widely discussed in newspapers since the mid-1870s.
From the start, the Society placed most emphasis on the third proposal: a new
theater modeled on the Paris Opéra (Fuhara 1965: 29–30). Members of the
Shintomi-za were involved to some extent in the Society's plans, but they
doubted the effectiveness of so radical a reform program instigated by people
with little knowledge of and regard for their art. Indeed, the Society's proposed
reforms would have created a genre so radically modern and westernized in style
that it would have stripped kabuki of its essential aesthetic balance and beauty.

With hindsight, we can see that the Drama Reform Society's ideals of progress and sophistication were not so much incorrect as inappropriate. For
members, theater reform was only conceivable in terms of modifying what was
already available in Japan, namely kabuki, rather creating a new genre. Knowing
no alternative, they assumed that kabuki was able to adapt to their design, no

30   *R. Payne*

matter how alien. In the end, few of their plans came to fruition, although they did open the way for major participation in all aspects of kabuki's artistic and managerial processes by those outside the traditional kabuki world. The Society's major success was the organization in 1887 of kabuki's first performance before the Emperor, albeit of a repertory of selected auspicious classics, and performed on a specially constructed stage in Inoue's garden. This was nevertheless a considerable achievement for kabuki, which had been officially despised until only two decades earlier.

The imperial kabuki performance would have attracted less attention if it had not coincided with rumors of scandalous behavior at a Rokumeikan Ball and revelations of suspicious secret diplomatic negotiations (Tomita 1994: 177–86). These provoked a conservative backlash and intense criticism of Inoue (now Foreign Minister in Itō's first cabinet, 1885–7) and his overt westernization policy. The next cabinet, under Ōkuma, adopted a more conservative approach to social reforms and played no official role in theater reform. The radical Western-inspired ideals of the Drama Reform Society had also prompted heated dispute in the press, with some critics calling for recognition of the limits to which kabuki could modernize while still maintaining its artistic integrity (Mine 1996: 120–2).

Conclusions

By the mid-1880s, the Shintomi-za was rapidly losing its leading edge, struggling with debts incurred in following the government's reform guidelines. The rumored state patronage never materialized, and major actors transferred to new rival theaters where artistic reforms were less radical. Both *zangirimono* and *katsurekigeki* began to lose their appeal, and neither survived beyond the lives of their creators. Kabuki had come to be valued more for its cultural and artistic heritage rather than its contemporary relevance, with the theatrical depiction of *chōnin* culture generating feelings of nostalgia for a disappearing world. After the rise of new radical political movements in the 1880s and 1890s, censors concentrated on controlling artistic genres that promoted potentially subversive contemporary political material. They had more to worry about from the new *sōshi-shibai* (plays of young amateur political agitators), which sought to encourage wider political awareness through the production of plays with intense critical commentary. The nature of these plays demanded extensive reference to real names and events, and their choice of subject matter made them more likely to excite social unrest than kabuki's tales of warriors and domestic tragedies of a bygone age.

Overall, friction between kabuki and the state lessened during the early Meiji era. The Meiji government's aims for kabuki were achieved less through the strict policing of censorial regulations and more through the encouragement of certain progressive individuals who grasped the new opportunities for advancement and incorporated elements of official policy into their own reform programs. The unevenness of the Meiji kabuki community's response to the

Censorship in Meiji kabuki theater 31

authorities' ideals caused a split in the official approach between, on the one hand, universally applied censorship controls and, on the other hand, manipulative endorsement of keen reformers in a private relationship that closely resembled patronage.

Questions can be raised over the justification of the attempts of politicians to appropriate aspects of kabuki to aid their own domestic and diplomatic interests. Their actions deserve criticism for their blatant disregard of kabuki audience tastes and ignorance of its artistic heritage. However, with hindsight we can see the importance of the early Meiji censorship edicts in initiating kabuki's rise in social status, which in turn provided opportunities for a wider sector of society to engage with kabuki. The new perception of kabuki as a cultural treasure is one of the greatest legacies of the Meiji theater controls, which ultimately changed the way that people thought about art, performance and the theater as an institution.

Notes

1 See Mitchell (1983: 8–10) for a detailed account of the early Meiji literary restrictions, and Bolitho (1993: 144–5) for a discussion of the wider social controls.
2 Brandon and Leiter (2002: 25) provides a comprehensive list of theater restrictions from 1837 to 1842.
3 Actors are referred to by their stage name and the ordinal number denoting the generations to have had that name.
4 The Tempō theater reforms issued in Osaka also limited the number of theaters and banned the sale of merchandise and publications adorned with actors' family crests (Brandon and Leiter 2002: 27).
5 Translated by Anne Phillips in Brandon and Leiter (2002: 220–48).
6 Regarding the indifference with which the audience of men, women and children watched scenes of 'indescribable grossness', Alcock notes, '... these people in some aspects are altogether bewildering when we try to judge them by our canons of morality and taste' (1863: vol. 2, 114).
7 The *Shinbun zasshi* was directly supported by the influential statesman Kido Takayoshi, who regarded its remit as the education of the nation regarding thought and actions appropriate to the new age (Mitchell 1983: 38–9). The *Tokyo Nichinichi shinbun* was closely connected to Fukuchi Gen'ichirō (Ōchi), a participant of, and interpreter for, several official visits to the West. When he became chief editor in 1874, the paper's connections to officialdom became so close he boasted it was a *goyō* (patronage) *shinbun*. Ōchi played an important part in the next chapter of Meiji kabuki history as a keen reformer, patron and theater manager and dramatist.
8 Translations are the author's own work.
9 In Edo kabuki, it was the convention to refer to the warlords Hashiba Hideyoshi and Oda Nobunaga as Mashiba Hisayoshi and Oda Harunaga respectively, to avoid censorial restrictions on the use of real names.
10 *Bunmei kaika* was a popular slogan of the early Meiji Western-inspired reform movement.
11 The Office of Shinto Worship (Jingi-kan) was subsumed into the Department of Religious Affairs (Kyōbushō) in 1872.
12 See Bach (1995) for a detailed analysis of the effects of the new licensing laws on actors' salaries and status and the capital's minor theaters.
13 Edo kabuki was one of the few social entertainments enjoyed by both men and women. Parents often took their children to performances, and even as late as the 1880s breast-feeding women could still be seen in the auditorium, as recorded by the

32　*R. Payne*

French cartoonist Georges Bigot (1860–1927) in his sketch of a working-class family at the theater (Takahashi 1995: 144–5).

14　The rowdiness of the auditorium and the gaudiness of theater architecture were criticized, as were plays with immoral or illogical content. Actors were censured for their opulent lifestyles and scandalous private lives, and praised for wearing fashionable Western clothes and socializing with haiku poets (Matsumoto 1974: 48–51).

15　These were treaties signed in the 1850s that allowed Western nations extraterritoriality and limited Japan's autonomy to set its own trade tariffs. Japan considered these contrary to its status as an independent nation.

16　This account is available in full: see Kume *et al.* (2002).

17　Translations of this book were extremely popular for their inspiring tales of men of low social status succeeding through determination. See Kinmonth (1981).

18　Toita (1956: 215–16) noted that Osaka/Kyoto kabuki was in some respects more advanced than Tokyo in terms of modern plays, although the motive there was to continue incorporating new elements into kabuki, rather than to reform it.

19　Until 1881 this playwright's name was Kawatake Shinshichi.

20　Ironically, the lawsuit was brought by Yoda Gakkai, an active supporter of the historically accurate plays that most closely reflected official calls for kabuki to be educational and inspiring.

21　*Woman Student* is translated by Valerie Durham in Brandon and Leiter (2003: 120–200).

22　Translated by Faith Bach in Brandon and Leiter (2003: 260–79).

23　See also Takahashi (1995).

24　Around this time Inoue Kaoru, having returned from his second trip to Europe, took over as head of foreign affairs. His predecessor had fallen from favor after failing to repeal the Unequal Treaties, which Japan still considered a humiliating negation of its status as a civilized nation. Inoue was among those convinced that their repeal could be achieved if Japan asserted its cultural parity with Western nations. This was the reasoning behind renewed efforts to westernize Japan's high-class social institutions (Tomita 1994: 6–10, 51–60).

References

Alcock, Rutherford (1863) *Capital of the Tycoon: A Narrative of Three Years' Residence in Japan*, 2 vols., London: Longman Green.

Anthony, Douglas W. and Healey, Graham H. (1996) *The Itinerary of the Iwakura Embassy in Britain*, Cardiff: Cardiff Centre of Japanese Studies.

Bach, Faith (1995) 'Breaking the *Kabuki* Actors' Barriers: 1868–1900', *Asian Theatre Journal*, 12(2): 264–79.

Barr, Pat (1968) *The Deer Cry Pavilion*, London: Macmillan.

Bolitho, Harold (1993) [1989] 'The Tempo Crisis', in Marius B. Jansen (ed.) *Cambridge History of Japan Vol. 5: The Nineteenth Century*, Cambridge: Cambridge University Press, 116–67.

Brandon, James, R. and Leiter, Samuel L. (2002) *Kabuki Plays on Stage Vol. 3: Darkness and Desire 1804–1864*, Honolulu: University of Hawai'i Press.

Brandon, James, R. and Leiter, Samuel L. (2003) *Kabuki Plays on Stage Vol. 4: Restoration and Reform 1872–1905*, Honolulu: University of Hawai'i Press.

Chang, Richard T. (1969) 'General Grant's 1879 Visit to Japan', *Monumenta Nipponica*, 24(4): 373–92.

Cobbing, Andrew (2005) 'Early Japanese Visitors to Victorian Britain', in Gordon Daniels and Tsuzuki Chushiki (eds.), *History of Anglo-Japanese Relations 1600–2000 Vol. 5: Social and Cultural Perspectives*, Basingstoke: Palgrave Macmillan, 43–59.

Censorship in Meiji kabuki theater   33

Craig, Teruko (1994) *The Autobiography of Shibusawa Eiichi: From Peasant to Entrepreneur*, Tokyo: University of Tokyo Press.

de Lange, William (1998) *A History of Japanese Journalism: Japan's Press Club as the Last Obstacle to a Mature Press*, Richmond: Japan Library (Curzon Press).

Fuhara Yoshiaki (1965), 'The Theatre Reformation Movement in the Early Meiji Era of Japan: a preliminary sketch', *Hitotsubashi Journal of Arts and Sciences* 6 (1), 25–33.

Gakkai Jiroku Kenkyū-kai (ed.) (1992) *Gakkai jiroku* (Gakkai's diary), 12 vols., Tokyo: Iwanami Shoten.

Griffis, William E. (1876) *Mikado's Empire*, New York: Harper and Brothers.

Ihara, Toshirō (1933) *Meiji engeki-shi* (Meiji Theatre History), Tokyo: Waseda University Press.

Ihara, Toshirō, Kawatake, Shigetoshi and Yoshida, Teruji (eds.) (1973) [1956] *Kabuki nenpyō* (Kabuki Chronology), 8 vols., Tokyo: Iwanami Shoten.

Kawatake, Shigetoshi (1959) *Nihon engeki zenshi* (A Complete History of Japanese Theatre), Tokyo: Iwanami Shoten.

Kawatake, Toshio (1993) *Mokuami* (Mokuami), Tokyo: Bungei Shunjū.

Keene, Donald (1976) *World Within Walls: Japanese Literature of the Pre-Modern Era, 1600–1867*, London: Secker and Warburg.

Kimura, Kinka (1943) *Morita Kan'ya* (Morita Kan'ya), Tokyo: Shin Taishūsha.

Kinmonth, Earl (1981) *The Self-Made Man in Meiji Japanese Thought: From Samurai to Salary Man*, Berkeley: University of California Press.

Kobitsu, Matsuo (1988) *Nihon shingeki rinen-shi* (An Ideological History of Modern Japanese Drama), 2 vols., Tokyo: Hakusuisha.

Kume, Kunitake, Healey, Graham and Tsuzuki Chushichi (eds.) (2002) *The Iwakura Embassy, 1871–73: A True Account of the Ambassador Extraordinary & Plenipotentiary's Journey of Observation through the United States of America and Europe*, Richmond: Curzon.

Mason, Richard H.P. (1979) 'Suematsu Kenchō and Japanese Patterns of Cultural and Political Change in the 1880s', *Papers on Far Eastern History*, 20: 1–55.

Matsumoto, Shinko (1974) *Meiji zenki engekiron-shi* (A History of Early Meiji Drama Theory), Tokyo: Engeki Shuppansha.

Mehl, Margaret (1993) 'Suematsu Kenchō in Britain, 1878–1886', *Japan Forum*, 5(2): 173–93.

Metzler, Mark (1994) 'Capitalist Boom, Feudal Bust: Long Waves in Economics and Politics in Pre-Industrial Japan', *Review* (Fernand Braudel Center), 17(1): 57–119.

Mine, Takashi (1996) *Teikoku Gekijō kaimaku* (Curtain-rise at the Imperial Theatre), Tokyo: Chūō Kōron.

Mitchell, Richard H. (1983) *Censorship in Imperial Japan*, Princeton: Princeton University Press.

Morse, Edward S. (1990) [1917] *Japan Day by Day*, 2 vols., Cary, NC: Cherokee Publishing.

Payne, Rachel (2003) *Meiji Theatre Design: From Communal Participation to Refined Appreciation*, Oxford: Nissan Occasional Papers Series 34.

Powell, Brian (2005) 'Theatre Cultures in Contact: Britain and Japan in the Meiji Period', in Gordon Daniels and Chushichi Tsuzuki (eds.), *The History of Anglo-Japanese Relations 1600–2000*, Vol. 5, Basingstoke: Palgrave, 103–17.

Rubin, Jay (1984) *Injurious to Public Morals: Writers and the Meiji State*, Seattle: University of Washington Press.

34 *R. Payne*

Shively, Donald H. (1976) 'The Japanization of the Middle Meiji', in Donald Shively (ed.), *Tradition and Modernization in Meiji Japan*, Princeton: Princeton University Press, 77–120.

Shively, Donald H. (1982) 'Tokugawa Plays on Forbidden Topics', in James R. Brandon (ed.), *Chūshingura: Studies in Kabuki and the Puppet Theater*, Honolulu: University of Hawai'i Press, 23–57.

Soviak, Eugene (1976) 'On the Nature of Western Progress: The Journal of the Iwakura Embassy', in Donald H. Shively (ed.), *Tradition and Modernization in Meiji Japan*, Princeton: Princeton University Press, 7–35.

Takahashi, Yuichiro (1995) 'Kabuki Goes Official: The 1878 Opening of the Shintomi-za', *The Drama Review*, 39(3): 131–50.

Tamura, Nariyoshi (ed.) (1922) *Zokuzoku kabuki nendai-ki* (Kabuki Annals), Tokyo: Ōtori Shuppan.

Toita, Koji (1956) 'Kabuki and Shingeki', in Komiya Toyotaka (ed.), *Japanese Music and Drama in the Meiji Era*, Tokyo: Ōbunsha, 177–236.

Tomita, Hitoshi (1994) [1984] *Rokumeikan Jidai: giseiyō-ka no sekai* (The Rokumeikan Era: A World of Fake Westernization), Tokyo: Hakusui-sha.

Yokoyama, Toshio (1987) *Japan in the Victorian Mind: A Study of Stereotyped Images of a Nation 1850–1880*, Basingstoke: Macmillan.

3 Seditious obscenity/obscene seditions

The radical eroticism of Umehara Hokumei

Jonathan Abel

From the post-earthquake publishing boom of the 1920s to the crackdowns of the early 1930s associated with the Manchurian Incident, erotic and proletarian literatures flourished in Japan despite redoubled efforts of censors to suppress their supposedly obscene and seditious material. Rather than being immobilized during this high period of state control of public discourse, some writers, editors, and publishers were able to manipulate censorship to make money and cultivate marginal literary forms, thereby achieving fame and notoriety. Mentioning this productive role of censorship should not diminish the force of the censors and the harshness of the increasingly severe punishments they meted out – the confiscations and destructions of valuable stocks of banned books, the dissolving of the capital investments of publishers and printers alike, the severe fines on producers of banned material, the lengthy prison terms, and the surveillance and torture of members of the literati. Nevertheless, recognizing the productive capabilities of censorship enables us to gauge the violence of the censors against the force of discourse and dissemination of/by the censored, displacing solely top-down visions of power and hierarchical notions of the locus of censorial authority in a society. Acknowledging the productive power of censorship also reminds us that whether offense-giving is an act of resistance or complicity depends less on the categories for and content of offense than on the context of the act. For a brief moment in the late 1920s in Japan when crimes against mores and social order were equally declared by censors, giving offense through publication of material under either of these categories was necessarily an act of resistance – albeit one quickly contained by the increasing enforcement of regulations.

The censors and the censored were well aware of the intersections between obscenity and sedition, two supposedly separate legal classifications for offense. The career of a key figure of the literary underworld, Umehara Hokumei (1901–46), highlights these connections and provides a telling example of the ambivalent relations between the so-called producers and destroyers of cultural material. Novelist, translator, editor, and publisher, Hokumei both overcame and succumbed to these seemingly disparate categories of the censors, managing to equally offend censorious sensibilities for both. Hokumei's multiple offenses allow us to consider how these classifications for suppression affected literary productivity and the limits of the representation of violence as Japan moved toward war.

36 *J. Abel*

Crossing categories: sex and politics

Typically two major subcultural trends of Taishō democracy (a period roughly spanning the 1910s and 1920s characterized by relative liberalism, said to have preceded the march towards war) are thought of in mutually exclusive terms. It seems self-evident that those involved in the bourgeois nightlife cultures of cafés and dance halls would not have been interested or involved with the farmer and laborer struggles and strikes of the period. And yet the cultures were intertwined in interesting and important ways.

In industrialized countries shaken by war and by the threat perceived in the Russian Revolution, the subjects of sex and politics were linked not only by explicit government decrees and social ideologies, but also by the discourses produced by an international intelligentsia responding to new controls on cultural production. In Japan, these fears of subversion, categorically defined by the mid-Meiji Publishing Laws of the 1890s, were exacerbated by the tragedy of the 1923 Great Kantō Earthquake, the adoptions of the 1927 and 1932 Comintern Theses (*Kominterun teze*) by the Japanese Communist movements, and later by the Manchurian Incident of 1931, the attempted coup of 1936, and the escalation of war in China in the late 1930s, not to mention the beginning of the Pacific War in 1941. Mounting fears manifested themselves not only in continual expansion of the duties and purview of the censor, but also in temporary booms of the two kinds of literature most likely to be banned. From a publisher's standpoint, topics defined as risqué by the censors appeared as potentially big sellers and could be deemed risk worthy, despite the potential for losses incurred from fines, bans, and seizures. Though the breaking point for the publication of these products would come, risky and risqué publications flourished for nearly a decade after the earthquake of 1923.

A former Home Ministry censor, Tachibana Takahiro, included a chapter entitled 'Eroticism, The Proletariat, and Censorship' in his 1932 memoirs in which he locates a link between leftism and eroticism in a certain kind of modernism.

> [I]t seems that the *raison d'être* of the censor is to protect against the publication of seditious propaganda, which is rooted in Sovietism, and the products of eroticism (the so-called ero-publications), which are influenced by Americanism. In his short essay 'Modernity,' F.L. Wheeler states that the characteristics of modernism are, as a result of war, the demand for freedom in actions and morality and a desire for the moment's pleasure and physical enjoyment; and in that sense, we can then say that the censor's work confronts modernism directly.
>
> (Tachibana 1932: 55)[1]

Here the censor declares his dual role not only as the enforcer of a two-pronged publishing law aimed at suppressing both sedition and obscenity, but also as a guardian against a certain brand of modernism. For Tachibana, this is a front-line battle against seditious (Sovietist) and obscene (Americanist) publications.

The logic evident here – modernism is both Sovietism and Americanism, and, therefore, to fight against modernism we must fight against both of their representatives – neatly shows how sedition and obscenity were connected by an enforcer of the single two-pronged Japanese law.

The censored, too, recognized and commented on the connections. The preface to the 1930 *Dictionary of Modern Terminology* characterizes contemporary times as follows:

> It is said that the present day is particularly a period of the three Ss; at the same time, we can say it is a period of the three ROs. The 'three Ss' are speed, sports, and screen, while the 'three ROs' points to eRO [erotic], guRO [grotesque], and puRO [proletarian].
>
> (*Modan yōgo jiten* 1995 [1930])

While the three Ss represented some kind of ubiquitous mainstream culture, the three ROs (referring to the erotic, grotesque, and proletarian) represented a tangible but less visible back alley culture.[2] Here the 'puro' element is added to what is typically remembered as solely erotic and grotesque.[3]

For Japanese historians and gender theorists it might seem obvious that there was a radical politics linked to what is generally characterized as *ero-guro-nansensu* (a booming Japanese discourse of erotic, grotesque, and, presumably nonsensical culture prevalent in the interwar period), or a base bourgeois sexual oppression within the proletarian movement in Japan. So why highlight these connections here yet again? Simply because the connections were so explicit then, yet instantly marginalized as derivative versions of some pure essential wholes or then later forgotten. The political and the sexual were explicitly and openly connected by some of the key players in these discourses, despite the revisionist and nostalgic views of critics who continue to fetishize radicality and subversiveness in purely political or erotic content. What is still remembered as merely *ero-guro* even in our day, for instance, was in fact occasionally recognized as *ero-puro* (as in the case of the censor Tachibana) or, at least, as *ero-guro-puro* (as in the case of the terminology dictionary). Though these connections may have been marginalized, they are by no means of marginal importance; they provide key junctures where state force and the power of cultural production, discourses on the public and private, and the political and the sexual intersect.

Shades of pink[4]

Jay Gertzman (1999) has used the sociological concepts of 'pariah capitalism' and 'middleman minority' to describe a group of American immigrant booksellers and publishers dedicated to erotic publications who were active during the interwar period.[5] In Gertzman's description, pariah capitalists worked outside the bounds of both mainstream culture and capitalism, and were uniquely positioned to thrive by bending and exaggerating accepted business practices.

38   *J. Abel*

Such characteristics also apply to underground booksellers and publishers in Japan during the same period. They used the techniques of the regular publishing world in order to sell materials that mainstream writers and publishers specifically avoided or simply could not sell. Their publications often circulated outside the bounds of legality and mainstream commerce. The discourse they produced existed both in spite of and because of explicit and implicit censorship pressures. And, while much of the erotomania evident in the late Taishō and early Shōwa publishing boom may seem at first glance to rest entirely within bourgeois modes of desire, theirs was a period when the publication of the erotic itself was seen to have radical import and further was linked to radical publication. Those producers of culture who believed in the radicality of sexual expression depended on a significant degree of internalization of and sensitivity to the taboos of the mainstream as well as on newly defined left-wing concerns.

Purveyor of porn

The story of Umehara Hokumei and his creations tells not only of the varying yet related censorships in the late Taishō and early Shōwa literary worlds, but also about the degree to which an offender of sensibilities (an offense-giver) can ever be said to be entirely removed from or insensitive to the mores and breaking points of the offense-takers. It takes at least two to tango in the give and take of offense. Hokumei is representative of the nuanced understanding those censored often have of their censors. To push the limits of acceptability, one must first know very well what those limits are. To this extent, Hokumei's career and works reveal the inadequacy of rashly concluding that the censored were either entirely subversive or wholly complicit. In the interwar moment of post-Russian Revolution fears when offenses for immorality in Japan equaled and, at times, exceeded offenses for sedition, Hokumei reached the height of his literary activity. Cultural critic Tanizawa Eiichi comments: '[T]he mysterious intermingling of socialist, neoperceptualist, and pornographer could only have appeared in this brief period' (1981: 74). The two-sidedness of his offenses is the direct result of a similar two-sidedness of a censorship system which helped both to define the unpublishable and to encourage the publishing of that material defined as unpublishable.

Hokumei may be considered a shrewd pariah or marginal businessman – an outsider to the publishing world. He is perhaps most often remembered as the only translator to have successfully skirted the censors and published Boccaccio's *Decameron* in prewar Japan. Though this 1925 work was not the first translation of *Decameron* in Japan, it was the first not to be banned. While differences in the various translations abound – for instance, Hokumei's *Decameron: The Complete Translation* has fewer *fuseji* (deletion marks generally Xs and Os used to blank out potentially offensive type) than the previous Togawa Shūkotsu and Ozawa Teizō versions – the most significant difference was that Hokumei anticipated the potential for censorship (Umehara M. 1968: 226). On the occasion of the publication of the translation, Hokumei threw a huge shindig in Asakusa in

The radical eroticism of Umehara Hokumei   39

honor of the 500th anniversary of Boccaccio and cleverly invited the Italian ambassador. It would seem like a national affront against Italy if the Japanese government then banned the translation, so it was published without a hitch. Hokumei was even reportedly presented with a cultural award by the ambassador, which, in a drunken stupor, he gave to a café waitress (Umehara M. 1968: 227).

Stunts like these have led critics to note rightfully that Hokumei resided in a liminal underground world. Yamaguchi Masao focuses his critical attention on Hokumei's escape from Japan to Shanghai that followed several successive bans. For Yamaguchi, Hokumei's literal position outside of Japan during these months in Shanghai is of utmost importance in explaining his role in early Shōwa discourse (1995: 349).[6] This narrative of exiled, renegade rogue of the publishing world depicts Hokumei as firmly against or opposed to censorship while nevertheless requiring censorship to survive.

But the numerous ways in which Hokumei's subversions required the censor and the mainstream are rarely sought by critics such as Yamaguchi who suggest this relationship between center and periphery. To be sure, in his comments on erotomaniacal booksellers of the interwar US cultural landscape, Gertzman is more nuanced than Yamaguchi is for Hokumei; Gertzman claims that pariah capitalists sold their wares outside normal markets, but, nevertheless, required that the normal markets would not sell similar wares in order to make a buck. This seems to be much closer to the historical situation where Hokumei was intermeshed with and dependent on more mainstream culture.

Hokumei was neither an ethnic pariah figure, as were the Jewish immigrants of Gertzman's narrative, nor as wholly outside the Japanese elite as Yamaguchi's narrative would suggest. On the contrary, he held an aristocratic pedigree, descended from the Toyama clan of samurai. Like many upper-class Meiji and Taishō intellectuals, Hokumei left home for school in the big city while still a youth. His sword-maker father supported his study for entrance to medical school. But Hokumei derailed his career by squandering the money his father sent for medical textbooks on literature by Chekhov and the like. Although he had dropped out of school and, to some extent, the mainstream economy, Hokumei was very much a product of those important bourgeois institutions of modern Japan. Moreover, the list of subscribers to his own oft-banned magazines included high-ranking military and government officials, attesting to the fact that his readers were not necessarily subversives living on the fringes of social acceptability. Hokumei ended his career by writing stories for the widely popular wartime magazines *New Youth* (*Shinseinen*) and *Story Club* (*Kōdan kurabu*).[7] In short, Hokumei's relationship with mainstream middlebrow culture was deep, extending back to his childhood and through to the end of his life.

These connections to the mainstream should remind us that one need not have been a member of a marginalized minority or an exile to take part in 'middleman minority' markets. Hokumei, having dropped out of the mainstream economy, created publications that could not long remain within mainstream discourse – although his publications and his livelihood relied on the trends and taboos of

40   *J. Abel*

that market. By a combination of financial necessity and self-righteous sense of freedom, he used the categories of the censor to sell books. Highlighting the connections of Hokumei with mainstream culture should not obviate the view of him as an 'outsider' but rather qualify what could constitute an outside and, further, an outsider.

Purveyor of politics

The very next month after the release of the first volume of his *Decameron*, Hokumei published his translation of Albert Rhys Williams' *Through the Russian Revolution*, promptly banned by the authorities for seditious content. Williams himself had been forbidden to return to the US via Japan after his field research for the book (Kunitz 1967), so the fact that his reportage narrative would be offensive to the Japanese authorities should have been clear to Hokumei. The reliance on the attractiveness of potential censorious materials and on the censor's approval as a lure for buyers is also made clear on the final page of the book which advertises Hokumei's *Decameron*. The ad seems to presume that readers of the overtly politically charged reportage and the ribald tales of Europe might be the same. It reads, '[O]nly Mr. Umehara Hokumei's *Decameron: The Complete Translation* passed the sharp EYES OF THE CENSOR without incident' (Umehara and Uyama 1925). Extra large font for the phrase the 'eyes of the censor' draws attention to the potential taboo of the content and the permissibility of this particular version. This appeal to the readers of the class-conscious history through the sensational allure of the potentially censorable sexually explicit tales illustrates commonalities between prurient interest and political dissent as selling points. The ad appeals to the same mode of desire for the transgressive. In 1930 Hokumei repeated this method of using one form of taboo to sell another, when the cover to a pamphlet advertising his collection *The Hidden History of the Pavilion of Bizarre Tales* (*Dankikan hisshi*) re-describes the titular volume as 'The Strange Sanctuary of Leftist Erotica' (*Sayokuha ero no kaidendō*) (Umehara 1930).

Skirting the censor

In order to maintain his ability to publish and sell despite his proclivities toward working with material that would offend, Hokumei devised schemes to avoid fines, incarceration, and sometimes publishing objectionable material. Though he was in a business that would taunt censorship, Hokumei navigated the line between the offensive and the acceptable so closely that he occasionally advertised more than he provided readers.

In September of 1926, while still editor at the 'anti-authoritarian and radical' *Arts Market* (*Bungei shijō*), he began another magazine, *Perverse Matters* (*Hentai shiryō*), pandering to the growing market for sexological studies.[8] It was banned seven consecutive times, leading Hokumei to dedicate the June 1927 issue to *hikka* or 'troubles of the pen.' In 1927, every issue from June to October of *Arts Market* was also banned. That magazine, too, dedicated an issue to the topic of censorship. The August 1927 cover of *Arts Market* (with variant Japanese title *Bungei ichiba*) depicted a map of the tortuous path a publication must follow only to be banned (see Figure 3.1). With explanatory notes titled 'Secrets Revealed: the Road to Magazine Bans under the Newspaper Act,' the map depicts how a galley travels via post, telegraph, and truck through various levels of the bureaucracy – revealing the irrationality, waste, and irritation involved in attempting to get something past the censors. Following the arrows across the front and back covers the reader sees that one might even encounter a government minister in receiving a ban. The minister is depicted as sitting back smoking a cigar.

Successive encounters with the censors led Hokumei to invent several other methods for avoiding bans, such as the aforementioned banquet in honor of Boccaccio. For instance, his article on Mirabeau in the January issue of his magazine *Grotesque* (*Gurotesuku*) ended abruptly by beseeching interested readers to send more money for a book length study of which 'only 300 are being printed' (Umehara 1928: 146–9). Direct mailings and private publications were far more difficult for the censors to track than widely distributed and sold publications.[9] Between 1929 and 1932, Hokumei edited several book-length compilations of banned Meiji-period newspaper articles, some of which were themselves banned.

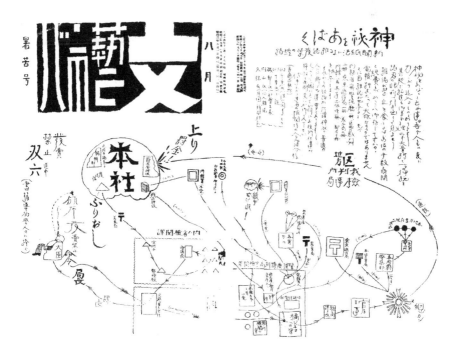

Figure 3.1 A cover of *Arts Market*, here with variant title *Bungei ichiba*, mapping the tortuous path a publication must follow through the censorship process. Note the government minister with the cigar at bottom left.

42   *J. Abel*

In the preface to one of the compilations, *A Complete History of Modern Social Trends* (*Kindai sesō zenshi*, 1931), he describes the process of obtaining the permission of the Minister of Education to use the materials held in the Ueno library as *etsuran kinshi* or 'forbidden from viewing' (Umehara 1931b). This preface, like the Boccaccio party, functioned as a way to avoid censorship – seemingly saying to would-be censors that 'I have permission, so had you better not censor me.' By mentioning the status of the man from whom he received permission, Hokumei repeated the strategy for avoiding censorship that he had used for launching *Perverse Matters*, a magazine for which he would claim to have subscribers as diverse as businessmen, university professors, high-ranking military men, and public prosecutors. One of the reasons he was able to return to publishing again after successive bans was the grand power of his subscribers. For instance, the Dongxiang field marshal Ogasawara Naganari was an ardent fan, and Hokumei apparently used his name to escape from a few sticky situations (Jō 1991; Umehara M. 1968).

Though Hokumei devised intricate schemes for evading the censors, they were not always successful, and successive bans took serious tolls. In 1932, after having been jailed, banned, and fined, Hokumei escaped to Osaka with the thought police (*shisō kenji*) hot on his trail for an issue of *Grotesque* deemed particularly offensive. In Osaka, he worked briefly as a teacher of English. He moved back to Tokyo in 1933 and secured a job compiling a social history of the Yasukuni Shrine, infamous today for its association with nationalism and militarism as the place enshrining the spirits of the war dead. From 1938 to 1940 he published under the pseudonym Azuma Tairiku in the popular magazines *New Youth* and *Story Club* to avoid the raising the censors' ire.[10] During the Pacific War, he joined the war effort by participating in the Society for the Promotion of Science and Technology (Kagaku gijutsu shinkōkai), an officially sanctioned society that specialized in pirating and translating technical books from English on engineering and medicine. Overall he suffered more fines, bans, and jail-time than his Meiji-period forefather in radical and erotic publishing, Miyatake Gaikotsu (Umehara M. 1968: 235). His curious life continued to have an influence long after his death from typhus in May of 1946, inspiring the scandalous Nosaka Akiyuki to write a fictional portrayal of Hokumei's career titled *A Sexual Spirit* (Nosaka 1968).

Receptions

Whether as an editor or writer, for profit or out of ideological concerns, Hokumei pushed the envelope of allowable discourse. In so doing, he reaped profits and at other times suffered monetary and personal loss. Hokumei seems to have adhered to the modernist school of thought, which historian of Japanese sexuality, Ueno Chizuko, has summed up as believing that 'the "radicality" of sexual expression depends upon the level of how revealing it is' (Ueno 1998: 42). And if we think about the simultaneous offenses given by certain modes of realism, naturalism, and later social realism in Japan, which sought to continually reveal

The radical eroticism of Umehara Hokumei   43

more and more, we can see how Hokumei was not alone in using that which was openly declared most taboo to his benefit and at great risk. From Shimazaki Tōson and Tayama Katai through Tanizaki Jun'ichirō and Nagai Kafū to Kobayashi Takiji and Itō Sei, other more prominent literary personae also benefited as well as lost from their encounters with censorship. However, while literary history has viewed these writers as cutting edge or idiosyncratic geniuses, it has not been so kind to Hokumei. While this may have much to do with the quality and quantity of his own personal literary output, it is certainly not unrelated to his tainted reputation in the literary worlds in which he worked.

The reception of Hokumei, both in his day and since, has been mixed at best. Nakano Masato, a proletarian writer who worked with him on *Arts Market*, wrote that

> Umehara himself did not think of his standpoint as either bourgeois or proletarian, so he comfortably associated with them all. He wanted to take the good and the bad together, but amongst the proletarian authors he was condemned as a flunky.
>
> (Umehara M. 1968: 230)

This seems to square with the accounts of Umehara standing out in a sea of overalls at a workers' protest rally by wearing a tuxedo (Suzuki 1930: 306). Others have been more kind in their appraisals. Kaneko Yōbun, Hokumei's coeditor at *Arts Market*, saw his work as genuinely proletarian, citing as evidence of his radical inclinations Hokumei's June 1927 article in *Arts Market* which discussed the history of the Takebashi incident, the first army insurrection in modern Japanese history (Kaneko 1976: 2).[11] Hokumei's son, Umehara Masaki, too, claims that Hokumei at first was using his jaunts into the erotic world as a way to finance the proletarian magazine (Umehara M. 1968: 232). Jō Ichirō, an independent scholar of banned books, wants to have it both ways, arguing that Hokumei was not merely a pornographer but a shrewd businessman and political activist (1991: 103). This seeming contradiction – the pariah capitalist as a person with proletarian-minded motives and actions – signifies Hokumei's hybrid existence at the crossroads of several discourses. The desire to deny this hybridity and judge Hokumei on the basis of an assumption about the possibility of purely erotic or of unadulterated proletarian discourses is widespread, if somewhat misleading and ahistorical.

These contesting accounts – alternatively lambasting Hokumei as a tainted radical or mere pornographer and praising him purely for his politics or for reveling in sexual liberation – ignore the facts that the erotic and the political were connected methods of offense-giving and -taking, and that very few figures in literary history produced wholly in one mode or the other over the course of their careers. This period should be evaluated less on the essential ideological and radical purity of the key players than on the way in which they freely appropriated and mixed modernist tropes, be they proletarian, erotic, or any of the myriad other possible thematic choices.

44 *J. Abel*

The renowned cultural critic Ōya Sōichi suggests that modernism on the whole was always already compromised: 'Modernism is that which lies between the bourgeois and the proletarian and is rooted in the nihilism particular to the middle class, which has lost its hopes for the future through its life philosophy and the guiding principle of consumerism' (cited in Ōuchi 1967: 458). If we agree with Ōya, we might categorize nearly every writing intellectual of the time as a middle-class flunky of one kind or another, including those writers, like Kuroshima Denji, who were held up as exemplars of the working-class artist.[12] So if this can be recognized as the case for many of the discourses subsumed under the rubric of modernism (whether described as radical proletarian or avant garde Dadaist), why does the issue of complicity in the interwar period continue to plague critics of Japanese culture? The historical outcome of the war and the succeeding Cold War left Japanese critics questioning the efficacy of the interwar Japanese Left. Knowing that even some of the most radical intellectuals were complicit to some degree with mainstream ideologies, why have critics of Japan persisted in their desires for unadulterated radical intentions and texts from that period?

One root of this fetishization of the pure proletarian in the Japanese case may be the famed postwar critical debate among three major literary figures, Hirano Ken, Ara Masahito, and Nakano Shigeharu, which centered on the seeming contradiction between the prewar proletarian literary movement's political call to arms and its naïveté about issues of gender relations. Using as evidence the 1932 novel *Lifetime Party Member* (*Tō seikatsusha*) written by the über-proletarian writer Kobayashi Takiji, Hirano Ken launched the first volley of this debate in his 1946 article 'Politics and Literature' (*Seiji to bungaku*) claiming that the treatment of the male protagonist's girlfriend betrayed the problems with the prewar proletarian movement. The modern girl, Kasahara, for instance, financially supported her leftist boyfriend Sasaki's ability to pass out leaflets at the factory. Notably, Sasaki reads bourgeois detective fiction in *New Youth* and not the more openly subversive proletarian fiction. If we were to follow the logic of this argument we might indict Hokumei's radicality on similar grounds, as Hokumei financed his proletarian endeavors with money earned through a reliance on sexual desire and prurient interests.[13]

Accusing the proletarian movement of complicity with mainstream gender oppression may be a fitting assessment of the period, but incriminating either Kobayashi or Hokumei on these grounds is not as important as its arguers would have it. There was sexual discrimination underlying the proletarian project and fictional representation of class dissolution may be impossible to separate from representations of sexual relations, but the work of Kobayashi and Umehara does not deny this or aim for essences of either *ero* or *puro*. Rather than holding texts of the period to standards seldom achieved and perhaps impossible to attain, we might do better to embrace the hybrid possibilities of the fluid genres within which they worked.[14]

What is forgotten in the Cold War nostalgia for prewar literature on the part of leftist activists and by critics of sexology is how close the explicit ties

The radical eroticism of Umehara Hokumei 45

between sexual liberation and expression, on the one hand, and political movement and revolution, on the other, had been. The initial postwar desire to divorce the two was sustained by both incremental shifts in policies by the Cold War censors and the willingness of intellectuals to disregard these links. In short, while the tendency among postwar leftists was to forget the prevalence of erotica in the 1920s and 1930s and its connections to anti-capitalist, anti-imperialist, and anti-war discourses, postwar eroticists and pornographers tended to elide the party politics involved.

Certainly, from the viewpoint of proletarian ideology, Hokumei was a flunky, interested in pandering to faddish tastes in order to earn money. Through the lens of gender critique we may see him as yet another male eroticist continuing phallocentric oppression by appealing to typical modes of bourgeois desire. But what Gertzman writes of the sexual transgressions of pariah capitalists and the erotic literature they produced can hold for proletarian literature as well: 'In reality, they were themselves a form of repression – and a safety valve providing fantasies whose satisfaction allowed people to tolerate, not rebel against conventional ideas of decency' (1999: 23). The eroticism of the interwar period was as much an aspect of modernism as were proletarian leanings.[15] Merely to turn the equation 'modernism equals liberation' into 'modernism equals repression' is to be insensitive to the historical intentions (failed in practice as they may have been) and to the moment in which he was working, moments when erotic and proletarian literature (were) crossed.

However justified by our latter day theoretical frameworks and knowledge, there are particular reasons in Hokumei's case to read beyond these charges. Such a 'reading beyond' does not absolve him of his complicity with various modes of oppression and suppression and violence, but it can follow the degree to which his intended acts of transgression were indeed subversive by the contemporary standards within which he worked.

Transcendental conversions: the fictional turns of Hokumei

Even those critics who have read the literary works of Hokumei do not offer extended interpretations.[16] Yamaguchi, for instance, relies on summary of contents alone to explain how the texts work within the contexts of the author's careers. In this way critics parallel censors, assuming that the censored works are monologic in tone. While the parallels between censors and critics are perhaps unavoidable, extended treatment of some of the works may allow us to answer larger questions. Comparing early works in his career with later works written after his multiple brushes with censors reveals a sustained interest in offense-giving, one which gradually diminishes, but never disappears. While Hokumei's overtly political and erotic aesthetics fade in his later novels, these novels can still be read as radical and obscene within the context of war.

In 1924, Hokumei published his first novel *Murder Incorporated: The Heyday of Diabolism* (*Satsujin gaisha: Akumashugi zensei jidai*), a grotesque story loaded with erotic and proletarian content and banned for disrupting morals upon

46   *J. Abel*

its release. He published the novel under the sobriquet Hokumei from the characters meaning the 'north' and 'bright.' As such, the name was intended to evoke images of looking toward the Russian Revolution with hope.

The novel opens with a framing story featuring an author who is frustrated in his attempts to come up with a story worth writing. Fortuitously, an old school acquaintance, Santarō, who has been in America for five years, turns up with fantastic tales of his foreign escapades. The episodic novel revolves around Santarō's involvement with the F Murder Joint Stock Company or FMJC, a corporation that makes a business out of assassination and murder, with a sideline of canning and selling human flesh.[17] With a drugstore as the front, the company operates in the middle of the banking district in San Francisco. The nonchalance with which Santarō relates his exploits as a company man shocks and intrigues the author, so he continues to listen to the stories through the night. Ranging from the white sex-slave trade and necrophilia to assassinations of leaders of black rights movements, anti-Japanese movements and the lynching of Jews, Santarō's stories of the Murder Company appeal to the narrator with their grotesqueries. Santarō tells the I-narrator that the company is unlike run-of-the-mill cult groups who just sit around and philosophize. Instead, the Murder Company does things; the company is productive both socially and economically – the perfect social unit in capitalism.

The final chapters of the novel recount Santarō's discovery of another secret society – the *jisatsu kurabu* or Suicide Club. Unlike the formal capitalist structure of Murder Company, the Suicide Club is based on friendship. Removed from the financial districts, the Suicide Club takes place in a peripheral, seedy part of town. Santarō is led there by a regular who he finds in a Prohibition era underground bar where scoundrels, sailors, gentlemen, and ladies alike would gather. But before he goes into the Club he witnesses a scene through a keyhole of one of the doors upstairs from the bar. A gentleman is role-playing with a prostitute, who calls him 'dear master Duke,' while he 'the duke' refers to her as his 'Marquise' (Umehara 1924: 272).[18] Then, at just the right moment, the 'boy' from the bar downstairs bursts in and throws the duke out of a presumably low window. The duke is happy. His fantasy of engaging in sexual intrigue with a woman of an unattainable social status and the masochistic pleasure of defenestration for his 'crime' are fulfilled. This scene of class fetishism precedes Santarō's being led to a 'dark, dank long and narrow underground room' (Umehara 1924: 309) where the Suicide Club meets, and ensures that class is in the reader's mind for the scene to come.

Unlike the positive, hard-working men of Murder Company, the members of Suicide Club are a destitute and distraught group with nothing left to live for; neither the thrill of killing nor the power of wealth tempt them to live any longer. The foppish group meets wearing tuxedos, and they play cards to the accompaniment of violins, in 'a decisive battle betting their life existence' (Umehara 1924: 310). It is the duty of the winner to kill the loser. The loser is blindfolded. As a scantily clad woman dances to the violins, the winner shoots the loser. On the night Santarō visits, the scene is particularly pathetic, as the winner whimpers

The radical eroticism of Umehara Hokumei 47

that all he wants is to be as fortunate as the loser – he wants to die. The twist comes when Santarō is asked if he himself (as an obviously depraved man) is ready to join and become a member of the Suicide Club: 'Can you bear to die easily for no purpose?' (Umehara 1924: 315). In the end, even Santarō, who is immune to most of the morals of the world, finds this group repulsive and escapes the club headquarters, presumably making it back to Japan to tell his tales soon thereafter.

Though this novel has been characterized as teetering between anarchism and nihilism (Jō 1991: 108), the contrast between the Suicide Club, built for individual gratification beyond the normalized realms of commerce, and the capitalist Murder Company, cultivated as a social service and for mutual gratification, tells a different story. Though no reducible sexual politics surface in the novel, what is most clear is the incessant disruption of Japanese literary norms and social mores, or what Yamaguchi Masao (1995: 358) called in another context Hokumei's 'anti-authoritarian radicality.' As Jō mentions, this is no ordinary Taishō novel and is, in fact, making fun of the one-time revolutionary Abe Jirō's novel *Santarō's Diary* (*Santarō no nikki*, 1914) in naming its protagonist. By 1924 Abe's philosophical novel of the awakening of the individual spirit on the order of Nietzsche's *Genealogy of Morals* had become passé, bourgeois fluff for the overly pedantic, while Hokumei's story seemed cutting edge and risqué (see Kohl 1990).

Although in 1924 *Murder Incorporated* challenged ideological, sexual, and literary norms and was banned for transgressions against public morals (obscenity), by 1938 Hokumei was publishing unctuous teen literature under a pseudonym in mainstream magazines. Whether this reflects some kind of informal *tenkō* (conversion) or truckling to the times seems beside the point, as change in practice does not necessarily equal an ideological conversion. But it is important to remember that, unlike Kobayashi Takiji, Hokumei pushed the censors and *lived* to write again, and his successive encounters with censors surely changed his literary output in tangible ways.

Critics who debate Hokumei's complicity with national ideological agendas of the wartime pay little attention to these later works from the late 1930s and early 1940s. Jō (1991) seems to ignore this period of Hokumei's production because none of the stories were deemed obscene by the censors, as if the effects of censorship are only to be seen in works actually censored. Yamaguchi (1995) is more interested in interrogating the rhetoric of 'frustration' or 'despair' (*zasetsu*) in early Shōwa than he is in proposing a way to read the late 1920s and early 1930s without recourse to a narrative of 'failure' and 'lost hopes.' And for Yamaguchi the fact that a 'centrifugal force' pulled Hokumei out of Japan to Shanghai and later out of Tokyo to Osaka is of overdetermined significance.[19] But the fact of having left of the metropolis is not inherently representative of a kind of radicality. Yamaguchi's structuralist approach does not get us beyond the limits of the rhetoric of failure in early Shōwa that he himself so thoroughly details. Instead of focusing on historical and biographical detail we may do better by turning our attention to Hokumei's later literary production for

48   *J. Abel*

evidence of the degree to which he gave up his radical inclinations during the war or the degree to which any *tenkō* may be said to have been complete. There may not be a way out of the monolith of wartime discourse, but only a way through it, subversive and transgressive though never entirely revolutionary. A look at the wartime material of Hokumei needs to recognize the earnestness of his irreverent efforts at liberation even while acknowledging the problem of finding actual revolutionary work under wartime repression.

Although we can read Hokumei's wartime endeavors as the jejune results of repeated clashes with the censors, there is reason to read beyond the surface meanings. Though Japanese readers had been trained to *read* between the lines by the prevalence of covering devices like *fuseji* and euphemism appearing in fringe publications like communist party organs, it was not always clear that they would do so, particularly in mainstream publications. However, Hokumei's theoretical writings about the function of writing itself reveal that he at least hoped that *writing* between the lines could have some success.

As early as 1926, Hokumei anticipated the problems of a continuing censorship and some of what would become the major issues in debates about writing with an ideological slant. In a short essay published in *Arts Market* on New Years Day, titled 'The Pickled-Overnight Revolutionary' (*Ichiyadzuke no kakumeiyasan*), Hokumei argued that publishing in a party organ was not necessarily the most effective way of transmitting proletarian ideas to the masses. Here he criticized the intellectuals who seemed to have just read Marx the night before and whose works blatantly touted leftist ideology. There were more subtle ways of conveying the Marxist line to a reader than the methods of pseudo-radicals who were merely 'pickled overnight' (an idiomatic phrase referring to cramming for an exam) in the brine of Marxism. Critical of the trendy Marx-boy types who clutched proletarian books as a fashion statement on their strolls through town, he wrote:

> Most works that cheat by advertising to members of society their inherent sense of purpose are not particularly effective. For instance, rather than giving a militant short story to a propaganda journal, publishing a literary work that skillfully adopts a socialist awareness in *Story Club* is far and away more socially effective...
>
> But, in short, walking around smugly thinking that we are obviously social revolutionaries because we carry about these works is ridiculous.
>
> (Umehara 1926a: 46)

Years after the demise of his openly proletarian and erotic magazines, Hokumei published a number of adventure stories under the pseudonym Azuma Tairiku, in popular venues. The 1939 January *Story Club* collection of 'patriotic, valiant, detective, mystery, and true story masterpieces' featured Azuma Tairiku's 'The Beckoning Spirit and the Scout' (*Shōrei to sekkōhei*) (Azuma 1939: 88–111). The story drips with sappy sentiment from the beginning. The plot is simple – Yae and Kazuo are lovers fated to be separated by class, war, and death. With

The radical eroticism of Umehara Hokumei   49

the war looming, Kazuo gets permission from his father to marry Yae. The lovers are ecstatic. The next day the go-between comes to Yae's house to give the mother and daughter permission to purchase wedding clothes on the family's tab. They travel to Tokyo and buy what they think is a stylish and modern gown embroidered with plums, bamboo, and cranes, pleased at finding such a great bargain. On their return, they learn that Kazuo has been called up for war, so they rush to make arrangements. At a meeting of the two families they take out the gown only to realize they have been swindled: the golden thread is not real gold, and what they assumed was a new gown had in fact been used. Embarrassment and tears ensue, and Kazuo's father cancels the wedding. The next day, as Kazuo is about to set off with the troops, Yae comes to give him a thousand-stitch belt, a garment given to soldiers leaving for the front to protect them. She begs his forgiveness and tells him she will wait for him for years or even decades if he only forgives her. Kazuo holds back both his tears and his words. She takes this to mean he is done with her. He goes off to war. She drowns herself. Then, when he is lost behind enemy lines in China, her ghost comes to him and leads him back to safe Japanese territory where he delivers his report and is made a hero. He admits he owes everything to Yae. Eternal (unconsummated) love and nation are preserved.

Gone are the explicit sexual liaisons of the episodic 1924 *Murder Incorporated*. Gone are references to Marxist ideology. If there were ever a story that would seem suitable to the words 'patriotic' and 'valiant' in the title of the collection in which was published, this would be it. What we are left with seems a fairly straightforward narrative of juvenile fluff. But if we take Hokumei's 1926 essay, 'The Pickled-Overnight Revolutionary,' denigrating explicitly ideological novels and proposing more mainstream publishing venues like *Story Club* to be significant, our reading of this and other insipid stories published by Hokumei in *Story Club* might change. Following his logic in 'The Pickled Overnight Revolutionary,' the degree to which a story is subsumed in the standard tropes and ideologies and published in mainstream publications is not only the degree to which a text is potentially complicit, but also the degree to which a text might be subversive. It is the very ability of the text to remain within mainstream discourse, its very complicity, that may provide the opportunity for radicality.

To read the story along these lines is to downplay the previous plot summary in favor of other themes. In reading the 'Beckoning Spirit' we might focus on the way the meaning of the opening poem is subverted by that which follows. The story begins with a familiar traditional poem: 'Minanogawa, every man and woman's river, flows from the shadows atop the twin peaks of Mount Tsukuba and gathers like love into a swelling *pool*' (quoted in Azuma 1939: 88, emphasis added). Yozeiin's famed love poem (circa ninth century) from the *Hyakunin isshu* bespeaks a burgeoning love that runs a natural course. But Hokumei's appropriation of the poem hinges on the doubled meanings of *fuchi* – a deep pool and an impassable abyss – suggesting a burgeoning love that is always on a treacherous precipice, a passionate love that can overflow to disastrous consequences. Hokumei draws on the double meaning by following the love poem with a sharp contrast – war. The poem's proximity to nature is shattered by the hard prose directly following it: 'And at the foot of those two peaks of Tsukuba Mountain in T. Village, a rising sun flag fluttered in the crisp autumn wind. In this village, today, the famed soldier named OO was sent off with cheers' (Azuma 1939: 88). Here we are completely within the realm of the human, nation, and war. The first few lines then, poem and prose, foreshadow all that is to come.

In this story, Hokumei was trying his hand at something more subversive along the lines set out in his earlier article. The problem of class inequality is central to this story of ill-fated love. Kazuo's father is the wealthy landowner and mayor of the town, while Yae and her mother are essentially sharecroppers on his land. When Kazuo's father deigns to grant permission for the wedding, he is transgressing traditional family and class norms. Concern for class divisions is further reiterated when Yae and her mother, country bumpkin field hands, go to the big city and are swindled by the wedding store clerk. Their gaffe is the mistake of low-class farmers – a people presumably devoid of middle-class taste or sense of decorum. This fact alone explains Kazuo's father's rage, the termination of the wedding, and the sudden class consciousness of the son at the end of the story. His individual realization both of his error in not resisting his father's decision and of the value of Yae's life is enabled by their class difference. Hokumei uses a popular and acceptable plot line to surreptitiously convey the notion that class divisions are artificial, the source of tragedy and even the troubles in war.

Hokumei's career and writings not only reveal the complicity of Japanese proletarian and obscene writing with bourgeois discourse, but also highlight the potential radicality of the mere expression of certain kinds of bourgeois sexual relations. While Jō (1991) correctly points out the backstreet life of the *enpon* or sexual books at the time of the main street *enpon* or one-yen books, he does not remark on the fact that they were two streets created and maintained by a group of the city planners with mutually productive interests – the censors, pariah capitalists, and artists. The boom of one kind of *enpon* contained the boom of the other. Thus, there is no contradiction in the fact that the period of publishing and reading which brought about the world's first *Complete Works of Marx and Engels* also brought with it a boom in magazines with names like *Kama Sutra*, *Erotic Life*, and *Sex Crimes*.

Criminalized sex, glorified violence, and banned wounds

Making the connection between the erotic and the proletarian explicit can begin to explain the mass canonization of violent representation through disparate venues from detective fiction and adventure stories to war narrative. Neither sexually nor politically radical, but, nevertheless, titillating and escapist, war narratives represent the displacement of what was sought after in the suppressed erotic and proletarian fiction – ever-more realistic and bald depictions of taboo subjects (Yano 1996: 292–3). The *ero-puro* sense provides the basis for a rereading of the decriminalization of representations of violence in wartime cultures.

The radical eroticism of Umehara Hokumei   51

What is left after the vanishing of this *ero-puro* connection? If the erotic and proletarian are suppressed, where might we find their traces, their return in mainstream publications during the war? A preliminary answer may be found in what we have neglected in the standard *ero-guro* characterization thus far – that is, the grotesque itself. Though violent and sexual stories considered grotesque also experienced a boom during the period, the amount of banned grotesque fiction – whether noir/bizarre (*ryōki*), detective (*tantei*), or mystery (*suiri*) fiction – extant in the archives of the Home Ministry in Japan between 1923 and 1945 is particularly low when compared to other genres.[20] Pointing to the discrepancy since the mid-1920s between the banning of erotic art and the mass popularity of detective fiction in the US, independent scholar of American folklore Gershon Legman wrote that 'we are faced in our culture by the insurmountable schizophrenic contradiction that sex, which is legal in fact, is a crime on paper, while murder – a crime in fact – is, on paper, the best seller of all time' (1949: 19).

The fact that there were statistically insignificant numbers of bans on detective fiction in Japan throughout the interwar period should not signify that censorship had no effect on the more grotesque genres. Major figures like Edogawa Ranpo did suffer the occasional ban and eventually moved to different genres, though as Sari Kawana (2003: 203–8) points out, these moves may have been more voluntary than the result of censorial coercion. While Legman's notion that detective fiction went unscathed may be usefully questioned in the case of Japan, we should not ignore the larger claims he makes which do seem to hold as well for the Tokyo publishing world as they did for the one in New York.

Legman's point that certain *representations* of violent crimes are not themselves criminal, and therefore not censorable, raises several issues: Have some representations of violence been historically less offensive than others? Have censors or the market been the dictators of what kinds of representations of violence are deemed offensive? Discussing actual cases of state violence and not the representations thereof, Ueno Chizuko argues persuasively that the one kind of violence universally decriminalized is state violence: 'It can be said that the basis of military power is the decriminalization of state violence. After all, an act of violence committed under any other circumstances is a criminal act' (2004: 161). If we take Ueno's point to be violence in the name of the state is routinely justified (if rarely justifiable), what of the *representations* of violence in the name of country, nation, emperor, or democracy? Are these representations of war to be less targeted than others?[21] What kinds of images of state violence are deemed offensive? What images of violence at the national level are criminalized? Which ones are decriminalized? Who decides?

The June 1927 issue of Hokumei's magazine *Perverse Matters* carried a series of five photographs under the title 'The War Against War' (*Sensō ni tai suru sensō*). These disturbing images of the ravages of war were reproduced from Ernst Friedrich's German book *Krieg dem Krieg* (The War Against War, 1924). One of the photos included was particularly telling. The Japanese caption reads, 'Even with this, he lives!' and below, 'This is a sacrifice of the German Army in the European War.' Ernst Friedrich's caption from the original

52   *J. Abel*

reads: *'Die "Badekur" der Proleten: Fast das ganze Gesicht weggeschossen'* ('The "health resort" of the proletarian: Almost the whole face blown away') (Friedrich 1987 [1924]: 233). In the context of late 1920s Japan, it is understandable that the Japanese caption does not translate the overt Marxist overtones of the original caption. The combination of the two Japanese captions wavers between appealing to morbid curiosity at the grotesque image and to the pacifist message of the German original minus the overt connection to proletarian ideology.[22]

Significantly, this interwar collection of photographs was published in *Perverse Matters*, not Hokumei's other magazines, *Arts Market* or *Grotesque*. Interwar 'perversion' and erotics had a further political reach than we might expect. The influence of this kind of anti-war sentiment,[23] published in the seemingly liminal *Perverse Matters*, was deep. The year after this series of five photos was first published, its title, *The War Against War*, was borrowed for the first ever collection of anti-war short stories published in Japan. Most of the writers assembled in that collection were renowned proletarian writers; wartime rape is a feature of several of the stories. Writers in the collection included Eguchi Kan, Hayashi Fusao, Kaneko Yōbun, Kuroshima Denji, Maedakō Hiroichirō, Murayama Tomoyoshi, Takeda Rintarō, and Tsuboi Shigeji. As raw portrayals of the experience of war devoid of prolonged philosophical reflection, these anti-war stories were the stylistic forerunners of even the most jingoistic of canonical war literature.[24]

Foucault's caution that 'we must not think that in saying yes to sex, we are saying no to power' (1978: 157), has been thrown to the wind historically by a number of radicals from the 1920s through the 1970s. Yet, in light of the demise of the *ero-puro* moment in prewar Japan, the possibilities entailed in such a saying yes to sex need to be well heeded. And, while bodies and pleasures may provide one useful starting place for interrogating the idea of a monolithic wartime discourse, a look at bodies and pain may be more helpful for examining the rise in literatures of violence. Foucault's 'microphysics of power' does not suggest a specific path for resistance to censorship or the power censorship seeks to consolidate. Recognizing that 'cultural forms are hybrid, mixed, impure and the time has come in cultural analysis to reconnect their analysis with their actuality' (Said 1994: 14), we can begin to delineate a path understanding moments of historical resistance – their failures and successes.

Notes

1 Wheeler (1929: 65) writes that the 'modern generation' have 'a virus in their blood – the virus of universal chaos consequent upon war; of a world of spiritual, intellectual, and economic principles in a state of flux.' He also writes:

> The results of war are many and varied, and are of course of paramount importance in arriving at an adequate understanding of the tendencies of any post-war generation. First of all we have a social chaos amid which moral values, national and individual, undergo considerable modification.

(1929: 66)

The radical eroticism of Umehara Hokumei 53

2 The phrase the 'period of three Ss' (*san S jidai*) referred to speed, sports, and screen in the early 1930s and not 'sports, screen, and sex' until the postwar era when the US Occupiers were said to have brought in a '3S policy' (*san S seisaku*). For examples of the 'period of three Ss' referring to speed, sports, and screen see 'San esu jidai' (1932) and Harada (2002 [1933]). For more on the postwar 'three S policy' see Buruma (2003: 135).

3 For instance, see numerous volumes of *Modan* (1995 [1930]).

4 'Shades of pink' is a phrase intended to draw a bilingual pun. In Japanese, *pinku* refers to a whole genre of magazines and film subsuming Hollywood's distinctions between hardcore and softcore pornography, and has come to refer to eroticism itself. 'Pinko' was a derogatory American epithet used in the post-McCarthy Era Cold War as a way of silencing opinions that gave any tangential credence to Socialism, deriving from the association of Communism with the color red. This pun does not work in Japanese because *aka*, or 'red,' alone is used for Communism there, though there have been jokes such as Sasaki Hiroaki's referring to a conversion (*tenkō*) from *aka* (Communist red) to *momo* (peach color of erotica). I thank Asuka Sango for helping me think through this idea. Silverberg (2006: 29) cites a similar point by Maruyama Masao, that youth 'could become "pink" – indulgent in sexual pleasures (the preferred choice of their parents) – or they could become "red" – adherents of "dangerous thought".'

5 Gertzman (1999: 23, 28, 37–8) borrows these terms from Max Weber.

6 See also Driscoll (2000: 73–4). Both Yamaguchi and Driscoll overemphasize the geographical importance of publishing from Shanghai, especially in light of Sasaki Hiroaki's note that only the first of the six volumes of Hokumei's *Kama Sutra* journal purported to be printed in Shanghai was actually printed there. See Shichimendō (2000).

7 See special issue of *Erochika* (1973); also Jō (1991) and Umehara M. (1968).

8 See Frühstück (2003) on the relation between sexology and the nation-state.

9 Hokumei's son recalled how one technique was to advertise a limited edition number of about one-tenth the actual pressing, ensuring a sellout. Hokumei would ask for advance pay for certain items, and even asked for donations for impending fines from the censor. See Umehara M. (1968: 232–7).

10 He may have published under Yoshikawa Eiji's name during this time, though this is in dispute: see Isogai (1991).

11 For more on the Takebashi incident see Umehara (1973 [1931]: 79–126). For more details on Hokumei's insurrectionary concerns, see the afterword to the republished edition by Kano Masanao, 'Hopes for Agitation of the Realm' (*Tenka jōran e no kitai*).

12 The problem of the subaltern identified by Spivak (1988) was precisely the internal crisis for the elite theorists of proletarian literature – the very moment we are said to have finally the words of the proletariat in writing, we find their credentials as members of the proletariat are questionable.

13 Hirano (1975 [1946]: 115–21) and Odagiri (1990: 168–75); also recounted in Shea (1964: 328–37).

14 Aramata (2000) goes a long way to removing the stereotype of proletarian literature as dry and ideological, reading proletarian novels variously as horror fiction, detective fiction, sexual fiction, and science fiction. That his position within the Japanese academy is liminal (he is an independent scholar) signifies the marginalized status of his viewpoint, though the mass appeal of his readings may be seen in the fact he has become a television celebrity. See also Shimamura (2005: 628–30). For a similar viewpoint on the breadth and depth of proletarian writers in America, see Wald (1994: 22).

15 Or as Barbara Foley claims more simply, 'the literary proletarians were part of modernism' (1993: 62); see also Silverberg (2006).

54 J. Abel

16 Akita (1994) and Kanno (2005) pay little attention to his fiction.
17 Grotesque and proletariat links bear noting here. Hokumei came back again and again to the selling of human corpses both as a way to appeal to base grotesque interest and as a critique of the ends of capitalism. Of particular interest are his 1931 story 'Corpse for Sale', depicting a destitute worker wanting to sell his soon-to-be-dead body to fund a strike, and the 1938 story ' "Asia" express' (attributed to Yoshikawa Eiji), featuring the body parts of a dismembered young girl circulating around the continent in a suitcase: see Isogai (1991).
18 This chapter was reprinted as 'Theater through the Keyhole' in *Arts Market* (Umehara 1926b). As Stallybrass and White (1986: 153–7) note of A.J. Munby and Sigmund Freud's 'Wolf Man,' the class position of a maid and her association with dirt created desire in the bourgeois European male, having been brought up in a society that cast out the poor, women, and dirt. That the opposite could be true for a person of a lower class seems likely.
19 Driscoll (2000) also employs the rhetoric of an outside.
20 By my count, fewer than ten such books exist in the archives of the Home Ministry censors.
21 The banning on both grounds of sedition and obscenity of the humorous comic book *Soldiering Life* (*Heitai seikatsu*) with its satirical vision of the life of soldiers in training, including jibes at their sexual jaunts, is an example of how these two categories could be conflated in times of war (see Imagawa 1943).
22 This connection is confirmed in Kanno Satomi's work on the age of 'perversion,' linking depictions of violence to the 'perverse' spirit of the mid-1920s (2005: 157–63).
23 Hokumei's own anti-war views can be read in his preface to his wartime translation of Otto Paust's *Volk im Feuer*, in which he warns that postwar Japan might become what Germany became after World War I (Azuma 1943: 1–4).
24 Yano Kan'ichi (1996: 292–3) argues that war narrative derived its penchant for realistic detail and conveyance of the facts 'as they really are' (*aru ga mama*) or 'direct records of experience' (*chokusetsu no keiken no ki*) from leftist literature. In this regard, also note that the examination copy of one of the rare books to have been banned both for reasons of morals (*fūzoku*) and sedition (*annei*), *Secret Stories of Blind Love, Crime, and Arrest* (*Chijō hanzai torimono hiwa*) has pencil markings of the censor around several passages relating to war. Sections dealing with war are titled 'Out of War Great Murderers Arise,' 'The Ravages of War: Powerless Antiwar Treaties,' and the like (*Chijō hanzai* 1939: 19, 203, 430).

References

Akita, Masami (1994) *Sei no ryōki modan* (The Bizarre, Sexual Modern), Tokyo: Seikyūsha.
Aramata, Hiroshi (2000) *Puroretaria bungaku wa monosugoi* (Proletarian Literature is Gruesome), Tokyo: Heibonsha.
Azuma, Tairiku [aka Umehara Hokumei] (1939) 'Shōrei to sekkōhei' (The Beckoning Spirit and the Scout), in *Aikoku buyū tantei kaiki jitsuwa kessaku shū* (Patriotic, Valiant, Detective, Mystery and True Story Masterpiece Collection), Shinnengō furoku (January special issue) of *Kōdan kurabu* (Story Club), 88–111.
Azuma, Tairiku [aka Umehara Hokumei] (1943) *Hi no naka no kokumin* (People in the Fire), trans. of Otto Paust, *Volk im Feuer* [1934], Tokyo: Shōbunkaku.
Buruma, Ian (2003) *Inventing Japan: 1853–1964*, London: Weidenfeld & Nicolson.
Chijō hanzai torimono hiwa (The Secret Stories of Crimes of Passion) (1939) Osaka: Yūbunkan. Censor's examination copy held at NDL as *toku* 501–3.

Driscoll, Mark W. (2000) *Erotic Empire, Grotesque Empire: Work and Text in Japan's Imperial Modernism*. Unpublished doctoral dissertation, Cornell University.

Erochika (1973) Special New Year's edition 'Erosu no kaitakusha: Umehara Hokumei no shigoto' (Pioneer of Eros: Umehara Hokumei's Work), vol. 42.

Foley, Barbara (1993) *Radical Representations: Politics and Form in U.S. Proletarian Fiction, 1929–1941*, Post-Contemporary Interventions, Durham: Duke University Press.

Foucault, Michel (1978) *The History of Sexuality, Volume I: An Introduction*, New York: Vintage Books.

Friedrich, Ernst (1987) *WAR against WAR!*, trans. of *Krieg dem Krieg*, Seattle: The Real Comet Press.

Frühstück, Sabine (2003) *Colonizing Sex: Sexology and Social Control in Modern Japan*, Los Angeles: University of California Press.

Gertzman, Jay A. (1999) *Bookleggers and Smuthounds: The Trade in Erotica, 1920–1940*, Philadelphia: University of Pennsylvania Press.

Harada, Yoshikatsu (2002) [1933] 'Dai-san: jojō fūkei yoru no eigakan' (The Third: Lyrical Scenes of the Movie Theater at Night), *Kyōdo fūkei* (Local Scenes): digitized version by Chi'iki shiryō dijitaruka kenkyūkai, September 2002, available at: www.mt8.ne.jp/digiken/archives/kyodo/vol. 327.html (accessed October 2003).

Hirano, Ken (1975) [1946] 'Seiji to bungaku' (Politics and Literature), in *Hirano Ken zenshū* (Collected Works of Hirano Ken) Vol. 1, Tokyo: Shinchōsha, 189–92.

Imagawa, Yoshio (1943) *Heitai seikatsu* (Soldiering Life), Tokyo: Kagaku Nihonsha.

Isogai, Katsutarō (1991) 'Yoshikawa Eiji to ' "Tokkyū Ajia" ': Umehara Hokumei no daisaku ka' (Yoshikawa Eiji and "the Asia express": is Umehara Hokumei the ghost-writer?), *Taishū bungaku kenkyū* (Research on Popular Literature), 94(April): 8–12.

Jō, Ichirō (1991) *Hakkinbon zoku* (More Banned Books), Tokyo: Fukutake Bunko, Fukutake Shoten.

Kaneko, Yōbun (1976) 'Umehara Hokumei to *Bungei shijō*' (Umehara Hokumei and *Arts Market*), in Senuma Shigeki (ed.), *Bungei shijō fukkokuban bessatsu* (Addenda to the Facsimile Edition of *Arts Market*), Tokyo: Nihon Kindai Bungakukan, 1–3.

Kanno, Satomi (2005) *'Hentai' no jidai* (The Age of 'Perversion'), Kōdansha gendai shinsho, Vol. 1815. Tokyo: Kōdansha.

Kawana, Sari (2003) *Undercover Agents of Modernity: Sleuthing City, Colony, and Body in Japanese Detective Fiction*. Unpublished doctoral dissertation, University of Pennsylvania.

Kohl, Stephen W. (1990) 'Abe Jirō and *The Diary of Santarō*,' in J. Thomas Rimer (ed.), *Culture and Identity: Japanese Intellectuals during the Interwar Years*, Joint Committee on Japanese Studies, Princeton: Princeton University Press, 7–21.

Kunitz, Joshua (1967) 'Albert Rhys Williams: a biographical sketch,' in *Through the Russian Revolution*, New York: Monthly Review Press, i–ix.

Legman, Gershon (1949) *Love and Death: A Study in Censorship*, New York: Breaking Point.

Modan yōgo jiten (Modern terminology dictionary) (1995) [1930] Jitsugyō no Nihonsha, ed. Kōjimachi, Kōji and Kita, Sōichirō, facsimile, in *Kindai yōgo no jiten shūsei* (Revised Modern Terminology Dictionary), Vol. 13, Tokyo: Ōzorasha.

Nosaka, Akiyuki (1968) *Kōshoku no tamashii* (A Sexual Spirit), Tokyo: Shinchōsha.

Odagiri, Hideo (1990) *Shakai bungaku, shakaishugi bungaku kenkyū* (Social Literature, Socialist Literature Research), Tokyo: Keisō Shobō.

Odagiri, Hideo and Fukuoka, Seikichi (eds.) (1965) *Shōwa shoseki, zasshi, shinbun*

56   J. Abel

hakkin nenpyō (Chronology of Banned Books, Magazines, and Newspapers during the Shōwa Period), 4 vols., Tokyo: Meiji Bunken.

Ōuchi, Tsutomu (1967) 'Ero guro nansensu,' in *Fashizumu e no michi* (The Road to Fascism), Tokyo: Chūō Kōronsha, 451–69.

Said, Edward (1994) *Culture and Imperialism*, New York: Vintage Books.

'San esu jidai' (The period of three Ss) (1932) *Fujin kurabu* (Ms. Club), 13(8): 16.

Sensō ni tai suru sensō: Anchi miritarizumu shōsetsushū (The War Against War: an anti-militarism novel collection) (1984) [1928] ed. Nihon Sayoku Bungeika Sōrengō, Tokyo: Fuji Shuppan.

Shea, George Tyson (1964) *Leftwing Literature in Japan: A Brief History of the Proletarian Literature Movement*, Tokyo: Hosei University Press.

Shichimendō, Kyūsai (2000) 'XX Bungaku no yakata, zasshi shiryō: kāmashasutora' (The Pavilion of XX Literature: magazine documents-kama sutra), available at: http://kanwa.jp/xxbungaku/Magazine/Kama/Kama.htm (accessed 8 August 2012).

Shimamura, Teru (2005) 'Ero, guro, nansensu,' in Teru Shimamura (ed.), *Korekushon modan toshi bunka: 15 Eroguro nansensu* (Anthology of Modern City Culture), Tokyo: Yumani Shobō, 627–36.

Silverberg, Miriam (2006) *Erotic, Grotesque, Nonsense: The Mass Culture of Japanese Modern Times*, Los Angeles: University of California Press.

Spivak, Gayatri Chakravorty (1988) 'Can the subaltern speak?' in Cary Nelson and Lawrence Grossberg (eds.), *Marxism and the Interpretation of Culture*, Champaign: University of Illinois Press, 271–318.

Stallybrass, Peter and White, Allon (1986) *The Politics and Poetics of Transgression*, London: Methuen.

Suzuki, Ryōzō (1930) 'Shinbun kasha jidai no kare' (When he was a Newspaper Reporter), in '"Hito wo kutta otoko" no hyōden' (Biographies of 'The Man Who Ate People'), *Gurotesuku* (January): 296–315.

Tachibana, Takahiro [aka Kōshirō] (1932) *Kore ijō wa kinshi: Aru ken'etsu kakarichō no shuki* (The Rest is Banned: a censor's memoir), Tokyo: Senshinsha.

Tanizawa, Eiichi (1981) 'Ero guro nansensu: "Kafe no jidai," Umehara Hokumei nado' (Erotic, Grotesque, Nonsense in the 'Café Period': Umehara Hokumei and the like), in Nihon Bungaku Kenkyū Shiryō Kankōkai (ed.), *Nihon bungaku kenkyū shiryō sōsho: Shōwa no bungaku* (The Japanese Literary Research Series: Shōwa Period Literature), Tokyo: Yūseidō Shuppan, 70–5.

Ueno, Chizuko (1998) 'Ratai no "roshutsudo" to sono "seijisei"' (The 'Exposure' of Nudes and the 'Politics' thereof), in *Hatsujō sōchi: erosu no shinario* (Mechanisms of Lust: the scene of eros), Tokyo: Chikuma Shobō, 41–3.

Ueno, Chizuko (2004) *Nationalism and Gender*, trans. Beverley Anne Yamamoto, Japanese Society Series, Melbourne: Trans Pacific.

Umehara, Hokumei (1924) *Satsujin gaisha: Akumashugi zensei jidai* (Murder Incorporated: the heyday of diabolism), Tokyo: Akane Shobō.

Umehara, Hokumei (1926a) 'Ichiyazuke no kakumeiyasan' (The Pickled-Overnight Revolutionary), *Bungei shijō* (Arts Market) 3(1): 46.

Umehara, Hokumei (1926b) 'Kagiana no shibai kenbutsu' (Theater through the Keyhole), *Bungei shijō* 2(7): 172–98.

Umehara, Hokumei (1928) 'Mirabō haku no chinpon' (Dr. Mirabeau's Rare Books), *Gurotesuku* 1(1): 146–9.

Umehara, Hokumei (1930) 'Dankikan hishi: sayokuha ero no kaidendō kindai yōkiteki hyakkaten' (The Hidden History of the Pavilion of Bizarre Tales: a strange sanctuary

The radical eroticism of Umehara Hokumei   57

of leftist erotica, an eerie department store of modernity), Nichibunken Pamphlet Collection UC71Um, Tokyo: Dankikan Shokyoku.

Umehara, Hokumei (1931a) 'Shitai o uru' (Corpse for Sale), *Gurotesuku* 4(1): 190–201.

Umehara, Hokumei (ed.) (1931b) *Kindai sesō zenshi: keiou kara taishō made no shinbun jūyō kiji shūsei* (A Complete History of Modern Life: a collection of important newspaper articles from the Keiō era to the Taishō era), Tokyo: Hakuhōsha.

Umehara, Hokumei (ed.) (1973) [1931] *Kinsei bōdō hangyaku henranshi* (A History of Early Modern Riots, Revolts, and Rebellions), Tokyo: Kaien Shobō.

Umehara, Hokumei and Uyama, Asatarō (1925) *Roshia daikakumeishi*, trans. of Albert Rhys Williams, *Through the Russian Revolution* [1921], Tokyo: Asakaya Shoten.

Umehara, Masaki (1968) 'Umehara Hokumei sono ashiato' (The Footprints of Umehara Hokumei), in Muraoka Kū (ed.) *Dokyumento Nihonjin* (Japanese People Documented), Vol. 6, Tokyo: Gakugei Shorin, 220–41.

Wald, Alan M. (1994) *Writing from the Left: New Essays on Radical Culture and Politics*, London: Verso.

Wheeler, F. L. (1929) *Modernity*, London: Williams & Norgate.

Yamaguchi, Masao (1995) *'Zasetsu' no Shōwa shi* (A History of 'Collapses' in the Shōwa period), Tokyo: Iwanami Shoten.

Yano, Kan'ichi (1996) 'Sayoku bungaku kara sensō bungaku e' (From Leftist Literature to War Literature), *Kindai sensō bungaku jiten Vol. 1: Izumi jiten shiriizu 3*, Osaka: Izumi Shoin, 279–93.

Yokote, Kazuhiko (2003) 'Ichiranhyō senzen senjiki hiken'etsu bungaku sakuhin shobun risuto' (A List of Prewar and Wartime Censored Literary Works), *Heiwa bunka kenkyū* (Peace Cultural Studies), 23(1): 153–76.

Yoshimura, Yoshiko (ed.) (1992) *Japanese Government Documents and Censored Publications: A Checklist of the Microfilm Collection*, Washington, DC: Library of Congress.

Yoshimura, Yoshiko (ed.) (1994) *Censored Japanese Serials of the Pre-1946 Period: A Checklist of the Microfilm Collection*, Washington, DC: Library of Congress.

4 The censor as critic

Ogawa Chikagorō and popular music censorship in imperial Japan

Hiromu Nagahara

Introduction

The advent of mass consumer society in the early twentieth century brought about new challenges and opportunities for the imperial Japanese state as it sought to extend its control over popular culture. Along with the rapid transformation of Tokyo after the devastation of the Great Kantō Earthquake of 1923, this period saw the flowering of an urban, cosmopolitan lifestyle that both attracted and disturbed contemporary observers. At the heart of this development were the growing demands and fantasies of the newly emerging urban middle class, who availed themselves of a widening array of entertainment and services, including cafés, dance halls, and department stores. Such imaginations and desires for consumer goods were, in turn, amplified and disseminated through the rapid growth of mass media during this period. These included mass journals, film, radio, and phonograph records.

This chapter focuses on the censorship of phonograph records in imperial Japan, which began in 1934. A close examination of the career and writings of Ogawa Chikagorō (b. 1896), the Home Ministry record censor, reveals the complex web of motives, ideas, and historical processes that went into the process of record censorship. Going beyond simply banning objectionable songs, Ogawa sought to reshape popular songs as a genre by joining in the contemporary discourses on music and mass culture as a whole. In the end, the record censorship of this period reveals not only how the state attempted to manage popular culture but also how such effort required a close cooperation with influential intellectuals and critics. These connections, in turn, laid the foundation for the continuation of popular music censorship long after the dismantling of the Home Ministry, and its censorship apparatus, under the Allied Occupation (1945–52).

The birth of popular songs in modern Japan

While the first record company was established in Japan in 1909, it was not until the first years of the Shōwa period (1926–89) that what had been a collection of various small record companies was consolidated into a major industry. In these years, three large companies emerged in the Japanese market under close cooperation with their Western counterparts. In 1926, Japanese importers of the Polydor label approached its German maker, Deutsche Gramophone, and won the right to press their records locally in Japan by establishing Japan Polydor. In 1927, the US-based Victor Talking Machine Company established its Japanese branch, including a full-scale factory that produced phonograph records as well as players. In the same year, the Japan Phonograph Company (Nihon Chikuonki Shōkai), originally established in 1909 by an American trader based in Yokohama, came under the control of the Anglo-American-owned Columbia Records, one of the largest record conglomerates in the world.

An oft-cited reason for the sudden deluge of Western capital in early Shōwa was the establishment of a luxury tax in 1924, which placed a 100 percent tariff on imported phonographs and records in order to encourage domestic production as part of the reconstruction efforts following the Great Kantō Earthquake. Clearly, it made sense for the Japanese record dealers as well as their Western associates to expand the local production of records and phonographs. At the same time, this was also an opportunity for the Western companies to establish themselves more firmly in what was seen as a promising market (Azami 2004: 93–4). Victor and Columbia, in particular, were eager to deploy their newly developed electrical recording technology, which quickly made the mechanical system obsolete.

This kind of investment paid off as the record industry expanded rapidly during the following decade. Between 1929 and 1936, the industry saw an almost threefold increase in its annual record production and a two-fold increase in its phonograph production.[1] While the increasing demand for and availability of inexpensive records of Western music, such as classical music and jazz, played a role in this growth, it was quickly eclipsed by the rapid increase in the number of locally produced popular songs, known as *ryūkōka* (fashionable songs).

The term *ryūkōka*, which came into use in the late 1920s, was a reformulation of an earlier term, *hayariuta*, which used slightly different Chinese characters and, more obviously, a distinct pronunciation. Together, these linguistic changes connoted the novelty of these songs as well as their close connection to the recording industry. Musically, many of these songs featured the syncretic *yonanuki* pentatonic scale that gave the song a distinctly Japanese feel despite the use of Western instrumentation. Many of the early hits in this vein came to be known as *shimpei-bushi* (Shimpei songs), in reference to their composer, Nakayama Shimpei (1887–1952). During the 1930s, Koga Masao further developed this syncretic style as he composed songs that came to be called *koga merodī* (Koga melodies). The unabashed syncretism of both *shimpei-bushi* and *koga merodī* embodied the cultural hybridity that ultimately became the hallmark of the vast majority of popular songs that were produced by the record industry during this period.[2]

Victor led the trend in producing *ryūkōka* with a series of hits in 1928 and 1929, signaling a shift in a phonograph record market that was hitherto dominated by Western imports and recordings of more traditional Japanese music.

60   H. Nagahara

One such hit, 'Longing for You' (*Kimi koishi*), reportedly sold as many as 250,000 copies (Azami 2004: 112; Kurata 2006: 180). By 1937, there were reports of hits that sold as many as 500,000 copies (Ogawa 1941: 148).[3] The internal reports circulated within the Home Ministry verify this development. At the end of 1935, one such report indicated that the number of new popular songs that were produced in that year easily outnumbered that of other genres of music.[4] As another report noted a year earlier, popular songs clearly had become 'the principal source of profit for the record companies,' which now devoted their marketing efforts almost exclusively to this genre (*NK* 1934: 289–90).

The rapid expansion of popular songs as a genre, however, also led to a growing chorus of criticism and the expression of misgivings regarding this new mass entertainment. One of the first groups to voice such concern was that of educators in primary and secondary schools. These teachers were fearful of the moral, and in particular sexual, degradation that the 'plaintive, lewd, and lustful tunes' allegedly caused among their students (Kamita 2007: 18). Just as Victor was producing its first hit songs in 1929, newspapers in Tokyo began to cover various anti-popular song movements led by teachers as well as officials from institutions like the Tokyo Music School and the Tokyo city government's Education Department (Kurata 2006: 184). An *Asahi shinbun* article from 13 November 1929 reported the rapidity with which popular songs apparently spread throughout Japan, prompting educators not only to seek a ban on popular songs but also to reform the music curriculum in order to provide what they saw as more 'healthy' music.[5]

Reflecting such concern among educators, the Education Ministry established the Committee of Popular Culture in 1931, which was designed to discuss and combat the negative social effects of mass entertainment, including film, theater, radio, and popular songs (Anon. 1931a).[6] One of the first activities of the committee was to create a list of approved records that were deemed suitable for popular consumption. Tanabe Hisao, a member of the committee and a music scholar, also published a treatise entitled *How to Choose and Listen to Phonographs and Records* (*Chikuonki to rekōdo no erabikata kikikata*, 1931), in which he argued that the Home Ministry should join the fight against popular songs through censorship. Tanabe's opinion was shared by Education Ministry officials, who approached their Home Ministry counterparts in the same year to begin discussing precisely such measures (Anon. 1931b). Finally, after three years of preparation, the Home Ministry drafted the revisions to the Publication Law, which included a provision for record censorship, and saw it enacted on 2 May 1934.

Record censorship in practice

The Home Ministry officially began record censorship three months later on 1 August 1934. Records were now censored according to the provision of Article 19 of the Publication Law, which stipulated that any material that 'disturbed public order' or 'endangered manners and morals' was liable to be banned from

Ogawa Chikagorō and popular music censorship   61

sale and distribution (Ogawa 1935: 71–3).[7] The revised law also required record companies to submit two copies of each new record three days prior to the date of release, thus placing records under pre-publication censorship.

How, then, did the censorship of popular songs work in the following years? The most obvious sources necessary to understand the process come from the Home Ministry, including the *Publication Police Report* (*Shuppan keisatsuhō*) and the *Publication Police Summary* (*Shuppan keisatsu gaikan*), both of which were internal reports of censorship activities that were circulated within the Home Ministry.[8] Given the well-earned reputation of prewar and wartime censorship as a draconian system, some of what emerges from these documents may be surprising at first glance. The first thing that we can see from these reports is that relatively few popular songs were actually banned from sale and distribution under Article 19 throughout the period during which the Publication Law was in effect. Between August 1934 and December 1937, only twenty popular song records were actually banned from sale. Given that 2,166 popular song records were submitted for censorship in 1935 alone, this is a notably small number. Not surprisingly, all twenty records were banned for disturbing manners and morals rather than endangering public order.

Notably, the majority of these records were banned under either one of two specific circumstances. The first of these emerged in 1936, when Victor's 'Don't You Forget Me' (*Wasurecha iyayo*) became a runaway hit following its release in March. The song featured Watanabe Hamako, one of the most celebrated female singers in the early to mid Shōwa era, who ended each verse by pleading with her lover in a sugary voice, 'Oh, don't forget me. Don't you forget me.' While the song initially passed the censor's inspection, its growing popularity alarmed the Home Ministry officials and prompted them to prohibit its public performance after May (*NK* 1936d: 24–5). Even more problematic for these officials, however, were the numerous imitations that 'Don't You Forget Me' spawned, most of which allegedly accentuated the original song's amorous tone. Consequently, they banned eight such records between June 1936 and June 1937, under Article 19, while Victor was also ordered to suspend production of the original song (*NK* 1936c: 24–5). Ogawa Chikagorō later recalled that, when he first examined the song in March 1936, he did not feel that anything was particularly wrong with it, 'except for the very last line of each verse, which felt a little too sweet' (Ogawa *et al.* 1936: 15). This impression ultimately gave way to alarm as the song became a massive hit.

The second set of circumstances emerged as a direct consequence of the outbreak of the second Sino-Japanese War (1937–45), which began with skirmishes surrounding the Marco Polo Bridge near Beijing on 7 July 1937 and quickly turned into a full-scale offensive by the Japanese forces in Northern China. As the military operation escalated overseas, the government used the rhetoric of *hijō jikyoku* (wartime emergency) to assert greater control and demand a new sense of urgency among the inhabitants of what was increasingly seen as the home front. Almost immediately, the Home Ministry strengthened its censorship standards, beginning with newspaper coverage of the war and quickly expanding

62   H. Nagahara

to all other forms of media including records. As a result, six records were banned for featuring popular songs that were deemed to be 'unsuitable to the current emergency situation' between September and December 1937 (*NK* 1937b: 91–2; *NK* 1937c: 146, 205–6). Most of these records featured songs that, while not as directly sensual as the likes of 'Don't You Forget Me,' were nevertheless accused of being inappropriately focused on romance in such serious times.

The ban on the twenty popular song records was not the full extent of record censorship, as several other records were, in fact, banned under Article 19 in the years 1934–37. Most of these records were *manzai*, *rakugo*, and other forms of speech-based entertainment. These records largely fell into two categories: (1) those that contained language and themes that were deemed to be overtly erotic, and (2) those that were seen to disturb public order by using the key institutions of the nation for comic relief, including the military, the Yasukuni shrine, and, in one case, Prince Shōtoku, an ancient imperial prince long venerated as one of the key figures in Japanese history (*NK* 1936b: 162–3). All together, twenty-two such records were banned from sale and distribution during this period.[9]

In the early years of record censorship, there were many other records that also came under the sanction of the Home Ministry but not under the provision of the Publication Law. These were records that were originally produced before the implementation of the new law and were regulated, to the extent that they were, by Article 16 of Public Peace Police Law. This article gave police the authority to ban public performances that were deemed to 'violate public order' or 'endanger manners and morals.' After August 1934, records within this category that were deemed to be harmful continued to be regulated under the Public Peace Police Law, while further production of those records was suspended. Between 1934 and 1935, 128 records in this category were banned.

The effect that this particular provision had on popular song production was, however, minimal. As was true in the case of records that were produced after August 1934, most of these banned records were not popular songs. Also, the record companies themselves were much more focused on producing new hits rather than reproducing old records. From their perspective, they had already made as much money as they could make on old popular songs, most of which had been already distributed.

Kondan

In short, the banning of songs did not define the extent or the core of what constituted popular song censorship. What, instead, lay at the heart of the censor's task was what the Home Ministry officials termed *kondan* (consultation), an extra-legal system involving an ongoing contact between the censor and record producers.[10] An early report in the *Publication Police Summary* already expresses satisfaction with the low number of banned songs and attributes much of their success to the 'communication and cooperation' that they had established with the record companies (*NK* 1936a: 561). At the very basic level, this took the form of record companies discussing the viability of their new song with the censor during the planning phase, a practice known as *naietsu* (internal review).[11] There are indications that this was in practice for record censorship as early as September 1934 (*NK* 1934: 294).

From the Home Ministry's perspective, the task of a censor was not only to implement the law but also, more importantly, to give direct guidance to the record companies in order to prevent the production of songs that would be banned in the first place (Ogawa 1941: 111). There was also a clear financial incentive for record companies to cooperate, since they faced significant loss whenever songs were banned. Understandably, most record companies submitted their records for formal censorship long before the legally mandated date (Ogawa *et al.* 1936: 19–20).

The outbreak of the war with China in 1937 quickly led to further intensification of this process. On 28 August, the Home Minister summoned executives from film and record companies in order to discuss how to make entertainment media adhere to the 'aims of the total mobilization of the national spirit that have emerged in this state of emergency' (*NK* 1937a: 21–2). Three days later, on 31 August, the director of the Criminal Affairs Bureau convened a similar meeting, this time inviting record company officials, musicians, critics, journalists, and other bureaucrats to discuss specific steps to implement changes in popular song production. The discussion covered a diverse range of topics, including choice of theme in lyrics, choice of tunes, performers, methods of advertisement, and the need for further coordination between record producers and censors. As one Home Ministry official put it, all of this amounted to a demand for the record companies to shift their attitude from 'a singular focus on making profit' to 'public service for the sake of overcoming the current emergency' (Ogawa 1941: 168).

In an internal report written shortly after these consultation meetings, the record censor notes, with satisfaction, how very few records have proven to be problematic since the outbreak of the war (*NK* 1937a: 22). This was, in part, due to the fact that the record companies were increasingly focused on producing songs with war-related themes, which displaced songs along the lines of 'Don't You Forget Me.' As one record company official recalled in the postwar period, war songs sold well in the early years of the war against China, helping to revitalize an industry that was struggling to produce new hits (Andō 1963a: 2). In other words, the change of course demanded of them by the Home Ministry coincided with their business interest to a greater degree than one might presume.

At the same time, the day to day consultation process undeniably became even more thorough in the last months of 1937, as the censor came to be more consistently involved with such basic aspects of song making as the choice of words in the lyrics and the singers who were assigned to each song (Ogawa 1941: 192–3). Maruya Yoshizō, who worked at Columbia during this period, recalled in a postwar memoir how one of his colleagues visited the censor's office almost every day to discuss ongoing projects (1961: 4). One example of the songs that emerged out of this process was 'China Nights' (*Shina no yoru*), which became a major hit after its release in 1938 and a popular souvenir among the American GIs in the Occupation period. Sung by Watanabe Hamako, the song featured melody and lyrics that evoked sweet, exotic memories of a romantic night in China:

> China nights, China nights.
> In the harbor light, in the purple night,
> A dream-like Chinese boat emerges.
> I hear the unforgettable sound of *erhu*.
> China nights, nights of dream.[12]

While the censor did not object to the general content of the song, Maruya was nonetheless forced to change certain parts of the original lyrics, such as 'opium smoke,' which became 'harbor light,' and 'nights of love,' which became 'nights of dream.'

Censorship as cultural critique

The intensification of the consultation system in 1937 clearly indicated the state's growing determination to mold and manage mass culture in the context of wartime mobilization. The centrality of the consultation system, however, also highlights the significance of the individual censors who were at the frontline of implementing such efforts. This is especially true in the case of record censorship, which was largely conducted by a single censor, Ogawa Chikagorō, for the period stretching from 1934 to 1942 (*NK* 1936a.2: 221; Ogawa *et al.* 1936: 26).

Ogawa was a particularly visible figure throughout his tenure as a censor, and actively sought media exposure, writing at least five journal articles and participating in three roundtable discussions (*zadankai*) hosted by music journals. In 1941, he published a 200-page monograph on the history of popular songs and censorship. In addition, he was interviewed by newspapers and journals on multiple occasions, in which he described his work.[13] Ogawa's writings, which were almost exclusively devoted to discussing popular songs, give us insight into the logic that undergirded his work. In particular, they reveal a censor who quite freely expressed his appreciation for the very object of his censorship and sought to intervene in the broader public discourse on popular songs.

While very little is known about Ogawa's personal biography, there is little indication in his life before the Home Ministry that he was destined to become a censor. Born in Oita prefecture in 1896, Ogawa did not go directly into the government after his graduation from Senshū University in Tokyo, but instead worked in other fields for about ten years, including stints at a trading company in Tokyo and the Taiwan Electric Company. In 1928, he joined the Bureau of Reconstruction, an organization established under the Home Ministry that was given the task of overseeing the ongoing reconstruction of Tokyo in the years following the Great Kantō Earthquake. By the following year, he was transferred to the ministry's Criminal Affairs Bureau.

Ogawa Chikagorō and popular music censorship   65

In a 1942 magazine-sponsored roundtable discussion, Ogawa emphasizes the more or less coincidental nature of his appointment as a record censor:

> I didn't 'understand' music but I liked it. I liked it but I had no academic knowledge of it. I understood music as sensation but not in a logical way. And then, by coincidence, it was decided that I was the one who had a musical sense within the Home Ministry.
>
> (Ogawa *et al*. 1942: 41)

Perhaps liking music was a natural prerequisite for a job that required one to listen to hundreds of records every month. In another roundtable on the so-called *keiongaku* (light music) held in 1941, Ogawa confesses that he even grew to appreciate jazz as a form of music, after persevering through the initial shock (Ogawa *et al*. 1941: 25). What is important to note here is that Ogawa's selection as a record censor was not based on any particular expertise he possessed but, instead, on his appreciation of music as a lay consumer.

Ogawa's enthusiasm for recorded music is further substantiated in the entries regarding record censorship within the Home Ministry's monthly censorship report. These monthly reports, almost certainly authored by Ogawa between 1934 and 1935, featured lists of songs, ranging from Western classical music to popular songs, that were deemed to be 'particularly excellent' by the censor. These lists featured several popular songs sung by some of the most famous singers of the time, including Katsutarō, Shōji Tarō, Fujiyama Ichirō, and even Watanabe Hamako, whose 1936 hit 'Don't You Forget Me' had the distinction of being one of the few songs that was banned by Ogawa, as noted earlier.

Special commentaries were attached to songs that were considered to be particularly noteworthy, as was the case for Katsutarō's 'Hidden Tears' (*Himeshi namida*), which Ogawa describes as follows: 'Featuring lyrics and tune that are calm yet full of emotion, this is a very suitable piece for Katsutarō' (*NK* 1935b: 274). What these lists effectively signify is the infiltration of a consumer's pleasure into the work of censorship – a realm that is more often seen to be hostile to such sentiment. Selected by his superiors for his appreciation of music as a lay consumer, Ogawa did not restrain this impulse even in an official capacity.

Following his appointment as a record censor, Ogawa developed a more sophisticated appreciation of popular songs, as is apparent from his appearances in the media. In 1936, Ogawa participated in his first roundtable discussion, hosted by the music journal *Music World* (*Ongaku sekai*). In this discussion, entitled 'Trends in Popular Songs and Issues in Censorship' (*Ryūkōka no keikō to ken'etsu no mondai*), Ogawa argues that the essence of popular songs lies in the fact that they are easily accessible to a mass audience, featuring tunes that are not placed in rigid form and, instead, maintain 'softness' and common sensibility (Ogawa *et al*. 1936: 11–34). Consequently, he argues that it would be a mistake to try to insert anything solemn in its content. In his opinion, 'it would be unavoidable to have some amount of sensuality in it, like jazz' (Ogawa *et al*. 1936: 21). Ogawa declares that careful consideration of such fundamental

66   H. Nagahara

characteristics of popular songs was indispensible in his work as a censor. In the same discussion, however, Ogawa also goes on at length to explain that, as a censor, he is under the 'rule of the political trend' of his time, which he defines as 'the opinion of the dominant forces within society' (Ogawa *et al.* 1936: 11). While it was his personal opinion and hope that he would not have to crack down on most songs, such actions were inevitable given the relationship between 'politics, government administration, and the trend of the times' (Ogawa *et al.* 1936: 22). As we will see, the tension he expressed here between his understanding of the nature of popular songs and his role as a censor remained a consistent feature in his writings throughout his career.

In an article written in October 1937, following the outbreak of the Sino-Japanese War, Ogawa reiterates the stance that he had taken since the inception of record censorship (1937: 15–16). In his belief, every popular song emerged as a reflection of the social realities of the time of its birth and, in particular, the sentiments of the masses. Consequently, it was natural for songs to reflect the times of decadence as well as discipline. His policy had been to accept such natural tendencies of popular songs as much as possible, while simultaneously working gradually 'to improve' their quality. In other words, while it was his ultimate aim to 'elevate the tastes of the masses,' he had to allow for some amount of 'vulgarity' if he were to preserve the natural characteristics of popular songs, while acknowledging that such a stance would not lead to the immediate production of songs that matched the tastes of the educated, social elites of his time. In the same article, however, Ogawa also admits that such policy needed to be modified in a time of national emergency. According to him, wartime society demanded 'popular songs that could be sung by anyone, anywhere, and at any time' (1937: 16). In other words, the home front required what he later called 'public popular songs' (*kōteki ryūkōka*) that positively motivated the masses as they were mobilized in the war effort (1941: 170). Nonetheless, Ogawa closes the article by suggesting that, even in a time of war, 'human sentiments, melancholy, and even love' could continue to exist as themes in popular songs, 'so long as they do not lose a sense of cleanness and wholesomeness.' Rather than demanding that all popular songs become like military marches, Ogawa argues that the ideal popular song would continue to express realities of life 'without falling into nihilistic hedonism' (1937: 17).

Ogawa reiterates the tension between the demands of national emergency and what he sees as the unchangeable characteristics of popular songs in the book he published in 1941, entitled *Popular Songs and Social Currents (Ryūkōka to sesō)*. In it, he narrates the history of popular songs in Japan from the Meiji Restoration to his own time. As he does this, he is careful to emphasize that, in each historical period, popular songs have reflected the social climate and the sentiments of the masses. While much of the book reads somewhat like a litany of regrets regarding songs that he did not but should have censored in hindsight, Ogawa insists that popular songs, with all of their 'natural characteristics,' will always be sung by the people. He emphasizes this point by juxtaposing 'public popular songs' with 'private popular songs,' arguing that, despite the best efforts of educators and police officials, the former will never eliminate the latter (1941: 170). Consequently, he suggests that, while people should be encouraged in their singing of patriotic songs in public, they should also be left alone to sing songs like 'China Nights' in private.

Ogawa's rhetorical shuffle between his sympathy for the 'fundamental characteristics' of popular songs and the need to regulate their perceived negative effects remained a constant feature in his writings throughout his career, even as censorship standards were tightened steadily in those years. This seems to suggest that Ogawa's affinity towards 'private' popular songs remained remarkably consistent even amid wartime emergency. At the same time, however, Ogawa's stance was perhaps ultimately self-serving in that it also functioned to justify his position, and by extension that of the state, as an arbiter in the contemporary discourse on mass culture. As indicated earlier, Ogawa recognized that many of the social and political elites of his time considered popular songs to be highly problematic. In the portion of his 1941 book where he discusses the beginnings of record censorship, Ogawa acknowledges his awareness of such misgivings as well as the broader contours of the competing opinions regarding popular songs at that time. In his view, the public opinion in 1934 was divided between supporters of popular songs who dismissed any potential for harm and critics who seemed to 'criticize for the sake of criticizing' (1941: 116–17). Acknowledging some validity in the arguments of both sides, Ogawa notes that his primary task was to find a middle ground between these opinions.

Even as he presented himself as an arbiter in the discourse on popular songs, however, much of Ogawa's understanding of popular songs was borrowed from other critics of his time. By 1934, many of the critics had, in fact, chosen the middle ground that Ogawa aimed for – a stance characterized by a certain level of excitement for this new media that was nevertheless tempered by an ever-present ambivalence. A series of articles in the *Asahi shinbun* written in 1933 by Sugiyama Heisuke, a critic and regular contributor to the newspaper, is a good example of this. In the series, entitled *On Modern Popular Songs* (*Gendai ryūkōkaron*), Sugiyama praises popular songs for their ability to attract the masses and reflect their emotions, regardless of how vulgar or sentimental the songs may be. At the same time, Sugiyama also expresses concern that these songs are fundamentally warped by the fact that they are mass produced by a profit-driven industry. Finally, he suggests that the increasing rapidity of song production and distribution expands the social influence of such songs, making it necessary for them to be subjected to social critique. Sugiyama declares that he is writing the series in an attempt at precisely such an intervention, and he calls on other 'specialists' to join him in this endeavor.

Ogawa, in short, found natural allies in the community of mass culture critics from the outset of his career as a censor. His reliance on this community is especially apparent in the first and last roundtables in which he participated in 1936 and 1942. Hosted by prominent music journals, both meetings featured some of the leading musicians and music critics of his time, including Yoshida Shin (composer), Yoshimoto Akimitsu (critic), Shioiri Kamesuke (critic and editor of

Music World), Nakayama Shimpei (popular song composer), Sonobe Saburō (critic), and Yamane Ginji (critic). In these roundtables, Ogawa calls on the 'specialists' who sat with him to join him in his work by 'entering into the politics' of popular song censorship as leaders of society (Ogawa *et al.* 1936: 31; Ogawa *et al.* 1942: 35–6). On both occasions, the critics who participated in the discussion responded positively to such calls for involvement.[14]

Ogawa was not, in fact, the only censor who ventured into the realm of mass culture critique. A notable example was Tachibana Takahiro, who started at the Tokyo Metropolitan Police as a film censor in 1917 and eventually became the head of a police station in Tokyo. Throughout his time as a censor, Tachibana maintained a parallel career as a film critic (Makino 2006: 321). Tachibana began his activity as a critic even before he became a censor, by contributing articles to various film journals, in which he discussed every aspect of film and film making. As his journal contributions grew, he compiled many of them into books, including *A Study of Popular Entertainment* (*Minshū goraku no kenkyū*, 1920), *On Educational Film* (*Kyōiku eigaron*, 1929), and *The History of the Development of Film Art* (*Eiga geijutsu hattatsushi*, 1935). These works covered a wide range of topics from theories of popular entertainment to film history. Not only that, Tachibana also hosted a film study group at his home, attracting university students in the Tokyo area, many of whom continued on to be involved in film making and critique.

The careers of Ogawa and Tachibana betray the censors' desire to directly intervene in the contemporary critical discourse on mass culture, thus taking censorship beyond the idea of simply removing objectionable materials. On the one hand, this meant that the censors were increasingly joining the process of cultural production as supporters of mass culture. As noted earlier, Ogawa made no secret of his appreciation for popular songs, both as a lay consumer and a cultural critic. On the other hand, this also highlights the existence of a highly effective and insidious form of mass culture control by the state, in which the production, consumption, and regulation of popular songs were, in the end, part of the same process. In fact, this is precisely what enabled popular song censorship to survive the dismantling of the imperial state after 1945.

Continuities beyond 1945

As Japan's war with the Allied forces intensified, the line between the state and the producers of popular songs became increasingly blurred, culminating in the establishment of the Japan Association of Phonograph Record Culture (JAPRC) in 1942. Like many other industry 'control groups' that were created during this period, the main purpose of JAPRC was to strengthen the record industry's cooperation with the war effort by coordinating all aspects of its operation, from song selection to product distribution. Board members included record company executives and representatives from related organizations, including the Japan Association of Music Culture, which was another control group set up to manage

Ogawa Chikagorō and popular music censorship   69

musicians.[15] Not surprisingly, several government officials also joined JAPRC as 'councilors'; Ogawa represented the Home Ministry, while the Information Bureau was represented by Miyazawa Jūichi, who became a well-known music critic in the postwar period.

Soon after the association's establishment, the Home Ministry delegated to the JAPRC the task of inspecting product proposals submitted by record companies. At this point, record companies were required to submit such proposals to the JAPRC prior to the recording of each song. While the Home Ministry monitored this process through its representative, this effectively placed much of the record censor's duties in the hands of JAPRC officials. Recalling this transition in a postwar memoir, Andō Minoru, a JAPRC board member, attributed this delegation of authority to the increasing shortage of personnel within the Home Ministry as well as to the Ministry's sense that its censorship standards had been sufficiently internalized by the record producers (1963b: 8). Shortly after this, Ogawa was transferred to head Nara Prefecture's Office of Labor Affairs, ending his career as a censor.[16]

Notably, JAPRC continued its activities even after Japan's military defeat in 1945. While the Home Ministry and its censorship apparatus were dismantled by the Allied Occupation forces in September 1947, JAPRC continued to coordinate the music industry's efforts at recovering their production capacity, which were gravely damaged in the last years of the war. The end of Home Ministry censorship did signal the end of JAPRC's official censorship duties. The Occupation forces' Civil Censorship Detachment, which took over record censorship, ultimately proved to be quite lenient towards records and popular songs in particular, in contrast to their stance towards other forms of media. By 1949, popular song records were no longer subject to censorship.[17]

By the early 1950s, however, a growing coalition of mass culture critics revived the prewar critique of popular songs and demanded the introduction of some form of content regulation for phonograph records, especially within the context of the movement to protect children's cultural environment that gained steam from the late 1940s.[18] JAPRC responded by establishing the Record Production Standard Committee in 1955.[19] Made up of prominent music critics as well as record company officials, the committee was given the authority to examine all songs before they went on sale and, when deemed necessary, to order record companies to make changes.[20]

In short, by the mid-1950s, the regime of popular music censorship that had been developed during the war was effectively resurrected, albeit in the name of 'self-regulation' by the industry. At the heart of this transwar continuity were the activities of the many social and cultural critics who not only continued their careers as intellectuals but also as active participants in the politics of mass culture. In the course of the 1950s, these critics joined the producers of not only popular songs but also other forms for media as regulators. While Ogawa may not have approved of the dismantling of the Home Ministry, these developments do not seem far off from what he envisioned as he called on the critics to join him in the politics of popular songs.

70   H. Nagahara

Conclusion

Popular song censorship conducted by the Japanese state during the 1930s and 1940s ultimately suggests an understanding of censorship that de-centers the role of the state in what has been one of the quintessential functions of governments throughout history. In contrast to the censorship of more established forms of media like press and even film, the Home Ministry's stance towards popular songs, as seen through the experience of Ogawa Chikagorō, appears to have been characterized less by a unique sense of purpose as it was by reliance on existing critical discourse surrounding music and mass culture. That reliance need not, however, be interpreted as a sign of weakness. As seen in the postwar period, the enduring role of critics outside the government is ultimately what enabled the reestablishment of popular song censorship within a political context wherein the more overt form of censorship by the state was no longer a possibility. In that sense, the significance of popular song censorship in imperial Japan lies as much in its postwar legacies as in its activities before 1945.

Notes

1 See Komota (1994: 171); Nihon rekōdo kyōkai (1993: 44). Annual record production jumped from 10,483,364 to 29,682,590; sales peaked in 1936 and did not reach this level again until 1961. Phonograph production in the same period increased from 130,982 to 265,295.
2 On the connections between *ryūkōka* and both the prewar and postwar manifestations of *enka*, see Yano (2002). On *ryūkōka*'s connection to jazz, see Atkins (2001). Both works touch on musical genres that are, in many ways, better remembered today by scholars than the general public. Despite important connections between these three, it is nonetheless important not to conflate them in the period stretching from the 1920s through the 1950s.
   Enka, in prewar context, referred largely to a genre of popular ditties that were composed and disseminated by street performers known as *enka-shi*, the most famous one being Soeda Azembō (1872–1944). The postwar *enka* emerged from the 1960s when songs that were previously categorized as *ryūkōka* were recast as the musical representation of 'traditional Japan'; this happened as *ryūkōka* was increasingly marginalized in the face of the increasing diversification of the Japanese popular music scene.
   Elements of jazz, while recognizable in earlier hits like 'Longing for You,' ultimately remained distinct from *ryūkōka*, especially as a growing number of songs in the latter category came to be identified with the 'Japanese' tunes of Nakayama and Koga. As Atkins (2001: 47) notes, however, the term *jazu* in the Japanese usage oftentimes referred less to the musical characteristics of popular songs in the technical sense of the term as it did to their connection to broader socio-cultural phenomena like Americanization and mass consumption. As such, even *ryūkōka* with distinctly 'Japanese' tunes continued to be recognized and critiqued by many observers as part of the *jazu* phenomenon.
3 According to Ogawa (1941: 148), the song was titled *Aa sorenanoni*, which loosely translates to 'Oh, even though....'
4 See *Naimushō keihokyoku* (1935a: 559), hereafter referred to as *NK*. In this report, 3,983 out of a total of 12,210 songs were categorized as 'popular songs'; second place was 'Western music' with 2,467 songs.
5 A notable example of an early controversy on *ryūkōka* centered on Victor's 1929 hit,

'Tokyo March' (*Tokyo kōshinkyoku*). Created to promote a Nikkatsu film of the same title, the song featured Nakayama Shimpei's syncretic tune and Saijō Yaso's lyrics that highlighted the love life in modern Tokyo. The song's reference to a couple eloping on the Odakyū train, however, led NHK, the national radio broadcaster, to ban the song from its airwaves under the instruction of the Tokyo Metropolitan Bureau of Communication. What is important to note here, however, was the fact that this ban was limited to radio broadcasting and never affected the production or sale of the song's records.

6 The committee members included Gonda Yasunosuke, the social critic, and Takano Tatsunobu, a professor at Tokyo Music School.

7 As Kasza (1988: 9) notes, this twin principle, which remained at the heart of media censorship from the time of its establishment in the Meiji period, left a vast space for the censor's personal discretion due to its vagueness.

8 The former was a monthly report of censorship and the latter was an annual summary of the former.

9 The Home Ministry documents also indicate that other types of records were banned, including two Chinese popular songs that were imported to Japan and were seen to be anti-Japanese (*NK* 1937c: 146) and a Korean *manzai* with an erotic undercurrent (*NK* 1938: 48–9). These, however, were exceptional cases that were not repeated. Records produced for the Korean and Taiwanese markets were generally censored by the local governor general's office and the Home Ministry usually deferred to their judgment.

10 For a historical overview of the 'consultation' system in press censorship, see Kasza (1988: 172–5).

11 *Naietsu* was already well-established in other forms of media censorship.

12 *Erhu*, or *kokyū* in Japanese, is a two-stringed musical instrument sometimes called the 'Chinese violin' in the West.

13 See for example Takazawa's interview in *Music World* or the staff interviews in *Yomiuri shinbun* 1934; Anon. (1937); Anon. (1938).

14 In fact, two of the participants in the last roundtable, Yamane Ginji and Sonobe Saburō, continued to be involved in the critique of popular songs in the postwar period, indicating that their assent was not merely a product of wartime rhetoric.

15 The Japan Association of Music Culture was represented by Sonobe Saburō, a prominent music critic.

16 Shortly after Ogawa's departure, the Cabinet Information Bureau issued the famous ban of records of over a thousand American and British songs. While this may suggest a tightening of regulatory stance, it was more likely the product of wartime rhetoric, which became increasingly heated as Japan's fortunes waned in the battlefields of the Pacific. The delegation of censorship to JAPRC indicates, in fact, that the state no longer saw the recording industry as in need of a strict surveillance. In the course of the 1940s, record production ground to a halt, as few Japanese were able to afford such luxury and many of the recording industry's facilities were converted into munitions factories.

17 For an overview of popular song censorship during the Occupation period, see Nagahara (2011: 86–98).

18 On the postwar child protection movement and its role in the establishment of 'self-regulation' in the recording industry, see Nagahara (2011: 120–53).

19 By this time the JAPRC (Nihon chikuonki rekōdo bunka kyōkai) had been renamed the Record Industry Association of Japan (Nihon rekōdo kyōkai) in 1949. This was, in fact, the second time that the association's name was changed, as JAPRC was first changed to Japan Record Association (Nihon onban kyōkai) in 1944. The use of *onban* (disk/record) here successfully avoided the word *rekōdo* (record), which was borrowed from the Anglo-American enemy. The change in 1949 amounted to the Association's attempt at distancing itself from its wartime origins.

20 The first members include the music critics Horiuchi Keizō and Yoshimoto Akimitsu.

72   H. Nagahara

References

Andō, Minoru (1963a) 'Rekōdo kyōkai 20 nen no ayumi <1>' (20 Years of the Record Association), *Record*, 6: 2–3.

Andō, Minoru (1963b) 'Rekōdo kyōkai 20 nen no ayumi <3>' (20 Years of the Record Association), *Record*, 6: 8–9.

Anon. (1931a) 'Monbushō no ero torishimari' (The Education Ministry Tackles Eroticism), *Tokyo Asahi shinbun*, 8 February: 2.

Anon. (1931b) '"Ero" "aka" bayarikara rekōdo nimo ken'etsusei: naimushō yōyaku ugokidasu' (Popularity of 'ero' and 'red' Prompts Move to Introduce Censorship for Records: The Home Ministry Finally Begins to Act), *Yomiuri shinbun*, 5 April: 7.

Anon. (1937) 'Nē kouta no junan' (The Sufferings of *nē* Songs), *Yomiuri shinbun*, 14 May: 5.

Anon. (1938) 'Jikyokuka no ken'etsugan 2' (The Censor's Eye in Wartime), *Yomiuri shinbun*, 24 August: 3.

Atkins, E. Taylor (2001) *Blue Nippon: Authenticating Jazz in Japan*, Durham, NC: Duke University Press.

Azami, Toshio (2004) *Popyurā ongaku wa darega tsukurunoka* (Who Makes Popular Music?), Tokyo: Keisō Shobō.

Kamita, Seiji (2007) 'Ongaku kyōshikara tekishisareta merodī no kyōikuka: "Tokyo ondo" kara "kenkoku ondo" e' ('Educationalization' of Melodies Antagonized by Music Educators: Transformation of 'Tokyo Ondo' into 'Kenkoku Ondo'), *Kyōikugaku kenkyū* (Research on Education), 74(1): 13–27.

Kasza, Gregory (1988) *The State and the Mass Media in Japan: 1918–1945*, Berkeley and Los Angeles: University of California Press.

Komota, Nobuo (1994) *Shinpan nihon ryūkōkashi* (New History of Japanese Popular Songs), Vol. 1, Tokyo: Shakai Shisōsha.

Kurata, Yoshihiro (2006) *Nihon rekōdo bunkashi* (Cultural History of Japanese Records), Tokyo: Iwanami Shoten.

Makino, Mamoru (2006) 'Katsudō shashin kaidō wo kakenuketa nisoku no waraji no shōgensha' (The double-careered witness who ran through the moving picture highway) in Makino Mamoru (ed.), *Saisentan minshū goraku eiga bunken shiryō shūsei* (Source Collection on Advanced Popular Culture and Film), Vol. 15, Tokyo: Yumani Shobō: 321–5.

Maruya, Yoshizō (1961) 'Kaisō zakki <I>: "Shina no yoru" no kotodomo' (Memoir Essay <I>: 'China Nights' and Other Memories), *Record*, 9: 2–4.

Nagahara, Hiromu (2011) *Unpopular Music: The Politics of Mass Culture in Modern Japan*. Unpublished Ph.D. dissertation, Harvard University.

Naimushō keihokyoku (Home Ministry, Criminal Affairs Bureau) (1934) *Shuppan Keisatsuhō*, Vol. 72 (Publication Police Report).

Naimushō keihokyoku (Home Ministry, Criminal Affairs Bureau) (1935a) *Shuppan keisatsu gaikan* (Publication Police Summary).

Naimushō keihokyoku (Home Ministry, Criminal Affairs Bureau) (1935b) *Shuppan keisatsuhō*, Vol. 77 (Publication Police Report).

Naimushō keihokyoku (Home Ministry, Criminal Affairs Bureau) (1936a) *Shuppan keisatsu gaikan* (Publication Police Summary).

Naimushō keihokyoku (Home Ministry, Criminal Affairs Bureau) (1936b) *Shuppan keisatsuhō*, Vol. 88 (Publication Police Report).

Naimushō keihokyoku (Home Ministry, Criminal Affairs Bureau) (1936c) *Shuppan keisatsuhō*, Vol. 89 (Publication Police Report).

Naimushō keihokyoku (Home Ministry, Criminal Affairs Bureau) (1936d) *Shuppan keisatsuhō*, Vol. 94 (Publication Police Report).

Naimushō keihokyoku (Home Ministry, Criminal Affairs Bureau) (1937a) *Shuppan keisatsuhō*, Vol. 108 (Publication Police Report).

Naimushō keihokyoku (Home Ministry, Criminal Affairs Bureau) (1937b) *Shuppan keisatsuhō*, Vol. 109 (Publication Police Report).

Naimushō keihokyoku (Home Ministry, Criminal Affairs Bureau) (1937c) *Shuppan keisatsuhō*, Vol. 110 (Publication Police Report).

Naimushō keihokyoku (Home Ministry, Criminal Affairs Bureau) (1938) *Shuppan keisatsuhō*, Vol. 113 (Publication Police Report).

Nihon rekōdo kyōkai (ed.) (1993) *Shadan hōjin nihon rekōdo kyōkai gojūnenshi* (Fifty-year History of the Record Industry Association of Japan).

Ogawa, Chikagorō (1935) 'Chikuonki rekōdo torishimari ni kansuru gaikan' (Summary of Phonograph Record Regulation), *Keisatsu kenkyū* (Police Research), 6(9): 71–80.

Ogawa, Chikagorō (1937) 'Hijō jikyoku to rekōdo no torishimari' (The Time of National Emergency and the Regulation of Records), *Ongaku sekai* (Music World), 9(10): 14–17.

Ogawa, Chikagorō (1941) *Ryūkōka to sesō: jihenka ni okeru kayō no shimei* (Popular Songs and Social Currents: The Mission of Popular Songs in the Sino-Japanese War), Tokyo: Nihon Keisatsu Shinbunsha.

Ogawa, Chikagorō *et al.* (1936) 'Ryūkōka no keikō to ken'etsu no mondai' (Trends in Popular Songs and Issues in Censorship), *Ongaku sekai* (Music World), 8(8): 10–34.

Ogawa, Chikagorō *et al.* (1941) 'Keiongaku zadankai' (Roundtable Discussion on Light Music), *Gekkan gakufu* (Sheet Music Monthly), 7: 14–26.

Ogawa, Chikagorō *et al.* (1942) 'Ryūkōkaron' (On Popular Songs), *Ongaku kōron* (Music Review), 2(12): 32–51.

Sugiyama, Heisuke (1933) 'Gendai ryūkōkaron' (On Contemporary Popular Songs), *Asahi shinbun*, 11–15 June.

Takazawa, Motoo (1934) 'Rekōdo ken'etsujo wo ken'etsusuru' (Censoring the Record Censorship Office), *Ongaku Sekai* (Music World), 6(9): 101–2.

Tanabe, Hisao (1931) *Chikuonki to rekōdo no erabikata kikikata* (*How to Choose and Listen to Phonographs and Records*), Tokyo: Senshinsha.

Yano, Christine (2002) *Tears of Longing: Nostalgia and the Nation in Japanese Popular Song*, Cambridge, MA: Harvard University Asia Center.

5 Kawabata's wartime message in *Beautiful Voyage* (*Utsukushii tabi*)

Hiromi Tsuchiya Dollase

Introduction

The stance of Kawabata Yasunari (1899–1972) toward war has long been discussed by critics. Hatori Tetsuya, for instance, states that 'Kawabata did not encourage war. He could ... do nothing but watch the sad fate of human beings' (1981: 157). After the war, Kawabata himself stated,

> I am one of the Japanese who was affected least and suffered least because of the war.... I was never caught up in a surge of what is called divine possession, to become a fanatical believer in or blind worshiper of Japan.
> (*Tokyo shinbun* 1948; trans. Keene 1984: 823)

During the war, Kawabata maintained a low profile. Unlike Kawabata's contemporaries such as Kikuchi Kan, Yoshikawa Eiji, Yoshiya Nobuko and Hayashi Fumiko, to name a few, who joined the *Pen butai* (Pen corps) and accompanied the Japanese military to write war reports, Kawabata neither enthusiastically involved himself in such activities nor wrote mainstream stories which encouraged war sentiments.[1] However, Kawabata's hesitation does not equate to indifference to Japanese imperial ambitions. He supported Japan's policy of creating pan-Asian unity through his involvement in children's education.

Prior to 1937, Kawabata wrote many stories for adults which emphasized Japanese beauty and tradition, including *Snow Country* (*Yukiguni*), but after 1938 his output of stories for mature audiences suddenly reduced drastically (Yamanaka 2004: 3–4). Instead, Kawabata devoted himself to the development of juvenile literature. Between 1937 and 1942, he started to become deeply involved in a girls' magazine called *Girls' Friend* (*Shōjo no tomo*), in which he published serialized stories such as *Maiden's Harbor* (*Otome no minato*), *Flower Diary* (*Hana nikki*), and *Beautiful Voyage* (*Utsukushii tabi*), as well as serving as a commentator on readers' compositions. His activities and stories for this publication tend to be underestimated because of the entertaining nature of the magazine. However, these materials provide insights into his stance toward the war, because of their clear exposition of his thoughts about Asia – in particular Manchuria – and his own trans-racial utopian visions. In *Girls' Friend*, Kawabata projected himself as a writer, an educator, and a Japanese citizen. The connection between Kawabata's activities in girls' magazines and mainstream literature is seldom discussed by critics, but I believe that these two categories are closely related and worth exploring in the further investigation of his literature.[2]

In this chapter, I will focus on Kawabata as a girls' story writer, analyzing his war messages and argument for girls' culture in his work for *Girls' Friend* magazine, particularly the novella, *Beautiful Voyage*. By following the transformation of the magazine due to restrictions upon and censorship of the media, I will examine how Kawabata struggled to satisfy both his educational and literary ideals and governmental expectations, discussing how he eventually came to compromise his beliefs and alter his original messages. Kawabata's vision of girls' culture as a peaceful space apart from the war ultimately failed, as did *Girls' Friend* magazine.

Kawabata's involvement with girls' culture

Girls' Friend, established in 1908, was published by Jitsugyō no Nihonsha. It was one of the most popular girls' magazines of prewar Japan and one of only two girls' magazines which survived throughout the war.[3] The target audience was urban school girls. Containing fictional stories, pictures, readers' letters, and various articles on films, Western culture, and Takarazuka theater, it attracted a large audience with its modern and sophisticated air. *Girls' Friend* was an influential magazine and we can say that it helped create the foundation of modern Japanese girls' culture. Many renowned literary figures became involved with this magazine. Hayashi Fumiko frequently contributed essays and short stories, and Yoshiya Nobuko, the most representative girls' story writer of prewar Japan, was a regular contributor of serialized stories.[4] Male writers such as Saijō Yaso (the poet) and Yamanaka Minetarō (an author of various war stories and boys' adventure stories) also contributed works.

Kawabata's involvement with *Girls' Friend* started in 1937. His first serialized story in this magazine was *Maiden's Harbor*, published between June 1937 and March 1938. This is a story about two school girls who have an 'S' relationship – a romantic relationship between an older and a younger girl, which was a trend in girls' school culture in the 1930s.[5] Cultivating mutual respect, love, and trust, the characters of the story grow up into compassionate and fair human beings. The attraction of this story was the depiction of girls possessing gentility, demureness, spiritual ambition, and, most importantly, intimacy. In this work, the dark shadow of the war is not present. Every episode included beautiful illustrations drawn by Nakahara Jun'ichi, the most popular illustrator among school girls at that time.[6] Nakahara's pictures of modern girls – with big dreamy eyes and slim bodies – matched the image of the girls that Kawabata presented in his story.[7] Unlike the sentimental and dreamy delineation of a girls' world presented by Yoshiya Nobuko (whose stories were also accompanied by Nakahara's illustrations), however, Kawabata's prewar stories emphasized reality, didacticism, and humanism.[8]

76   H.T. Dollase

Kawabata soon became an indispensable writer for *Girls' Friend*. His commitment to this magazine is witnessed in the fact that he not only contributed stories but also made other appearances in the magazine. For instance, he attended the *aidokusha taikai* (convention of girl readers) in 1939 and a picture of him interacting with the audience at this meeting was published in December of that year. In July 1939, he published a travelogue about Kamakura, including pictures of him with his adopted daughter who at that time was a schoolgirl, just like his audience. To young readers, Kawabata was a familiar figure and a trusted mentor. In short, he was an important member of the girls' magazine community.

Kawabata and the *tsuzurikata* movement

In Kawabata's mainstream literature, young virgin girls often play significant roles.[9] In *The Izu Dancer* (*Izu no odoriko*), for instance, a male character observes a young, beautiful, and poor dancing girl, and by interacting with her, he acknowledges the beauty of life and finds a cure for his emotional problems, eventually regaining power for living.[10] A young girl is often presented as an oasis and a source of life for a male character. Kawabata's literary treatment of girls is often criticized by scholars who read his works from feminist perspectives, because Kawabata objectifies women and young girls; they are often treated as tantamount to decorative scenery.[11] They exist chiefly to provide succor for the male protagonist, their own selfhood being secondary. In this sense, it seems that Kawabata's literature could be taken as 'unethical,' for he exploits women and girls. But although young women represented escape and refuge for Kawabata in his mainstream literature, within the realm of his girls' literature he seems to have held genuine respect and admiration for what he saw as qualities of innocence and beauty, showing interest in the betterment and education of the girls themselves. Kawabata seems to have found peace and comfort in interacting with young readers. In 'Thoughts through Books' (*Hon ni yoru kansō*), Kawabata states:

> It is only women and children who are able to picture things directly.... Childlike things and feminine things are bright mirrors of creatures and nature: they are fresh spring. When language is used by women and children, it is revived and turns into a joy.[12]

In the fields of girls' and children's culture, Kawabata was an 'ethical' writer, and tried to be an 'ethical' educator. He clearly stated in the *Yomiuri shinbun* (16 August 1936) that 'we need to spread good literature and heighten literature in order to nurture children's *jōsō* (sentiments).... There are not so many stories that children can read' (qtd. in Fukasawa 1996: 74). 'Children's sentiment' is an important concept here. The idea, which originally emerged at the turn of the twentieth century with the introduction of juvenile literature, is closely related to the *tsuzurikata undō* (composition movement), which was started by Suzuki Miekichi, the editor and founder of *Red Bird* (*Akai tori*) magazine.[13] In 1936,

Composition Classroom (*Tsuzurikata kyōshitsu*), a collection of essays written by an elementary school girl, Toyoda Masako, was published and created a *tsuzurikata* boom. One of her works – depicting the everyday life of a working class girl – was adapted into a play which created a great sensation (Nakaya 2001: 44). Kawabata was impressed by Toyoda's writings, stating that her compositions were 'free, bold and innocent.... They reflect her untainted human eyes' (qtd. in Nakaya 2001: 46).[14] He valued unpretentious and honest writings, which came from 'children's sentiments' such as the *junsui na tamashii* (pure soul) and the *sunao na kokoro* (honest heart) (see Nakaya 2001: 49). In his 'On Compositions' (*Tsuzurikata ni tsuite*), Kawabata elaborates on his ideas:

> Children live selfishly, but because of their honest hearts, they emit the light of innocence and wisdom. Through their compositions, we understand that human beings are naturally good and beautiful. We understand that language is for revealing how good and beautiful humans are. The role of *tsuzurikata* is not just for adults to feel nostalgic about their childhood days.
>
> (*KYZ* 27: 239)

In a society filled with war sentiments and capitalism, children's writings taught adults good humanity and the fundamental virtues of human beings. Nurturing children's innocence, particularly in a difficult time, was an important mission for Kawabata.

To promote *tsuzurikata* education, Kawabata served as an editor/commentator for compositions submitted by the readers of such girls' magazines as *New Women's Garden* (*Shinnyoen*) and *Girls' Friend*.[15] In 1939, with Shimazaki Tōson and Morita Tama (a girls' story writer and essayist), he edited six volumes of *A Collection of Model Compositions* (*Mohan tsuzurikata zenshū*), collections of good compositions written by school children, and published them through Chūō Kōronsha. Kawabata wrote:

> The number of submissions reached 26,000. We received compositions not only from Japan, but also from Taiwan, Karafuto, Korea, Manchukuo, China, South Asia and America. This is truly a grand project. We also received works from leper hospitals and schools for the deaf and blind. We feel responsible to complete this ethnically and nationally important project.
>
> (quoted in Nakaya 2001: 51)[16]

In this comment, Kawabata revealed his humanitarian ambition and utopian vision. He believed that the cultivation of the 'pure soul' would erase differences among people and, having common sentiments, people would be emotionally unified. Kawabata regarded the value of the 'pure soul' as an alternative to a violent, aggressive, and forceful society. He was a center of the *tsuzurikata* movement and an avid preacher of its importance.

It is interesting to see that Kawabata emphasized that *tsuzurikata* was a 'national project.'[17] Donald Keene, however, states that 'Kawabata's writings in the 1930s were in no sense nationalistic, nor were they aimed at ingratiating himself with the military,' and that 'Kawabata does not seem to have been interested in presenting political or social views' (1984: 804–5). I also agree with Keene's views. At this point, I believe Kawabata's statement had no colonial implications. However, later, the 'pure soul' which was emphasized in the *tsuzurikata* movement came to be equated to a Japanese traditional virtue called *yamato-gokoro*.

Yamato-gokoro indicates 'Japanese sentiment.' Motoori Norinaga, a leading figure of the *kokugaku* (national learning) movement in the eighteenth century, emphasized this concept and considered the untainted human feelings and sensitivity toward nature, which were hallmarks of ancient Japanese literature, to be Japan's heritage. The idea of *yamato-gokoro* is also associated with the virtue of purity, which was believed to be traced back to the origin of Japan's imperial line, the gods. By the 1930s, however, *yamato-gokoro* had been co-opted into essentialist nationalistic discourse. The Japanese government started to stress their stance that the Japanese, descendants of the Yamato race, purer than other races genetically and morally, had a mission to lead and enlighten the other Asian races.[18] The educational message of the *tsuzurikata* movement conveniently matched the justification the government concocted for its colonial expansion. The gradual transformation of the goal of the *tsuzurikata* movement may be observed in Kawabata's work.

Beautiful Voyage

Beautiful Voyage (July 1939 to October 1942) was written at the height of the *tsuzurikata* movement, at a time when Japan was embroiled in war with China and entering the Pacific War. The story deals with a deaf, dumb, and blind child named Hanako. Kawabata was inspired by the life of Helen Keller, and wanted to write a similar story which would inspire others.[19] In the June 1939 issue of *Girls' Friend*, there is an advertisement for this work with Kawabata's picture. The ad states: 'this story depicts the struggles of a deaf and blind girl, as well as the birth and development of a new spirit. I want to let you know that Kawabata-sensei has great passion toward this work...'.[20] Interestingly, in this advertisement, the title of the story is indicated as *The New World* (*Atarashiki sekai*), instead of *Beautiful Voyage*. The original title provokes a grand utopian image. Shifting people's attention away from society, he probably envisioned an idealistic inner human world and relationships based on love, compassion, and trust.

The story opens with the description of a six-year-old child, who is deaf, dumb, and blind. Lacking proper education, this pretty little girl does not know how to communicate with people. She looks like a 'doll without a soul' (*KYZ* 20: 409). An encounter with two young children from Tokyo – Akiko (a high school student) and Tatsuo (a junior high school student) – opens up her world. Becoming sick as soon as he arrives in the town, Tatsuo ends up staying with Hanako's family. He plays with Hanako every day, attempting to communicate with her. He eventually teaches her the meaning of some words such as her name, *haha* (mother) and *chichi* (father). Through learning to communicate with people, Hanako's soul gradually awakens. Her soul, which had been 'secluded in a dark place, has been released to a wide world' (*KYZ* 20: 456).

After the death of her husband, Hanako's mother decides to take her to Tokyo and look for a school for her. Akiko and Tatsuo are delighted to be reunited with the family and help them out. Hanako's mother visits some schools and talks with the teachers there. Learning about the great education system of the Perkins School for the Blind in America, from which Helen Keller graduated, she feels that Japan lags behind in the field of special education compared to Western countries. When she visits the Christian school for the deaf, she hears that the school was created with the financial help of the Union Church in America. She sees children there are writing letters to American donors, and is impressed by their beautiful interaction beyond ethnic and geographical borders. She states that 'the problems that deaf children are dealing with are universal.... People's compassion, their desire to help the children and to remove their problems, is universal as well' (*KYZ* 20: 570). It is important to note that the suggestion of war is absent here. The story admires the advancement of deaf and blind education in the West and presents the Christian philanthropic spirit as something from which Japan should learn. The focus of the story is neither war nor society, but the connection of human beings through their hearts.

Finding a school which accepts a girl like Hanako, who is triply handicapped, proves extremely difficult. Coincidentally, Akiko's friend Ms. Tsukioka, who graduated from Akiko's school and used to be her 'sister' (the partner of her romantic love relationship), happens to be a teacher for the deaf and blind. Tsukioka-sensei, who had observed deaf and blind schools in America, has a strong passion for working for poor children and the improvement of Japanese special education. She agrees to become Hanako's teacher. Just like Anne Sullivan and Helen Keller, Tsukioka-sensei and Hanako are about to share their lives and to set out on a beautiful 'voyage of life' together (*KYZ* 20: 643).

In April, 1941, the first part of *Beautiful Voyage* – 'Hanako's Childhood' – was concluded. Kawabata's original plan was to continue on to 'Hanako's Girlhood' to further show the preciousness of life, through Hanako's struggles and development. However, the harsh war situation forced him to change his original plan and deprived him of his utopian ambition.

War and the magazine

According to Masui Takashi, 1938 is a significant year in discussing censorship, as the government's control of the press became increasingly strict (Masui 1997: 146).[21] In 1938, under the principle that children's magazines should have their own standard which was different from magazines for adults, the government issued *Jidō yomimono kaizen ni kansuru shidō yōkō*, the guide for the improvement and *jōka* (purification) of stories for children (Masui 1997: 145). The government ambitiously worked to make it into an innovative guide. Japan's Home Ministry and nine educators and writers, including Yamamoto Yūzō, Ogawa

80   *H.T. Dollase*

Mimei, and Tsubota Jōji, were involved in its creation (Satō 1993: 86). The guide condemned commercialism, prohibiting excessive self-promotion within magazines and vulgarity in illustrations, stories, and comics, etc. It instead encouraged children's education, instructing publishers to teach children above age ten the importance of cultivating the Japanese spirit, specifying the qualities of 'religiousness, loyalty, service, honesty, faithfulness, humility, courage and affection' (Satō 1993: 88). It is noteworthy that the guide also stressed the necessity of teaching children about China and helping them understand Chinese children's lives (ibid.).

Publishers and editors were gathered together by Japan's Home Ministry and were instructed on the content of the guide. We may assume that, in order to avoid problems, Kawabata practiced self-censorship according to the editor's suggestions, based on governmental guidelines and expectations. The Archive Division (Tosho-ka, which later changed its name to Ken'etsu-ka, the Censorship Division) of the Home Ministry was in charge of press censorship. They checked publications and drew red and blue lines over the parts which were considered to be problematic. The final decision on whether to issue a warning to the publisher or ban the publication was entrusted to the division's section head (Masui 1997: 145).

Masui Takashi reports that The National Archives of Japan (Kokuritsu kōbunshokan) stores *The Record of Censorship for Juvenile Magazines* (*Jidō zasshi ken'etsubo*) of 1938. This record shows how warnings were given to specific magazines. *Girls' Friend*, which was known as a modern and fashionable magazine, had been attentively marked by the authorities. Articles about the Takarazuka theater and beautiful gravures of Takarazuka actors and scenes disappeared from the magazine at this time (Jitsugyō 1997: 150), and the fancy pen names that readers conventionally used in their letters were condemned and banned. In *New Women's Garden*, Hayashi Fumiko's essay on Manchukuo, 'Frozen Land' (*Kōreru daichi*), received a harsh warning from the government which found the title offensive, for Manchukuo was regarded as the land of peace and prosperity (Jitsugyō 1997: 150).

Censorship intensified over the next two years, making 1940 the most tumultuous year for *Girls' Friend* magazine. It was in this year that Nakahara Jun'ichi's illustrations were removed from the magazine. The images of young girls Nakahara drew in his trademark style best described the ideal image of a 'girl' which fascinated adolescents. The pictures were of girls – neither children nor women – possessing female sexuality, but still lacking bodies suitable for reproduction. This idealized image of a girl was (and is still now) called *shōjo*. The *shōjo* body depicted in the pictures represented 'a privileged body' of 'unused sexual resources' (Takahashi 2008: 116). It was free from the burdens of production and reproduction. The beautiful and modern pictures that Nakahara drew had been the symbol of *Girls' Friend*.

However, they were now considered unfit for the time and the government's standards. According to the company history of Jitsugyō no Nihonsha, the editor in chief, Uchiyama Motoi, was threatened by the censorship division that if

Nakahara's pictures were not eliminated, the publication of *Girls' Friend* would be suspended (Jitsugyō 1997: 150). Uchiyama reluctantly made the decision to remove Nakahara's illustrations from the magazine. As a result, *Beautiful Voyage* acquired a new illustrator in Hatsuyama Shigeru, whose pictures were simple and abstract (see Figure 5.1). With this change, the representative image of *shōjo* changed drastically. Furthermore, the cover illustrator of the magazine also changed from Nakahara to Miyamoto Saburō. The *shōjo* that Miyamoto drew were girls with realistic bodies. Uchiyama told the readers of his decision to remove Nakahara's pictures thus:

> Nakahara-san's pictures are now gone from *Shōjo no tomo*. I am sure that many readers are feeling sad and disappointed by our decision.... His pictures are beautiful and his artistic skills are excellent; however ... the pictures of girls he drew do not look healthy or strong enough.... Now, we Japanese have to proceed to our goal. The goal, as you know, is the completion of our sacred war. We Japanese have to be healthy.... Nakahara-san's pictures will disappear for a while.
>
> (*GF* 1940, 33[7]: 244)

Figure 5.1 Comparison of Nakahara Jun'ichi's illustration for *Beautiful Voyage* on the left (*GF* 1940, 33[6]) and Hatsuyama Shigeru's illustration from the next issue on the right (*GF* 1940, 33[7]).
© JUNICHI NAKAHARA/himawariya
© Shigeru Hatsuyama/*Shōjo no Tomo*

82   *H.T. Dollase*

The girls that Nakahara drew were unrealistic *shōjo* who looked weak and fragile. What the society needed at that time were young women who would eventually join the system of 'production' by becoming mothers and bearing strong boys. *Shōjo*'s 'privileged bodies' were thus obliterated.

In the September issue, many sad and angry reader letters can be seen (Dollase 2008: 329). One girl says that 'I grew up with the atmosphere of *Girls' Friend*. Now I feel like my hometown has disappeared' (*GF* 1940, 33[9]: 237). Another girl writes 'Nakahara-sensei taught us the importance of having a beautiful dream. Is the government going to deprive us of our dream for the sake of a sacred war?' (*GF* 1940, 33[9]: 238). There is a letter which touches upon *Beautiful Voyage*: 'I am so sad that Jun-sensei's pictures are gone. *Beautiful Voyage* drawn by H-sensei (Hatsuyama Shigeru) looks too serious and so the story is difficult to read' (*GF* 1940, 33[9]: 238). We can understand how significant a role the pictures had played in supporting the popularity of the stories and how much they had provided dreams and comfort to the readers amid the difficult social conditions. The magazine's decision was not overturned and Nakahara never came back to *Girls' Friend*.

However, it is important to note that we can also witness many letters which accept the decision. One girl writes 'it is sad that Nakahara-sensei's pictures are gone, but the new drawings are realistic and also beautiful' (*GF* 1940, 33[9]: 327). Another girl writes: 'I am glad to see that the front cover was drawn by Miyamoto-sensei. His pictures of healthy and lively girls are more suited for war time Japan' (*GF* 1940, 33[9]: 241). In fact, many of the girl readers accepted the change and their new image of a strong and healthy girl on the home front.

The fictional stories published after this incident in *Girls' Friend* came to promote war propaganda more obviously.[22] Articles written by educators and military authorities also increased, attempting to discipline the readers and to correct their conduct and sentiments. By comparing Japanese girls with German girls, for instance, they rebuked the readers for not being strong enough physically or mentally. Articles which explained the idea of *gozoku kyōwa* (the cooperation of five ethnic groups) and the concept that the Japanese were the leaders of Asia filled the pages.[23] At the same time, images of Western culture, which had previously dominated the magazine, quickly disappeared, replaced by pictures of Japanese working girls in rural areas and factories as well as images from the Japanese traditional arts. Phrases which pushed war propaganda such as '*kono issen naniga nandemo yarinuku zo*' (we will win this battle at all costs) or '*aoge hinomaru warera ga kokoro*' (look up at the Japanese flag, our heart) started to appear in the corner of the front covers.

Writers were also encouraged to promote a strong and healthy image of girls in their works. Ultimately, Kawabata also succumbed to the pressure from his publisher and the government. Kawabata, just like all the writers and magazine editors at that time, had no choice but to obey the authorities. As Hatori Tetsuya (1981: 155) argues, Kawabata tried to rationalize that the war was unavoidable for the creation of an ideal society, which would be based on love and compassion. I agree with Hatori's assessment. Unfortunately, however, this logic was

Kawabata and wartime in Beautiful Voyage   83

exactly the same as the Japanese government's manipulative premise that the sacred war was not for colonial expansion but for the construction of harmonious pan-Asian unity.

In September 1941 *Beautiful Voyage, the Sequel* (*Zoku utsukushi tabi*) began, accompanied by the illustrations of Fukiya Kōji.[24] However, soon after Kawabata started this sequel, he was invited to travel to Manchukuo and became occupied with the trip.

Kawabata and Manchukuo

1941 was a significant year for Kawabata. He spent many months on his trips to the protectorate; he was in Manchukuo from April through May at the invitation of the *Manshū Nichinichi* newspaper, in September at the invitation of the Kantōgun (Kwantung army), and from October through November, at his own expense.[25] Kawabata's interest in Manchukuo, which at that time was described by the Japanese government as 'utopia' and 'the land of hope' (Yamamuro 1993: 351), is strongly evident.[26] During these trips, he had meetings with Manchurian writers to discuss the future of Manchurian literature, was interviewed by newspaper companies, and appeared on radio shows (Okude 2004). Kawabata's primary interest was children's education. He visited girls' schools, co-ed elementary schools and schools for the deaf and blind. He also gave a talk entitled 'Manchukuo and Compositions' (*Manshū to tsuzurikata*) which was broadcast on the radio.[27] During the speech, he emphasized that in this new country, where everything, from culture to literature, was new, children's writings were the most wonderful form of art.[28] He encouraged the children of Manchukuo to cultivate good writings with the help of Japanese teachers and to connect with Japanese people. He believed that children's literature 'conveys a superior understanding of Manzhouguo (Manchukuo) than does typical reporting, which can only express surface reality' (Cabell 1999: 267). He also thought that by sharing their 'pure soul' through reading and writing compositions – the core message of *tsuzurikata* education – people with different cultural and ethnic backgrounds or handicaps could establish affectionate, respectful, and honest relationships in the future (Kawabata 1942: 66).

The Japanese government at this time was investing in Japanese language education in pan-Asia; it believed that language was the best way to influence people with its utopian visions and create a sense of national unity.[29] Japanese had become one of the official languages of Manchukuo in 1937, and had come to be the 'dominant means of communication at the top of a hierarchy where the Chinese and Korean languages were relegated to a semi-colonial status' in Manchukuo (Culver 2008: 255). The Japanese government had enthusiastically sent Japanese teachers there and utilized radio programs, children's literature, advertisements, and lectures by writers to promote the Japanese language.[30] Regardless of Kawabata's original educational intention, he was invited to Manchukuo as part of this governmental scheme.

Kawabata's aim was for human beings to truly understand each other through writing, and it did not take much time for him to conclude that having a common

84   *H.T. Dollase*

language, in this case Japanese, was indispensable. In this attitude we can see that, although he detested war, he was not immune to some imperialism in his mindset. In 'Book of Manchukuo' (*Manshū no hon*) published in *Literary World* (*Bungakukai*) in March 1942, one of a few essays which he wrote about his trips, he stated:

> The development of Japanese *tsuzurikata* provided Japanese children with a true voice. Their voice is the purest form of language in today's Japan. I wonder if children in China and Manchukuo write through their own voice. Their compositions (written in Japanese) that I saw were antiquated and stereotypical. Their writing lags behind Japan.
>
> (Kawabata 1942: 66–7)

He then stressed that children there should master the command of Japanese language, and then their 'souls' would flourish (Kawabata 1942: 67). The original goal of *tsuzurikata* education was to promote the development of the aesthetic aspect of the lives of children regardless of race. However, eventually *tsuzurikata* simply meant language education, teaching children how to write like the Japanese. Kawabata emphasized that children of Asia should understand the importance of mastering the Japanese language; he said that as the children of Manchukuo interacted with teachers and Japanese children through writings, their souls would be enlightened – the exact message that the government enthusiastically extolled. Kawabata's own aims thus to a large extent overlapped those of the Japanese government and language educators.

Beautiful Voyage, the Sequel and nationalism

Beautiful Voyage, the Sequel began serialization in September 1941, but soon after that, Kawabata departed for Manchukuo, this time by the invitation of the Kwantung army, commemorating the tenth anniversary of the establishment of Manchukuo. Besides Kawabata, four other writers including Ōya Sōichi and Hino Ashihei were invited. According to Okude (2004: 256), Kawabata's interest was to observe Japanese language education there.

In January 1942, Kawabata finally returned to *Girls' Friend*. He apologized to his readers for the delay of his stories. Then, he explained how wonderful his trips were and how much he had learned from the experience. In the readers' compositions section, he emphasized the significance of the improvement of Japanese girls' compositions:

> Your writings printed in magazines will be read by people in Manchukuo and China. Please remind yourself. The readers of the magazine are not limited to Japan. The readership outside Japan is increasing. As Japanese girls, I want you to improve your writings.... In Manchukuo, I had a chance to look at children's compositions, but their writings are so far behind. We need to help them improve their level of culture. I believe that composition

Kawabata and wartime in Beautiful Voyage   85

education is the best way. Your good writings should be the model for those who live outside Japan.

(GF 1942, 35[1]: 185)

Kawabata had previously never expressed the superiority of Japanese culture, but here he clearly emphasizes the idea of Japanese leadership. *Tsuzurikata* education – teaching children to write through their pure soul – was now translated into the education of people of a still young 'country' to write as Japanese. The humanistic goal of children's education – to cultivate children's sentiments – similarly changed to the goal of teaching the precious Japanese cultural value called *yamato-gokoro*. Here we observe strong racial discourse: the Japanese are the 'leading race' in Asia and it is the mission of Japan to raise the cultural standards of other Asian races (Dower 1986: 9). Education was a perfect cloak in which to hide racist intention, and it was a practical means for the government to indoctrinate the people of Asia and justify their own colonial expansion.

Kawabata's change is obvious in *Beautiful Voyage, the Sequel*, which resumed in January 1942, after his return to Japan. The story abruptly starts with the departure of Tsukioka-sensei to Manchukuo and takes the format of letters addressed to Akiko. In the letters, Tsukioka-sensei explains her thoughts on the situation of the country. Witnessing that the education of deaf and blind children is lagging behind, she wonders what she, as a Japanese, can do for them. Also, she describes the great and hard work of the Japanese teachers who have gone to Manchukuo to realize their educational ideals, stating that 'the ones who provide brightness have to be us, the Japanese. I feel like I want to work for the deaf and blind children of this land' (679). She later states that 'this kind of job cannot be trusted to Western women. We Japanese have to be in charge' (690). Hostile and competitive sentiments against the West are witnessed here, while celebrations of Japan and Japanese superiority are emphasized. Reading the letter from Tsukioka-sensei, Akiko thinks that 'I am sure she will teach the "Japanese kind heart (*nihon no yasashii kokoro*)" to children in Manchukuo' (681). The compassionate heart which was previously presented as a Christian virtue has now become a Japanese virtue, strongly reminiscent of *yamato-gokoro*. Cloaked by philanthropic ambition, the message of *gozoku kyōwa* (the harmonious unity of five ethnic backgrounds), an idea set out by the Japanese government, is obediently delivered, glorifying Japanese colonial power in Manchukuo.

How can we account for such a dramatic transformation in Kawabata? Surely the escalation of the war – with America's entrance in December of 1941 – increased government propaganda activity, including oversight of publications. Since December 1940, the Information Bureau (Jōhō-kyoku) had been established within the cabinet for the total control and censorship of all the publications. All publications were examined before they were published. Also, each publisher was required to obtain a registration number and print it in the colophon (Jitsugyō 1997: 156). The government's goal was to 'maintain the social order' by controlling the content of magazines. Kawabata's drastic change reflects this condition of the press. It is evident that the *tsuzurikata* movement, rooted as it was in Japanese language education and the promotion of Japanese sentiment, was consumed by war. It was impossible to 'go beyond the policies decided by the Cabinet Information Bureau' (Jitsugyō 1997: 156).

Because *Girls' Friend* followed the government loyally, its contribution was recognized and it received the Children's Culture Award (Jidō Bunka-shō) in the magazine category of 1941 (*GF* 34[9]: 40). The award was a badge of honor given to the publisher for raising good Japanese citizens. However, *Girls' Friend* maintained its position as a leading Japanese girls' magazine by suppressing the voices of and depriving freedom from girl readers.

The celebration of Japanese empire continued in *Beautiful Voyage, the Sequel*. Kawabata inserted an episode explaining the idea of *tsuzurikata shisetsu* (composition delegation) (Figure 5.2). The *tsuzurikata shisetsu* was formed by ten children of different ethnic backgrounds: they were chosen at a composition contest organized by South Manchuria Railways. The purpose of the delegation was the promotion of cultural exchange and mutual understanding of Japan and Manchukuo through children's writings. The ten selected children traveled to major cities both in Japan and Manchukuo for half a year. Their travelogue was later published. In *Beautiful Voyage, the Sequel*, Kawabata uses quotes from their compositions which emphasized how they were impressed by the Yasukuni Shrine and the Imperial palace, and how they admired Japanese religiousness and the kindness and greatness of the Japanese people (*KYZ* 20: 705–7). The greatness of Japan is presented, through their 'pure eyes,' delineating the nation as compassionate, respectful, and culturally advanced.

In the final published chapter of *Beautiful Voyage, the Sequel*, Tsukioka-sensei returns to Tokyo, where Hanako and her mother welcome her. With joy, Hanako suddenly says 'sensei' (teacher), a word that she has been practicing with Tatsuo. Holding Hanako in her arms, Tsukioka-sensei rubs her cheek against Hanako's with joy. She exclaims 'Nippon! Nippon!' Tsukioka's exclamation, 'Nippon,' can be taken as the celebration of *yamato-gokoro*, pointing not only to 'Japanese people's spirits' but also to more nationalistic sentiments. Kawabata's educational stance that he, as a Japanese, needed to teach Japanese language to the children in Manchukuo is translated to Tsukioka-sensei's ambition to teach handicapped children how to communicate. Hanako and the non-Japanese children of Asia are regarded as 'lacking,' needing to be taught and educated to become 'full Japanese.' Hanako's miracle is connected to Japan's ambitions for the children in Manchukuo. Through 'Japanese sentiment' and the expression of Yamato identity, Kawabata's *tsuzurikata* ambition thus came to be interconnected with nationalism and geopolitical expansion.

Ultimately, the story was a failure. It ended without completion in October, 1942. Kawabata's artistic productivity decreased as his output of colonial messages increased, which suggests the deterioration of his enthusiasm and his surrender to the reality of war. Kawabata was probably tired of the increasing governmental and publisher control over his writings.[31] As the war heated up, the number of pages in *Girls' Friend* magazine was reduced and it contained nothing but patriotic stories and militaristic articles. Amid this situation, the only

Figure 5.2 Beautiful Voyage illustrated by Fukiya Kōji, showing a 'composition delegation' formed by ten children of different ethnic backgrounds (*GF* 1942, 35[4]). © Fukiya Koji. (The authorization for the usage of this picture was facilitated by Mr. Shizuo Hasegawa at the Fukiya Koji Museum.)

resistance by Kawabata that we can witness was that he never chose readers' compositions based on militaristic content. Although he complied with the promotion of pan-Asian unity, he did not believe in violent force. He believed in the importance of the 'pure soul' to the end. Kawabata's passive attitude toward the war displeased the authorities; he was finally removed from the position of commentator for *New Women's Garden* and *Girls' Friend* in 1943, because the government considered that the way he selected compositions was not 'suited for the war situation' (Jitsugyō 1997: 158). Kawabata seems to have been disappointed by the government's decision. He states:

88 H.T. Dollase

I have been in charge of this corner for seven years. I took it seriously with love and high ideals.... While choosing good compositions, I saw Japanese women's beautiful hearts, innocence, and gentleness. I was encouraged and consoled by them. Now my corner will be gone. But I want you to keep improving your writing...

(quoted in Jitsugyō 1997: 159)

Kawabata's deep sorrow for letting go of girls' culture is observed here. Kawabata attempted to establish his ideal community through 'pure soul' and 'female sentiments' and tried to awaken handicapped children both inside and outside Japan. Ironically, however, there was enough overlap between the virtues of the 'female sentiment' that he extolled and the 'Japanese virtues' that the government promoted for its own purposes that he found himself co-opted into promoting ideas of Japanese nationalism and military expansion into Asia – ideas with which he may not have truly agreed.

Conclusion

During the war, Kawabata maintained a low profile; unlike his contemporary writers, he was not enthusiastic about delivering war messages in his literary works. But this does not mean that he resisted the government. He did not worship military Japan, yet he believed in and promoted 'Japanese sentiments.' He accepted his wartime role as a writer by promoting *tsuzurikata* education and Japanese language education.[32] The government knew that children's magazines were influential media with which to influence people and to nurture future adult Japanese citizens; militaristic power could thus be enforced behind the cloak of innocent culture.

Just as Kawabata did not resist power, eventually, neither did the readers. They gradually responded to the newly constructed image of a girl who was healthy and physically strong. They welcomed the new image of *gunkoku shōjo* (military girl) with great enthusiasm, having accepted their future social roles as mothers. The state forced Japanese *shōjo* (who refuse to grow up) to change into good girls with 'pure souls' (who agree to grow up). The educators' (including Kawabata's) promotion of *tsuzurikata* education, which taught girls that they should listen to adults and have pure and innocent minds, ultimately weakened girls' assertiveness. Viewed in this light, the new image of *gunkoku shōjo* (military girls) actually represented girls who did *not* fight for themselves.

Notes

1 Twenty-two literary figures were chosen for the *Jūgun butai* or *Pen butai* (Pen corps) in 1938, a year after the Sino-Japanese War broke out. The goal of this organization was to accompany the Japanese military to China and the battlefront and write war reports. Writers like Kume Masao, Ozaki Shirō, Kataoka Teppei, Hayashi Fumiko, and Kishida Kunio served in the army, while Kikuchi Kan, Sugiyama Heisuke, Satō Haruo, Yoshikawa Eiji, Kojima Masajirō, and Yoshiya Nobuko served in the navy.

Their responsibility was to write *jūgunki* (reports on accompanying the military) (Yoshino 2008: 170).

2 See also Miura Taku (2006).

3 *Girls' Club* (*Shōjo kurabu*) published by Kōdansha was another popular girls' magazine. Its target audience was younger than that of *Girls' Friend*, which approximately targeted the upper grades of elementary school through middle and high school. I have referred to the issues of *Girls' Friend* which are stored at the International Institute for Children's Literature (Kokusai Jidō Bungakukan) in Osaka.

4 Yoshiya Nobuko (1896–1973) is one of the most well-known girls' story writers of prewar Japan. Her *Flower Tales* (*Hana monogatari*), a collection of short stories about school girls, published in *Girls' Club* and *Girls' Pictorial* (*Shōjo gahō*) between 1916 and 1923, created a great sensation.

5 On the phenomenon of the S-relationship see Robertson (1998) and Shamoon (2008). *Maiden's Harbor* may be found in the *Kawabata Yasunari zenshū* (*Complete Works*), 20: 9–183. Hereafter the complete works are denoted *KYZ*.

6 Nakahara Jun'ichi (1913–83) was an illustrator and doll artist. When his artistic talent was discovered by Uchiyama Motoi, the chief editor of *Girls' Friend*, and he was asked to work for this magazine, he was just nineteen years old.

7 Nakahara's drawings inherit the tradition of *jojō-ga* (lyrical illustration). See Takahashi (2008: 118–19).

8 See Dollase (2008; also 2003: 193–202).

9 Donald Keene explains that 'Kawabata throughout his career was attracted especially by virginal, inviolable young women ... for Kawabata they seem to have represented the essence of beauty' (1984: 794).

10 *The Izu Dancer* appears in *KYZ* 2.293–324.

11 Komashaku Kimi, for instance, argues that, in *The Izu Dancer*, 'the hierarchical relationship between the dancer and the protagonist is concrete.... The dancer is always in the position of serving him' (2001: 187).

12 *KYZ* 18: 401–2. The full text of 'Thoughts through Books' is in *KYZ* 18.394–402.

13 Suzuki Miekichi (1882–1936), also a fiction writer, helped establish modern juvenile literature in Japan.

14 It was originally published in *Home of Literature* (*Bungaku no kokyō*) in *Monthly New Tsukiji Theatrical Company* (*Gekkan shin tsukiji gekidan*), March 1938 (Nakaya: 2001: 46).

15 *New Women's Garden* was a 'sister magazine' of *Girls' Friend*, and was targeted at an audience which had graduated from girls' high school.

16 It was originally published in *Central Review* (*Chūō kōron*), September 1939 (Nakaya 2001: 51). It is important to note that Manchukuo is mentioned here. Manchukuo, a nation which consisted of five ethnic groups (Japanese, Chinese, Korean, Manchurian, and Mongolian) was established in 1932 in the northeast region of China. 'Manchuria' or 'Manshū' often refers to a geographical region in Northeast China (however, this term is not acknowledged by the Chinese government). For details, see Tamanoi (2000: 249). 'Manchukuo' or 'Manshūkoku' refers to the puppet state created by Imperial Japan in 1932. Manchukuo was proclaimed an independent state, but it was under rigid control by the Japanese as part of the expansion of their power into Asia. According to Annika Culver,

> Japanese policy makers in Manchukuo actively promoted the creation of a new national culture, art and literature in addition to a body of work describing the physical and symbolic construction of the new multi-ethnic nation ... [however,] culture in Manchukuo was in reality characterized by a primary focus on imperial Japan as the center.

(2008: 255)

For further readings on Manchukuo, see Louise Young (1998).

90 *H.T. Dollase*

17 For the *tsuzurikata* movement in Manchukuo, see Kawamura (1998).
18 On the implications of *yamato-gokoro* for imperial expansion and nationalistic discourse see Dower (1986: 205). While Japanese ultranationalism was certainly in effect in the 1930s, the concept of *yamato-gokoro* dates back to ancient times. It indicated gentle feminine feelings in contrast to the masculine tenets of Chinese education which were important to male aristocratic culture at the time. *Yamato-gokoro*, which, according to Kobayashi Hideo disappeared after the Heian period, reappeared in the Edo period as an aestheticism representing Japan's independent heritage (Kobayashi 1983: 25–6) and continued to be passed on as a part of Japanese spiritual identity presented with pride to the outside world in later eras (see Kanokogi 1997).
19 Helen Keller visited Japan in 1937. The translation of her autobiography, *The Story of My Life*, was Kawabata's favorite book (Fukasawa 1996: see also *KYZ* 27: 283–4). *Beautiful Voyage* is found in *KYZ* 20.401–658.
20 *Girls' Friend* 32 [7]. The magazine is hereafter denoted *GF* in citations.
21 For discussions of strict governmental control of the press, see Mitchell (1983) and Kasza (1988).
22 Yoshiya Nobuko, for instance, started to write about soldiers and *imonbukuro* (a comfort bag which was sent to soldiers on the battle field) in 1940 and revealed obvious patriotism (Dollase 2008).
23 For literature on Manchukuo, see Kawamura (1998).
24 Fukiya Kōji (1889–1979) was a popular illustrator and a poet who drew for various girls' magazines. *Beautiful Voyage, the Sequel* appears in *KYZ* 20.659–733.
25 For details about Kawabata's trips see Okude (2004).
26 'Book of Manchukuo' (*Manshū no hon*), is an essay Kawabata wrote after he came back from the second trip. See Kawabata (1942).
27 According to a letter submitted by a reader who lives in Harbin, Kawabata gave a talk on 22 December 1941. According to her, Hayashi Fumiko was going to come to Harbin on the 25th (*GF* 1941, 34[12]: 190).
28 This was also mentioned in 'Book of Manchukuo'. See Kawabata (1942: 65).
29 Tsukase (1998: 75); see also Seki (2003).
30 One of Kawabata's activities included editing *Anthology of Compositions by Each Ethnic Group in Manchukuo* (*Manshūkoku kaku minzoku sōsaku zenshū*), a collection of Japanese short stories and poetry written by Japanese and writers living in Manchukuo for the promotion of new literary culture (Culver 2008: 260).
31 In a congratulatory message marking Jitsugyō no Nihonsha's forty-fifth anniversary in 1952, Kawabata looked back on the difficulty he had writing stories during wartime, stating,

> Just before the Pacific War broke out, I started the sequel of *Beautiful Voyage*. The story takes place in Manchukuo.... The stories I wrote before were helped by illustrations by Nakahara Jun'ichi who was extremely popular in *Girls' Friend*. At that time, I was hated by the military government and was subject to oppression. The way I selected compositions also fell under their displeasure.
>
> (Jitsugyō 1997: 189)

32 In 1942, he also joined the Japanese Literature Patriotic Association (Nihon Bungaku Hōkokukai) and in 1944 he served as the judge of a war literature prize (Keene 1984: 823).

References

Cabell, Charles Richard (1999) *Maiden Dreams: Kawabata Yasunari's Beautiful Japanese Empire, 1930–1945*. Unpublished Ph.D. dissertation, Harvard University.

Culver, Annika A. (2008) 'Manchukuo and the Creation of a New National Literature: Kawabata Yasunari and "Manchurian" culture, 1941–1942,' *PAJLS* (Proceedings of the Association for Japanese Literary Studies) 9: 253–63.

Dollase, Hiromi Tsuchiya (2003) *Mad Girls in the Attic: Louisa May Alcott, Yoshiya Nobuko and the Development of Shōjo Culture.* Unpublished Ph.D. dissertation, Purdue University.

Dollase, Hiromi Tsuchiya (2008) 'Girls on the Home Front: An examination of *Shōjo no tomo* magazine 1937–1945,' *Asian Studies Review* 32(3): 323–40.

Dower, John W. (1986) *War without Mercy: Race & Power in the Pacific War*, New York: Pantheon Books.

Fukasawa, Harumi (1996) '*Shōjo Kurabu Shōjo no tomo* ni okeru Kawabata Yasunari' (Kawabata Yasunari in *Girls' Club* and *Girls' Friend*), *Geijutsu Shijōshugi Bungei* (Literary Art for Art's Sake), 22(12): 70–85.

Hatori, Tetsuya (1981) 'Kawabata Yasunari to sensō' (Kawabata Yasunari and War), *Kokubungaku kaishaku to kanshō* (Interpretation and Appreciation of Japanese Literature) 46(4): 152–7.

Jitsugyō no Nihonsha (ed.) (1997) *Jitsugyō no Nihonsha hyakunenshi* (A Hundred Years of Jitsugyō no Nihonsha), Tokyo: Jitsugyō no Nihonsha.

Kanokogi, Kazunobu (1997) *Yamato kokoro to doitsu seishin* (*Yamato-kokoro* and the Spirit of Germany), Tokyo: Ōzorasha.

Kasza, Gregory J. (1988) *The State and the Mass Media in Japan, 1918–1945*, Berkeley: University of California Press.

Kawabata, Yasunari (1942) 'Manshū no hon' (Book of Manchukuo), *Bungakukai* (Literary World), 9(3): 64–7.

Kawabata, Yasunari (1981–84) *Kawabata Yasunari zenshū* (Complete Works of Kawabata Yasunari), 35 vols., Tokyo: Shinchōsha.

Kawabata, Yasunari *et al.* (eds.) (2000) *Manshūkoku kaku minzoku sōsaku senshū* (Selected Works of Fiction by Authors of Every Ethnic Background in Manchukuo), vols. 1 & 2, Tokyo: Yumani Shobō.

Kawamura, Minato (1998) *Bungaku kara miru 'Manshū': 'Gozoku kyōwa' no yume to genjitsu* (Manchukuo through Literature: dream and reality of the cooperation of five ethnic groups), Tokyo: Yoshikawa Kōbunkan.

Keene, Donald (1984) *Dawn to the West: Japanese Literature of the Modern Era (Fiction)*, New York: Holt, Rinehart and Winston.

Kobayashi, Hideo (1983) 'Kobayashi Hideo mihappyō kōen sokkiroku: *Yamato-gokoro* to *yamato-damashii*' (A record of an unpublished lecture by Kobayashi Hideo: *yamato-gokoro* and *yamato-damashii*), *Shokun* (You), 15(5): 24–33.

Komashaku, Kimi (2001) '"Izu no odoriko" fureai no kōzō' (Hierarchy of Interactions in 'The Izu Dancer') in *Kawabata Yasunari 'Izu no odoriko' sakuhin ronshū* (Collection of Research Articles on 'The Izu Dancer'), Tokyo: Kuresu Shuppan, 177–88.

Masui, Takashi (1997) 'Naimushō toshoka "Shōwa 13-nen jidō zasshi ken'etsubo" ni tsuite' (Concerning the Record of Censorship of Juvenile Magazines in 1938 by the Home Ministry), *Kokusai jidō bungakukan kiyō* (Bulletins of International Children's Library), 12: 141–71.

Mitchell, Richard H. (1983) *Censorship in Imperial Japan*, Princeton: Princeton University Press.

Miura, Taku (2006) 'Watashitachi dake no sekai no yukue: *Shōjo no tomo* nettowāku to Kawabata Yasunari' (Fate of a World of Our Own: networks in *Girl's Friend* and Kawabata Yasunari), in *'Kōdansha' nettowāku to dokusha: Kindai bungaku gōdō*

92   *H.T. Dollase*

kenkyū ('Kōdansha' Network and Readers: A collaborative study of modern literature), vol. 3, 44–62.

Nakaya, Izumi (2001) ' "Tsuzurikata" no keisei: Toyoda Masako *Tsuzurikata kyūshitsu* o megutte' (Creation of "tsuzurikata": discussing Toyoda Masako's *Composition Classroom*), *Nihon daigaku kokubungakkai* (Association of Japanese Literature of Nihon University), 111(12): 43–54.

Okude, Ken (2004) 'Kawabata Yasunari: Senjika Manshū no tabi o megutte' (Kawabata Yasunari: discussing a trip to Manchukuo during wartime), *Kokugakuin zasshi* (Kokugakuin Journal), 105(11): 251–63.

Robertson, Jennifer (1998) *Takarazuka: Sexual Politics and Popular Culture in Modern Japan*, Berkeley: University of California Press.

Satō, Hiromi (1993) 'Jidōbunka seisaku to kyōiku kagaku: Naimushō "Jido yomimono kaizen ni kansuru shishiyōkō" (1938, October) o megutte' (The Policy of Juvenile Culture and Science of Education), *Jinmon gakuhō, Kyōikugaku* (Academic Bulletin of Enquiry, Pedagogy), 28: 83–118.

Seki, Gō (2003) *Shokuminchi shihai to nihongo: Taiwan, Manshūkoku, tairiku senryōchi ni okeru gengo seisaku* (Japanese Language in the Colonies: Japanese language policies in Taiwan, Manchukuo and the colonies on the continent), Tokyo: Sangensha.

Shamoon, Deborah (2008) 'Situating shōjo in shōjo manga: teenage girls, romance comics, and contemporary Japanese culture', in Mark W. MacWilliams (ed.), *Japanese Visual Culture: Explorations in the World of Manga and Anime*, New York: M.E. Sharpe, 137–54.

Takahashi, Mizuki (2008) 'Opening the Closed World of *Shōjo Manga*,' in Mark W. MacWilliams (ed.), *Japanese Visual Culture: Explorations in the World of Manga and Anime*, New York: M.E. Sharpe, 114–36.

Tamanoi, Mariko Asano (2000) 'Knowledge, Power, and Racial Classifications: The "Japanese" in "Manchuria",' *The Journal of Asian Studies*, 59(2): 248–76.

Tsukase, Susumu (1998) *Manshūkoku: 'Minzoku kyōwa' no jitsuzō* (Manchukuo: reality of the cooperation of five ethnic groups), Tokyo: Yoshikawa Kōbunkan.

Yamamuro, Shin'ichi (1993) *Kimera: Manshūkoku no shōzō* (Kimera: portrait of Manchukuo), Tokyo: Chūō Kōron.

Yamanaka, Masaki (2004) ' "Jūgonen sensō" to sakka "Kawabata Yasunari" (oboegaki): Shōwa Jūnendai no "sakuhin" o chūshin ni' (The Fifteen Years' War and the Writer, Kawabata Yasunari: discussing his works during the tenth year of Shōwa), in *Ōkagakuen daigaku jinbungakubu Kenkyū Kiyō* (Ōkagakuen University bulletins on juvenile literary study), 7:1–16.

Yoshino, Takao (2008) *Bungaku hōkokukai no jidai* (Age of Patriotic Association for Japanese Literature), Tokyo: Kawade Shobō.

Young, Louise (1998) *Japan's Total Empire: Manchuria and the Culture of Wartime Imperialism*, Berkeley: University of California Press.

6 Banned books in the hands of Japanese librarians
From Meiji to postwar

Sharon H. Domier

Introduction

In Imperial Japan, the last visitor the staff of any library wanted to see coming through the doors was a policeman. But come they did, first sporadically and then more frequently as the government attempted to combat social unrest by eliminating dangerous thoughts. They came to check the book request slips. They came to examine graffiti in bathroom stalls and in the marginalia of books. They came to arrest staff and users for seditious comments and political activities. But most often they came bearing lists of banned books to confiscate.[1] Generally it was a constable from the local police station, but it could also be a plain clothes detective from the Special Higher Police (*tokkō*), and towards the end of the war the military police (*kenpeitai*) also came to libraries to confiscate any books that might pose a risk to national security. Sometimes they even competed with each other to confiscate the same book.

No libraries were officially off-limits to police. After the promulgation of the Peace Preservation Law in 1925, from the smallest private library run by a local young men's association to the Imperial Library itself, policemen had the right to enter the reading rooms and book stacks looking for threats to national security. They had the right to confiscate books that they believed to be 'injurious to public morals,' whether or not the Home Ministry had declared an official ban. As the number of seizures increased in the mid-1930s, some librarians devised procedures that would allow them to protect their books and follow the letter of the law at the same time. As a result, a book that was confiscated from one library could evade capture in another library. This essay describes the prevailing patterns of behavior by librarians in handling materials that were banned subsequent to being added to their collections between the late Meiji period and the immediate postwar era.

Establishing a pattern of selective access to library materials

Fukuzawa Yukichi introduced the Western concept of public libraries in his book *Things Western* (*Seiyō jijō*), published in 1866. Members of the Iwakura Mission also saw the value of libraries during their visits to the British Library and the New York Public Library in 1872–73. As early as 1872 the government-sponsored Tokyo Library (Tōkyō Shojakukan) opened its doors 'in order to assist the education of men of talent and cultural advancement' (Ishii 1978: 66). But the library quickly became so popular with the general public that the library administration had to put rules in place to minimize frivolous use (such as reading novels) and to provide separate reading facilities for serious users. The early excesses of Western-based education that so displeased the Emperor during his tour of the countryside in 1878 also had a profound effect on the development of libraries.[2] All libraries, public, private, and academic, reported to the Education Ministry and were expected to follow a dual track similar to its education system. Research libraries (both academic and public) with rich collections would support the needs of scholars and men of talent, while popular libraries with small and strictly carefully chosen collections would support vocational studies and recreational reading of the common people. By 1882 the Education Ministry made clear its belief that the value of libraries lay in censoring out the bad books that could cause social and moral unrest, and presenting good ones that supported governmental motives and promoted good behavior (Itō 1927: 21). Scholars would be permitted as much freedom as possible, but the types of readers who would use popular libraries needed much more supervision because their minds were more susceptible to dangerous thoughts.

The Tokyo Library, later renamed the Imperial Library (Teikoku Toshokan), and in the postwar period the National Diet Library (Kokuritsu Kokkai Toshokan), was one of the earliest and best known Japanese libraries open to the public. It first opened its doors in 1872, serving as both a research library and a popular library, keeping separate reading rooms so the scholars would not be disrupted by the general populace reading for pleasure. It began serving as the depository library for the nation in 1875, and received a copy of every item submitted to the Home Ministry. But that didn't mean that every item received was actually available to the public. Books received on deposit from the Home Ministry that had been approved for publication were divided by the library into three categories: *kō*, *otsu*, and *hei*. *Kō* books were deemed acceptable for use by the public. These books were added to the collection and retrievable through the public catalog (card or book). *Otsu* books, on the other hand, were determined to be inappropriate for the general public. They were kept and cataloged in the staff catalog, but only people who had a good reason would be allowed to use the materials (and would have to be on good enough terms with the library staff to find out that the library had the book). This category also included some Edo period 'pillow books' and stitch bound books that the librarians were not comfortable adding to their public catalog because of their erotic images. Materials falling in the *hei* category were deemed to have no discernible value to the collection. They were frequently non-book materials such as calendars and other printed matter that had been submitted as part of the deposit program. The decision to not add all materials received likely goes back to at least 1885, per a notice in the Tokyo Library's annual report that states 'The library will not permit the public to view obscene (*hiwai*) materials' (Ōtaki 2006: 199).

Because books were received 'on deposit' from the Home Ministry, the library served more like a caretaker, and books were returned to the Home Ministry as requested. Such requests were made in some cases because censors in the Home Ministry needed to refer to something; in other cases they decided later that a book should be banned and therefore removed from the Tokyo Library's collection. From research done by Ōtaki Noritada, now director of the National Diet Library, we know that there are no banned books in the National Diet Library that date back prior to 1887 (Ōtaki 2006: 200). Earlier research by Ōtaki unearthed correspondence between the Home Ministry and the Tokyo Library requesting the return of books received on deposit that had been banned. A number of times the library responded that the books had been given the *otsu* category upon receipt and sent to storage, and later mixed up with other materials that had been discarded (Ōtaki and Tsuchiya 1976: 20). In 1908, for example, the Home Ministry wrote to the Imperial Library asking them to return Kōtoku Shūsui's *Essence of Socialism* (*Shakaishugi shinzui*) and withdraw it from their public catalog, although it had not yet been banned (Ōtaki and Tsuchiya 1976: 29).[3]

As the Education Ministry had made clear in 1882 and reinforced periodically thereafter, one of the major values of libraries lay in restricting access to 'bad' books and presenting 'good' books that supported governmental motives (Itō 1927: 21). But little attention was actually given to smaller libraries until the Home Ministry began a campaign for local improvement at the end of the Russo-Japanese War in 1906. The Home Ministry believed that rural libraries could solve a number of problems such as countering civil unrest and providing continuing education opportunities for young men through the provision of 'appropriate reading material.' This interest by the Home Ministry in turn prompted the Education Ministry to take another look at libraries, both for the possibilities of playing a role in social education and for their cost, which was equivalent to building a school for much less benefit to the nation. The number of libraries increased dramatically, but most were very small collections housed in elementary schools or erected as memorials. Komatsubara Eitarō, the Minister of Education, was particularly concerned about the harmful effects of naturalism and socialism and thought that popular libraries would be one way to promote 'wholesome reading beneficial to public morals' (Gluck 1985: 171).

The High Treason Incident of 1910 and its effect on libraries

On 25 May 1910 police arrested a small group of anarchists who were collecting bomb making material and hoping to spark popular unrest through violence. Coming on the heels of the Red Flag Incident of 1908, in which several prominent anarchist Communist leaders were arrested for political unrest, authorities used the High Treason Incident as an opportunity to put a choke hold on the increasing popularity and spread of political activism. As part of their investigation, the police interviewed and arrested hundreds of people who had ties to the anarchist and socialist organizations. By the time the case came to trial, 26

96 S.H. Domier

people faced the death penalty under charges of *lèse-majesté*. Although the trial was conducted in a closed court, it caught the attention of the public and garnered a great deal of press.

One of the ways that the Home Ministry attempted to deal with the public reaction to the High Treason Trial was to retroactively ban Socialist and anarchist books.[4] For the first time, the Home Ministry issued a lengthy list of banned books. Since these materials had been previously approved for publication, many libraries had them on their shelves and in their public catalogs (Ishii and Maekawa 1973: 186). Notifications about banned books went from the Home Ministry to the police and the Education Ministry, which then relayed them to all libraries. Okada Ryōhei, Vice-Minister of Education, notified prefectural officers to remove all dangerous materials from libraries across Japan (Ōtaki 1971: 44). Akashi Takaichirō, Secretary to the Minister of Education, also sent out a notice to school principals because many popular libraries were housed within schools. The notice read:

> Recently, among the books being collected in private libraries one finds for offer, not only books containing dangerous theories which might harm morals, but also books that are on the Home Ministry's banned-for-sale-or-distribution list. This cannot help but to have a considerable effect on the nation's morals. Especially in the case of popular libraries, this interferes completely with their purpose. Check the stacks of each library, and if there are any books previously mentioned, they should be withdrawn from public view and in the future this policy should be followed in collecting books.
>
> (Ishii 1975: 165)

The Imperial Library reported back promptly that it did have a number of socialist materials in its collection but would only allow special scholars to use them and not the general public. The Education Ministry agreed that the library could keep the materials, but requested that the banned titles be removed from the public catalog (Ōtaki 1971: 44). The process that the Imperial Library staff followed set a pattern that we may see in other libraries at a later date. Each title on the banned list was checked against library holdings. If the book had been in the public catalog, the cards were removed, the information transferred into a staff catalog for banned books, the book relabeled with an accession number starting with *kin* (forbidden) and put under lock and key. This information has been compiled in an unpublished catalog called *The Classified Catalog of Books Banned for Sale or Restricted for Use* (*Hatsubai kinshi etsuran seigen tosho kangō mokuroku*), which includes title, author, date received, number of volumes, original call number, and date of transfer (actually the Japanese term is *shobun*, meaning 'disposed of'). There are 245 titles, beginning with the 45 designated during the aftermath of the High Treason Trial of 1910–11 (Ōtaki 1971: 49).

At the same time as the Education Ministry was exhorting its officials to exercise due caution over the amount of dangerous materials in libraries, the Home Ministry decided it would not advertise which books had been banned because it didn't want to encourage people to seek out those materials. In 1910 the Home Ministry announced that it would no longer publish the titles of banned books in the *Official Gazette* (Mitchell 1983: 151). Now the first time that librarians knew an item had been banned was when the local police walked into the library with an order to confiscate such and such a title because it contravened the law on public peace or public morality. From all indications, though, neither school principals nor local police took their role in the censorship process very seriously for many years. In 1921, the Head of the Police Bureau sent a notice of complaint to all prefectural governors, saying that there were still banned books in libraries and asking that in the future the governors notify each library to do its duty properly, so that the purpose of the prohibition of sale and distribution orders could be accomplished (Mitchell 1983: 243–4).

The police became a more frequent presence in libraries after the passage of the Peace Preservation Law in 1925. In addition to the local police, the Special Higher Police (*tokkō*) increased in numbers and activities.[5] Also known as the thought police, the Special Higher Police were originally established in 1911 to control political groups and ideologies. The thought police kept tabs on people that they suspected held thoughts that might be dangerous. They prepared case files, questioned the suspect's family and employers, checked the suspect's shelves and reading habits, his involvement in social protest movements, and changes in his ideological positions (Mitchell 1976: 116). More and more books were banned by the government, many retrospectively, and police fanned out with their lists to confiscate the banned books. Local police stations were responsible for carrying out surveillance on trains, in boats, in libraries, and in public waiting rooms (Mitchell 1983: 262).

Over the years librarians received considerable criticism over the number of banned materials held in libraries, but they defended themselves by pointing out that they only found out about which books had been banned when the police came barging in to confiscate the books. They argued instead that the censors should do a better job so that 'dangerous materials' would not accidentally reach library shelves (Domier 2007: 555). In 1928, at the Japan Library Association, librarians also rejected the Education Ministry's proposition that they become more involved in providing thought improvement. Only one librarian stood up to the Education Ministry to say that removing 'dangerous' books from their collections was shortsighted and inappropriate for libraries (Ogawa and Yamaguchi 1998: 114–15). The passivity shown by librarians, neither stepping forward to support nor reacting against the Education Ministry's proposals, was at odds with reality.

With or without the assistance of librarians, the Home Ministry ordered police to investigate study groups, associations and individuals, which resulted in the arrests of thousands of people labeled as Communists, anarchists, and socialists. One raid took place in 1933 that included the arrest of 203 teachers labeled as 'red.' Many of these had been teaching in rural areas and supervising private libraries run by young men's associations. It was not only the left-wing elements that troubled the government. It found itself under attack from increasingly

98   *S.H. Domier*

violent right-wing elements as well.[6] Internal unrest from both ends of the spectrum coupled with an army that was making its own decisions in China led the country into a state of emergency.

A new breed of librarian

As the authorities attempted to control unrest by increasing the power of the police, so too were changes implemented in the library community. The Education Ministry, under pressure from the Home Ministry, began to insist on greater responsibility and oversight over libraries. Changes in the library legislation enacted in 1934 mandated a central library system that gave the director of the central library responsibility for oversight over all libraries for the prefecture – public and private, large and small. Otobe Senzaburō, director of the central library in Nagano Prefecture, took his responsibility seriously and visited a number of small private libraries run by young men's associations in his district. He found their shelves to be full of left-wing material (Domier 2007: 558). Otobe pointed out to his colleagues that library directors should not sit back and wait to be told what had been banned, but should actively reach out to the head of police and ask for lists so that they could do their part in keeping banned books out of the libraries (Otobe 1934: 107).

Otobe certainly wasn't the only person to have noticed the number of left-wing publications in private libraries run by young men's associations. The Tokyo Evening News (*Tōkyō yūkan shinpō*) reported on 28 March 1933 that prefectural police across the country had found red cells among the young men's associations, and as a result of extensive investigations found that their libraries, as well as libraries under the supervision of elementary school teachers, were full of left-wing publications. The new central library system would rectify the situation by providing appropriate thought guidance to the rural libraries and lending them healthy reading materials (Koreeda 1983: 125). One of the best descriptions of young men's association libraries and how they operated in this period is available through the research done by Koreeda Eiko in *Raising a Tree of Knowledge* (*Chie no ki o sodateru*, 1983). Koreeda's research is based on the records of Shinshū Kamisato Library in Nagano Prefecture, one of the libraries under Otobe's supervision at the time.

Shinshū Kamisato Library started out as a young men's association library. Young men in the village pooled their money together to purchase books that they wanted to read. When the legislation changed to mandate central library supervision over their activities, they received occasional visits from both police and central library staff. But in 1941, young men's associations across the country were disbanded and replaced with a new organization better suited to defending the nation. As a result, administration of the Shinshu Kamisato Library was turned over to the town and the principal of the local school became the library director (Koreeda 1983: 166–7). The new director actively tried to promote reading among village members, but at the same time he took a hard line against what he considered to be inappropriate reading materials. In addition

Banned books and Japanese librarians   99

to the banned titles that were removed by the police, the new director ordered the removal of a number of titles, including everything that was on the topic of sex (Koreeda 1983: 170).

Fully developed system of book protection for some public libraries

The Tokyo metropolitan library system had been a role model for public and popular libraries across the country since the Hibiya Library opened in 1908. By the mid-1930s, the most liberal librarians had left public service for private libraries, and the new library staff hired to manage the library system were strongly encouraged by upper administration in the Tokyo municipal government to be more responsible about handling banned books. Like the Imperial Library and some of the larger academic libraries, Tokyo public libraries had established a procedure to put books in protective custody during the period of emergency. When a policeman delivered the list of banned book titles to the library he did not enter the stacks himself but relied on the library staff to research the titles. The staff would research each title to see if the library owned it. If so, the cards were removed from public catalogs, and the books put into boxes closed with the director's seal across it. The director signed an affidavit saying that the boxes were in his custody and safe from viewing. According to a 1937 collection report of the Tokyo Municipal Library system, six libraries (Hibiya, Surugadai, Kyōbashi, Fukagawa, Ryōkoku, and Honjō) had 7,557 books placed in protective custody and their cards pulled from public catalogs (Satō 1998: 158).

In July 1940, local policemen fanned out to the libraries in their district with a list of 157 titles. The earliest title on the list was Sakai Toshihiko's *From the Perspective of Historical Materialism* (*Yuibutsu shikan no tachiba kara*) published in 1919 (Chiyoda-ku 1968: 197). The Tokyo Metropolitan government issued a memo to all library directors to review the collection for any left-wing materials and lock up anything that was on the police list and anything else that might have a taint of left-wing philosophy (Satō 1998: 158). Surugadai Library (now Chiyoda Library) found that they only had six titles from the list of 157. To that they added another 31 that they thought should also be removed from circulation. These 37 titles were boxed, sealed with the director's seal and locked away from both staff and users. The cards for these books were removed from the public catalogs and the library director signed an affidavit guaranteeing that these books were prohibited from use. In addition to removing the information from the public catalogs, the library staff added the information about the banned books to a separate 'staff only' catalog of banned books. Figure 6.1 shows an example of a paper 'staff only' catalog of banned books held by Fukagawa Library.

Library staff members were not allowed to tell users that a book had been banned. An anecdote by Meiji University professor Hagiwara Tatsuo illustrates the situation nicely. Hagiwara had a friend working at the Imperial Library in

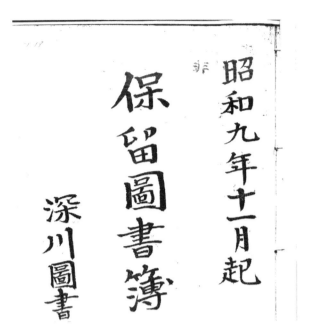

Figure 6.1 The cover of a catalog of books put into protective custody by the Fukagawa Public Library.

Ueno and used to get preferential treatment. Yet some books that he knew the library had he was never allowed to use. His friend would just make a face and tell him they were unavailable. Not once did he ever let him know that he had been asking for books that had been banned (Chiyoda-ku 1968: 204). Although staff members were not allowed to tell the public which books had been banned, they were expected to cooperate with all police inquiries. For example, in 1939 the director of the Surugadai Public Library in Tokyo received a request from a policeman in Korea, who needed help with information for an investigation. A suspect had copied pages from a book that was believed to be titled *Collections of Essays on Life* (*Jinsei zuihitsu-shū*). He asked if the library had a copy, and if so, to provide details about the author, title, date of publication, and whether or not it had been banned. The library responded that it didn't have a copy of a book by that title but it did have one called *Essays on Life* (*Jinsei zuihitsu*) published by Hakubunkan in 1929 that was not banned (Chiyoda-ku 1968: 194).

In exchange for taking a proactive role in removing dangerous books from public circulation (and the eyes of the library staff), police delivered a copy of *Censorship Weekly* (*Ken'etsu shūhō*) to the directors of the larger libraries so that they could check their shelves themselves (Ishii and Maekawa 1973: 188). *Publications Police Materials* (*Shuppan keisatsu shiryō*) regularly reported on reading trends at the Imperial Library and the five largest public libraries in Tokyo (an example for 1937 is provided in Yamazaki 1986: 229–30). But police, whether in uniform or plain clothes, could always walk into a library and demand to see the reader request slips.

In addition to actual police visits, there could be any number of informants working in or using libraries. Nakata Kunizō, at the time director of the Ishikawa Prefectural Library, and later director of Tokyo Imperial University Library and then Tokyo Metropolitan Library, made an off-hand comment to a group of nine librarians in 1937 about the violence committed by Japanese soldiers in Shanghai and the anti-Japanese sentiment of the Chinese. He was brought in for questioning, severely admonished and kept under surveillance through the end of the war, although none of his colleagues ever knew about it (Yamazaki 1986: 224–5). Yamazaki's research also shows that library users were arrested for writing comments in books and graffiti on the bathroom walls. One young man in Kyoto received a two-year sentence for writing anti-Emperor and anti-capitalist slogans in a library book on the Japanese constitution (Yamazaki 1986: 224–5). Library staff who did not cooperate with police were threatened with arrest. Akioka Gorō, director of the Fukagawa Public Library in Tokyo, was officially reprimanded for not having reported graffiti in the men's washroom, and was later removed from his post and demoted for having hired an employee (named Tosaka Jun) who was suspected of being a Communist (Yamazaki 1986: 229).

Differentiating between students and scholars

There are scattered reports in library histories about how academic libraries handled the banned books in their collections. Most university libraries used a closed stack policy, whereby only faculty members were allowed free access to the stacks. Students had to fill out request forms, and library staff would retrieve items for them. As a result, it was fairly simple to control student access to materials in the general collections. Academic libraries had always had some books listed as *etsuran kinshi* (forbidden to view) because of their erotic content. These materials required special permission to view. Meiji University Library, however, made a decision in 1930 to remove all cards that carried *etsuran kinshi* labels on them from the public catalog because the staff found that some students were making a systematic study of them just because they were banned (Ukizuka 2005: 176). On a much more serious note, beginning with the Takigawa Incident in 1932, academic librarians found themselves being asked to remove books that had been a staple on their shelves.[7] The first reports about the effects of purges of academics and increased censorship on academic libraries became clear in 1934. An article in the *Capital Daily News* (*Teito nichinichi shinbun*) reported that university libraries were no longer purchasing left-wing materials, forbidding lending of the ones they already owned, and that they had started refusing gifts from scholars who were trying to weed their own collections (Ukizuka 2005: 176).

Keio University had already worked out its own system for protective custody of problematic books, much earlier than the Tokyo Imperial University. Keio

University built separate facilities for two 'special collections,' the first of which was for rare books. The second special collection was for problematic materials, and was only accessible to faculty, usually under supervision. At first, these materials were chiefly erotica but later included hundreds of books on social issues that the library director thought would be problematic. In 1936, a young officer involved in the February 26th Incident was found to have books by Kita Ikki in his home that had been checked out from Keio University.[8] When the Special Higher Police came to investigate, they found out that the officer's father (a Keio professor) had borrowed them at his son's request. The library history notes that the thought police never returned the books, but the father did come and apologize for causing them trouble (Keio 1972: b4–6).

The library history also provides an anecdote about what happened when the plain clothed officer came to Keio with the secret order to deliver the most recent list of banned books to the police station in 1940. Apparently he had been making rounds in his district and thought that Keio would be like the other libraries he had to visit. When he showed them the list of banned books, one member of the staff said that they owned almost all of them. He didn't believe them and insisted on being taken to the stacks. After reviewing the shelves, he was thoroughly disgusted with what he saw and left without taking a thing. The chief librarian spent several days negotiating with the police station until they were allowed to keep their books, but it took the staff five days to remove all the catalog cards from the public catalogs (Keio 1972: b4–6).

Susuki Hisayo's book on the library of Tokyo Imperial University (later the University of Tokyo) during the war years provides a fairly detailed account of the amount of consultation and level of negotiation that went on in order to come up with a way to comply with the Home Ministry's directives without giving up custody of the books. For example, on 15 July 1940, a policeman came from Ueno Station with a secret order to get rid of all left-wing materials and anything that would be injurious to public order. Two librarians went directly to the Home Ministry to consult on the directive. They were told that since the directive at that time did not list any specific titles, they did not have to hand anything over to the police if they came back. Instead they were to tell the police that they had received this permission from the Home Ministry and that details would be forthcoming on how to handle the materials (Susuki 1987: 104).

Another policeman returned on 24 July, with another document marked 'secret' that did give details for handling banned materials and said that as long as the materials were disposed of appropriately they would not have to be turned over to the police. The procedures that the Tokyo Imperial University developed were as follows:

1 Books would be pulled from the general stacks and be relabeled as 'special collections.'
2 The catalog cards would be annotated to note 'special collections.'
3 Anyone wishing to use material in this 'special collection' would need to fill out a request slip and receive permission from the library supervisor.

Banned books and Japanese librarians   103

4   The library supervisor would review the requestor's name, rank, and research interests before deciding whether or not to grant permission. If necessary, the request would be reviewed by the library director.

5   Use of 'special collections' would be in designated (and supervised) areas only.

After developing this procedure, library staff no longer felt any obligation to turn banned books over to the police. They would consider them 'cultural assets' that needed to be preserved for future generations (Susuki 1987: 105).

It took a significant amount of bravery to stand up to the thought police, but once the pattern had been established it became easier to repel demands to turn over banned books. According to the daily reports of the Hōsei University Library, a policeman from the Kōjimachi station came to confiscate 161 left-wing materials on 22 February 1940. On 24 April, they received a notice from the Education Ministry that 660 items had banned at once (Hōsei 2006: 132). After investigating, the library found that they had 109 items in 174 volumes on the list, and since some items had been banned previously they pointed out the duplication. Titles on the list included many by Marx, Lenin, Engels, Ōsugi Sakae, and Kawakami Hajime. The library director signed an affidavit that all of the items listed had been placed under protective custody and banned from viewing (Hōsei 2006: 132–3). When the Chief of Police from Kōjimachi police station sent a letter to the Hōsei University president dated 20 April 1943 reprimanding him for not having delivered banned books to the station as required, the president responded that he would follow the protocol of other university libraries: prepare a catalog of books in their collection that had been banned, remove them from public circulation, and deliver the list but not the books to the police station. The president of the university supported the library director's desire to protect the books, and told him not to hand books over to the thought police no matter how insistent they were (Hōsei 2006: 136–7). In Hōsei University Library's case, the secure location was a locked bookcase in the director's office. It could only hold 300 books, however, so when it filled the president allowed the staff to bundle up and hide the rest of the books deep within the closed stacks of the library (Hōsei 2006: 139).

Theoretically for most of the period, faculty could still receive permission to use the banned books for their research. Some faculty, however, could not. One example that bears more investigation is the case of Ōtsuka Kinnosuke. Ōtsuka was a professor at the Tokyo Higher Commercial School (now Hitotsubashi University) in economics. He was arrested in 1933 and forced to resign from the university, losing his library privileges. After his release from prison, he was forbidden to publish anything but he did manage to gain access to libraries. Although he had lost his faculty privileges at the Tokyo Higher Commercial School library, Ōtsuka successfully petitioned the library director to allow him reading privileges, meaning he would have to fill out request forms like the students. Ōtsuka also tried using the Imperial Library, but found the Keio University library more to his liking (Hosoya 1982: 466). Under police surveillance

104 *S.H. Domier*

until the end of the war, Ōtsuka burned his private research collection over the winter of 1940–41 to try to minimize police harassment (Matsumoto 1993: 192).

While librarians had been vigilant in protecting library materials – both from access by students and from the threat of confiscation by the police – faculty offices and departmental reading rooms were not in their jurisdiction. In 1944, the Education Ministry's Department of Educational Affairs tried to reach out to university presidents to get their cooperation to exert more control over students' reading habits. Specifically, they wanted library staff to provide oversight to books in faculty offices and departmental reading rooms because students were still gaining access to prohibited materials (Hōsei 2006: 138–9).

Protecting national secrets and checking for crumbs

In addition to books that were banned for moral or political reasons, librarians also had to exercise due caution and carefully screen users wishing to see materials that might compromise national security. The staff records for a register of shipping companies, for example, included an annotation 'release with caution' (*kōkai chūi*). A paper catalog of books put into 'protective custody' (*horyū tosho*) is available at the Fukagawa Library in Tokyo (see Figure 6.1). Articles that were designated as restrictive access included prefectural statistics, weather charts, maps, guides to natural resources, and other types of government documents. While Japanese businessmen and scholars had a legitimate need for this kind of information, the military did not want foreigners or spies to have access, so library staff were expected to question users about their occupations and needs for those kinds of materials.

One of the favorite anecdotes of Japanese librarians who were active at the time involves playing the military police (*kenpeitai*) against the thought police (*tokkō*) in order to keep possession of a library book.[9] In 1943 the military sent the *kenpeitai* out across the country to confiscate copies of *Compendium of Japanese Geography and Customs* (*Nihon chiri fūzoku taikei*), because the detailed maps posed a threat to national security. The chief librarian at the Municipal Library in Osaka told the officer that he only took orders from his superior, which was the Education Ministry, so if the officer wanted to confiscate library property he would need to have the Minister of the Army write to the Minister of Education first (Ogawa and Yamaguchi 1998: 131).

Even the Imperial Library, which had been allowed to put banned books under protective custody, had to negotiate constantly over the fate of books because different police came at different times. Okada Narau, then deputy librarian, refused to turn books over to the police towards the end of the war and told them that because the books were on deposit from the Home Ministry, he would only return them directly to the Home Ministry. Instead he had his staff box up the books and hide them until he could get permission from the Home Ministry to keep them, which he did (Ōtaki 1971: 50).

The records of Kōfūkai Library in Chiba prefecture showed that not only did the library staff need to deal with separate visits from official entities to check

Banned books and Japanese librarians   105

their collections but also with more coordinated efforts towards the end of the war. For example, the *kenpeitai* came on 12 July 1944 to notify the library that the *Compendium of Japanese Geography and Customs* was prohibited because of national security. The *tokkō* came in January 1945 to recheck the stacks and remove biographies of Marx and Lenin that were on the prohibited list. On 12 February 1945 the prefectural *tokkō*, local *tokkō*, and head of the Department of Social Education came to the library together to check the stacks (Suzuki 2001: 59–60).

After the war

What happened to all the books in protective custody after the war? Sadly, much of the collection held by the Tokyo Metropolitan libraries had been moved to Hibiya Library for safekeeping and was destroyed by B-29 bombers. The remaining books were set free from protective custody on 26 April 1946 (Chiyoda-ku 1968: 226). University libraries also unboxed most of their books right away and returned them to their previous call numbers. But not all books made it back to the stacks as quickly. Otokozawa Tadashi, a librarian at the University of Tokyo Library, recalled that all the Russian books had been removed from the stacks, their cards removed from the public catalogs, and boxed up and stored someplace deep inside the library during the war. But 20 years later, they still had not been unearthed and put back on the shelves (Otokozawa 1965: 286). Likewise at the National Diet Library, books that had been banned for their political content were returned to their original shelves right away, but books that had been banned for their moral content were for the most part left the way they were and remained inaccessible to the public (Ōtaki 1971: 51).[10]

These days there is little interest among academic librarians in Japan about the handling of books before 1945. When I attended a librarians' meeting at Kyoto University in 2005, I asked the managing director of the libraries about banned books in their collections during the war. He sounded surprised and said that he doubted that the library had ever held banned books. But then one of his young staff spoke up and said she had some in her collection and took me to see them. We went back behind the circulation desk into the closed stacks, and there were exactly the kinds of books I expected to see: Marx, Engels, Stalin, Lenin, and Kropotkin. In some cases the labels had been scraped off, but there was an entire set of shelves of books that still had visible markers of their previous status, such as the *etsuran kinshi* (prohibited from reading) labels still stuck on the covers. Because the labels remain, we can see that in the case of the *Collected Works of Stalin* (*Sutārin chosakushū*), it was number 202 based on the Prohibited from Sales or Distribution List from 7 April 1941 (see Figure 6.2).

Attempts to find other library collections with visible scars of banned book handling have been largely unrewarded. Keio University, with its extensive collection of books found on banned lists, yielded no treasures and few clues. Its books do not have *etsuran kinshi* stamps on them. It was not until I located old copies of print catalogs (containing reproductions of the old public catalog cards)

Figure 6.2 The sticker on the *Collected Works of Stalin* (*Sutārin chosakushū*) showing that it was added as number 202 to the Prohibited from Sales or Distribution List on 7 April 1941.

containing the term *teishi* (suspended) that I could go back and check individual volumes again. Then I was able to verify that the titles with *teishi* on the cards had new labels on the spines. Because librarians had completed retrospective conversion of the card catalogs, the old staff cards have been destroyed, with any detailed information about the banned book status lost to posterity.

Hitotsubashi University Library has not yet discarded its staff catalog, so I was able to check both the public information (the book itself) and the staff information for several of its books. Using the example of *Outlook of Monopoly Capitalism in Japan* (*Nihon dokusen shihonshugi no tenbō*), the title page has only an ownership seal for the library, the handwritten call number in pencil, and a stamp showing that the library had purchased the book on 31 October 1931. The spine of the book shows only that a new label has been affixed over another one. Fortunately, a request sent to a librarian in the cataloging section of the library yielded a card from the staff catalog showing a red stamp with the word *hakkin* (banned), which may be seen in Figure 6.3.

Any researcher wishing to see a large and intact collection of banned books should visit the Sankō Library in Tokyo. The collection used to belong to the Ōhashi Library, a large public library financed by the publishing giant

Banned books and Japanese librarians 107

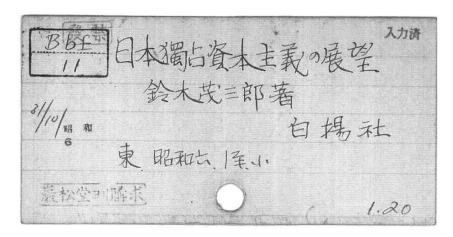

Figure 6.3 The card from the staff catalog for *Outlook of Monopoly Capitalism in Japan* held by Hitotsubashi University Library. The red stamp on the top left over the call number says *hakkin* (banned).

Hakubunkan. The book collection survived the damages of the war and the library has kept its staff card catalogs, which contain a great deal of data helpful to scholars. The catalog cards include detailed information about when the book was purchased, when it was banned, and why (whether for morals or politics) (see Figure 6.4). Because of its special nature, using the staff catalog for banned

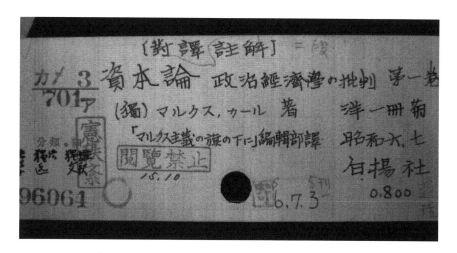

Figure 6.4 A card from the staff catalog of Sankō Library (the former Ōhashi Library). There is a red stamp in the center of the card that says *etsuran kinshi* (banned from viewing) October 1940, and to the left of that a stamp that says it was banned for political reasons.

108 *S.H. Domier*

books might be one of the easiest ways to get a feel for the types of banned materials held in public libraries before the war.

Conclusion

Despite the broad search and seizure laws of the police, and the vast numbers of materials actually seized and disposed of, copies of many of the banned books survived the war and are available today in libraries today because of arrangements made between the directors of the large libraries and authorities to put the books into protective custody rather than turn them over to the police for 'disposal.' In exchange for being allowed to protect and preserve these materials, library directors were expected to be proactive in sharing information with authorities on the reading habits of library users, graffiti in books and in bathroom stalls, and the political activities and opinions of its staff. Libraries with staff who were not accorded the same level of trust by police (including local constables, thought police, and later military police) continued to have their stacks monitored and offending books removed and destroyed. In fact, towards the end of the war, so few books were being published and so many were being confiscated and destroyed, that one senior librarian wondered if there would be any printed knowledge left (Tsuboya 1943: 473).

In conclusion, this essay has examined the ways that librarians and other 'keepers of the books' handled banned books in Japanese libraries during the period between late Meiji and the immediate postwar. Three major practices are evident from the study: books were confiscated by the police and destroyed, kept under protective custody by the library director with the knowledge of the police, or surreptitiously hidden. Minor variations included snipping offending portions of books under directive and limiting the use of particular materials to appropriate users. The success rate of libraries being allowed to retain banned books in their collections appears to have been directly related to the ability of the library director to negotiate with various governmental agencies including the police, Home Ministry, and the Education Ministry. The backroom drama faced by librarians, whether to follow the letter of the law of the time or to protect the intellectual property of the nation for the future, went largely unnoticed by the public. Although the number of items banned after publication is very small today, librarians still limit access to certain materials that they believe are problematic.[11] This practice continues to affect the kinds of materials that researchers can use in libraries. The emphasis on negotiation and individual discretion in making decisions on banned materials – formed in the first half of the twentieth century – is thus still in place, restricting the kinds of materials that researchers can use in libraries in Japan.

Notes

1 For the sake of convenience, I am using the term 'banned books' to encompass all notices of prohibition to the library including books, journals, and newspapers. In

some cases librarians were asked to remove particular articles or images from books, journals, and newspapers so that the rest of the item could still be used by the public. To get a sense of the numbers of items banned, please consult Martina Tayek's 2008 master's thesis on the topic.

2 See Duke (2009: 268) for an explanation of how displeased the Emperor was with the effects of the liberal Western education that the students received. Students were able to memorize English words and phrases but were unable to explain their meanings in Japanese.

3 In addition to the research done by Mr. Ōtaki on the books held on deposit at the Imperial Library, Professor Asaoka of Chukyo University is conducting research on the books held on deposit by Chiyoda Public Library and other branch libraries in Tokyo (Chiyoda 2011).

4 See Oguro (1990) for an in-depth study of libraries and the High Treason Incident.

5 See Tipton (1990) for a comprehensive study on the Special Higher Police.

6 Kasza (1988: 137–48) points out that right-wing activism attracted a significant amount of censorship and regulation through the 1920s and 1930s, following the enactment of the Peace Preservation Law of 1925.

7 Takigawa Yukitoki was a professor of Law at Kyoto Imperial University who had been accused of incorporating Marxist philosophies into his theories of criminal law by the Education Ministry. The Ministry forced the university to suspend him from teaching and his colleagues resigned in protest. The incident is dramatized in Kurosawa Akira's 1946 film *No Regrets for Our Youth* (*Waga seishun ni kuinashi*).

8 The February 26th Incident was an attempted *coup-d'état* by young military officers in 1936, who were frustrated by extreme poverty in rural areas and supposed corruption of senior government officials.

9 See Tajima (1975), for example. His memoirs are echoed in many other memoirs written by librarians in the decades after the war ended.

10 Ōtsuka Nanae did a survey of the books that had been banned subsequent to being added to the collection. She not only provides a title-by-title list of banned books in the NDL collection, but also provides very clear instructions on how to search for those titles in the public catalog. See her paper for details (Ōtsuka 2010).

11 See Wakiya (1987) for an example of how libraries dealt with postwar prohibitions on viewing sensitive materials. See Ishii (2003) for an example of how libraries dealt with a journal article that was banned after it had been added to the collection.

References

Chiyoda-ku (1968) *Chiyoda toshokan hachijū-nenshi* (80 Year History of Libraries in Chiyoda), Tokyo: Chiyoda-ku.

Chiyoda Kuritsu Chiyoda Toshokan (2011) *Chiyoda Toshokan zō 'Naimushō iitakubon' kankei shiryō* (Materials Relating to the Censored Books in Chiyoda Library's Collection), Tokyo: Chiyoda Kuritsu Chiyoda Toshokan.

Domier, Sharon H. (2007) 'From Reading Guidance to Thought Control: Wartime Japanese Libraries,' *Library Trends*, 55(3): 551–69.

Duke, Benjamin C. (2009) *The History of Modern Japanese Education: Constructing the National School System, 1872–1890*, New Brunswick, NJ: Rutgers University Press.

Gluck, Carol (1985) *Japan's Modern Myths: Ideology in the Late Meiji Period*, Princeton, NJ: Princeton University Press.

Hōsei Daigaku Toshokan (2006) *Hōsei Daigaku Toshokan 100-nenshi* (100 Year History of Hosei University Library), Tokyo: Hōsei Daigaku Toshokan.

Hosoya, Shinji (1982) 'Kurai tanima no jidai to toshokan' (Libraries during the Dark Valley Period), *Toshokan zasshi* (The Library Journal), 76(8): 465–7.

110   S.H. Domier

Ishii, Atsushi (1975) 'Senzen ni okeru "toshokan no jiyū" no mondai: toshokanshi, shinbun, zasshi kiji kara (tokushū toshokan no jiyū 1)' (Library Freedom in the Prewar Period: as seen in library histories, newspapers and magazine articles 1), *Gendai no toshokan* (Libraries Today), 13(4): 163–8.

Ishii, Atsushi (1978) *Toshokangaku kyōiku shiryō shūsei. Toshokanshi, Kindai Nihon hen* (Collection of Materials for Library Science Education. Library History, Modern Japan), Tokyo: Shiraishi Shoten.

Ishii, Atsushi and Maekawa, Tsuneo (1973) *Toshokan no hakken: shimin no atarashii kenri* (Discovering Libraries: the new right of citizens), Tokyo: Nihon Hōsō Shuppan Kyōkai.

Ishii, Masayuki (2003) ' "Ishi ni oyogu sakana" jiken no kyōkun' (Lessons Learned from 'The Fish Swimming in the Stone' Incident), *Toshokan hyōron* (The Library Review), 44: 39–51.

Itō, Heizō (1927) 'Yonjūgo-nen mae no Mobunshō: Toshokan shiyu jikō' (The Ministry of Education 45 Years Ago: admonitions for libraries), *Toshokan zasshi* (The Library Journal), 21(1): 19–22.

Kasza, Gregory J. (1988) *The State and Mass Media in Japan, 1918–1945*, Berkeley, Los Angeles and London: University of California Press.

Keio Gijuku Toshokan Mita Jōhō Sentā (1972) *Keio Gijuku Toshokanshi* (History of Keio University Library). Available online: www.mita.lib.keio.ac.jp/history/history.html (last modified 2002; accessed 17 April 2012).

Koreeda, Eiko (1983) *Chie no ki o sodateru: Shinshū Kamisato Toshokan monogatari* (Raising a Tree of Wisdom: the Shinshū Kamisato Library story), Tokyo: Ōtsuki Shoten.

Matsumoto, Tsuyoshi (1993) *Ryakudatsu shita bunka: Sensō to tosho* (Plundered Cultures: war and books), Tokyo: Iwanami Shoten.

Mitchell, Richard H. (1976) *Thought Control in Prewar Japan*, Ithaca: Cornell University Press.

Mitchell, Richard H. (1983) *Censorship in Imperial Japan*, Princeton, NJ: Princeton University Press.

Ogawa, Tōru, and Yamaguchi, Genjirō (1998) *Toshokanshi. Kindai Nihon hen* (Library History. Modern Japan), Tokyo: Kyōiku Shiryō Shuppankai.

Oguro, Koji (1990) 'Taigyaku jiken to toshokan' (Libraries and the High Treason Incident), *Toshokankai* (Library World), 41(6): 280–7.

Ōtaki, Noritada (1971) 'Senzenki shuppan keisatsu hōseika no toshokan: sono etsuran kinshibon ni tsuite no rekishiteki sobyō' (Libraries under the Prewar Publication Police System: historical sketch of books prohibited for viewing), *Sankō shoshi kenkyū* (Reference Service and Bibliography), (2): 39–54.

Ōtaki, Noritada (2006) 'Toshokan to yomu jiyū: kindai Nihon no shuppan keisatsu taisei to no kanren o chūshin ni' (Libraries and the Freedom to Read: how it relates to the publication police system in modern Japan), in Shiomi Noboru and Kawasaki Yoshitaka (eds.), *Shiru jiyū no hoshō to toshokan* (Libraries and the Protection of the Right to Know), Kyoto: Kyōto Daigaku Toshokan Jōhōgaku Kenkyūkai, 165–242.

Ōtaki, Noritada and Tsuchiya Eiji (1976) 'Teikoku Toshokan bunsho ni miru senzenki shuppan keisatsu hōsei no ichi sokumen' (A Look at the Publication Police System through Imperial Library Correspondence), *Sankō shoshi kenkyū* (Reference Service and Bibliography), (12): 14–32.

Otobe, Senzaburō (1934) 'Hakkinbutsu to kōkyō toshokan' (Banned Books and Public Libraries), *Toshokan zasshi* (The Library Journal), 28(4): 105–7.

Otokozawa, Tadashi (1965) 'Haisengo no Tōdai toshokan' (University of Tokyo Library after the War), *Toshokan zasshi* (The Library Journal), 59(8): 286–9.

Ōtsuka, Nanae (2010) 'Ukeirego ni hakkin to nari etsuran seigen sareta tosho ni kansuru chōsa: senzen shuppan hōseika no kyū Teikoku Toshokan ni okeru rei' (Research of Books and Materials Banned or Restricted after Acceptance: examples from the Imperial Library under the publication statutes in the pre-war period), *Sankō shoshi kenkyū* (Reference Service and Bibliography), (73): 27–53, plus images. Available online as a pdf file through the National Diet Library website: http://dl.ndl.go.jp/view/download/digidepo_3051631_po_73–04.pdf?contentNo=1 (last accessed 20 January 2012).

Satō, Masataka (1998) *Tōkyō no kindai toshokanshi* (History of Modern Libraries in Tokyo), Tokyo: Shinfūsha.

Susuki, Hisayo (1987) *Iro no nai chikyūgi* (Colorless Globe), Tokyo: Dōjidaisha.

Suzuki, Eiji (2001) *Zaidan Hōjin Kōfuūkai Toshokan no gojūnenshi* (50 Year History of the Kofukai Library), Chiba-ken Noda-shi: Zaidan Hōjin Kōfuūkai.

Tajima, Kiyoshi (1975) *Kaisō no naka no toshokan* (Libraries in our Memories), Tokyo: Kōbundō.

Tayek, Martina J. (2008) *A Statistical Analysis of Banning of Literature in Japan Between 1926 and 1944*. Unpublished M.S. thesis, Bowling Green State University.

Tipton, Elise (1990) *The Japanese Police State: The Tokkō in Interwar Japan*, Honolulu: University of Hawai'i Press.

Tsuboya, Suisai (1943) 'Surikogi no jūbako sōji' (Cleaning out the Lunch Box with a Toothpick), *Toshokan zasshi* (The Library Journal), 37(7): 7–9.

Ukizuka, Toshio (2005) 'Senjika no Meiji Daigaku toshokan' (Meiji University Library during the War), *Tosho no fu* (Book Notes), 10: 170–82. Available online: www.lib.meiji.ac.jp/about/publication/toshonofu/ukidukaI05.pdf (last accessed 29 May 2012).

Wakiya, Naohiro (1987) 'Kokka Himitsuhō to toshokan' (National Secret Protection Law and Libraries), *Minna no toshokan* (Libraries for All), 123: 24–33.

Yamazaki, Gen (1986) 'Tokkō keisatsu ni yoru toshokan dan'atsu' (Library Oppression by Special Higher Police), *Bunka hyōron* (Cultural Critique), 308: 223–31.

7 Self-censorship

The case of wartime Japanese poetry

Leith Morton

Introduction

In a review of a book on the media by James Hardy published in the *Daily Yomiuri* newspaper in March 2006 the issue of self-censorship was raised. Hardy cites Noam Chomsky and Edward Herman's 'propaganda model' where it is argued that self-censorship is a fundamental problem facing journalists, since they tend to 'subordinate their own beliefs to an assigned ideology' (2006: 18). This issue is linked to the role of the media in wartime, specifically during the war in Iraq in 2003. However, the same issue can be, and has been raised in respect of World War II, where much of the vast outpouring of patriotic and propagandist literature written by Japanese writers seemed extremely difficult to find once the war ended. Although censorship of militaristic literature by the Occupation authorities was one cause of this, it is unlikely that it was the main cause, especially after the end of the Occupation.[1] In collection after collection of poetry and prose published in the first two decades after the war, gaps were left where writers appeared to have written very little from the late 1930s to the war's end. In recent years, much of this lacuna has been filled by the large array of archival series of wartime writings published in ever-increasing numbers over the last decade or two. And this trend has extended to individual collected works published over the last few decades where the missing literary works have reappeared (although some exceptions remain).

This study will investigate how and why these 'missing' works came to be missing and in doing so will focus on the issue of self-censorship by the writers concerned, as there is no doubt that this was the reason many of the works disappeared from view in the first place. The specific topic of discussion will be wartime Japanese poetry (mostly limited here to *shi*, modern *vers libre*, but not traditional genres of verse like tanka and haiku), an area in which fierce and frequent debate and exhaustive research has been carried out over a number of decades. In these debates, the role of ideology is accepted by all concerned as one of the causes behind the production of such poetry. However, once the prewar and wartime fascist ideology collapsed with Japan's surrender to the Allied Powers in 1945, so did the justification for the production of these works.[2] Due to limitations on length, the focus here will be on poetry written during the

Self-censorship and wartime Japanese poetry 113

Pacific War, fought primarily against the Anglo-American powers, rather than during the war in China.[3] Critics have regarded most of these writings as largely devoid of literary merit, a viewpoint more than justified by the examples that follow. The new democratic, liberal ideology which replaced the Japanese version of fascism espoused a distinctly different set of values to those held during the war, which left such poetry as shameful relics of a discredited past. This process was not simple or straightforward, however, and the complex questions arising out of these debates concerning censorship, poetry, ideology and war responsibility do not provide any easy answers for students of self-censorship in the early years of the twenty-first century.

Censorship and self-censorship

Virtually all literature, including poetry, written during the war years was subject to censorship, although the kind and degree depends upon the particular circumstances and the period in which publication took place. Ben-Ami Shillony has described the process of censorship in some detail in his book *Politics and Culture in Wartime Japan*, looking at intellectuals and writers in particular (1991: 110–33), and Jay Rubin has also documented this process in his 1984 study *Injurious to Public Morals: Writers and the Meiji State* where he focuses in his last chapter on the general liberal magazines *Central Review* (*Chūō kōron*) and *Reconstruction* (*Kaizō*). Rubin traces the increasing censorship of such journals by the military to the point where, as he writes, 'the publishing industry police[d] itself', that is, it was engaged in self-censorship (1984: 256–78). Both Shillony and Rubin cite Donald Keene's essay 'Japanese Writers and the Greater East Asia War' (included in Keene 1971), among other sources, as evidence of the fact that there was a 'lack of literary resistance to the war in Japan', with most writers exulting in Japan's military triumphs (see Rubin 1984: 272).

The most detailed English-language study of literary censorship during the Allied Occupation is Sharalyn Orbaugh's 2006 volume *Japanese Fiction of the Allied Occupation*, documenting censorship exercised by the Occupation authorities. Orbaugh argues that it was 'surprisingly lenient ... although ultranationalist sentiments were expressly prohibited' (2006: 88). In recent years, various series have been published in Japan reproducing literary works censored by the Occupation authorities, and it often appears that the motive for the censorship was explicitly political, designed to protect the Occupation from criticism by removing any references to crimes committed by Allied soldiers (Yamamoto 2009: 11). These two categories of removing ultranationalist sentiments and protection of the Occupation itself, probably cover most incidences of censorship of verse published during the Occupation.

The exact nature of wartime self-censorship emerges in memoirs published by the editors in question. Hatanaka Shigeo, wartime editor-in-chief of *Central Review*, noted that editors corrected texts in various ways to make them read more in line with military objectives, that is, more patriotically. In his own words, 'We were truly callous in how we changed manuscripts ... what we did was certainly a violation of the author's copyright' (Hara 2001: 534). Some editors even destroyed the integrity of the texts by removing whole sections. The wartime editor-in-chief of the popular children's magazine *Juvenile Club* (*Shōnen kurabu*), Katō Ken'ichi, repeats the same story, an indication of just how pervasive the censorship was. Katō also notes that a certain Colonel 'S' threatened his editors with a sabre in order to enforce the military's will over the magazine (Hara 2001: 534). The threat of violence was all too real: John Solt in his biography of the modernist poet Kitasono Katue (1902–78) notes that experimental poets in Kobe had been arrested as subversives in 1940, and in the same year Katue himself (amongst other poets) was questioned by the thought police about his verse (Solt 1999: 148).

The replacement and rewriting of texts by editors is important when assessing postwar self-censorship; it could be argued that changes to the texts of poems or essays on poetry were merely an attempt by the authors to reclaim the original text (although, in fact, this claim is seldom made). The degree of wartime censorship testifies to the strength of the ideology which inspired the 'patriotic' verse flowing from the pens of poets in vast numbers during the war years.

Just how much poetry was published during this period? Sakuramoto Tomio, a scholar who has played a leading role in the collection of data relating to wartime poetry, states that his research has shown that over 146 anthologies of poetry were published during the Pacific War, and over 300 individual volumes of poetry (cited in Tsuboi H. 1997: 167, 361). Ben-Ami Shillony (1991: 110) increases that figure by citing 863 poetry books published in 1942 alone, presumably, unlike Sakuramoto who is solely concerned with *shi*, including traditional genres of verse. It is unlikely that all of these texts are still extant given the small print runs of some individual volumes, and the widespread destruction wrought on the metropolitan centers – especially Tokyo – by the massive Allied bombing raids carried out during the war. It is quite possible therefore that all the facts about self-censorship among poets will never be known, but much has been uncovered by such investigators as Abe Takeshi (1980, 2005), Sakuramoto (1983, 1996), Takahashi Ryūji (1975), Tsuboi Hideto (1997), Tsuruoka Yoshihisa (1971) and, last but not least, Yoshimoto Takaaki (1970).

The issue of self-censorship hinges on the regret, shame or simply embarrassment that poets felt after the war concerning their wartime poetry. The fear of retribution by the Occupation authorities probably played a role but it appears to be only a minor one, as it seems few poets were actually arrested in the postwar purges, although the most famous jingoistic poet Takamura Kōtarō (1883–1956) may have fled to the mountains to escape Occupation scrutiny. But why should this be so? If poets were determined to eliminate every inferior work from their *oeuvre* then the collected poems of many great twentieth century poets would be decidedly thinner. This is especially the case in Japan where for most of the twentieth century, literary works have been widely made available in individual collections, either collected or selected works or collected poems. The assumption has generally been that such collections should contain all published works by the authors concerned (and, in some cases, unpublished works), an assumption not really challenged after World War II, as we shall see later. Also, collections of war poetry by Australian, US and British poets are widely available, and patriotic verse in these countries is generally not held in low esteem, as it is in Japan. And, as a number of critics have pointed out, this negative evaluation of patriotic poetry in Japan applies usually only to verse written during the so-called Pacific War, not to verse written during earlier or later wars (Rabson 1998: 3–5). What is it about poetry written at this time that makes it so objectionable?

As mentioned earlier, as a result of the defeat, the governing ideology changed from fascism to democracy, and values changed accordingly. The facts that democratic, liberal, secular values were those of the victors, and that for seven years Japan was under military occupation and rule by the same victors who attempted to impose those values on Japanese society at large, obviously played a major role in persuading poets that their wartime verse needed to be self-censored – in many cases concealed or rewritten entirely. However, if this were the only factor, then one would expect to see over the past half century since the war a gradual reversal of judgment, away from ideology or politics towards an evaluation based primarily on literary or aesthetic grounds. This is in fact beginning to happen, as demonstrated by Takahashi Ryūji's attempt to differentiate between wartime poetry that has literary merit and verse that has none, and the poet Seo Ikuo's recent study of wartime poetry where he attempts to reevaluate patriotic poetry on the grounds that there is no *a priori* reason to condemn such verse, while criticizing pro-war poetry on aesthetic grounds (Seo 2006; Takahashi cited by Hara 2001: 530–1).

Takahashi defines 'war poetry' (*sensōshi*, a word connoting a negative evaluation of wartime poetry) on the grounds of both content and form, as poetry that supports a fascist totalitarian ideology, or actively rejoices in the imperial myth, or that deliberately utilizes an archaic style or the specialized military jargon sanctioned by the authorities (Hara 2001: 530–1). But, as seen here, politics still plays a crucial role in determining judgment. As secular and liberal democratic values have taken root in the Japanese consciousness over the decades following World War II, aesthetic values have inevitably taken on a political coloration that finds much patriotic war poetry simply unacceptable as literature. Part of the reason for the continuing debate over war poetry and the issue of self-censorship – some critics have long alleged that this exercise, especially as undertaken by Sakuramoto and his allies, is actually a witch-hunt – lies in the immediate postwar environment and the polemics over war responsibility.

Who is guilty? The controversy over war responsibility

It is broadly acknowledged that the debate over the responsibility that writers had in promoting fascist values during the Fifteen Years' War was touched off by an article written by the leftist critic Odagiri Hideo (1916–2000) titled 'Pursuing War Responsibility in Literature' (*Bungaku ni okeru sensō sekinin no tsuikyū*), published in June 1946 in the newly formed journal *New Japanese Literature* (*Shin Nihon bungaku*). Odagiri states his premise at the outset: 'war

116   *L. Morton*

responsibility in respect of literature is, more than anything else, first and foremost our problem. This problem commences with our self-criticism' (1972: 115). But then Odagiri goes on to name 25 writers who 'have the prime responsibility' for promoting the war, thus beginning a climate of denunciation and counter-denunciation. The poets named include Takamura Kōtarō, Saitō Mokichi (1882–1953), Noguchi Yonejirō (1875–1947), Saijō Yaso (1892–1970) and Satō Haruo (1892–1964) (see Odagiri 1972: 116). The critic Kobayashi Hideo (1902–83) was also named; two months later Kobayashi resigned his professorship at Meiji University and around that time fell onto the rail tracks at Suidōbashi station, sustaining minor injuries (Takamizawa 2001: vii). Odagiri's article originated in a speech given at the inaugural meeting of the Association for New Japanese Literature (Shin Nihon Bungaku Kai) and signalled the start of a political struggle for dominance over literature. The issue of war guilt was the rallying cry of writers involved with this association which centered upon prewar, proletarian authors, most of whom – like one of the association's most prominent members, the poet Nakano Shigeharu (1902–79) – had committed *tenkō* (an ideological turnabout). Under government pressure, Nakano committed *tenkō* in 1934 and underwent a conversion to pro-military values, although in his case this was a camouflage (Silverberg 1990: 199, 203–5).

The distinguished postwar literary historian Hirano Ken (1897–1978) was the leader of the literary opposition after the publication of his essay 'An Anti-Proposition' (*Hitotsu no hansotei*) in May 1946 in the journal *New Life* (*Shinseikatsu*) (Hirano 1972). J. Victor Koschmann has characterized this essay as a classic statement of the doctrine that the end never justifies the means (1996: 70–1). Clearly this is not a direct response to Odagiri but it represents a drawing of the lines between the group of writers like Hirano associated with the postwar journal *Modern Literature* (*Kindai bungaku*), and the *New Japanese Literature* group, whom they criticized on various grounds but primarily objected to what they saw as the instrumentalist Communist ideology of the group, which dictated a political approach to literature (Koschmann 1996: 41–87; Schnellbächer 2004: 72–110).

The debate over war responsibility and self-censorship had new life breathed into it by a series of articles published by the poet and critic Yoshimoto Takaaki (1924–2012) starting in 1955 that focused on the concealment and rewriting of patriotic war poetry. The articles dating from 1955–6 were collected together and published in a single volume, together with four articles by Takei Akio, in September 1956. Yoshimoto continued to explore this issue with further articles published between 1956 and 1960 subsequently reprinted in various of his books. Some of the 1957–8 pieces were republished as late as 2006. It would be instructive and useful to describe in detail all these articles here, and further references to them will occur later, but at this juncture it is only necessary to summarize a few of the most important, as Yoshimoto is generally recognized as the chief theorist of the self-censorship issue.

Yoshimoto is of a younger generation than the earlier protagonists in the debate and, as Oguma Eiji suggests in his 2002 examination of Yoshimoto, the

Self-censorship and wartime Japanese poetry 117

fact that he did not go to war and instead survived it, inflicted a deep psychological trauma on him that has driven his pursuit of writers who concealed their wartime activities (Oguma 2002: 598–655). One of the earliest and most famous of his polemics 'Poets of the Previous Generation – on the Evaluation of Tsuboi and Okamoto' (*Zensedai no shijin tachi – Tsuboi Okamoto no hyōka ni tsuite*) was first published in the journal *Poetics* (*Shigaku*) in November 1955. Yoshimoto castigates the two prewar modernist poets Tsuboi Shigeji (1897–1975) and Okamoto Jun (1901–78) for concealment of their wartime patriotic poetry. What angered Yoshimoto most was the fact that in the prewar era both poets espoused leftist, anarchistic values and at the war's end both men declared themselves in the democratic, progressive camp. Yoshimoto particularly savages Tsuboi who was lauded as a 'resistance poet' after the war. Yoshimoto sees this as hypocrisy of the worst kind since both poets wrote collaborationist pro-war poetry during the war and tried to conceal these activities later (1970: 38–54).

Yoshimoto also developed a complex critique of the 'Four Seasons' (*Shiki-ha*) school of prewar verse. This school of poetry included one of the greatest Japanese poets of the century, Miyoshi Tatsuji (1900–64), and was the dominant current in prewar poetry circles. Many of the poets belonging to the school wrote xenophobic, pro-war verse, including Miyoshi. Yoshimoto's main critique of this school is his essay 'The Essence of the Four Seasons Group' (*Shiki-ha no honshitsu*), first published in April 1958 in the journal *Literature* (*Bungaku*). He is not as harsh in his judgment on these poets as he is on modernist avant-garde poets because he regards them as primitive romanticists who yearn for a Japanese arcadia – in this sense he finds continuities in their prewar and wartime writing, although he still condemns their barbarous wartime verse (1970: 119–35). Yoshimoto's most famous critique of prewar and wartime verse is his essay 'Artistic Resistance and Collapse' (*Geijutsuteki teikō to zasetsu*), first published in April 1958 but later reprinted in his 1959 book of the same name. Focusing on poetry, the carefully argued essay investigates the issue of why artistic resistance to the war collapsed in the face of government oppression. Yoshimoto's answer is that both the prewar proletarian poets' poetry movement and avant-garde poets were fatally flawed in their political sensibility and in their failure to grasp the true nature of the consciousness of ordinary Japanese. He also criticizes individual poets belonging to both schools for their inability to write poetry free from political dictates. This powerful critique must be read against the background of the debate over politics, literature and subjectivity raging at the time.[4] It should also be noted that these three essays – 'Poets of the Previous Generation', 'The Essence of the Four Seasons Group' and 'Artistic Resistance and Collapse' – are taken from a much larger number of such critiques written by Yoshimoto at the time.

Two essays summarize the general reaction to Yoshimoto's decisive intervention in the debate: first, the critic Hanada Kiyoteru's (1909–74) July 1957 essay 'Younger Generation' (*Yangā zenerēshon*) which defends Okamoto Jun and argues for the existence of a different kind of resistance that Yoshimoto is not prepared to countenance (Hanada 1972); and, second, the poet Akiyama Kiyoshi's (1905–88) pro-Yoshimoto essay 'Democratic Literature and War

118   *L. Morton*

Responsibility' (*Minshushugi bungaku to sensō sekinin*) published in 1956, where Akiyama further attacks Okamoto and argues that the *New Japanese Literature* group's views are imprisoned in the rigid straightjacket of Communist ideology (Akiyama 1972). Whether supporting or opposing Yoshimoto's views, critics after Yoshimoto had to start from the premises that he established; as Ōkubo Norio, the editor of a volume of essays on war responsibility wrote, 'it was Yoshimoto Takaaki who established self-criticism in respect of the issue of responsibility regarding war literature' (1972: 167).

Miyoshi Tatsuji's self-censorship

Donald Keene's assessment of Miyoshi's jingoistic, xenophobic war poetry is short and succinct: 'His wartime "Japanism" was quite dissimilar to Takamura Kōtarō's; his love of Japan was absolute and did not imply a rejection of the West ... he did not recant after the defeat' (1984: 317). How accurate is this assessment? Miyoshi wrote seven volumes of verse between 1940 and 1945 of which three books are made up of unabashed pro-war poetry: *News of Victory Has Come* (*Shōhō itaru*, 1942), *Wooden Clappers in the Cold Night* (*Kantaku*, 1943) and *Martial Music* (*Kanka eigen*, 1945). The title poem of the first collection reads as follows:

> News of victory has come
> News of victory has come
> To the clear sky of early winter
> And the cloudless islands of Yamato
> News of victory has come
> At the mouth of Pearl Harbor, US warships have capsized
> On the far shores of Malaya, British warships have been destroyed
> Thieves for a hundred years in East Asia
> Ah you despicable red-haired blue-eyed merchants
> Why is your greed and bluster so strong?
> Why are your warships so flimsy and weak?
> Tomorrow Hong Kong will fall
> The day after, the Philippines will bow before us
> On the next day Singapore will fly the white flag of surrender for the third
>   time
> Ah a hundred years of blight in East Asia
> Aged thieves with wrinkles and bent backs
> Already the pomp of your cannon and fortress is in vain
> In the end they could not support
> Your cunning trade of blackmail and extortion
> On the seas of the eastern hemisphere
> The dawn of our sphere of divine ideals
> The cool breezes of daybreak will blow

(Miyoshi 1965a: 29–30)

Self-censorship and wartime Japanese poetry   119

An extract from the second poem in the collection, 'The US Pacific Fleet is Destroyed' (*Amerika Taiheiyō kantai wa zenmetsu seri*) reads as follows:

Ah your threats
Ah your show
Ah your economic blockade
Ah the ABCD line
Is laughable! The fat President of an obese democracy
All our intrigues of last night were sweeter than sweet
The US Pacific fleet is destroyed
Mile upon mile through the stormy sea
Running against the massive waves
Ah warships under the leadership of the mediocre Admiral Kimmel
After a sound night's sleep
Deep in the so placid Pearl Harbor
The line of warships sank
…
The true sons of the Imperial Land under the eastern sun released all at once
   a thunderous assault
Their submarines all sank forever
…
Depart our oceans, shame on you!

(Miyoshi 1965a: 31–2)

It would be tedious to translate much more as these poems are typical of most of the verse found in the three collections. One of the poems in *News of Victory Has Come*, 'A Personal Message to Mr Winston Churchill, John Bull's Principal Agent' (*Jon Buru karō sahai Winsuton Chāchirushi e no shigen*) has the words: 'Your precious democracy was totally useless' and is marked by the presence of sarcasm in almost every line (Miyoshi 1965a: 43–4). There is also a number of tanka in this collection. *Lasting Words on Autumn Days (Shūjitsu eigen)* is a sequence of nine tanka extolling Japan – the first four tanka read exactly the same except that one word or phrase differs in each poem, so the first tanka, 'Good friends live in this country Japan that I believe is peerless' (*Yoki tomo no kokodaku sumeba hinomoto o muni naru kuni to waga omounari*) is changed slightly for the second variation which substitutes 'good books' (*yoki sho*) for 'good friends', and so on (Miyoshi 1965a: 63).

In content I do not find these poems to be any less jingoistic than Takamura Kōtarō's wartime verse, and they certainly read like a rejection of the West. To date no critic has found such verse to have any literary merit, but Yoshimoto Takaaki argues that the following two tanka by Miyoshi from *The Rape of Malaya (Marei no kankatsu)*, a sequence of 11 tanka in *News of Victory Has Come*, are cruel and primitive but less 'mechanical' than Nazi cruelty: 'Using shells made with Japanese iron, wipe out this enemy!' and 'The enemy has filthy hearts, don't pity them, kill them!'[5]

120   *L. Morton*

Following their original appearance, these poems did not materialize again in any collection of Miyoshi's verse until the publication of the 1965 *Collected Works* (from which they are taken) shortly after the poet's death, over a quarter of a century later. That this was due to Miyoshi's self-censorship is verified by Ishihara Yatsuka's bibliographical notes appended to the second volume of the *Collected Works* where he quotes Miyoshi's postwar admonition, 'Apart from these few poems, do not reprint [these three wartime collections]', and confirms that the first reprinting since the war was in the *Collected Works* (Miyoshi 1965a: 503).

After the war, Miyoshi undertook a kind of recantation with his attacks on the Emperor, most notably in his essays 'Nostalgic Japan' (*Natsukashii Nihon*), the first part of which was published in *New Tides* (*Shinchō*) in January 1946, and 'Those around the Emperor' (*Tennō o meguru hitobito*), published in the same magazine in February 1950. Miyoshi wrote in the former essay, 'On reflection we men of culture ... are all burning with shame', in reference to their failure to stop the madness. He also criticized the Emperor trenchantly:

> The Emperor is the head of the state, and as the one most responsible must take the responsibility for the war and defeat. ... The Emperor neglected his duties shamefully by permitting the military clique to do as it wished, and did not conduct his duties as necessary. ... His responsibility extends beyond merely losing the war...
>
> (Miyoshi 1965b: 9–34)

But such critics as Abe Takeshi and Tsuruoka Yoshihisa are unwilling to accept Miyoshi's repentance as genuine. Tsuruoka (1971: 157–78) observes that in his postwar writings, Miyoshi portrayed himself as a victim, not as part of an aggressive war effort. Further, he asserts that Miyoshi's gifts as a lyric poet were turned totally over to the service of Japan's wartime rulers, and therefore his war poetry was not faked but totally sincere. Abe repeats the sentiments, with the comment that Miyoshi was the 'running dog' of the military (1980: 18). The real issue is that of self-censorship. In his lifetime Miyoshi forbade any republication of the three volumes of his jingoistic patriotic poetry, and not only expressed few regrets about this work but created the illusion that his wartime verse was slight and insignificant. He was aided and abetted by the many Japanese editors and critics (named and condemned by Abe, Tsuruoka and Sakuramoto) who hardly mention these poems in their postwar anthologies, books and articles on Miyoshi. Together, these observations permit the conclusion that it was a form of subterfuge, a refusal to face the issue. Miyoshi stands in stark contrast to Takamura Kōtarō who confronted the past openly with his poems of 1950, *Confession of an Idiot* (*Angu shōden*). A number of Japanese commentators on Miyoshi, like Tsuruoka Yoshihisa and Tsuboi Hideto, agree with Donald Keene: they feel he was perfectly sincere in his sentiments but, if that is the case, why the self-censorship, the 25 years of cover-up? Perhaps the answer to the question is because just about everyone followed suit.

Tsuboi Shigeji as a resistance poet

Before discussing the much-discussed case of Tsuboi, two quotations will demonstrate how widespread and common self-censorship was among modern poets. First, from the distinguished poet Ayukawa Nobuo's (1920–86) article 'My Attitude towards Debates over War Responsibility' (*Sensō sekinin no kyoshū*) first published in 1959: 'Without exception "Selected" and "Collected Poems" put together after the war had all war poetry and patriotic poetry of the poets of the previous generation excised and left blank' (2005: 100–1). The second quote comes from a leading contemporary critic of modern poetry Tsuboi Hideto in his magisterial 1997 study *A Celebration of Voices: Modern Japanese Poetry and War* (*Koe no shukusai: Nihon kindai shi to sensō*):

> While still alive, authors excluded topical war poetry from their collections. After their deaths, editors who took into consideration the 'honor' of their surviving family members removed such poetry from their 'Collected Works' or 'Collected Poetry'.... Naturally, it is not unusual for sections dealing with the war to be expunged from biographies, studies and articles in dictionaries and encyclopedias. Generally speaking, what supports this massive, systemic amnesia, i.e. cover-up, is the logic that this period was a disaster since free speech was nullified and everybody had to create works unwillingly.
>
> (Tsuboi H. 1997: 159)

Both these statements are supported by the massive body of evidence collected by Sakuramoto, Abe and Tsuruoka which lists publication after publication carefully vetted so that little remains of the poets' wartime verse.

Tsuboi argues that the justification offered by poets themselves for their collective amnesia about their war poetry is especially weak given the nature of poetic creation – ultimately poetic expression is a creation of the heart, it emerges voluntarily (Tsuboi H. 1997: 160). Yoshimoto Takaaki in his 1959 article 'The Debate over Poets' War Responsibility – a Literary Classification' (*Shijin no sensō sekinin ron – bungakuteki ni ruikeika*) argued that the notion that the past is the past – used to justify omissions and excisions of wartime verse – is a typical example of the Japanese logic of amnesia and indifference arising out of 'populist sentimentality'. This kind of thinking is supported by the 'fundamental, objective lack of substance in Japanese society' and the 'strong intrinsic authority of the mentality possessed by the Japanese ruling class' (Yoshimoto 1969b: 467–8). Yoshimoto here traces the sources of the self-censorship of verse (whitewash may be a better term) to Japanese society itself. One of the most flagrant examples of self-censorship cited by Yoshimoto is the poet Tsuboi Shigeji.

The clearest example of the rewriting that Yoshimoto finds reprehensible in Tsuboi's work is the prose poem 'A Poem Dedicated to an Iron Kettle' (*Tetsubin ni yoseru uta*), published in June 1943 in the journal *Ladies Review* (*Fujin kōron*), which reads as follows:

When I found you for the first time in the corner of a curio shop, you were covered in rust. When I had any spare time, I polished you. The more I polished the more my love permeated your skin. You became more dear to me than my dearest friends. You are stubborn and silent but when your bottom is warmed over a flame-red charcoal fire you begin to sing. Ah, when I hear that song, I think how many harsh winters have we passed together. But now the times have added to the harshness still more. The tumult of war has entered my living room. You can no longer sing on and on in my living room, I can no longer enjoy your songs forever. Oh, my Nanbu iron kettle. Goodbye! There to be melted anew, straightened out, for our warships, to make unbreakable steel plates! Repel all the uncounted millions of enemy shells that fall upon your skin!

(Tsuboi S. 1988: 150–1)

What enraged Yoshimoto about this 'monumentally patriotic poem' (in Yoshimoto's words) is the fact that after the war when it was published under the title 'A Song of the Iron Kettle' (*Tetsubin no uta*) in October 1952, the poem was rewritten with no reference to the war whatever, thus the last two sentences disappear (Tsuboi S. 1954: 278–9, 294; Yoshimoto 1970: 43–4). The original version of the poem is now available in the 1988 *Collected Works*, published after Tsuboi's death.

Tsuboi was a radical, avant-garde poet before the war, with a fervent attachment to the left. After the war, he reinvented himself as a 'resistance' (*teikō*) poet, who did not succumb to wartime nationalism, as he wrote in the preface to his September 1946 collection *Fruit* (*Kajitsu*):

I did not abandon the composition of poetry during the oppressive climate of the war years. But however insignificant these works were, they were an effort at resistance. I tried hard to express my true feelings that welled up within me, without being swept away by the tenor of the times.

(Tsuboi S. 1954: 224)

Also in the postscript to his 1952 collection *War Eye* (*Sensō no me*), Tsuboi wrote, 'Editing this collection amid the reactionary climate of Japan today, I realized clearly how passive my posture of resistance was' (1954: 293). He was publicly taken up by both Odagiri Hideo and Nakano Shigeharu as one of the leaders of the artistic resistance. It was this postwar reinvention of his poetic self, which necessitated self-censorship or, more properly, concealment of his wartime poetry, that so incensed Yoshimoto and his collaborators (Yoshimoto 1970: 38–41).

Yoshimoto's pursuit of Tsuboi was relentless and motivated by intense emotion. Yoshimoto wrote that he remembers in 1949 'swearing in his heart' not to forgive people like Tsuboi for wearing the masks of democrats. He observed that 'A Poem Dedicated to an Iron Kettle' ended in 'pseudo-fascist demagogy' while the rewritten version ended in a 'pseudo-democratic spirit'. Yoshimoto described his reaction to the original poem in the following way: 'I feel shame, humiliation and despair' (1970: 43–5). It is true that Tsuboi criticized Yoshimoto's study of Takamura Kōtarō but such vehemence could not arise from mere pique.

Yoshimoto found one war poem by Tsuboi worthy of a kind of praise, 'a brave, sad poem' called 'A Poem Admonishing Myself' (*Mizukara o imashimeru uta*) published in *Japan Review* (*Nihon kōron*) in 1943 (see Yoshimoto 1970: 47). The poem reads as follows:

> Swords must be polished sharply
> The skin of the blade without imperfection
> Rifles are heavy
> So shoulders must be broad and powerful
> Walk straight ahead
> Sometimes zig zag
> But charges must be quick and daring
> Battle cries must echo like thunder
> An enemy ten times as many must be met with a hundred times more
>   courage
> On the road to war
> Advance singing war anthems
> When advancing
> Do not count the number of lives
> Your gallantry and cowardice
> Will be decided for the first time when the battle ends
> Only a donkey
> Disputes glorious deeds in the midst of war

(Tsuboi S. 1988: 157)

I can see two possible reasons why Yoshimoto praised this poem: one is that it is a poem of praise and encouragement for the ordinary soldiers for whom Yoshimoto had much sympathy, and second it could be read as an anti-war poem (but Yoshimoto does not say this): one reading of 'donkey' (*roba*) is to see this animal as referring to the poet himself, admonishing himself for not speaking out against the war but also providing a justification for remaining silent. This poem was not reprinted in the decade following the war.

Critics other than Yoshimoto also criticized Tsuboi. Murata Masao condemned 'A Poem Dedicated to an Iron Kettle' as a pro-war work, and criticized the changes made to conceal it (Murata 1971: 38–9), as did Abe Takeshi, who cited Tsuboi's defense of 'Iron Kettle' written after the war:

> This poem was written in response to a request from the poetry section of the Patriotic Writers' Association. ... To refuse would mean that I was clearly signaling my opposition to the war ... I did not possess sufficient courage [to refuse] and nor was I able to keep silent.

(Abe 1980: 232)

124 *L. Morton*

Two other wartime, jingoistic poems often mentioned by critics that were subject to self-censorship are 'To the South' (*Nanpō e*, 1944) and 'A Finger's Journey' (*Yubi no tabi*, 1942) (Tsuboi S. 1988: 140, 157–8). And one can easily see why Tsuboi concealed these poems since they are close relatives of the martial verse written by Miyoshi Tatsuji and Takamura Kōtarō. Overall, however, in volume and content, Tsuboi did not write anything like the wartime verse of these two poets.

The bibliographical note (*kaidai*) attached to volume one of Tsuboi's *Collected Works*, which includes all the war poetry, remarks about these poems that they 'are a matter of deep regret', but cites Kaneko Mitsuharu (1895–1975) – whom Yoshimoto conceded was a true 'resistance poet' – saying that, 'I am happy to [declare] that Tsuboi did not retreat from a position of resistance to the war during World War II' (Tsuboi S. 1988: 468). This comment seems to refer to Tsuboi's private position rather than the one he revealed to the wartime public, as Tsuboi's own defense cited earlier suggests. Yoshimoto's ire was chiefly aroused by Tsuboi's postwar posturing as a resistance poet which concealed completely his wartime verse, and also by his postwar poetry which Yoshimoto despised and openly ridiculed, primarily because he saw it as politically motivated, thus being an exact analogue to the wartime poetry (Yoshimoto 1970: 46–8). Ironically, Tsuboi's postwar poetry ended up being censored by the Occupation authorities (Dower 1999: 416–17).

Kaneko Mitsuharu: self-censorship or plain, old irony?

Kaneko Mitsuharu was championed by a number of critics in addition to Yoshimoto as a poet who actually did write resistance poetry during the 1930s and the 1940s.[6] These poems were later collected in three volumes: *Sharks* (*Same*, 1937), *Parachute* (*Rakkasan*, 1948) and *Moths* (*Ga*, 1948). The argument made for Kaneko is that he wrote anti-war poetry using difficult, ambiguous, ironic and highly symbolic or allegoric language that could not be understood by Japanese censors. This reading of Kaneko's work was promoted assiduously by the poet himself, for example, in his 1957 autobiography *Poet* (*Shijin*):

> *Sharks* was a taboo book, but as I had elaborated a heavy camouflage, it was not obvious even to the censor … 'Foam' (*Awa*) was an exposure of the Japanese army's atrocities. 'Angels' (*Tenshi*) was a rejection of conscription and pacifist … seen from the government side, I must be a person who deserved liquidation, when I wrote such things … I very naturally opposed the war with a feeling which on my side I was definitely up to that time unwilling to give up and I continued to write poems … in opposition to the state apparatus.
>
> (Kaneko 1988: 182–6)

A. R. Davis, the translator of this volume, has also translated selections from all three poetry books which, whether read in English translation or Japanese, confirm that his poetry was indeed ironic and, to an experienced reader, quite clearly anti-war.

But in 1983 with the publication of Sakuramoto Tomio's volume *The Vacuum and the War: Poets in Wartime* (*Kūhaku to sensō: senjika no shijin tachi*), Kaneko's reputation underwent a mauling, at least in the eyes of Sakuramoto's supporters. Sakuramoto alleged that Kaneko had self-censored his own wartime poetry when it was published later. Sakuramoto cites three examples of such poems 'The Harbor' (*Minato*), 'Flood' (*Kōzui*) and 'Bullet' (*Dangan*). He also disputes the 'ironic' reading of various resistance poems (Sakuramoto 1983: 96–129). Sakuramoto's arguments seem to be fairly slight for the first two poems. For example, the October 1937 version of 'The Harbor', published in the magazine *Literature* (*Bungei*), basically just adds the following four lines to the second part of the poem:

> We must fight
> For the necessity
> We must win
> For our faith
> (Kaneko 1975: 70–5; Sakuramoto 1983: 99)

The other changes are inconsequential but Sakuramoto feels the excision of a two-line quotation from Hegel, 'For the people to enjoy eternal peace/Is nothing other than simple depravity', in the postwar version is sinister rather than (in my view) comic (Sakuramoto 1983: 101). The 1975 *Collected Works*, published at the time of Kaneko's death, does not include the earlier versions, reproducing the 1948 *Parachute* as first published, and therefore differs from the previous editions of *Collected Works* by other poets examined here. 'The Harbor' as published in 1948 reads as a highly ambiguous poem which may be calling readers to take up arms against the war whereas the 1937 version is more a call to arms, however neither version is explicit or jingoistic. 'Flood' can by no stretch of the imagination be described as a 'war poem' but 'Bullet' is different, as the translation of the original 1939 version demonstrates:[7]

> When a bullet flies out of a gun barrel
> Immediately, it becomes a pigeon and takes flight,
> Fighting for peace in East Asia.
>
> Don't be afraid.
> The bullet is whistling
> At play.
>
> Into the dry, cracked creek the swaying
> wild fleabane heading towards sleep
>
> Following a steel helmet between flesh and bone
> the bullet rests its head cocked.

Bullet.
The smallest angel
Innocent, dirty life. Do as you wish.
The swiftness
Of heaven caught by you.

(Sakuramoto 1983: 109–10)

The version of the poem that appears in *Parachute*, and the *Collected Works*, is very similar to the original but lacks the line 'Fighting for peace in East Asia' and is more overtly sarcastic. Sakuramoto notes the 1948 version has been acclaimed as an outstanding example of an anti-war poem, full of irony, that may appear otherwise. He argues the original published in a 1939 collection of patriotic poetry reveals how pro-war the poem is.

The poem is certainly an unsettling mixture of playfulness and menace, but the ugliness of its overall tone – celebrating murder – enables this reader to see it as not all that different from the revised version. The dissonance between the angelic heaven promised by death (and the Blakean innocence of the tone) and the ugly reality of death itself, graphically displayed in the second-last stanza, results in a condemnation of war and violence, a sarcastic, brutal reminder of the evil of war. However, such a reading is anathema to Sakuramoto who is determined to convict Kaneko for his crime of self-censorship. Politics, as Yoshimoto noted decades ago, determines meanings before they emerge as a negotiation between reader and text, but only if the reader prefers politics to reading.

A good example of how a reader can be initially excited and stimulated by Sakuramoto's logic, only to reject it altogether on many close readings of the text, is the poet and critic Shimaoka Shin's detailed rebuttal of Sakuramoto's view of Kaneko (Shimaoka 1983: 61–7). This rebuttal is matched by Kaneko's biographer Hara Masaji who also mounts a convincing argument against Sakuramoto on Kaneko while acknowledging that one prose piece written for children and published in October 1938 titled 'Behold! The Indomitable German Soul' (*Miyo! Fukutsu no Doitsu-damashii*) may stand as the sole example of 'pro-war literature' authored by the poet (Hara 2001: 521–34).

The latest instalment (to the time of writing) in this long-running saga of charge and counter-charge is Nakamura Makoto's 2009 volume *Kaneko Mitsuharu: The Poetics of War and Life* (*Kaneko Mitsuharu: 'sensō' to 'sei' no shigaku*), which is clearly in the camp that absolves the poet from Sakuramoto's continuing salvo of criticism. Using newly discovered articles by Kaneko to bolster his case, Nakamura subjects all the verses discussed above (as well as other wartime verse by Kaneko and other poets investigated here) to a careful and detailed analysis, and agrees that the evidence confirms Kaneko's anti-war position, although he also believes that Kaneko's wartime verse production is more complex than a simplistic categorization of it as a sarcastic parody of wartime jingoism (Nakamura 2009: 81–112). This characterization agrees with James Morita's English-language study of the poet, and also with Steve Rabson's volume on war in modern Japanese poetry (Morita 1980: 60–83; Rabson 1998: 215–17).

Takahashi Shinkichi: uncomplicated patriot?

Takahashi Shinkichi (1901–87) is a fascinating poet whose work is far more complicated than the labels of 'Dadaist' or 'Zen poet' that have been applied to his verse both in Japan and abroad suggest. Abe Takeshi argues that Takahashi's reputation as a Buddhist poet is undeserved with a number of non-pacificist poems being published in *Pilgrimages to Shrines* (*Jinja sanpai*, 1942) and *Kirishima* (*Kirishima*, 1942) (Abe 1980: 170–4). The 1982 *Collected Works*, published five years before the poet's death, explains in the bibliographical note attached to the first volume:

> At this time [during the war] pilgrimages to shrines and purification ceremonies became popular among the people who, for the first time, began to feel a crisis in the strength of Japan during the course of this long war. Takahashi as a Japanese had a profound interest in the origins of various divine festivals unique to Japan, and decided on his own initiative to visit many old shrines throughout the country. Virtually the whole of 1941 was spent in this way. He wrote various things which were collected into a single volume but, on this occasion, is deleted from this collection. ... In addition the two poems 'South Seas' (*Minami no umi*) and 'The Conquest of Singapore' (*Shingapōru kanraku*) have been deleted at the author's request.
>
> (Takahashi S. 1982: 723–4)

Kirishima is reprinted in the *Collected Works*, with the two poems listed above deleted as stated.

'South Seas' is a typical war poem:

> Let's go
> Into the southern ocean
> Singapore has fallen
> India is next
> And then comes Australia ...
> Asia is tomorrow
> Europe is the past ...
> To the Hawaiian Islands
> The US is weak
> Panama is next
> And then comes New York ...
> The Pacific is free
> The world is small
> 　　　　(Abe 1980: 171–2)

'The Conquest of Singapore' is similar in tone and content to 'South Seas'. However, many other poems in *Kirishima* are nothing like as patriotic or jingoistic as these verses. So, the charge of self-censorship is justified but on rather thin grounds. What of *Pilgrimages to Shrines*?

128   *L. Morton*

This work is primarily a series of prose essays on various shrines visited by the poet, with only a few poems included. The tone of the essays is respectful and pious (using the honorifics typical of the time to refer to the Emperor), with due attention being paid to the Imperial mythology undergirding many of the legends and tales associated with the shrines. The poems refer more directly to the war, but also act to extol the mystery of the Imperial myth. The poem 'Meiji Shrine' (*Meiji jingū*) begins with the following three lines:

> How pure, cool and spacious
> Is the shrine
> Where the Emperor's soul is still
> (Takahashi S. 1942: 10)

The first half of the poem proceeds along these lines until we come to, 'Nanking the capital of China has fallen/In North China an independent government has been established', decidedly unpoetic, but the last four lines resume the initial theme:

> Why do all our countrymen united
> Burn with loyalty?
> Because of the unbroken Imperial line
> How lovely the myriad islands of Japan
> (Takahashi S. 1942: 12–13)

This mixture of patriotic reverence for the Imperial mythology combined with references to sacrifices and victories in the war mark all of the few poems in this volume. For example, 'The Altar on Mt. Torimi' (*Torimiyama no matsuri no ni wa*) repeats the line (or variations of) 'Fighting is the greatest joy' a few times, although the ostensible theme of the poem is the legends associated with three sacred mountains in Nara (Takahashi S. 1942: 8–9).

Takahashi became an extremely religious man – he turned to nihilism and then religion after his father's suicide in 1930. In the autobiographical summary attached to a collection of his verse published in 1954, Takahashi wrote:

> World War II began. My distrust of Japanese Shintō deepened and I embarked upon a tour of old temples throughout the country ... and came to feel that they were an extension of the real world and were constructed on the basis of lies but I was not able to publish this at the time ... two forces contended within my heart – the struggle between Shintō and Buddhism ... my heart was broken by this struggle.
> (Takahashi S. 1954: 1, 4)

In later life, Takahashi turned once more to Buddhism but the statement above seems to indicate that his wartime Shintō poetry was also a kind of camouflage, although it is clear he was struggling with the question of religion. Read in this light, the self-censorship of his wartime verse was not solely or even primarily due to embarrassment at the nature of his emperor worship but rather, as a result of his struggles with Shintō, he reinvented himself as a failed Shintōist, and eventually turned once again in the direction of Buddhism. His self-censorship indicates a profound loss of faith in the national creed.

Concluding note

From the studies of self-censorship examined here, it is easy to see that self-censorship is also a form of self-invention, a rewriting of the self in the direction of a different intellectual, emotional or literary program, whether inspired by ideology, history, circumstances in general, or internal forces. Writers are, it can be argued, naturally prone to such an exercise as writing is, literally, the invention of worlds on a blank page, and identity becomes one element in a complex construction that eventually results in literature. In that sense, the discarding or rewriting of certain works of poetry in favor of others is a normal part of literary production, and something practiced by most poets. In this study, literary reasons for self-censorship have not been given the same degree of consideration as non-literary factors, and if this is a failing, then it is a failing common to the debate as a whole and to many of the critics who initiated it. However, as James Hardy noted of the Iraq war at the beginning of this study, the exigencies of war, and its aftermath, change many things, including the reading, production and interpretation of literature.

Notes

1 See Dower (1999: 405–40), Molasky (1999: 93–101), Orbaugh (2006: 88–102) and Rubin (1985).
2 'Fascist' is the preferred nomenclature by many of the Japanese critics involved in the debate – and fascist ideology is now a subject of much interest by Western scholars reappraising the issue of fascism in Japan. See Tansman (2009a, 2009b).
3 The author has engaged in research on this topic elsewhere: see Morton (2011a, 2011b).
4 This debate is described in detail by J. Victor Koschmann and Thomas Schnellbächer. See Koschmann (1996: 41–87), Schnellbächer (2004: 48–110) and Yoshimoto (1969a: 145–72).
5 In Japanese the two tanka read: '*Shinshū no kurogane o mote kitaetaru hozutsu ni kakete tsukuse kono zoku*' and '*Kono zoku wa kokoro kitanashi mononofu no nasake na kake so uchiteshi tsukuse.*' See Miyoshi (1965a: 38), Yoshimoto (1970: 130–1).
6 See Keene (1984: 358–63), Morita (1980: 60–82), Tsuboi H. (1997: 179), Tsuruoka (1971: 85–111) and Yoshimoto (1970: 456).
7 The original title was '*Tama*' (also meaning 'bullet').

Bibliography

Abe, Takeshi (1980) *Kindaishi no haiboku: shijin no sengo sekinin* (The Failure of Modern Poetry: Poets' Postwar Responsibility), Tokyo: Ōhara Shinseisha.
Abe, Takeshi (2005) *Kindai Nihon no sengo to shijin* (Postwar Japan and Poets), Tokyo: Dōseisha.

130 L. Morton

Akiyama, Kiyoshi (1972) 'Minshushugi bungaku to sensō sekinin' (Democratic Literature and War Responsibility) in Usui, Yoshimi (ed.), *Sensō bungaku ronsō* (Debates on War Literature), Vol. 1, Tokyo: Banshō Shobō, 147–59.

Ayukawa, Nobuo (2005) 'Sensō sekinin no kyoshū' (Wartime Responsibility) in *Sengo 60 nen 'Shi no hihyō' sōtenbō* (60 Years after the War: A Discussion), *Gendai shi techō: tokushū han* (Contemporary Poetry Handbook: Special Issue), Tokyo: Shichōsha, 100–9.

Ayukawa, Nobuo (2008) *America & Other Poems*, trans. Shogo Oketani and Leza Lowitz, New York City: Kaya Press.

Dower, John (1999) *Embracing Defeat: Japan in the Aftermath of World War II*, London: Allen Lane.

Hanada, Kiyoteru (1972) 'Yangā zenereshon' (Younger Generation) in Usui, Yoshimi (ed.) *Sensō bungaku ronso* (Debates on War Literature), Vol. 1, Tokyo: Banshō Shobō, 139–46.

Hara, Masaji (2001) *Hyōden: Kaneko Mitsuharu* (Biography: Kaneko Mitsuharu), Tokyo: Hokumeisha.

Hardy, James (2006) 'Hitting the Press', *Daily Yomiuri* 12 March: 18.

Hirano, Ken (1972) 'Hitotsu no hansotei' (An Anti-proposition) in Usui, Yoshimi (ed.), *Sensō bungaku ronsō* (Debates on War Literature), Vol. 1. Tokyo: Banshō Shobō, 117–20.

Kaneko, Mitsuharu (1975) *Kaneko Mitsuharu zenshū* (Collected Works of Kaneko Mitsuharu), Vol. 2, Tokyo: Chūō Kōronsha.

Kaneko, Mitsuharu (1988) *Shijin: Autobiography of the Poet Kaneko Mitsuharu (1895–1975)*, trans. A. R. Davis, ed. A. D. Syrokomla-Stefanowska, Sydney: Wild Peony.

Keene, Donald (1971) *Landscapes and Portraits: Appreciations of Japanese Culture*, Tokyo: Kodansha International.

Keene, Donald (1984) *Dawn to the West: Japanese Literature of the Modern Era (Poetry, Drama, Criticism)*, New York: Holt, Rinehart and Winston.

Koschmann, J. Victor (1996) *Revolution and Subjectivity in Postwar Japan*, Chicago: University of Chicago Press.

Lento, Takako and Miller, Wayne (eds.) (2011) *Tamura Ryuichi: On the Life and Work of a 20th Century Master*, Warrensburg, MO: Pleiades Press.

Miyoshi, Tatsuji (1965a) *Miyoshi Tatsuji zenshū* (Collected Works), Vol. 2, Tokyo: Chikuma Shobō.

Miyoshi, Tatsuji (1965b) *Miyoshi Tatsuji zenshū*, Vol. 8, Tokyo: Chikuma Shobō.

Molasky, Michael S. (1999) *The American Occupation of Japan and Okinawa: Literature and Memory*, London and New York: Routledge.

Morita, James (1980) *Kaneko Mitsuharu*, Boston: Twayne Publishers.

Morton, Leith (2004) *Modernism in Practice: An Introduction to Postwar Japanese Poetry*, Honolulu: University of Hawai'i Press.

Morton, Leith (2011a) 'Wartime *tanka* Poetry: Writing in Extremis', in Jacob Edmond, Henry Johnson and Jacqueline Leckie (eds.), *Recentring Asia: Histories, Encounters, Identities*, Leiden, Boston: Global Oriental, 256–84.

Morton, Leith (2011b) 'Japanese Poetry and the Legacies of War', in Roman Rosenbaum and Yasuko Claremont (eds.), *Legacies of the Asia-Pacific War: The Yakeato Generation*, London and New York: Routledge, 164–82.

Murata, Masao (1971) *Sensō/shi/hihyō* (War/Poetry/Criticism), Tokyo: Gendai Shokan.

Nakamura, Makoto (2009) *Kaneko Mitsuharu: 'sensō' to 'sei' no shigaku* (Kaneko Mitsuharu: The Poetics of War and Life), Tokyo: Kasama Shoin.

Self-censorship and wartime Japanese poetry   131

Odagiri, Hideo (1972) 'Bungaku ni okeru sensō sekinin no tsuikyū' (In Pursuit of Writers' War Responsibility) in Usui, Yoshimi (ed.), *Sensō bungaku ronsō* (Debates on War Literature), Vol. 1, Tokyo: Banshō Shobō, 115–17.

Oguma, Eiji (2002) *'Minshū' to 'Aikoku': Sengo Nihon no nashonarizumu to kōkyōsei* (The People and Patriotism: Postwar Japanese Nationalism and the Public Interest), Tokyo: Shin'yōsha.

Ōkubo, Norio (1972) 'Kaidai' (Bibliographical note) in Usui, Yoshimi (ed.), *Sensō bungaku ronsō* (Debates on War Literature), Vol. 1, Tokyo: Banshō Shobō, 163–7.

Orbaugh, Sharalyn (2006) *Japanese Fiction of the Allied Occupation: Vision, Embodiment, Identity*, Leiden, Boston: Brill Academic Publishers.

Rabson, Steve (1998) *Righteous Cause or Tragic Folly: Changing Views of War in Modern Japanese Poetry*, Ann Arbor: Center for Japanese Studies, University of Michigan.

Rubin, Jay (1984) *Injurious to Public Morals: Writers and the Meiji State*, Seattle and London: University of Washington Press.

Rubin, Jay (1985) 'From Wholesomeness to Decadence: The Censorship of Literature under the Allied Occupation', *Journal of Japanese Studies*, 11(1): 71–103.

Sakuramoto, Tomio (1983) *Kūhaku to sekinin: senjika no shijin tachi* (The Vacuum and the War: Poets in Wartime), Tokyo: Miraisha.

Sakuramoto, Tomio (1996) *Hon ga dangan datta koro: senjika no shuppan jijō* (When Books Became Bullets: Publishing during Wartime), Tokyo: Aoki Shoten.

Schnellbächer, Thomas (2004) *Abe Kōbō, Literary Strategist: The Evolution of his Agenda and Rhetoric in the Context of Postwar Japanese Avant-garde and Communist Artists' Movements*, Munich: Iudicium Verlag.

Seo, Ikuo (2006) *Sensōshiron 1910–1945* (A Study of War Poetry), Tokyo: Heibonsha.

Shillony, Ben-Ami (1991) *Politics and Culture in Wartime Japan*, Oxford: Clarendon Press.

Shimaoka, Shin (1983) *Shijin to shōsetsuka no sekai* (The Worlds of Poets and Novelists), Tokyo: Meicho Kankōkai.

Silverberg, Miriam (1990) *Changing Song: The Marxist Manifestos of Nakano Shigeharu*, Princeton, NJ: Princeton University Press.

Solt, John (1999) *Shredding the Tapestry of Meaning: The Poetry and Poetics of Kitasono Katue*, Cambridge, MA: Harvard University Asia Center.

Takahashi, Ryūji (1975) *Sensō bungaku tsūshin* (Dispatches on War Literature), Nagoya: Fūbaisha.

Takahashi, Shinkichi (1942) *Jinja sanpai* (Pilgrimages to Shrines), Tokyo: Meiji Bijutsu Kenkyūsho.

Takahashi, Shinkichi (1954) *[Zenshishū Taisei] Gendai Nihon shijin zenshū* (Library of Modern Poets), Vol. 12, Tokyo: Sōgensha.

Takahashi, Shinkichi (1982) *Takahashi Shinkichi zenshū* (Collected Works of Takahashi Shinkichi), Vol. 1, Tokyo: Seidosha.

Takamizawa, Junko (2001) *My Brother Hideo Kobayashi*, trans. James Wada, with an introduction by Leith Morton. Sydney: University of Sydney East Asian Series No. 14, Wild Peony, and Newcastle University.

Tansman, Alan (2009a) *The Aesthetics of Japanese Fascism*, Berkeley, Los Angeles, London: University of California Press.

Tansman, Alan (2009b) (ed.) *The Culture of Japanese Fascism*, Durham and London: Duke University Press.

Tsuboi, Hideto (1997) *Koe no shukusai: Nihon kindaishi to sengo* (A Celebration of Voices: Modern Japanese Poetry and War), Nagoya: Nagoya Daigaku Shuppankai.

132 L. Morton

Tsuboi, Shigeji (ed.) (1954) *[Zenshishū Taisei] Gendai Nihon shijin zenshū*, Vol. 10, Tokyo: Sōgensha.

Tsuboi, Shigeji (1988) *Tsuboi Shigeji zenshū* (Collected Works of Tsuboi Shigeji), Vol. 1, Tokyo: Seijisha.

Tsuruoka, Yoshihisa (1971) *Taiheiyō sensōka no shi to shisō* (Poetry and Thought during the Pacific War), Tokyo: Shōshinsha.

Yamamoto, Taketoshi (ed.) (2009–11) *Senryōki zasshi shiryō taikei bungaku hen* (Compendium of Occupation Literary Journal Materials), 5 vols., Tokyo: Iwanami Shoten.

Yoshimoto, Takaaki (1969a) *Yoshimoto Takaaki zencho sakushū* (Collected Works of Yoshimoto Takaaki), Vol. 4, Tokyo: Keisei Shobō.

Yoshimoto, Takaaki (1969b) *Yoshimoto Takaaki zencho sakushū*, Vol. 13, Tokyo: Keisei Shobō.

Yoshimoto, Takaaki (1970) *Yoshimoto Takaaki zencho sakushū*, Vol. 5, Tokyo: Keisei Shobō.

Yoshimoto, Takaaki (2006) *Shigaku josetsu* (An Introduction to Poetics), Tokyo: Shichōsha.

Yoshimoto, Takaaki and Takei, Akio (1956) *Bungakusha no sensō sekinin* (Writers' War Responsibility), Tokyo: Awaji Shobō.

8 Kurosawa Akira's *One Wonderful Sunday*

Censorship, context and 'counter-discursive' film

Rachael Hutchinson

Introduction

Released in July 1947, *One Wonderful Sunday* (*Subarashiki Nichiyōbi*) by Kurosawa Akira (1910–98) follows the difficulties of a young couple trying to enjoy a day out in Tokyo on a strictly limited budget. Masako (played by Nakakita Chieko) and Yūzō (played by Numasaki Isao) meet at the train station, inspect a model home, tour the zoo, attempt to purchase tickets to a symphony, visit a café and end up in an abandoned amphitheater, creating their own fantasy symphony out of thin air. Along the way the couple meet with various unscrupulous characters as well as street children and shopkeepers, resulting in happiness or despair depending on the nature of the encounter. Throughout, the lovers follow the ups and downs of any couple, quarreling and embracing by turns, but in the end promising to meet again next Sunday. Galbraith describes the film as 'resolutely apolitical' and a 'sweet, uncomplicated story' (2001: 87). Others have a similar assessment, Stephen Prince listing the film among Kurosawa's 'heroic' humanist narratives (1999: 73). Part of the reason for this view is that critics cannot help reading *One Wonderful Sunday* in the context of Kurosawa's previous film, *No Regrets for Our Youth* (*Waga seishun ni kuinashi*, 1946), widely hailed as Japan's first pro-democratic film in the aftermath of defeat. Even in the most general terms, the persistent view of *One Wonderful Sunday* as a simple romantic comedy is encouraged by the use of 'wonderful' in the English title, no doubt reminding later critics of Frank Capra's *It's a Wonderful Life* from 1946.[1] While the film is most often taken as an uncritical and straightforward piece of positive, life-affirming filmmaking, however, a close reading of *One Wonderful Sunday* reveals details and themes which seem to go against the strict Occupation policies regarding what could and could not be shown on screen. When considered in this context, the film is more critical than it first appears.

Just three weeks after Japan's defeat in 1945, the administration of the occupying forces, collectively known as SCAP,[2] issued a ten-point Press Code regulating media expressions. The Press Code covered newspapers, books, magazines, radio, film and theater, and was later expanded by follow-up directives. The Code was enforced by two arms of the SCAP administration: the CI&E (Civil Information and Education section) focused primarily on civil

134   *R. Hutchinson*

censorship, while the CCD (Civil Censorship Detachment) focused mainly on military and intelligence censorship. Total media control was achieved through a combination of prescriptive and proscriptive measures. 'Positive' propaganda was forwarded by CI&E officials, responsible for guiding filmmakers towards acceptable themes and content, while 'negative' enforcement concerned the scrutiny of media products by the CCD, leading to punishment for any infractions. The people primarily responsible for censoring film products in accordance with the Press Code were the staff of the PPB – the Press, Pictorial and Broadcast division of CCD.[3] The two main directives of the Press Code were the prohibition of any criticism of SCAP and the prohibition of Japanese militarism, while an overarching policy of invisibility forbade any mention of the occupation of Japan.[4]

In effect, this meant that filmmakers could not show images of soldiers, military vehicles or the effects of Allied bombing – whether from the atomic bombs in Hiroshima and Nagasaki or the air-raids on the city of Tokyo. Relationships between military personnel and Japanese women, labeled 'fraternization', were not to be shown, and representation of the economic effects of war – rationing, food shortages, overcrowding on public transport and the thriving black market – were also discouraged. If such images were to be shown, they had to be shown as the deserved result of Japan's militaristic activities during the war. In *One Wonderful Sunday*, Kurosawa seems to fly in the face of all these policies, vividly portraying the desperate situation of postwar Tokyo through images of war orphans, the homeless, bombed-out ruins, scavenging, hunger and poverty, the limbo and confusion of rebuilding, the veiled presence of the US military and the injustice of the black market and gangster-run cartels. According to the letter of the Press Code and SCAP law, the representation of all these things was banned. In this light, it is possible to read *One Wonderful Sunday* as a piece of counter-discursive film, which problematizes and critiques the struggle of day-to-day life in Tokyo under the Allied Occupation.

This second, more critical reading of *One Wonderful Sunday* fits the image of Kurosawa as a self-reflexive, counter-discursive filmmaker, put forward by critics like James F. Davidson (1972) and Yoshimoto Mitsuhiro (2000). It seems that there are two contrasting images of Kurosawa – the humanist and the subversive – which affect the way in which we read his films. The two opposing images seem to accord with the two possible outcomes of the censorship process in 1947: either the film would be taken as a 'sweet, uncomplicated story' and not be subject to censorship, or it would be seen as flouting SCAP policy and be censored or banned. As it happened, the film was not censored at the time, so a reading of *One Wonderful Sunday* as a 'counter-discursive' film seems to beg the question – 'how did Kurosawa get away with such direct representation?'[5] However, this kind of question has an assumption embedded within it, that Kurosawa somehow pulled the wool over the eyes of the unwitting censors. I hope to demonstrate that the non-censorship of Kurosawa's film was more a function of context, as well as the complexity of the censorship process in 1947. First, I examine how Kurosawa's track record with censorship may have affected the contemporary reception of *One Wonderful Sunday*, as well as his reception in recent academic criticism. I then undertake a close reading of *One Wonderful Sunday* as a case study of 'counter-discursive' film, and end with a consideration of factors which may have had an impact on the SCAP censorship process in 1947. Rather than saying that Kurosawa did or did not 'get away with' a particular kind of representation, it becomes clear that censoring the film or labeling it either 'pro-democratic' or 'counter-discursive' are outcomes equally dependent on contextual circumstance.

Censorship and creativity: expression within the limits

By the time he made *One Wonderful Sunday* in 1947, Kurosawa was experienced in dealing with censors and guidelines from both the Japanese military and the American administration, striking a balance between creative expression and external demands. Working at Tōhō studios, renowned for its large numbers of Communist party idealists and notorious for asking filmmakers to rewrite and reshoot scenes (Hirano 1992: 205–13), Kurosawa was also accustomed to complying with studio and union requests. The complexity of such a balancing act has led critics to view Kurosawa's filmmaking in terms of a spectrum of compliance. Galbraith (2001) emphasizes Kurosawa's 'apolitical' stance and focuses on studio and union directives in the making of *No Regrets for Our Youth* and *One Wonderful Sunday*, minimizing the impact of the Allied Occupation and SCAP policies in favor of Tōhō's Scenario Review Committee (2001: 70–1, 76, 91). In contrast, Hirano focuses entirely on SCAP policy, arguing that Kurosawa made *No Regrets for Our Youth* according to a set of guidelines put forward by CI&E (1992: 148). While it is naïve to think that Kurosawa would not have to take SCAP policies into account, Hirano's more direct charge of compliance deserves closer examination. A brief consideration of Kurosawa's dealings with censorship to 1946 will contextualize the issue of compliance regarding *No Regrets for Our Youth* and help us better interpret Kurosawa's expectations regarding censorship in the making of *One Wonderful Sunday*.

Kurosawa experienced censorship from the Japanese military government very early in his career, as assistant director on Yamamoto Kajirō's *Horses* (*Uma*, 1941) (Kurosawa 1983: 110–12). Throughout his autobiography, Kurosawa displays a venomous hatred of the Japanese censors, calling them 'mentally deranged' and obsessed with sexuality (1983: 118–19). Kurosawa emphasizes the random and arbitrary nature of the censors' judgments as well as their inflexibility: 'The verdict of the censors was final; there was no recourse' (1983: 117). The Japanese censors are represented as ignorant targets for Kurosawa's witty counterattacks, as in the treatment of *Men Who Tread on the Tiger's Tail* (*Tora no O-wo fumu otokotachi*, 1945). In response to the Japanese censor's comment that the film was a 'distortion' of the kabuki play *The Subscription List* (*Kanjinchō*) and 'a mockery of that classic', Kurosawa countered that *The Subscription List* was itself 'a distortion of the Noh play *Ataka*'. When the censors

136   *R. Hutchinson*

retorted that the film was boring and meaningless, Kurosawa apparently left the room (1983: 143).[6] Although Kurosawa undoubtedly plays up his own actions as heroically resistant, his experience with the Japanese censors was not all negative. While some of his scripts were censored or even abandoned in pre-production,[7] others won prizes,[8] and his films made during the war – *Sanshiro Sugata* (*Sugata Sanshirō*, 1943), *Sanshiro Sugata II* (*Zoku Sugata Sanshirō*, 1945), *The Most Beautiful* (*Ichiban utsukushiku*, 1944) and *Men Who Tread on the Tiger's Tail* – were very successful, popular with audiences and the military alike. The fact that Kurosawa continued to release successful titles during the war years shows his determination to make films, even at the expense of compromise.

Throughout the autobiography, Kurosawa discusses censorship in terms of compromise, self-censorship, free artistic expression and human subjectivity. In the early 1940s, Kurosawa knew roughly what the Japanese censors expected and worked accordingly. Kurosawa tells us that his scripts in 1942 were

> stories that the times required, about the aircraft industry and boy aviators. Their aim was to fan the flame of the national war spirit, and I did not undertake them out of any personal inclination. I just dashed them off in the suitable formulas.
>
> (1983: 121)

It seems that directors were well aware of what was likely to win approval or attract censorship, and Kurosawa admits to calculating the response of the censors before submitting his work.[9] Kurosawa's self-professed shame at 'ingratiating myself when necessary and otherwise evading censure' during the war (1983: 145) has been criticized,[10] but the absence of directorial creativity in this atmosphere seems to be genuinely lamented:

> In wartime we were all like deaf-mutes. We could say nothing or, if we did, all we could do was to repeat in parrot fashion the tenets taught by the militarist government. In order to express ourselves, we had to find a way of doing so without touching on any social problems.
>
> (1983: 146)

As an artist, Kurosawa strove for artistic expression within the limits. Coming into the Occupation, Kurosawa had high hopes for the new creative freedom and relief from oppressive Japanese military censorship, albeit balanced by a skeptical realism. In 1945, he writes, 'freedom of speech was recovered (within the limits permitted by General MacArthur's military policies)' (1983: 144). The bracketed aside may reflect the priorities in Kurosawa's filmmaking: freedom of expression being the main aim, with any restrictions to be considered as a secondary challenge. By the time CI&E distributed its list of guidelines and prohibitions in 1945, it seems Japanese filmmakers were accustomed to dealing with the idea of such rules and working within and around them to best effect.

Kurosawa Akira's One Wonderful Sunday   137

On 22 September 1945, CI&E officials met with representatives from the Japanese film industry to discuss a 'motion picture industry guide', requesting the 'abolition of Japanese militarism and military nationalism themes and encouragement of liberal tendencies and processes in Japan including the basic freedom of religion, speech and right of assembly' (SCAP 1945: 1.160). Hirano places great emphasis on this meeting, where the Japanese were encouraged to follow the principles of the Potsdam Declaration and contribute to the rebuilding of society. Possible subjects for new films were suggested, encouraging democracy, free speech, equal rights and individualism (Hirano 1992: 5–6, 37–9). In response, the immediate postwar period saw a new genre of so-called 'democratization films' as filmmakers explored the new ideals. Kurosawa's first film to be made under these conditions was *No Regrets for Our Youth*, which Hirano labels 'an archetypal democratization film made according to these guidelines' (1992: 148). This wording casts Kurosawa's actions in terms of compliance with CI&E's 'industry guide' rather than as an independent project. It is worth addressing this issue in detail, as the impact of *No Regrets for Our Youth* has heavily influenced the reception of *One Wonderful Sunday*.

No Regrets for Our Youth shows many aspects of freedom and democracy that would have pleased CI&E officials, dramatizing the story of Professor Takigawa Yukitoki from Kyoto Imperial University, persecuted by the Japanese government for liberalism in 1933. The film was also inspired by the real-life story of leftist Ozaki Hotsumi, executed as a spy in 1944 and seen as a martyr to the Japanese regime. In portraying the story of two men who stood for freedom, the film may be read as a critique of Japanese militarism. Further, it features a strong female heroine and demonstrates the results of agrarian reform in the early years of the Allied Occupation (Hirano 1992: 181–2). Hirano suggests:

> As may be guessed from the foregoing description of the film's themes, the idea for *No Regrets for Our Youth* may have originated within CI&E itself, or if not, within a company very conscious of and responsive to this occupation agency's suggestions.
>
> (1992: 184)

However, in interviewing Kurosawa, Hirano reports that 'he did not recall that CIE had a significant influence on the project' and that he decided the subject of the film himself (1992: 184).

Kurosawa makes no mention in his autobiography of working to the guidelines of CI&E, saying that the only changes made to the script were the result of requests from Tōhō studios, due to its similarity with another film being made that year (1983: 148). The SCAP records of the time summarizing developments in motion pictures do not reflect a close working relationship with Kurosawa, or indeed any director, as films are referred to by their studio and title only. While some films are singled out for their outstanding contribution to the democracy effort, no mention is made of *No Regrets for our Youth*.[11] According to the screenplay writer Hisaita Eijirō, the main idea and research for the film came

138   R. Hutchinson

from its producer, Matsuzaki Keiji, while Kurosawa 'cordially collaborated in the writing' (Hirano 1992: 184). It is notable that Hisaita also wrote the screenplay for *Morning of the Osone Family* (*Osone-ke no asa*, 1946), cited by Hirano as another great 'democratization' film,[12] and Yamada Kazuo states that Hisaita's heroine expressed more depth of feeling than any other woman on the Japanese screen to that point (1999: 65). Hisaita and Matsuzaki were well known in the proletarian movement and for their liberal ideas (Yamada 1999: 66), so they may have brought their own interests in these themes to the *No Regrets* project. The collaborative nature of the project makes it difficult to argue that Kurosawa took CI&E regulations as a starting point to purposefully produce a 'democratization film'.

This is not to say, however, that Kurosawa was uninterested in exploring democratic ideals. In his autobiography, Kurosawa says that *No Regrets for Our Youth* was about 'the problem of the self', because:

> The Japanese see self-assertion as immoral and self-sacrifice as the sensible course to take in life. We were accustomed to this teaching and had never thought to question it.
> I felt that without the establishment of the self as a positive value there could be no freedom and no democracy.
>
> (1983: 146)

While it is naïve to take the whole of Kurosawa's autobiography at face value, his stated reason for making a film about the individual 'self' in celebration of relief from fascist oppression is not unreasonable. Yamada's argument that Kurosawa's two main aims of the period were 'establishment of the self' (*jiga no kakuritsu*) and 'cinematic freedom' (*eiga no jiyū*) (1999: 59–65) seems to be borne out by Kurosawa's statements. The strength of emotion Kurosawa professes is not easily dismissed:

> I felt particularly deep emotions about this film, the first to be made in the post-war atmosphere of freedom. The locations we used in the old capital of Kyoto – the grassy hills, the flower-lined side streets, the brooks reflecting the sun's rays – are all employed in the most trivial films today, but at the time they held special meaning for us. For me it was as if my heart could dance, as if I had grown wings and could fly among the clouds.
>
> (1983: 150)

This joy in the freedom of expression was shared by many other postwar Japanese artists. Jay Rubin (1985) argues that postwar literature was dominated not by a feeling of suppression but of liberation as writers found new creative freedom in the Occupation years. Dower similarly writes of 'the hunger for words in print' (1999: 180) assuaged by an outpouring of magazines and books freely expressing writers' ideas on the defeat, surrender and the task of rebuilding a new Japan (1999: 180–7). Freedom of expression provided the subject for

Kurosawa Akira's One Wonderful Sunday   139

two of Kurosawa's essays in 1946 (Yamada 1999: 59–61), and continued to inform Kurosawa's discussion of his filmmaking.[13] Although Kurosawa made films throughout the Allied Occupation, from 1945 to 1952, *No Regrets for Our Youth* seems to be singular in its skeptical treatment by the critics as a case of compliance with SCAP guidelines. Based on the available evidence, however, it seems that this is too strong a reading. Taken together with his commitment to freedom of expression and artistic creativity, I would suggest that Kurosawa's interest in the liberation of the 'self' provides sufficient basis for his making of *No Regrets for Our Youth*.

The screening of *No Regrets for Our Youth* was Kurosawa's first major meeting with CI&E officials. Amazed by their warm reception and praise, Kurosawa was further impressed that 'a Mr Garky' gave a party in the film's honor (1983: 149).[14] Kurosawa's positive experience with the Americans would have made a strong impression, particularly in contrast to his dealings with Japanese military officials. His following films would not escape the blue pencil entirely (Hirano charts various amendments made to *Drunken Angel, Stray Dog* and *The Quiet Duel*) but perhaps this early experience would have made Kurosawa more willing to explore the boundaries of artistic expression and strive for artistic truth in his postwar films. In contrast to reading Kurosawa's filmmaking as 'compliant' with external demands, I would therefore argue that Kurosawa's strategy should be seen in terms of creativity, working within and around the guidelines and the Press Code to achieve the maximum freedom of expression. In making *One Wonderful Sunday*, Kurosawa certainly had to take SCAP policies into account, but he would do so in a creative way, drawing our attention to the process in a self-reflexive, self-conscious manner.[15] Kurosawa uses narrative, background setting, *mise-en-scène*, sound and music, to emphasize the constructed nature of the film, directing the audience's attention to specific points and using cumulative effect to produce a critical atmosphere in the film as a whole.

One Wonderful Sunday as counter-discursive film

Kurosawa's choice of narrative mode for *One Wonderful Sunday* – a light romance based on the difficulty of being young and in love and on a date with no money – seems at odds with the idea of a critical, counter-discursive film. But the strength of Kurosawa's critique lies in the very ordinariness of the characters and the simplicity of the story. Kurosawa writes that '[t]he story called for them to be the kind of young couple you might see anywhere in Japan at that time' (1983: 154–5), representing everyman and everywoman of postwar Japan. Kurosawa himself chose the actors for their ordinariness, and reports having trouble finding them in a crowd scene at Shinjuku (1983: 154). This ordinariness maximizes the audience's ability to relate to the main characters. From the very first shots of the man and the woman – she is on a packed train, and he is furtively eyeing a cigarette butt discarded in the street – we immediately understand their situation in life, dominated by poverty and struggle. For postwar audiences these

140 R. Hutchinson

images would have conjured up real and still relevant memories, reflecting the reality of daily life on screen.[16] As Hirano tells us in her description of prohibited subjects in postwar Japanese film, 'the censors required that the postwar social and economic confusion be explained as a consequence of Japanese militarism. They forbade criticism of food rationing, crowding on the trains, and such' (1992: 54). Not only is the overcrowded train not attributed to Japanese militarism, but later in the film Kurosawa directly shows a starving war orphan approaching the couple and demanding food, which he wolfs down ravenously. Throughout the day, the couple have to calculate their budget very carefully, and disaster strikes when a stray baseball, hit by Yūzō, smashes the wares of a *manjū* stall owner and they have to pay damages. Similarly, the couple cannot afford the extortionately high prices for coffee in a shop which charges extra for milk, and they fantasize about running their own establishment where milk would be included in the price. The shortage of food and resources is obvious, represented both visually and verbally. Moreover, the representation is negative, as it leads to anxiety, tension, complaints and escapist fantasy. The anxiety and frustration of the couple's day out give the simple narrative its meaning, and the film as a whole reads as a commentary on the difficulties of life in postwar Japan.

Stephen Prince has noted the strong escapist tones of *One Wonderful Sunday* (1999: 73, 307), most evident in the café fantasy sequence towards the end of the film. After leaving the tea shop, the couple wander into a deserted area of town where they find the flattened foundations of a building. This space serves as an imagined piece of real estate where the couple will one day open their own tea shop – the tables here, curtains here and so on. The poignancy of the scene is highlighted by Kurosawa's choice of background, as behind the couple stretches a scene of devastation, with tall buildings showing empty gaps and holes instead of windows, rubble all over the ground and pieces of masonry sticking up everywhere. Satō Tadao criticizes this 'childlike' scene and argues that the disjunctive realism/fantasy split in the film indicates Kurosawa's immaturity as a director, further noting that much of the film was shot on sets which could hardly be compared to the reality of Tokyo's rubble as shown in newsreels of the time (1969: 117–19). However, one could equally argue that the need for fantasy and escape underlines the grimness of reality, and that a deliberately constructed set provides excellent evidence for Kurosawa's commitment to portraying the postwar destruction. Set against the childlike play of the couple, the vision of Tokyo as a bombed-out ruin is extremely powerful in this scene. According to the Press Code, '[n]o visual or verbal description of the devastation resulting from the Allied attack during the Pacific War was allowed' (Hirano 1992: 54). Despite this prohibition, this scene provides the strongest visual critique of the Allied bombing in the film.

Even in the smallest of details, Kurosawa is acutely critical and observant in his choice of *mise-en-scène* to draw attention to the state of postwar Tokyo.[17] The choices are deceptively simple, as when Masako sits down to eat her *manjū* bun, arranging herself neatly in the mouth of a large concrete pipe that has been discarded in the street. The act of sitting fits perfectly into the diegetic sequence,

Kurosawa Akira's One Wonderful Sunday   141

providing a romantic hiatus as Yūzō stands protectively over her, but the choice of seat speaks volumes. The pipe is there because the city is under reconstruction, and Masako sits in the pipe because there is nowhere else to sit, no 'normal' benches or other signs of civilized city life. While a concrete pipe could signify mere 'building' in the sense of constructing new offices or new roads, it is doubtful whether a contemporary Japanese audience would see such an image as unrelated to the necessity of rebuilding Tokyo after the massive firebombing it sustained in the final stages of the war. Even for the modern viewer, there is a cumulative effect of the repetition of such seemingly simple scenes throughout the course of the film. It is on reflection after the film, when one has seen a number of such scenes in succession, that the viewer is left with an unaccountably overwhelming feeling of the couple's struggle, not just to enjoy their day out but to rebuild their entire lives in a context of extensive material and spiritual devastation. This cumulative effect continues to build right to the end of the film, where another seemingly simple choice of *mise-en-scène* brings the Allied Occupation to the viewer's attention.

The final scene takes place at the train station as Masako and Yūzō sit silently on a bench in the middle of an empty platform, awaiting her train at the end of the day. The shot is divided into halves, with the couple seated on the bench on the left, and the platform extending to the right. Appearing in the center of the shot is a rubbish bin next to the bench, printed with the strikingly incongruous English word 'trash'. Not only is the word in English, but it appears in capital letters, in stark black paint, leaping out from the light background: 'TRASH'. The modern viewer cannot help but notice the word, creating a strong disjunctive effect between the word's meaning and the romantic farewell scene on the station platform.[18] When the next shot places the couple in the center of the screen, the trash receptacle remains clearly at the right of the bench, although it disappears as the camera closes in on the couple. By placing the word in the forefront of an otherwise quiet and unremarkable scene, Kurosawa gives the viewer time to ponder its significance: is Kurosawa making a statement of some kind about 'trash'? Are this young couple seen as 'trash' to mainstream Japanese society, or are they meant to stand out in contrast to the dregs that they have encountered during the day? Is Japan 'trash'? Is the whole effort of rebuilding 'trash'? Or is the word pointing to the military administration responsible for placing the bin on the platform, with its English language and commanding implication ('put the trash in here, and understand the English command to do so')? This last possibility seems most likely, given the context of critique and commentary that has filled the film to this point. By commenting on 'postwar' Japan, Kurosawa must comment on 'Occupation' Japan. In the Press Code, all mention of the Occupation was forbidden. We know that scenes in other films were censored for depicting signposts in English, and although many of these were military signs regulating parking and vehicles and therefore more direct signifiers of the Occupation presence, some films of 1946–7 were subject to much stricter controls, with the English letters A, B, C, 'USA' and 'I love you' deleted from the final cuts (Hirano 1992: 56). While lapses from the censors

142   *R. Hutchinson*

were not unknown,[19] it is surprising that this word is allowed to feature so prominently and for such a long period of time on the screen. Kurosawa's careful staging and framing in the rest of the film suggest that he would have been aware of the impact of the English command.[20] From his prior experience of dealing with censorship, it seems that Kurosawa was able to work creatively within the limits to provide his own commentary, while providing the audience with just enough information for their imaginations to fill in the blanks.

Apart from narrative mode, background setting and *mise-en-scène*, Kurosawa's choice of sound and music also draws attention to the issues of postwar struggle. The most intrusive use of sound in the film occurs when the couple spend a brief time in Yūzō's run-down apartment. Yūzō is driven to despair at his failure to succeed in life and provide for their engagement and future together, in fact seeing no future ahead in such a negative and difficult atmosphere. Masako attempts to comfort him with words, but is frightened when Yūzō demands more physical attention. Masako leaves, but returns and begins disrobing in an extremely tense, awkward scene which takes place in almost complete silence, except for the dripping of water from the leaky ceiling. The drips are almost unbearably annoying, producing extremely uncomfortable viewing. This discomfort has been criticized (Yoshimoto 2000: 136), but Satō Tadao has noted this scene as one of the most sexually charged in Japanese cinema (1969: 118). While the charge of pent-up energy is certainly related to sexual tension, the tension also shows Yūzō's desperation, reflecting the exhaustion and despair (*kyodatsu*) that dominated postwar Japanese life.[21] This sense of exhaustion is highlighted by Kurosawa's choice of music halfway through the film. A famous Japanese ditty, 'The Apple Song' (*Ringo no uta*), plays in the background as Yūzō visits his friend's drinking establishment to ask him a favor. The use of this popular contemporary song superficially indicates the fashionable nature of the cabaret, but it also produces a strong contrastive effect. Dower states that 'The Apple Song' was synonymous with positivity and 'brightness' in specific contrast to the bleakness and exhaustion of the defeat (1999: 172–3). In the context of the narrative, it seems Kurosawa uses the song to emphasize the contrast between 'brightness' in the luxury of band music and the shame that Yūzō experiences as his friend takes him for a beggar and shunts him off to the back room for a free meal.

Kurosawa's use of music is consistently thoughtful, seen in the treatment of Schubert's *Unfinished Symphony*, a performance of which the couple fail to attend when scalpers buy up all the tickets. At the end of the day, the couple find themselves in an abandoned amphitheater swirling with dust and leaves. Masako seats herself in the audience as Yūzō climbs the stage and attempts to conduct his own version of the *Unfinished Symphony* for her. Moved by his first abortive attempts, Masako turns directly to the camera and asks the audience to clap loudly to inspire fresh hope in all young people of Japan, a tactic which failed miserably in Tokyo but was successful in Paris. Criticism of this scene has tended to focus on the success or failure of the applause experiment (Richie 1996: 46; Yoshimoto 2000: 137), missing the wider point of why Kurosawa may have used this particular piece of music so prominently. In this scene and throughout the narrative, it stands for something unobtainable, desirable and inspiring of hope. On the surface, the use of an Austrian composer points to this new hope coming from the West – a reading which would please the American censors and European audiences alike. However, Kurosawa has chosen a piece of music whose vernacular title indicates it is 'unfinished'.[22] The couple are unable to see the piece performed because of the strength of the gangsters who run the black market in a collapsed economy. They must fantasize their own version, in an empty and abandoned location – not only is the symphony unfinished, it is not even real. For contemporary Japanese audiences, this bleaker reading of the scene may have added to the discomfort of being asked to applaud in an unfamiliar setting.

Taking the narrative, *mise-en-scène*, sound and music into consideration, the overall construction of *One Wonderful Sunday* points to an extended commentary and critique on life in postwar Tokyo. Unlike the veiled critique in *Rashomon* (*Rashōmon*, 1950), which James F. Davidson (1972) reads as counter-discursive because of its ruined gate imagery and its sustained focus on the suspect nature of truth, nearly every shot of *One Wonderful Sunday* seems deliberately constructed to show the ruin of war and the hardship of living through it. Kurosawa describes the subject of the film as 'impoverished lovers struggling along in defeated Japan' (1983: 153), and Yūzō himself represents that defeat as a soldier returned from the war. *One Wonderful Sunday* poses a direct critique, not only in regard to the struggle of postwar life, but also to the Allied attacks that contributed to that struggle. When *One Wonderful Sunday* is taken together with *Drunken Angel* (*Yoidore tenshi*, 1948), *The Quiet Duel* (*Shizukanaru kettō*, 1949) and *Stray Dog* (*Nora inu*, 1949), Kurosawa's films from 1947 to 1949 provide very strong commentaries indeed. The films are tied together by the concept of a 'postwar', the meaning of which Kurosawa explored and problematized through his main characters' struggle to establish a new identity suitable for postwar life. The foremost meaning of 'postwar' points to war itself – it is impossible to have a 'postwar' without a war. The focus on 'postwar' also points to Japan's coping mechanisms after a war which ended in defeat and occupation at the hands of the American and Allied forces. Even though Kurosawa did not explicitly show extended scenes of the processes of Occupation, these films may be seen as thematically exploring the 'occupied postwar', rendered invisible by the processes of censorship and self-censorship. This overriding focus on the problematic postwar, as well as the carefully constructed critique outlined above, leads us to the question of how *One Wonderful Sunday* was released in 1947. While a counter-discursive reading leads us to expect that the film would be censored, an examination of factors affecting censorship practice in 1947 locates the censors' decision in its historical context and reveals the problems inherent in such expectations.

Censorship and 'non-censorship': contextual considerations

Taking the context of the film from the censors' point of view, it is clear that CI&E officials and the Allied administration as a whole wanted to encourage the idea of a fresh start for Japanese people after the defeat. As the narrative of *One Wonderful Sunday* is based on the idea of hope, one can read the film as a positive contribution to Occupation ideals of democracy and freedom. The narrative also accords with specific suggestions on SCAP's list of possible ways in which filmmakers could assist with the objectives of the Occupation. The first suggestion, to 'show Japanese in all walks of life cooperating to build a peaceful nation' (SCAP 1945: 1.160), is upheld by Masako's appeal to the audience to support the young couples of Japan in living for their dreams. The fourth suggestion, to 'demonstrate individual initiative and enterprise solving the post-war problems of Japan in industry, agriculture and all phases of national life' (ibid.), is met by the couple's plans to open a café – fantasy or otherwise, their plan for a new life demonstrates initiative. The film also accorded with SCAP's wider aim of showing individual rights, in Masako's relationship with Yūzō, as she participates in decisions and argues with him on an equal footing. Further, the couple seem to be in love without concern for their parents' feudalistic or patriarchal values, coming together of their own free will. The couple's embraces would also have been encouraged at the time as a free expression of love.[23] All these points accord with SCAP policies of encouraging freedom, enterprise and individualism.

Moreover, the 'big picture' of rebuilding may have been more important to the censors than the way that Kurosawa constructed specific shots. Scenes showing crowded trains and discarded cigarette butts were far preferable to blatant depictions of guns, soldiers or military vehicles. One war orphan asking for food and being given that food to eat was similarly preferable to scenes 'overplaying starvation'. There are no injured people in the film or direct discussion of the bombing that created the ruins in the city. While the entire narrative may be read in terms of struggle, the struggle itself may be read as no bad thing – endurance and fortitude would be necessary for rebuilding the nation, so these values were to be encouraged. In fact, the very first summary of SCAP's non-military activities in Japan noted that, once the strict control of the Japanese government was removed, 'a trend towards liberal themes and films dealing with the problems facing Japan has been stimulated' (SCAP 1945: 1.158). Such 'problematization films' are given the longest descriptions and greatest praise in the SCAP reports,[24] and it seems that the Japanese people were encouraged to make sense of their country's difficulties through the narrative possibilities of film.

With regard to specific shots and scenes, the way we read the film now may also be very different to the way in which the censors saw particular details in 1947. As an example, Hirano lists the promotion of baseball as one of the American aims in overseeing postwar films, citing Kurosawa's *One Wonderful Sunday* as one of the films that fulfilled this aim (1992: 175). The baseball game in *One Wonderful Sunday* is played in a street obviously under construction, by a ragged group of urchins with a ball, a bat and a motley assortment of gloves and caps. CI&E officials and PPB staff may have wanted to read the scene in a particular way, as a promotion of baseball as a healthy, positive, fun exercise enjoyed by children and other members of Japanese society. It is possible to read this scene now in terms of critique, as it is difficult to ignore the fact that the children are dirty, their clothes are tattered, and the couple who join in are poor and hungry. Kurosawa may be making quite a negative statement on the presence of American soldiers in Japan – as a result of the Occupation, Japan has baseball, but no food or money – but the American censors chose to read the scene in a positive light.

In terms of practical considerations, 1947 was a transition year for the American censors, as censorship practice was shifting from pre-production to a post-production system (Dower 1999: 407). This shift would have made the censorship of any one film more open to interpretation than in a time when procedures were more clear-cut. Monica Braw also cites CCD directives to the censors reminding them that 'censorship is a matter of judgment'. There was not one singular, overarching, monolithic policy on censorship 'but many of them, written and unwritten, some of which changed from day to day, and were based upon censorship experience and current developments of the occupation' (Braw 1991: 74). One of the most contentious of these 'current developments' was the so-called 'Reverse Course', in which the Allies, concerned at the growth of Communist and Socialist ideals in postwar Japan, were forced to quash the more liberal interpretations of their encouragement of free speech (Hirano 1992: 3–4). Similarly, the ideal of free speech led to a fundamental paradox in which censorship itself challenged the primary ideal of freedom so valued by the American administration. Anxiety over censoring free expression may have led some censors to be more lax than others (Braw 1991: 148–9).

Other practical details concerned the censors as individual people, working to strict schedules and deadlines. The offices of the CCD were responsible for checking a wide variety of materials. Takamae's history of GHQ activities notes that in mid-1947, the PPB was screening 'on a *monthly* basis (pre- and post-publication) 16 news agencies, 69 daily newspapers, 11,111 non-daily news publications, 3,243 magazines, 1,838 books, 8,600 radio programs, 673 films, 2,900 drama scenarios and 514 phonograph records' as well as *kamishibai* storytelling shows (2002: 387, emphasis in original). Even for those working primarily on films, the amount and variety of material submitted was daunting: the SCAP records of synopses, scenarios and complete films submitted for review by the various film studios every month include not only feature films but also shorter comedy reels, newsreels and educational films. CCD officials also had to sift through old prewar films for either banning or re-release, as well as importing American films and arranging their Japanese subtitles.[25] Censors depended on translators to provide English scripts, which took time. Further, while it was possible to notice large sections of films or lines of written dialogue which were obviously flouting Press Code protocols, these censors worked without the benefit of the pause, rewind and replay functions of video technology, and did

146   *R. Hutchinson*

not have the academic luxury of sitting back and analyzing the *mise-en-scène* of every shot. Films with the most noticeable images or extreme viewpoints would take up most of the censors' time, attention and resources, while films with an overall positive message would be seen in a more forgiving light.

In comparison to other films made around the same time, *One Wonderful Sunday* was more artistic than many of the cruder pro-democracy propaganda films being produced, and fitted well with those films that thoughtfully explored the ideas of democracy, individuality and living in a free world. Among the more mature films of 1946, Hirano lists Imai Tadashi's *People's Enemy* (*Minshu no teki*), Kinoshita Keisuke's *Morning of the Osone Family* (*Osone-ke no asa*) and Kusuda Kiyoshi's *As Long as I Live* (*Inochi ga aru kagiri*) (1992: 152–3). We have already seen that the screenwriter for *Morning of the Osone Family*, Hisaita Eijirō, also worked on *No Regrets for Our Youth*. Kurosawa's collaborative links to such writers and producers who worked on 'pro-democracy' films would have further improved his image by association. At the other end of the comparative spectrum, *One Wonderful Sunday* was far milder than films which pushed SCAP policy to the limit. In the years 1946–7, Kamei Fumio's films *The Japanese Tragedy* (*Nihon no higeki*) and *Between War and Peace* (*Sensō to heiwa*) caused many problems for the censors. The first, a documentary charting Japan's descent into militaristic and fascist ideology responsible for the war, was initially welcomed by SCAP but then rejected and banned in August 1946 due to its disrespectful attitude to the Emperor, whose sovereignty SCAP had sworn to uphold. The second, a long feature film titled after Tolstoy's novel and co-directed with Yamamoto Satsuo, was also first praised by CI&E for its dedication to anti-militarism, but then rejected by CCD for its Communist implications (Dower 1999: 427–9; Hirano 1988). The changing aims and goals of SCAP affected not only the treatment of particular films during their production and release, but also the decisions of different departments in different ways. One aim that the entire administration could agree on was the suppression of documentary footage showing the after-effects of the atomic explosions in Hiroshima and Nagasaki (Braw 1991). The veiled references to the Occupation in *One Wonderful Sunday* paled in comparison to these direct affronts to SCAP regulations.

While the context of films made by other directors is important, it is difficult to overstate the impact of Kurosawa's own previous work in the reception of *One Wonderful Sunday*. Even though Kurosawa's wartime films *Sanshiro Sugata I* and *II*, *The Most Beautiful* and *Men Who Tread on the Tiger's Tail* were all ordered destroyed as examples of nationalistic and feudal propaganda in 1945, the promotion of *No Regrets for Our Youth* as Japan's first real 'democratic' film after the defeat labeled Kurosawa squarely as a 'pro-democracy' filmmaker, wiping out his militaristic image. Released eight months after *No Regrets for Our Youth*, *One Wonderful Sunday* is often discussed in terms of the earlier film. Kurosawa himself acknowledges the strong thematic link between the two films, as they explore two different sides of Japanese youth. Where *No Regrets* envisions an ideal image of youth, free from nationalistic concepts of honor and

Kurosawa Akira's One Wonderful Sunday   147

glory, *One Wonderful Sunday* brings us back to reality. As Kurosawa explains: 'for Japan's post-war youth to regain its life breath, it would have to endure yet more hard times. These would be the subject of my next film' (1983: 150). *One Wonderful Sunday* thus problematizes the ideals of *No Regrets for Our Youth*, portraying the struggle necessary merely to be 'a youth' in the cold climate of postwar Japan. While Kurosawa saw *One Wonderful Sunday* in terms of 'enduring hard times', however, the contemporary audience and censors of 1947 focused more on the idea of 'overcoming adversity' than on the adversity to be overcome, and it is the ideal vision of youth that has persisted in the critical imagination. By casting *No Regrets* as 'A case study of a "Democratization Film"', Hirano at once elevated it to the finest or most complete film of its type and limited its reading to that type only. As the label of 'democratization' director sits more comfortably with the image of Kurosawa as the humanist than as the militaristic or the counter-discursive director, it is the humanist image that dominates academic reception, lessening the probability that *One Wonderful Sunday* – or any Kurosawa film – will be read in terms of serious critique.

Conclusions

One Wonderful Sunday has been read as a 'democratization film' (Hirano 1992), as a critical failure (Richie 1996; Yoshimoto 2000) and as an expression of 'cinematic freedom' and the 'establishment of the self' (Yamada 1999). While I have read *One Wonderful Sunday* in terms of counter-discourse, the CI&E officials of 1947 welcomed it as a useful 'problematization film' that would inspire audiences and give them hope for the future. The widely varying reception of the film demonstrates the relativity inherent in the process of reading a text, dependent on the contextual location of the viewer. The difference in context may be spatial, as seen in the example of audience reaction to the *Unfinished Symphony* scene in Tokyo and Paris; temporal, as in the difference between the audiences of 1947 and today; or bureaucratic, as in the different standards applied to films by different offices within the SCAP administration. When and where the film is viewed, by whom and for what purpose, all affect the way the film will be read.

Any system of censorship is based on a particular set of values that come from a particular historical, political and social context. Our expectations and assumptions about censorship can tell us much about our own contemporary context, including its value system and the usefulness of our theoretical frameworks. Examining the most common expectations about censorship in the case study of Kurosawa's *One Wonderful Sunday* brings us to a reconsideration of binary terms – censorship and non-censorship, discourse and counter-discourse – as well as an appreciation of complexity and relationality in the censorship process. One of the most problematic assumptions surrounding Kurosawa's *One Wonderful Sunday* is the linkage of expected censorship outcomes to particular readings of the film. In the academic criticism, the reading of 'sweet and humanist' has been equated with 'mainstream discourse' and linked to the expected

148   *R. Hutchinson*

outcome of non-censorship, while the reading of 'subversive' or 'counter-discursive' has been linked to the expected outcome of censorship being enacted. This automatic linkage is problematic for a number of reasons. When we judge a film to be 'counter-discursive' and expect it to therefore be subject to censorship, we imply that the contemporary censors failed – not to censor the film, but to judge it in the same way that we have judged it. Whenever we ask questions about the censorship or non-censorship of a particular work from the past, such questions carry with them a value judgment which is invalidated by shifts in the values on which the judgment is based. Not only these values but also the methods and purposes of such judgment are shifting all the time, as we see in SCAP's transition from pre-production to post-production censorship in 1947. To expect a specific reaction from SCAP based on our own assessments of the film would therefore be both anachronistic and shortsighted.

Given the context outlined above, SCAP did read *One Wonderful Sunday* as a problematization of the postwar situation, but this was not taken as criticism of the Allied Occupation because SCAP actively encouraged films that showed the reality of rebuilding after the war. The binary system of expectation, pitting 'sweet, humanist and uncensored' against 'subversive counter-discourse, which should be censored', is proved false. Such a binary simplifies the films themselves by painting all films as either threatening or unthreatening to the administration, and it simplifies the censorship process by reducing it to a rubber stamp embossed with 'censor' or 'don't censor'. But CI&E and CCD had different outcomes in mind when previewing the films and screening them for prescriptive and proscriptive purposes. Similarly, a PPB censor charged with passing or failing a film according to a set of standards, and seeing the film in the context of a large number of other films made in the same year, would have a very different reaction to an audience member who saw films for pleasure a few times a year.[26] The reception and censorship of any particular film depends heavily on context. Once that context is taken into account, we cannot reduce censorship to such black and white decisions, but are made to recognize the complexity of the censorship process as a whole.

Analyzing our own expectations and how they arise from our own context is naturally very difficult, if not impossible. Part of the problem arises from using terms which have become loaded with particular expectations themselves. I have used the term 'counter-discourse' to indicate Kurosawa's critical stance in problematizing his contemporary situation, and his critical opposition to the reigning 'discourse' of the Allied Occupation. However, the discursive practice of Occupation censorship was clearly strong enough to allow oppositional utterances on the margins of power, as long as that power remained unthreatened. My reading of *One Wonderful Sunday* as a 'counter-discursive film' does locate the film on the margins of power, but in no way negates or lessens the power of the reigning discourse. Conversely, it should be emphasized that the reaction of the 'discourse' to the 'counter-discourse' in no way negates the oppositional aspects of the counter-discursive text. This becomes significant for censorship studies when we consider the order in which works are censored and discussed in the critical literature. Too often we label an artist as 'counter-discursive' as a result of their being censored or banned. But a work can be 'counter-discursive' without censorship ever being involved. Examining works which have not been censored, and the process of 'non-censorship', can tell us much about the censorship system that we might not see if we concentrate only on censored works.

Terms such as 'discourse' and 'counter-discourse' are binary in nature, lending an equally binary cast to discussions of the censorship process. However, both terms are merely useful tools to discuss social interactions and power dynamics. In the case of Occupation censorship of Japanese films, 'discourse' and 'counter-discourse' are represented by 'Occupation forces' and 'Japanese filmmakers', where both sides coexist, are complicit with each other and are complex entities in their own right. Both groups are made up of factions and individuals, each with their own aims, motivations and problems, who may be at odds with each other at any time. The human specifics of social power give the lie to a monolithic, all-powerful 'discourse' which artists must meet with either resistance or compliance.[27] Perhaps a better way to think of censorship is in terms of inter-discursive space, where negotiation and complicity are the norm. This does not eliminate the terms 'discourse' and 'counter-discourse', both of which remain useful, but does draw our attention to the possibilities of human action, expression and choice in a more relational framework. More importantly, it disposes of the arbitrary linkage of 'counter-discourse' with 'censorship' and 'mainstream discourse' with 'non-censorship', instead placing the entirety of the censorship process in the in-between, contextualized space.

Notes

1 The story of *One Wonderful Sunday* may be based on D.W. Griffith's *Isn't Life Wonderful* (1912) (Richie 1996: 43; Yamada 1999: 74), but it is likely that Kurosawa was also influenced by Frank Capra's style (Richie 1996: 45).

2 While SCAP technically stands for 'Supreme Commander for the Allied Powers', referring to the person or office of General Douglas MacArthur, the acronym is generally used to refer to the administration in its entirety (see Hirano 1992: 3). The term points to the US rather than to the other Allied powers, and many critics refer to the occupation of Japan as the 'American Occupation', Hirano's rationale being a typical example (1992: 3). However, this usage not only minimizes the contribution of the other Allied powers, but overemphasizes the binary US–Japan relationship at the expense of other interactions in the period. I will therefore attempt to differentiate between SCAP's censorship offices, staffed mainly by American personnel, and the Allied forces as a whole, by referring to the 'American film censors' and the 'Allied Occupation'.

3 The PPB also issued monthly guidelines of taboos known as 'key logs' (Mayo 1991: 137). On the goals and responsibilities of the various offices involved in Occupation censorship, see Takemae (2002); also Braw (1991: 21–31), Dower (1999: 407–8), Hirano (1992: 6) and Mayo (1991: 136–8). On the prohibitions and enforcement of the Press Code in regard to film, see Braw (1991: 41), Hirano (1992: 36–7, 44–5) and Dower (1999: 410–15).

4 Dower explains this invisibility and its ramifications (1999: 407–10, 431–2).

5 A similar question was asked by Edward Fowler in his investigation of 'How Ozu Does a Number on SCAP' (2001).

150   *R. Hutchinson*

6 *Men Who Tread on the Tiger's Tail* attracted attention from both the Japanese and American censorship systems in 1945: while Japanese censors objected to the 'mockery' of the kabuki classic, American censors found the film too feudal in its outlook. On the convoluted history of the film's banning and release, see Kurosawa (1983: 142–4), McDonald (1994: 171, 180) and Yoshimoto (2000: 94–5). On its intertextual references to *The Subscription List* and *Ataka* (*Ataka*), see McDonald (1994: 170–80) and Yoshimoto (2000: 107–13).

7 *A German at Daruma Temple* (*Daruma-dera no Doitsujin*) was selected by the studio but rejected by the censors (Kurosawa 1983: 117), while *A Thousand and One Nights in the Forest* (*Mori no sen'ichiya*) and *The San Paguita Flower* (*San Paguita no hana*) were both 'buried forever by the Interior Ministry censorship bureau' (Kurosawa 1983: 118).

8 *Snow* (*Yuki*) and *All is Quiet* (*Shizuka nari*) won prizes in a contest sponsored by the Ministry of Information (Kurosawa 1983: 116).

9 Kurosawa expected the script of *Three Hundred Miles Behind Enemy Lines* (*Tekichū ōdan sanbyaku-ri*) to have an enthusiastic response, as the action-adventure set in the Russo-Japanese War told the story of a hero still alive and fighting in the Pacific theater: 'I had calculated that with this kind of subject and support the censors in the Ministry of the Interior were not likely to complain' (1983: 120). While the film would undoubtedly have been useful for propaganda purposes, it was rejected by Tōhō as too ambitious a project for an inexperienced director.

10 Hirano (2001: 223–4) compares Kurosawa's ambivalent statement with the agonized soul-searching of Itami Mansaku, who despite a similar level of complicity with wartime militarism was far more critical of himself and others after the war ended.

11 Daiei's *The Last Nationalist* is praised as 'technically the best moving picture produced since the Occupation' (SCAP 1945: 3.180); Shōchiku's *Victory of Women* is mentioned twice, as 'an outstanding treatment of the theme of equality of women' (SCAP 1946: 7.18) and 'the first feature produced which dramatically embodies the concept of women's equality with men' (SCAP 1946: 7.269).

12 This film is praised by SCAP as 'the story of a family during the later war years [showing] how the Japanese attitude changed from support of the war and its objectives to a complete renunciation' (SCAP 1946: 5.276).

13 Interviewed in 1991, Kurosawa lamented continued taboos on subjects such as the Emperor and contemporary politics, and complained about increased studio control (Schilling 1999: 58–9).

14 Kurosawa is referring to George Gercke, head of the Motion Picture and Drama branch of CI&E from November 1946 to 1952 (Hirano 1992: 102–3; Takemae 2002: 184).

15 Kurosawa's self-reflexivity is discussed in Hutchinson (2006: 174–7).

16 Dower reports that chaotic scenes of crowded trains were the subject of popular children's games in 1947, as children reenacted the postwar confusion through play (1999: 112).

17 I use the term *mise-en-scène* in the narrower sense of staging or the framing of shots, rather than the overarching sense of a particular director's 'signature style' or 'authorial sign'.

18 I have noticed that American undergraduate students shown this film tend to laugh at this scene and utter the word 'trash' out loud. Whether they are laughing at the incongruous effect of English in a Japanese film or at the humorous associations of 'trash' in a supposedly romantic farewell scene, it is noteworthy that the effect of the word is strong enough to produce a verbal response.

19 A striking example is the English sign in Shimizu Hiroshi's *Children of the Beehive* (*Hachi no su no kodomotachi*, 1948), stating 'This Area Off Limits to Occupation Personnel By Order of the Provost General' (Hirano 1992: 278 n35).

20 Higuchi notes the significance of framing in *One Wonderful Sunday* when only the

couple's feet are shown on the crowded streets, citing this as an example of the impact Kurosawa could produce with his framing technique (1999: 162).

21 See Dower, ch.3: '*Kyodatsu*: Exhaustion and Despair' (1999: 87–120).

22 The title of the work is *Symphony no. 8 in B minor*, which Schubert started in 1822 but left unfinished, hence the popular appellation.

23 See Hirano on the vogue for 'kissing films' (1992: 154–62), although suggestions of salaciousness due to American influence were discouraged (Dower 1999: 430).

24 These films may be given long descriptions for two reasons: to chart the development of desirable themes in the Japanese motion picture industry and to provide sufficient information for the careful monitoring of possibly inflammable topics.

25 Confiscation of banned films was conducted by a separate unit of CCD. Films made during the period 1931–45 deemed militaristic or ultra-nationalistic were listed by title, banned, confiscated and destroyed except for four copies of each text, which were sent to the US. A good summary of the variety of activities undertaken with regard to motion pictures is found in SCAP's summation journal (1945: 2.173).

26 Context also applies to our own current modes of viewing the film: for pleasure, or as part of a syllabus addressing Japanese censorship. My students saw the film in the latter context, which serves as a caveat to my observations on student reactions to it.

27 Haraszti (1987) claims the 'classical' model of censorship based on suppression and resistance is based on no more than a rumor, while Post (1998) describes how the classical model is giving way in recent scholarship to more Foucauldian models of dispersed social power.

References

Braw, Monica (1991) *The Atomic Bomb Suppressed: American Censorship in Occupied Japan*, Armonk, NY: M.E. Sharpe.

Davidson, James F. (1972) 'Memory of Defeat in Japan: A Reappraisal of Rashomon', in Donald Richie (ed.), *Focus on Rashomon*, Eaglewood Cliffs, NJ: Prentice-Hall International, 119–28.

Dower, John W. (1999) *Embracing Defeat: Japan in the Wake of World War II*, New York and London: Norton.

Fowler, Edward (2001) 'Piss and Run: Or How Ozu Does a Number on SCAP', in Dennis Washburn and Carole Cavanaugh (eds.), *Word and Image in Japanese* Cinema, Cambridge: Cambridge University Press, 273–92.

Galbraith, Stuart (2001) *The Emperor and the Wolf: The Lives and Films of Akira Kurosawa and Toshiro Mifune*, New York and London: Faber and Faber.

Haraszti, Miklós (1987) *The Velvet Prison*, trans. Katalin Landesmann and Stephen Landesmann with Steve Wasserman, New York: Basic Books.

Higuchi, Naofumi (1999) *Kurosawa Akira no eigajutsu* (Kurosawa Akira's Film Technique), Tokyo: Chikuma Shobō.

Hirano, Kyoko (1988) 'The Japanese Tragedy: Film Censorship and the American Occupation', *Radical History Review*, 41: 67–92.

Hirano, Kyoko (1992) *Mr Smith Goes to Tokyo: Japanese Cinema under the American Occupation, 1945–1952*, Washington, DC: Smithsonian Institution Press.

Hirano, Kyoko (2001) 'Japanese Filmmakers and Responsibility for War: The Case of Itami Mansaku', in Marlene J. Mayo and J. Thomas Rimer (eds., with H. Eleanor Kerkham), *War, Occupation, and Creativity: Japan and East Asia 1920–1960*, Honolulu: University of Hawai'i Press, 212–32.

Hutchinson, Rachael (2006) 'Orientalism or Occidentalism? Dynamics of Appropriation in Akira Kurosawa', in Stephanie Dennison and Song-Hwee Lim (eds.), *Remapping*

152   *R. Hutchinson*

World Cinema: Identity, Culture and Politics in Film, London and New York: Wallflower Press, 165–79.

Kurosawa, Akira (1983) *Something Like an Autobiography*, trans. Audie Bock, New York: Vintage.

Kurosawa, Akira (2007) [1947] *One Wonderful Sunday*, DVD. Toho/Criterion Collection: Eclipse Series 7 'Postwar Kurosawa'.

Mayo, Marlene (1991) 'Literary Reorientation in Occupied Japan: Incidents of Civil Censorship', in Ernestine Schlant and J. Thomas Rimer (eds.), *Legacies and Ambiguities: Postwar Fiction and Culture in West Germany and Japan*, Washington DC: Woodrow Wilson Center; Baltimore and London: Johns Hopkins University Press, 135–61.

McDonald, Keiko (1994) *Japanese Classical Theater in Films*, London and Toronto: Associated University Presses.

Post, Robert C. (1998) 'Censorship and Silencing', in Robert C. Post (ed.), *Censorship and Silencing: Practices of Cultural Regulation*, Los Angeles: Getty Research Institute for the History of Art and the Humanities, 1–12.

Prince, Stephen (1999) *The Warrior's Camera: The Cinema of Akira Kurosawa*, revised and expanded, Princeton: Princeton University Press.

Richie, Donald (1996) *The Films of Akira Kurosawa*, 3rd edn., Berkeley, Los Angeles and London: University of California Press.

Rubin, Jay (1985) 'From Wholesomeness to Decadence: The Censorship of Literature under the Allied Occupation', *Journal of Japanese Studies*, 11(1): 71–103.

Satō, Tadao (1969) *Kurosawa Akira no sekai* (The World of Kurosawa Akira), Tokyo: San'ichi Shobō.

SCAP (Supreme Commander for the Allied Powers) General HQ, Statistics and Reports Section (1945) *Summation of the Non-Military Activities of the Occupation of Japan and Korea*, vols. 1–3.

SCAP (Supreme Commander for the Allied Powers) General HQ, Statistics and Reports Section (1945–7) *Summation of the Non-Military Activities of the Occupation of Japan*, vols. 4–27.

Schilling, Mark (1999) *Contemporary Japanese Film*, New York and Tokyo: Weatherhill.

Takemae, Eiji (2002) *Inside GHQ: The Allied Occupation of Japan and its Legacy*, trans. Robert Ricketts and Sebastian Swain, New York and London: Continuum.

Yamada, Kazuo (1999) *Kurosawa Akira: hito to geijutsu* (Kurosawa Akira: The Man and the Art), Tokyo: Shin-Nihon Shuppansha.

Yoshimoto, Mitsuhiro (2000) *Kurosawa: Film Studies and Japanese Cinema*, Durham, NC: Duke University Press.

9 Censoring Tamura Taijirō's *Biography of a Prostitute* (*Shunpuden*)

Eleanor Kerkham

The novelist Tamura Taijirō (1911–83) deserves attention not only for his insights into sexuality, for which he is almost exclusively known, but also for his reflections on the contradictions and human effects of war, on Japan's use of Korean women as members (to use his term) of the 'young girls' army', and on the interrelationships of gender, class, and ethnicity in the Imperial Japanese army during the Asia-Pacific War.[1] I focus here on one short novel, *Biography of a Prostitute* (*Shunpuden*). Tamura began the work soon after his repatriation to Japan in February 1946, following almost seven years as an ordinary fighting soldier in North China, from 1939 to 1945. In April 1947, in accordance with established SCAP Press Code censorship procedures, the editors of the journal *Japanese Fiction* (*Nihon shōsetsu*) submitted galleys of their premier issue to the Publications unit of the Publications, Pictorial, and Broadcasting Division (PPB) of the Civil Censorship Detachment (CCD).[2] *Biography of a Prostitute* was its lead story.[3] The novella was illustrated by a well-known artist, Ihara Usaburō (1894–1976), whose sketches of voluptuous, naked women sitting around languidly in sumptuous, boudoir-like chambers, occupy over five pages of the twenty-nine-page, double-column text (see Figure 9.1).[4] The *Japanese Fiction* editors were ordered to remove Tamura's story, and the volume appeared in May with a work by Sakaguchi Ango as substitute.[5] The complex process of the *Biography*'s deletion reveals the inner workings of PPB and the uses, abuses, and difficulties of a censorship procedure set up by the Allied Occupation as part of its comprehensive attempts to control and reshape a defeated Japan. Viewing the suppression of this story from the perspective of the censors and of the lives of the young Korean women whose story Tamura wished to tell, provides insight into the effects of not only silencing a concerned writer, but also quietly covering up a war crime of broad significance and erasing from the public sphere images of abused and eminently worthy Korean women.

A truncated writing career

Tamura began his publishing career as a university student in the early 1930s.[6] Through the 1930s he associated with several different literary societies, editing and publishing essays and stories in a variety of coterie journals. While influenced

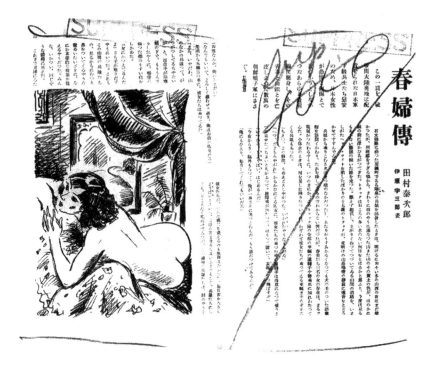

Figure 9.1 Suppressed *Shunpuden*, opening pages with Prologue and Ihara illustration. (Prange Collection galley.)

by Socialist thought and by the debates over politics and literature which were part of his historical era, Tamura's primary concern during his prewar career appears to have been to gain a place in the Tokyo literary world as a serious, modernist writer. With the publication of a series of works dramatizing student life and the lives of women employed in Tokyo's small cafés and bars, he had, by the late 1930s, gained recognition as a promising young writer. In 1940, at the age of twenty-nine, he was drafted into the army and sent to the China front.

After his repatriation to occupied Japan in February 1946, Tamura returned to his home, Yokkaiichi City, Mie Prefecture. Six months later he made his way back to Tokyo to resume a literary career profoundly influenced by his war experiences and by the realities of a devastated Tokyo.[7] Installments of his first two postwar novels, *Devil of the Flesh* (*Nikutai no akuma*) and *Gate to the Flesh* (*Nikutai no mon*), were serialized beginning in September 1946 and March 1947 respectively.[8] The setting of the first was the China front. He focused here on a Chinese prisoner of war – a woman suspected by the narrator of being a Communist operative. In a 1964 autobiographical essay Tamura states that the novel was based on his own experiences, and that it was the Chinese woman's extreme hatred of Japanese men, as well as her refusal to compromise her political ideals,

Censoring Tamura's Biography of a Prostitute   155

which motivated him to try to understand this female soldier's way of thinking.[9] In *Gate to the Flesh*, Tamura's most famous fictional work, the author's eye is on the lives of young streetwalkers or 'pan-pan' girls attempting to survive in a ravaged Tokyo immediately after the war's end. The work's vivid images of women openly defying conventional norms of behavior, and its descriptions of harsh, often violent human interaction attracted a wide audience. It became an instant bestseller and was soon adapted to stage and film.

The *Japanese Fiction* issue featuring *Biography of a Prostitute* was submitted for publication the same month that *Devil of the Flesh* and *Gate to the Flesh* came out in book form, April 1947. As in the first two works, Tamura focused on another spirited woman – a young Korean who is recruited and transported by the Japanese army to a remote mountain town on the Chinese fighting front.[10] Two years earlier, the girl had been sold by destitute parents to a house of prostitution in the Chinese city of Tienjin. Deceived by a young Japanese businessman whom she had hoped to marry, Harumi (the Japanese name assigned to her) impulsively volunteers for the new assignment. She and two friends also recruited by the Japanese army are placed in one of the two army-controlled brothels in Yu Xian, a remote castle town occupied by Japanese troops. The women are expected to service ten to twenty soldiers during the daytime, a non-commissioned officer or two in the early evening, and, if called on, an officer through the night. The feisty, outspoken Harumi, described by the narrator as 'having the type of face which appealed to Japanese men', attracts the attention of the cruel Company Aide-de-Camp, Lieutenant Narita. He decides, based on her reputation and on her open hatred of him, that she will be his companion each night. She is, however, strongly attracted to the officer's innocent young orderly, Mikami, and the two become secret lovers. After Mikami's imprisonment and release (when his shooting skill is needed in a night attack), he is wounded and abandoned by his comrades, whereupon Harumi faces enemy fire in order to find him. Both are taken captive by a Chinese Communist guerrilla band and are eventually returned to Yu Xian, where Mikami awaits court-martial. Unable to face the shame at having been taken prisoner by the enemy, the naïve country soldier persuades Harumi to steal a grenade. When she sees that he does not plan to escape with her as planned, she runs into his arms and the exploding grenade to die with him.[11] Mikami is reported as having died in battle; Harumi's ashes are scattered by her friends, and she is forgotten. While the *Japanese Fiction* version of *Biography of a Prostitute* was censored in its entirety, an apparently self-censored version, one in which the Korean women were transformed into Japanese women, was published in an anthology of Tamura's stories in May 1947.[12]

These three postwar works brought Tamura sudden monetary profits, eager publishers, public controversy, and the demand for more 'flesh stories'. Tamura took advantage of his name recognition and reputation as a writer of 'flesh literature' (*nikutai bungaku*) to produce within a three-year period over thirty-five works of fiction and numerous essays.[13] His fiction, journal articles, frequent interviews, and appearances in round-table discussions and public literary debates all helped to define him as the major *nikutai* writer and to promote what became his 'theory of the body' (*nikutai no ron*).[14] Critics suggest that Tamura's early postwar work soon lost the freshness and originality that characterized the three postwar novels named above.[15] After his popularity waned in the early 1950s, Tamura backed away from fiction for about ten years. When he returned in the early 1960s, his war memories became the basis of his work. According to his own account, these experiences and the themes they engendered – especially the relationships between the will to live, the sex drive, and death – called out for expression and held his attention for the rest of his writing career.[16] Tamura and his critics consider these works from the early 1960s to be his best. His prominent place in the postwar *nikutai* category of popular writers, however, and the continued assumption that he should be defined around this grouping, account in part for his relative critical neglect in Japan and in the West.

Suppressing *Biography of a Prostitute*

The usual censorship procedure for the Publications section of PPB was for Japanese nationals first to scan all materials for possible violations (see Figure 9.2). Suspect words or passages were circled and translations of worrisome portions, often with brief comments, were forwarded to one or several senior American censors who could assign a second or third re-examination. Occasionally, as in this case, chiefs of other divisions were consulted.

The first content sheet dealing with *Biography of a Prostitute*, checked as 'pre-censored' and dated 16 April 1947, was prepared in English by a Japanese examiner, Nakajima. It lists the table of contents of the April issue of *Japanese*

Figure 9.2 PPB examiners at work: Japanese nationals in print censorship scanning Japanese galleys, 1945 (General MacArthur's General Staff 1994: 237).

Censoring Tamura's Biography of a Prostitute   157

Fiction and calls attention to '*A story of a prostitute* (a novel)' as containing 'possible violations'.[17] A second five-page handwritten report by Nakajima, dated 17–18 April, begins with this translation of a portion of the *Biography*'s 'Author's Prologue':

> This story is dedicated to the Korean prostitutes who, counted by tens of thousands, went forward to the front lines on the battle fields of mainland China during the recent war. They having consumed their youth, destroyed their bodies at last.[18]

The word Nakajima translates as 'prostitutes', *jōshigun* (娘子軍, 'young girl's army'), is one of several euphemistic terms used by the Japanese military, this one as early as 1932, for groups of young, primarily Korean women supplied by the Japanese military to its troops in North China.[19]

Nakajima's report continues with this recommendation:

> As this statement indicates, this novel is a story of the Korean prostitutes at the fronts of the continent. Therefore it would better to be <u>suppressed</u> from the viewpoint of causing resentment of Koreans. And at the same time, from another viewpoint, as this story describes <u>the situations of the Japanese troops fighting against the Chinese armies and civilians</u> during the war, it is also objectional, I believe, despite of the author not intending to propagandize the militarism of the Japanese army.
>
> Even if the various parts objectional be deleted, the description of this story as a whole would suggest that the heroine is a Korean prostitute, though her name is called by the Japanese name 'Harumi'. For, the tendency of thinking of the heroine is somewhat different from the ordinary Japanese woman as to the customs and manner of her, through the narration of the author.

Nakajima's 'causing resentment of Koreans' is puzzling, given that Tamura (speaking in his own name in the author's prologue) dedicates the story to the 'tens of thousands' of Korean women who 'lost their youths and lives' serving the Japanese army, and that the story's unidentified narrator expresses only admiration for his Korean heroine. In the second paragraph Nakajima argues for complete rather than partial suppression because the story focuses throughout on a Korean prostitute and too much would have to be deleted given that 'the objectional parts scattered in various pages are counted to about thirteen pages totaled more than 100 columns'.

Nakajima objects first to the narrator's introduction to the three Korean women being transported in army trucks to the frontlines (p. 16):

> Harumi was born at the town of the neighborhood of Heijō in Korea, and Yuriko and Sachiko were born at Heian-Hokudō. They have true Korean names, of course, but they used the Japanese names since they <u>had been sold</u>

158   *E. Kerkham*

to the Akebono-cho in Tientsin on account of the poverty of their families in their native places.[20]

Nakajima's concern could be that Korean parents sold their daughters, although he seems to be most bothered by the fact that the three are clearly identified as Korean. His next example helps explain his concern that readers will think of the heroine as 'somewhat different from the ordinary Japanese woman', thanks to the way the author's narration presents her 'customs and manner':

> These women lived in unsophisticated naiveté – when happy, they would belt out a song, and when sad they would weep out loud. They possessed an extraordinary sort of passion. This was not something which came from logical reasoning or from knowledge found in books. It was a fierce life ideology, which they hammered out with their bodies. When their bodies liked something, they accepted it with complete abandon; when their bodies disliked a thing they rejected it completely. The intensity of their expression revealed the intensity of the life force within their bodies. The bodies of these women who ate garlic and red hot peppers, their very flesh and bones, contained a relentless, sharp will. And even after the strongest of passions, which might flare up following that will, they experienced no remorse. These were perhaps special ethnic characteristics of these women.[21]

While the narrator seems to find the women fascinating due to their ethnic differences, Nakajima is apparently worried because they are identifiably different, i.e., Korean.

Nakajima lists next a portion of a conversation among Japanese soldiers just after their truck convoy had been stopped by a land mine: '...We must fetch some persons [Chinese villagers] and butcher them! Look! They [Chinese villagers] look with an indifference' (Nakajima's translation and brackets). The conversation dramatizes a Japanese soldier's general willingness to murder Chinese civilians who may have 'indifferently' planted landmines. Nakajima notes: 'Underlined portion—Causes resentment of Chinese—'. Again, it is unclear whether Nakajima worries about stirring up 'resentment of Chinese' because they planted mines, or whether, as we might expect, Chinese will resent the fact that Japanese soldiers speak of butchering villagers.

Nakajima next translates a conversation between Harumi and the abusive Aide-de-Camp in which he calls her a 'Korean whore' (*Chōsen pii*), unworthy of considering herself a subject of the Japanese Emperor. The Lieutenant has forced his way into Harumi's room (a non-commissioned officer is there in her bed), and when she tells him to get out he responds (p. 22):

> 'Stupid bitch! What's a Korean whore like you talking about?'
>   Hearing this Harumi trembled and flushed red with uncontrollable anger.
> 'Korean? Korean you say? Wha'da ya mean? We have the same Emperor'.
>   She was agitated and deeply disturbed, but she knew the effect of these

words. This was not a phrase Harumi thought up on her own. These women used it time and again against Japanese men in all sorts of places and in many different situations. It was simply a kind of ethnic counter attack. Usually when they said this, the men would shut up.

'You fool! You think the Emperor knows the likes of women like you?' Without warning, the lieutenant struck her down. 'You speak of the Emperor! A dirty slut like you. How dare you!'[22]

Nakajima's note that this section 'causes resentment of Korean' is once again illogical. The concern here could only be that the scene would cause resentment among Koreans of cruel, ethnocentric/sexist treatment by a Japanese officer.

In his or her fifth example Nakajima quotes from a section of the story in which a Chinese is depicted as being 'a spy of the Japanese army', which again '—Causes resentment of Chinese—' (p. 38). Nakajima reasons that exposing the fact that some Chinese spied for the Japanese during the war would cause 'resentment of Chinese', rather than, as we might expect, that it would cause Chinese to resent other Chinese who were collaborators. In these examples Nakajima is invoking the Press Code category, 'criticism of an ally'.

Finally, Nakajima adds an 'Ex's Note' in which s/he explains: 'In this part of the story, some passages from '*Senjin-kun*' or the Military Lore delivered by Tojyō [sic] Hideki is quoted. It is, of course, objectional' (pp. 40–1). Nakajima then translates in full the recited Military Lore. The fear here would be that a scene in which Japanese soldiers are reciting the Military Lore might foster militaristic ideas.

Re-examinations of the text

Senior censors in PPB who received the Nakajima report apparently had questions and sent it on to a second examiner who responds first to Nakajima's general category, 'criticism of Koreans'. Over the top and down the right side of the first page of Nakajima's report s/he has handwritten this objection to the suggestion to suppress (see Figure 9.3):

Can't tell for sure about this without reading entire story. It seems to deal with a Korean girl and a Japanese soldier who fell in love with each other and finally committed *shinju*. Story would be passable if this can be excluded from 'crit. of Korean' category. The story of the two is treated sympathetically.[23]

The nameless second examiner continues through Nakajima's five-page report, adding in its margins different objections: a question mark next to Nakajima's translation of the sentence 'That might be a character of their race'; and two 'OKs' for the Japanese soldier suggesting butchering Chinese villagers and the Chinese who spied for the Japanese. The conversation between Harumi and the Aide-de-Camp has a 'retranslated' (p. 22), and an 'OK' and 'pass' are placed on

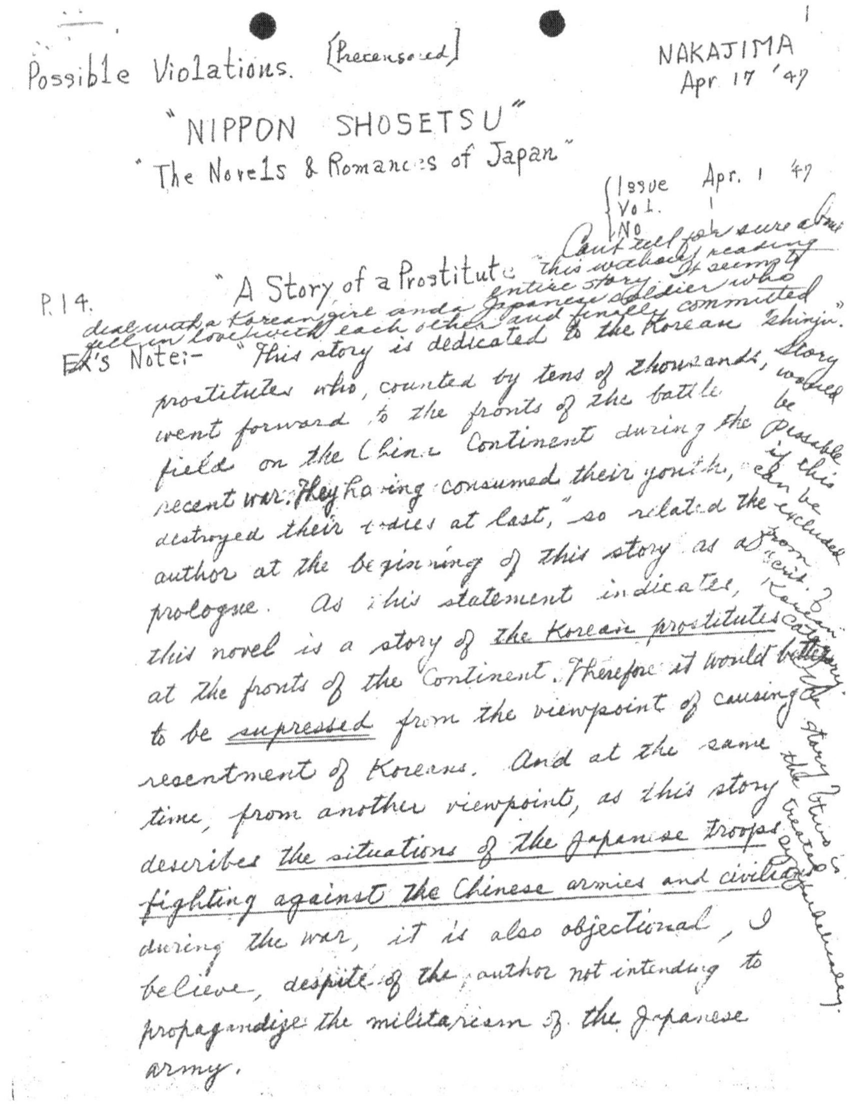

Possible Violations. [Precensored]   NAKAJIMA
                                     Apr 17 '47

"NIPPON SHOSETSU"
"The Novels & Romances of Japan"

(Issue   Apr. 1 47
 Vol.   1
 No.   1)

P.14.   "A Story of a Prostitute"

Ex's Note:- "This story is dedicated to tens of thousands,
prostitutes who, counted by tens of thousands,
went forward to the fronts of the battle
field on the China Continent during the
recent war. They having consumed their youth,
destroyed their ... at last," so related the
author at the beginning of this story as a
prologue. As this statement indicates,
this novel is a story of the Korean prostitutes
at the fronts of the Continent. Therefore it would ...
to be supressed from the viewpoint of causing
resentment of Koreans. And at the same
time, from another viewpoint, as this story
describes the situations of the Japanese troops
fighting against the Chinese armies and civilians
during the war, it is also objectional, I
believe, despite of the author not intending to
propagandize the militarism of the Japanese
army.

Figure 9.3 Nakajima report with second examiner's overlaid comments (National Archives II, RG 331, Box 8634, folder 25).

the Military Lore recitation (p. 40). This opinion is justified with these words written in the margin:

> The unit leader makes the soldiers recite this *Senjin–kun* after they receive news of the two lovers' 'shinju'. So the soldiers repeat it as ordered, but the 'I' who narrates the story cannot bring himself to censure the soldier or the girl.

Censoring Tamura's Biography of a Prostitute   161

Finally, in the left margin at the end of the Nakajima report, we find this query: 'Pass entire story?'

A handwritten document on the *Biography* dated 22 April 1947 identifies one K. Tsumura as a 're-examiner'. This suggests that it was s/he whose comments are on Nakajima's original report. The 22 April document reads as follows:

> 'A Life of a Prostitute'
> This short story narrates a miserable life of a Korean girl who followed the Japanese army to a firing line in Shansi Province as a drafted prostitute leading an abandoned life. She happens to come across a young Japanese soldier, unsophisticated and with 'Limpid eyes'. She feels a pure, uncalculating love toward him, and finally dies with the soldier when the latter has been severely wounded.
>
> Though our original examiner is prudent enough to recommend it to be suppressed in toto, I don't think it necessary to go so far. After the portions compromising the honor and integrity of Korea have been deleted,[x] the story may be permissible. The objectionable portions appear in the following pages:
>
> p. 14 (in the prologue) 'delete'
> p. 16 (upper & lower columns) 'ok'
> p. 20 (lower column)
> p. 22 (upper column)
> p. 25 (lower column)
> p. 34 (lower column)
> *x* or have been so altered as the reader cannot identify the heroine as Korean.

Tsumura's note (*x*) on 'compromising the honor and integrity of Korea' makes clear his or her belief, not stated elsewhere, that the women should not be presented as Korean. Thus the 'delete' for page 14, referring to 'Author's Prologue', would be crucial because the story is dedicated to all Korean 'comfort women.' The full Prologue reads:

> I offer this story to the tens of thousands of Korean women warriors who, to comfort lower ranked Japanese soldiers deployed to remote areas on the Asian mainland, risked their lives, losing their youths and their bodies on every possible battlefront, where Japanese women feared and disdained to go.
>
> (the author)[24]

Page 16 includes the narrator's introduction to the three Korean women being transported to the frontlines, translated above.[25] Page 20 describes the officers' attitudes towards the Korean women, as opposed to the attitudes of ordinary soldiers:

The officers had ample opportunity, under the pretext of the need for communications and such, to go to the towns along the railroad lines where there were Japanese women. There they could indulge in more humane delicacies. So for these men, playing with Korean women on the front lines was simply a physiological matter, like drinking a glass of sake or pissing. (Even if an ordinary soldier was sent into the towns along the railroad, with his one shoulder star and dirty, threadbare uniforms, he was despised and shunned by the Japanese women. Thus it was that all of the soldiers went to the Korean women, cursing the Japanese women as they went.)[26]

Page 22 represents the scene mentioned above in which Narita first bursts in on Harumi, insulting and striking her down. Page 25, lower column, includes several portions circled or crossed through on the galley copy. While it is unclear which sections Tsumura wished to delete, the most likely portion includes Harumi's feelings about sexual responses her body experiences when she is forced to sleep with the hated Aide-de-Camp and her memory of his earlier words, 'you're nothing but a Korean whore!'

The Aide-de-Camp's cruelty, expressed in the words 'You're nothing but a Korean whore', could not be opposed no matter what she might do. If she resisted him physically she would surely be defeated, and her body would then be given that pleasure about which she felt such shame. So every night she greeted the Aide-de-Camp in a blank stupor, as if she had already gone mad, feeling that her body was being forced to swim in dirty slime.

Tsumura is the only examiner to see as unacceptable portions of page 34, which include Harumi's memories of her native village in Korea:

The image of her mother and father in Korean dress floated up. She could hear the night music of the festival. It was the ancient Koguryo dance music. Scenes of the village shrine, where her parents had taken her to worship, drifted before her. Like a child she enjoyed the innocent memories and for several wonderful moments village scenes passed before her one after another.

The goal of this deletion is, of course, to erase her identity as Korean.

The 16 April information sheet discussed above, which lists journal title and table of contents, also has on it the handwritten words, 're-ex'd by K Tsumura numbers 2 & 6 only'. This further suggests that it was Tsumura whose handwritten comments are on the Nakajima report of 17–18 April.[27]

These two conflicting recommendations (either to delete the whole or to take out only suggested sections) prompted a third examination. An inter-office memo dated 24 April, sent by a JTF (probably examiner James Furukawa), to RRZ (Robert Zahn, Chief of PPB, District One, Tokyo) and VG (Victor

Censoring Tamura's Biography of a Prostitute   163

Groening, a senior censor who worked with Zahn) reveals that a third Japanese examiner, Mitsuoka, was next consulted.[28] The memo states: 'I had Mitsuoka look over this article and his comments is [*sic*] attached.' Mitsuoka's hand-written comments read:

1   This article depicts the tragic story of a Korean prostitute who killed herself together with a Jap. soldier in Chinese front. At the same time, it emphatically depicts the corruption of former Japanese army.
2   The article is written in sympathy with Korean prostitutes who were victimized by Japanese army. The general tone of the original version is pro-Koreans.
3   On the above grounds, it does not deserve suppression. I scanned this article. I think it can be passed with deletions.

These are followed by a two-page typed report, which begins:

'The Story of a Prostitute'
The story of the Korean prostitute is treated sympathetically and the whole story tends to be critical of the Japanese war of aggression, although there are no passages that can be labeled very anti-militaristic. However, there are a few passages which describe the superior attitude of the Japanese towards the Koreans. There seems to be no point in bringing this subject up at this time. It might aggravate the mutual resentment and/or hatred which some Koreans and Japanese feel.

Mitsuoka is the first to articulate the idea that dramatizations of Japanese ethnocentric attitudes of superiority towards Koreans might cause problems. He also argues, as did Tsumura, that the category 'criticism of Koreans' does not apply and that the story need not be removed.

Mitsuoka continues with a list of five sections recommended for deletion. Four of the five overlap with those named by Tsumura. Mitsuoka provides page numbers and brief translations of the offending passages. His first is the Prologue (he calls it a 'Dedication' and uses Nakajima's incomplete translation cited above). Thus all three examiners recommend deletion of the Prologue. The remaining common passages reveal Japanese attitudes towards the Korean women as of an inferior race/ethnicity. The third, for instance, from page 20, is that which deals with Japanese officers' and soldiers' contrasting attitudes towards the Korean women vis-à-vis professional Japanese women who work in Chinese 'towns along the railway'. The passage also depicts assumptions of superiority on the part of officers and of Japanese entertainment women towards ordinary soldiers. In his fourth example Mitsuoka translates more of Narita's violent response to Harumi's words, 'we have the same Emperor' (p. 22). Again, all three examiners saw his angry slur, 'You're nothing but a Korean whore', as unacceptable. Mitsuoka is the only examiner, however, who recommends that this speculation made later by the story's narrator be deleted:

164 *E. Kerkham*

Harumi did not understand the true nature of the Japanese Army – what they were trying to do in the depths of the continent and the good they had done. She did not understand why these young men submitted to the few who used them like beasts.

(p. 30)

Because Harumi did not understand the Japanese government's aims in China, she could not comprehend why Japanese soldiers, and particularly her own lover, had to accept abusive treatment from their superiors. This statement, which seems to signal the narrator's approval of 'the good' the Japanese had accomplished in China, might indeed have been construed as 'militaristic'.

At this point in the process, Robert Zahn and senior censor Victor H. Groening had three evaluations of the story – total suppression and two suggesting that certain passages, particularly those revealing discriminatory attitudes of the Japanese toward Koreans, should be deleted. These conflicting reports prompted a further check by Zahn with W. H. Fielding, identified in a later document as 'Chief of the Ryukyu-Korea Division, officer of the Executive Officer, chief of Staff'.[29] Zahn explains in a 28 April PPB 'Routing Slip' to his superior, Richard Kunzman,[30] that he considered the work to be too 'agitating':

Per check with Fielding, recommend suppression of the HELD article from Nippon Shosetsu. It deals with Korean prostitutes and Japanese soldiers during the war. Taichi Shobo publishes it. Original examiner suggested suppression, although re-examiners thought it was probably passable with deletions, particularly since it is more of a criticism of the Japanese army than of Koreans. It seemed to rather agitating [*sic*], however, so I asked Hank to check it with Fielding.[31]

This routing slip ends with a hand-written 'Suppress' and the initials RK (Richard Kunzman), which suggests that Zahn and Kunzman followed Fielding's recommendation. A 29 April 1947 'LOG OF STORIES REFERRED TO OR CHECKED WITH SCAP SECTIONS', signed RRZ, reveals Fielding's response:

SCAP Section(s), Person(s), and Title(s), Consulted:
Mr. W.H. Fielding, Chief of Ryukyu-Korea Division, Office of the Executive Officer, Chief of Staff

Action recommended by SCAP Section:
After reading the brief on the article, Mr. FIELDING stated: 'Leave this thing out! The mere mention of a Korean prostitute is dangerous, let alone the whole article.'

Action(s) taken: SUPPRESSED.[32]

Censoring Tamura's Biography of a Prostitute   165

The formal file report on this case of complete suppression dated 22 May 1947 has this heading:

'CCD, PPB District I, Press-Publications file report'
ACTION: Suppressed
REASON: Criticism of Koreans
MAGAZINE: Article in THE NOVELS AND ROMANCES OF JAPAN (Nippon Shosetsu) Published in Tokyo, April issue.
TITLE OF ARTICLE: 'The Story of a Prostitute' by Taijiro TAMURA.[33]

The report continues with an appended two-page typed summary of the story and ends with the name Kunzman listed as 'Examiner' with this note:

EXAMINER'S NOTE: Per check with Mr. W. H. Fielding, chief of Ryukyu-Korea Division, officer of the Executive Officer, chief of Staff.

The most revealing aspect of this instance of censorship in terms of SCAP's underlying aims and procedures is its final 'reason' for suppression as stated here. Nakajima, the first examiner, selected the categories 'criticism of Koreans', 'criticism of Chinese' (i.e., criticism of an ally) and militaristic propaganda as his/her reasons for complete suppression. Two subsequent readers suggested that the story did not fit these categories and should only be partially censored. As Tamura's prologue and the last two examiners' evaluations of the text suggest, 'criticism of Koreans' is inappropriate. The second and third examiners read the story 'more as criticism of the Japanese military than of Koreans' (Zahn). While it 'emphatically illustrates the corruption of the former Japanese army' (Mitsuoka), it suggests little that might be construed as criticism of Koreans. The story's narrator clearly admires the Korean woman whose life story Tamura is telling. She is depicted as a victim of several forms of Japanese violence and abuse – physical, psychological, and sexual. She alone runs into a fighting zone to save the life of her young Japanese lover, wounded and abandoned while defending his comrades; and only she finds ways to defy the cruel Aide-de-Camp and the Japanese army in her choice of whom to love, her theft of a grenade, plans for escape, and final desperate act of suicide.

Senior censors, however, chose Nakajima's 'criticism of Koreans' as the official reason for deletion. Did they believe that a masculinist, patriarchal Korean society would be criticized because selling a daughter was considered an acceptable way to relieve family poverty? Or would Korea's honor be damaged if it were known that its daughters were 'prostitutes'? Or was the desire to block the story related to the fact that officials in Occupied Japan were themselves indirectly involved in the control of Japanese women for the comfort and recreation of American forces?[34] (For this and other reasons, 'fraternization' was one of the unlisted but frequently employed grounds for censorship of written and other materials.) There is no indication that the problem of the use of Korean or other 'comfort women' was an open issue of concern to any of the parties involved

166   *E. Kerkham*

(Japanese, Korean, or American), and we are left with the question, why was 'criticism of Koreans' selected as the final, formal rationale for censoring the entire story?

A partially handwritten, partially typed draft of the 22 May final report in the Prange Collection sheds light on this question. It includes a three-page draft summary of the story with portions (words, phrases, and sentences) marked out on the typewriter or corrected by hand. The handwritten portion consists of the report's heading: 'SUPPRESSION REASON', 'MAGAZINE', 'TITLE OF ARTICLE'; plus its ending, 'EX. note'. After 'SUPPRESSION REASON', the words 'Incitement to Violence and Unrest' have been penciled out and 'Criticism of Koreans' written in by hand underneath. The document is not dated, but because it represents a draft of the Kunzman 22 May report, it would have to have been prepared between 29 April and 22 May. 'Incitement to violence and unrest' falls under SCAP's broad category, 'incitements to unrest or remarks disturbing to public tranquility'. Statements made by Mitsuoka, Zahn, and Fielding suggest that this was indeed the real reason for suppression. As Mitsuoka wrote:

> there are a few passages which describe the superior attitude of the Japanese towards the Koreans. There seems to be no point in bringing this subject up at this time. It might aggravate the mutual resentment and/or hatred which some Koreans and Japanese feel.

Zahn writes that the story is 'too agitating', and Fielding says emphatically: 'Leave this thing out! The mere mention of a Korean prostitute is dangerous, let alone the whole article.'

So why not retain 'Incitement to violence and unrest'? In the spring of 1947 SCAP officials and the Japanese government were indeed troubled by a complex 'Korean problem'. Large numbers of resident Korean nationals (close to 650,000, many of whom were forcibly brought to Japan as contract laborers during the 1930s and 1940s) had elected to stay in Japan rather than return to Korea. Other previously repatriated Koreans were attempting to return to Japan. Koreans were at odds among themselves along political and social lines and were agitating for the opportunity to work, for the right to have ethnically based educational institutions, for basic human rights, for legitimate legal standing or citizenship, and for protection both from hostile Japanese citizens and from the Japanese police. In addition, the Japanese government and Occupation authorities were clearly worried about what was perceived as unruly elements among different groups of Koreans.[35] Anxieties about 'incitement to unrest' were real. Occupation authorities did not want to stir up more feelings of resentment and hatred. And yet, they were also apparently not eager to have their own alarm about this danger become public knowledge. It was safer, perhaps, to appear to be concerned about their Korean allies. Perhaps it would have compromised 'the honor and integrity of Korea' (Tsumura) to reveal that Korean women had been sold by destitute parents. Or that young women had become, using CCD's term, 'prostitutes'. Fielding's words suggest that Occupation authorities did wish to

Censoring Tamura's Biography of a Prostitute   167

hide the fact that young Korean women had been used by the Japanese army to sexually service their fighting men. Whether actually concerned about such questions or not, it still appears to have been easier for Occupation officials to pretend to disallow criticism of an ally than to signal their apprehension about incitement to violence and unrest.

Book version of *Biography of a Prostitute*

One last document on the *Biography* case adds to its convolution. It suggests that the single volume collection of Tamura stories featuring *Biography of a Prostitute* was submitted to CCD's separate Book (as opposed to Magazine) Unit of PPB sometime late in 1946. The Prange Collection *Japanese Fiction* (*Nihon shōsetsu*) censorship file ends with the following brief, typed note, undated but signed VHG (Victor H. Groening):

> Shiro ITO came across a book in a book store 'A Story of a Prostitute' by Taijiro TAMURA, which was suppressed when it was presented in the magazine, NIPPON SHOSETSU, <u>May 47 issue.</u> It is a story about Korean prostitutes. Can you give any info concerning the book, was it censored, passed, or what?
>
> (VHG)

A cryptic, handwritten answer, apparently sent back to Groening on the original note reads simply: 'Passed, 2 Jan. 47!' As mentioned above, the Ginza Shuppansha anthology, entitled *Biography of a Prostitute* (*Shunpuden*), is dated May 1947 – the same month that *Japanese Fiction* was published without Tamura's story. It appears, then, that the Book Unit of PPB approved this collection of Tamura's short stories *before* the *Japanese Fiction* volume was submitted to the Magazine Unit. It includes seven other stories by Tamura, all but two of which were written, as he states in his introduction to the book, soon after his repatriation to Japan in 1946.[36] As mentioned above, the version of the *Biography* in this volume seems to have been self-censored by Tamura or his publisher. The story's 'Author's Prologue' is gone. Instead, in an introduction to the collection as a whole, Tamura comments briefly on each story. In his comments on the *Biography* he focuses on his warm feelings for 'frontline' women (not identified as Korean) and his resentment of Japanese women serving as pleasure workers for Japanese officers and businessmen in the cities:

> The story *Shunpuden* is a work of about 100 manuscript pages. During the war there were undoubtedly a great many women warriors (*jōshigun*) who, along with us lower ranked soldiers stationed deep in the Asian mainland, lived within gunfire and sacrificed their youths and their bodies, while held in contempt by Japanese officers and by the Japanese prostitutes serving as their war wives in the rear guard. The Japanese women, assuming they must not go out to the battlefields, conspired with officers and despised ordinary,

168   E. Kerkham

lower ranked soldiers. I have written this story with a heart wrenching longing towards those women warriors and with feelings of disdain toward the Japanese women.

(Tamura 1947: 1)

All uses of the word 'Korea' have been erased. Japanese readers or those (primarily men) familiar with the 'comfort women' system may have been aware that Tamura was referring to non-Japanese or Korean women, but his silencing of the women's voices as Korean, which continues through the narrative as a whole, erases images of women with special character traits which Tamura and his narrator admire. Harumi and her friends are now women from 'the peninsula' who were sold by poor parents to houses of prostitution in China. We are told that their birth names were changed to *genjina* (professional names given to bar hostesses and other entertainment women). Statements of cultural differences are removed – the women no longer eat 'garlic and red hot peppers'. Because Harumi and her colleagues are now not Korean, the issue of depicting discriminatory attitudes towards Koreans has disappeared; the Japanese military's attitudes towards Korean women as inferior female 'citizens' who could be used as needed are absent. With this de-Koreanization, the story would not have been tagged by the PPB book unit censors as 'criticism of Koreans' or as 'incitement to violence and unrest'. The author's emotional praise of the front-line women strengthens the impression that these less fortunate but more sensitive women kindly elected to comfort ordinary soldiers in dangerous areas. Because Korean voices are silenced, however, the impact of the story, originally dedicated to such women and centered on the snuffed-out life and unreported death of a vibrant Korean woman, is lessened, focusing rather on the author's resentment of the higher class professional Japanese women sitting snugly in the cities.

Reprints of the story in several different collections of Tamura's works from 1948 to 1949 reproduce this auto-censored account. Tamura's original text was, in fact, never published, so it is not surprising that stage and film adaptations of the work have replicated the transformation from Korean to Japanese women. The 1948 Tōhō stage production of *Shunpuden*, presented at the Tokiwaza in Tokyo, centers on a group of Japanese '*ianfu*' residing in two frontline brothels run by Japanese proprietors. The first film version, *Escape at Dawn* (*Akatsuki no dassō*, 1950), with original screenplay by Kurosawa Akira and Taniguchi Senkichi, went through at least seven revisions mandated by CI&E from September 1948 to January 1950. Even in its first disapproved script, however, Harumi was already a Japanese prostitute and by the time the film was released in 1950 she was a singer traveling with the Japanese military.[37] Director Suzuki Seijun's 1965 version, *Story of a Prostitute* (or *Joy Girls*), plays freely with Tamura's plot; Harumi is again a Japanese prostitute, and, as in *Escape at Dawn*, she and her lover die at the hands of the Japanese military.[38]

Tamura did not restore his original even after November 1949 when pre- and post-publication censorship ended. When he returned to fiction in the 1960s, however, he returned with a vengeance and with more skill as a writer to the

Censoring *Tamura's* Biography of a Prostitute   169

story of young Korean women sent to Japanese troops on the frontlines in his 1964 novel, *Locusts* (*Inago*) (Tamura 2005).[39] As if to signal the relationship between the two stories, he begins *Locusts* in exactly the same manner as *Biography of a Prostitute* – five women are being transported to a violent frontline world they had never imagined. Tamura eschews the romantic plot, however, to focus on the journey to camp and a Japanese sergeant's desperate and unsuccessful attempts to protect the women from multiple gang rapes by drunken Japanese troops, swarms of locusts, gunfire from American planes, and guerilla sniper fire. Charged with transporting the women and a trainload of bone boxes to his constantly moving unit, he manages to reach camp with only two of the five women. Romantic moments are gone (the woman to whom the sergeant is drawn is shot en route, and the party is forced to abandon her alive) and the only 'story' left of the women's lives is the description of a long, winding line of hot sweaty soldiers, each waiting his turn to alight for a few minutes on one of the two remaining women. The sergeant, patiently waiting his turn, sees the endless horde of soldiers as famished, locust-like creatures crawling between the women's legs.

Conclusion

Tamura was reaching the height of his popularity in the spring of 1947. His lead story in the inaugural issue of a respected literary journal would have provided prestige and a well-read audience. His name, along with Ihara's illustrations of ample, unclothed women, might have ensured greater circulation for the periodical, but it would also have placed Tamura with an impressive group of established writers, including Takami Jun, Dazai Osamu, Niwa Fumio, Hayashi Fumiko, Hayashi Fusao, and Mushakōji Saneatsu.

Twenty years of revelations and research on the 'comfort women' issue since the early 1990s has shown that the women, particularly those sent to the frontlines, were subject not only to daily sexual violence, but also to other physical and psychological abuse.[40] This form of violence against women was not named as a war crime and no individual in the Japanese military or government command was held to account at the Tokyo War Crimes Trials. Sexual slavery of this sort was not an issue in 1946–47. Although the narrators of *Biography of a Prostitute* and *Locusts* do not describe a direct military role in the original sale of the young Korean women from their homes to houses of prostitution in China, both works openly dramatize the direct role of the Japanese military in the women's subsequent induction for service on the front and transportation to frontline camps, as well as in their controlled, brutalized lives and unrecorded deaths in the service of swarms of frightened, roughened soldiers and of one specific sadistic officer.

Tamura's Prologue to the censored version of the *Biography* and his selection of the traditional term *den* (biography) in his title communicates the desire to re-create and dignify the 'lives', not just of one woman but of a larger group of ill-treated, forgotten women. At the same time Tamura also articulates the Japanese

170   *E. Kerkham*

military's and state's belief in the need for sexual relief of men in battle. Perhaps it was neither the supposed criticism of an ally, nor the fear of incitement to violence and unrest, which most bothered SCAP censors and officials. Occupation authorities were, it seems, not at all eager to have the topic of militarized sexual slavery become part of the public discourse. The original censorship action clearly interfered with a repatriated soldier/writer's attempts to shed light on an exploitative military practice, as well as to express strong personal emotions. Tamura's desire to give a voice and literary existence to the stolen 'youths and lives' of the 'tens of thousands' of young women in the 'Korean Girls' Army' was thwarted, but the curious case of the censorship of *Biography of a Prostitute* goes beyond the erasure of a single story and brings Tamura's original words back to a twenty-first century audience. It reveals a group of earnest examiners and censors who were not always aware of the meaning and significance of what they were reading, were sometimes uncertain of their goals, and were patriarchal and sexist in their assumptions about women's roles and duties. The complex censorship process illustrates the Occupation's media control, and at the same time exposes the mutual racism/ethnicism of the occupied and occupiers. The Japanese examiners were thoughtful and careful. The senior censors were cautious, and they were also willing to use their power to push a subject deemed 'dangerous' aside and to disguise their reasons for doing so. The censorship of *Biography of a Prostitute* not only affected the career and critical reception of Tamura Taijirō, but also contributed significantly to the shape of postwar Japanese discourse, both on Korean-Japanese relations and the broader issues of 'comfort women' and human rights.

Notes

1 Reprints of Tamura's works were not easily available after the late 1960s until 2005 when a five-volume collection appeared, *Tamura Taijirō senshū*, ed. Hata and Onishi (hereafter *TTS*). Onishi touches briefly on Tamura's relative critical neglect and possible reasons for it in his introductory essay (*TTS* 5: 217–18). For studies in Japanese see *TTS* 5: 281–3; on Tamura's war literature and his experiences as a soldier in China see Onishi (2008). Rubin (1985: 82–4) and Dower (1999: 157–8) discuss Tamura briefly in connection with postwar pulp literature. For more extensive considerations of his 'theory of the body' (*nikutai no ron*) and immediate postwar fiction see Kerkham (2001: 325–55) and Slaymaker (2004: 43–70).

2 Mayo (1991: 135–61) discusses SCAP (Supreme Commander for the Allied Powers) pre- and post-publication censorship procedures and regulations, the Press Code and its prohibited topics, and the organization of the Civil Intelligence Section of which CCD was a part. As Mayo indicates, 'the unit responsible for preventing the mass media from carrying materials harmful to the goal of demilitarization and democratization was the Press, Publications, and Broadcasting Division, or PPB...' (136).

3 The volume was the first of a renamed journal (formerly *Puromete*, meaning 'Prometheus'). See PPB Routing Slip, 28 April 1947, listing violations from the March *Puromete* and the upcoming May *Japanese Fiction* volume examined here: National Archives II, RG 331 (SCAP), Box 8634, folder 25. *Biography of a Prostitute* is twice the length of all but one other piece of fiction in the issue, most of which were installments of serialized fiction by well-known authors. The term *shunpu* (春夫, spring

spouse) is first used in Yokomitsu Riichi's novel *Shanghai* (1928–29) to identify primarily Russian women working as prostitutes in Shanghai in the 1920s. The term would have signaled to a postwar Japanese audience a prostitute or entertainment woman. The classical term *den* (伝) (to pass down or narrate a significant story) was used originally for biographies of important men.

4 A frequent producer of propagandistic art during wartime, Ihara was associated with a conservative group of artists popular in the immediate postwar period (Winther-Tamaki 2003: 348).

5 The Japanese galley proofs of the complete story and the partially complete PPB censorship files for this issue of the journal are in the Prange Collection, University of Maryland, College Park, MD; *Japanese Fiction*, April and May 1947. The May volume presents Sakaguchi's *Incident of a Discontinuous Murder* (*Furen satsujin jiken*) as lead story.

6 For more on Tamura's early literary career, see Onishi (*TTS* 5: 217–36, 255–72) and Kerkham (2001: 321–3).

7 For more on Tamura's postwar career see *TTS* 5: 237–53; Kerkham (2001: 323–5), and Slaymaker (2004: 41–70).

8 *Devil of the Flesh* appeared in the journal *World Culture* (*Sekai bunka*) and *Gate to the Flesh* in *Gathering Images* (*Gunzō*). For originals and brief commentary on each see *TTS* 2: 84–120 and 355–7; *TTS* 3: 28–54 and 334–6.

9 In 'The Woman who was Destroyed' (*Chūō kōron*, January 1964), Tamura writes that the Chinese heroine in *Devil of the Flesh* was based on a Chinese Communist prisoner with whom he had had a brief relationship. The essay is reprinted in *TTS* 2: 335–46.

10 On the system of 'comfort stations' set up and run by the Japanese military during World War II, see Yoshimi (2000: 88–9) and Soh (2008: 124–5). The situation described by Tamura closely matches Soh's 'embedded girls' army', in which women were 'kept within a military compound' usually located in remote frontline areas; and Yoshimi's 'military comfort stations directly managed by the military for the exclusive use of military personnel and civilian military employees'. For an analysis of the implications of the use of comfort stations as violations of international law and basic human rights, see Yoshimi's ch. 5, 'Violations of International Law and War Crime Trials'.

11 Their deaths, characterized as a 'love suicide' (*shinjū*) by Occupation censors (see below), should not be defined as such, since Mikami did not plan to allow Harumi to die with him.

12 The volume is in the Prange Collection.

13 Ōkubo Tadashi (1959: 80–81, 86) presents useful lists regarding these stories, including titles, types of leading male (for instance, criminal, soldier, black marketeer, writer, rapist) and female (prostitute, office girl, dancer, waitress, madam, mistress, pickpocket, and others) characters, types of relationships between the two, and presence of sexual material. This provides insight into Tamura's reputation as a 'lascivious literary writer' (Takayama 1948; see Tamura Yasujiro, first page, paragraph 2, 'records of writers', RG 331, Box 8593).

14 For more on Tamura's theories on the body and sexuality as expressed in the *Biography*, see Kerkham (2001: 325–35) and Slaymaker (2005: 41–70). On the 'flesh literature boom' and its sudden popularity immediately after the publication of *Devil of the Flesh* and *Gate to the Flesh*, see Mori (1972: 163–4). Rubin gives a brief account of *Gate to the Flesh* and places Tamura's immediate postwar works 'somewhere between the dregs and Sakaguchi Ango' (1985: 82–4).

15 Mori writes that in his late 1940s stories 'Tamura vulgarizes, rather than popularizes' what had earlier been his more serious *nikutai* theme (1972: 164). Hata and Onishi leave most of these works out of their selections.

16 See Tamura's 1965 essay, 'The Battlefield and Myself: Another Look at War Literature', *TTS* 5: 200–1.

172   *E. Kerkham*

17   *Nihon shōsetsu*, Prange Collection, April–May 1947; Nakajima, who could be male or female, is not otherwise identified.

18   National Archives II, RG 331, Box 8634, folder 25. My earlier brief account of the *Shunpuden* censorship process was based solely on the University of Maryland Prange Collection censorship file for the April and May issues of *Nihon shōsetsu* (Kerkham 2001: 335–42). Archives documents complete the censorship story. It is unusual to find handwritten reports such as this among Archives documents, which normally represent weekly interim and final PPB reports. I leave most English translations as they are. The underlined and double underlined words or passages are so marked in the English originals.

19   For discussions of the terms used by the Japanese to designate women taken by the military, including *jōshigun* (娘子軍, translated as 'girl's army'), see Yoshimi (2000: 47–8) and Soh (2008: 107, 124, 125, and 274 n89). The terms most often used today, *ianfu* (comfort woman) or *jūgun ianfu* (military or troop-following comfort woman), were not used by the Japanese during the Pacific War. Tamura does not use the word *ianfu* in the *Biography*. The 1948 stage adaptation of the novel (entitled 'Spring Breeze') does refer to the now Japanese women as *ianfu* (full script is available at National Archives II, Record Group 331, Box 5283, Folder 68). No censorship documents accompany the script. For more on the pejorative terms used by the Japanese government and military, such as *Sen-pii* or *Chōsen-pii* (Korean whores), see Soh (2000: 69–74; 2008: 69–77).

20   The Korean names for the cities are P'yongyang and Pyongan Pukto.

21   I use my own translation here for Nakajima's rough rendering.

22   My translation.

23   No date, examiner's name, or gender are given for the notes added to Nakajima's report. See Archives II, RG 331, Box 8634, folder 25.

24   My translation; the word in parenthesis, 作者 (*sakusha*) has a double strikethrough in the original Prange galley copy – included, presumably, by one of the PPB examiners. See Figure 9.1.

25   Tsumura provides no translations and does not make clear whether all or parts of the pages and columns listed should be deleted. The original Prange galley of the story, with passages circled, underlined, and/or drawn through, provides hints as to which passages were seen as problematic by this and/or other examiners.

26   The underlining and parenthesis in my translation are found in the original Prange galley. Nakajima, Tsumura, and a third examiner used this galley for their evaluations, so we do not know who marked these and other sections of the story.

27   While the *Biography* is the journal's lead story, it is preceded by a short piece entitled 'A Comment on "Cyrano De Bergerac" Through Pictures' by Suzuki Shintarō; Tamura's story is thus No. 2 in the journal's table of contents. No. 6 is the story 'A Nude Woman', flagged for its use of terms suggesting nationalistic sentiments. Select phrases were removed from the story.

28   RG 331, Box 8634, folder 25.

29   Fielding's title may reflect the fact that the Korean Division within SCAP's Government Section, set up in October 1945, was 'relieved of its responsibilities' in February 1947, although 'its small core of Korean experts would continue to deal with Koreans in Japan throughout the Occupation'. It is significant that at this time Korea experts in the Government Section were, together with Home Ministry officials, involved in the drafting of the new 2 May Alien Registration Ordinance (Takemae 2002: 449–50).

30   Richard Kunzman, a journalist by profession, was in charge of PPB District I, Tokyo (Mayo 1991: 137–8).

31   Prange Collection *Nihon shōsetsu* file. Hank is probably Victor H. Groening.

32   Archives II, RG 331, Box 8640, folder 4.

33   Archives II, RG 331, Box 8638, folder 11.

34 For a monograph on this topic see Duus 1985; see also Yoshimi (2000: 179–92) and Takeuchi (2010: 81–7).
35 For review of the 'Korean problem', particularly in early spring 1947, and of the cooperation between SCAP and BCOF (British Commonwealth Occupation Force) officials and the Japanese government see Morris-Suzuki (2004: 5–28); also Lee (1981: 58–90), Takemae (2002: 447–54), Caprio (2007: 1–22), and Caprio and Yu (2009: 179–99).
36 Tamura (1947: 2) states in his introduction that he selected two prewar stories, each set in Shinjuku, in order to contrast the pre- and postwar Shinjuku cityscape.
37 Hirano (1992: 87–95). Hirano's analysis of CI&E documents reveals that in disapproving successive revised film scripts the censors most often voiced concern with the sensational way that 'prostitution and sex', 'soldiers and "comfort girls"', or war and sex were depicted. The primary goal of CI&E was to infuse desired themes and topics into the media, so the film's potential antiwar theme was encouraged while the topic of war and sex was frowned on. On CI&E's indoctrination role see Mayo (1991: 135–6).
38 Available in re-mastered DVD, Criterion Collection, 2005. Suzuki might have read Tamura's 1964–65 story, *Locusts*, on the subject of Korean comfort women, but he elected to retell Tamura's earlier, more romantic and adventure-filled work. It appears that he did not suspect that the *Biography*'s original Harumi was Korean.
39 Appearing first in the journal *Literary Arts* (*Bungei*) in September 1964, the 100-page novella came out as the lead item in a collection of Tamura's war stories in October, 1965; for Tamura's original 'Introduction' see *TTS* 4: 331–2.
40 For succinct reviews of documents available and known facts on the 'comfort women' controversy, used by both Japanese deniers and activists in Korea, Japan, the US, and elsewhere, see Youn (2008: 213–28) and Roy (2009: 148–60, 239–42).

Bibliography

Caprio, Mark E. (2007) 'Resident Aliens: Forging the Political Status of Koreans in Occupied Japan', in Mark Caprio and Yoneyuki Sugita (eds.), *Democracy in Occupied Japan: The U.S. Occupation and Japanese Politics and Society*, London and New York: Routledge, 178–99.

Caprio, Mark E. and Yu Jia (2009) 'Legacies of Empire and Occupation: The Making of the Korean Diaspora in Japan', *Japan Focus* (September): 1–22.

Dower, John (1999) *Embracing Defeat: Japan in the Wake of World War II*, New York: Norton.

Duus, Masayo (1985) *Makaasaa no futatsu no bōshi* (MacArthur's Two Hats), Tokyo: Kōdansha. First published under the title *Haisha no okurimono* (A Present from the Defeated), Tokyo: Kōdansha [1979].

General MacArthur's General Staff (1994) *Reports of General MacArthur: MacArthur in Japan: The Occupation: Military Phase*, Vol. I, Supplement, Illustrations.

Gordon W. Prange Collection, University of Maryland Libraries. PPB documents on *Shunpuden* (*Biography of a Prostitute*), in *Nihon shōsetsu* (*Japanese Fiction*) folder.

Hata, Masahiro and Onishi Yasumitsu (eds.) (2005) *Tamura Taijirō senshū* (Select Works of Tamura Taijirō), 5 vols., Tokyo: Nihon Tosho Sentaa.

Hirano, Kyoko (1992) *Mr Smith Goes to Tokyo: Japanese Cinema under the American Occupation, 1945–1952*, Washington, DC: Smithsonian Institution Press.

Keene, Donald (1984) *Dawn to the West: Japanese Literature in the Modern Era (Fiction)*, New York: Holt Rinehart & Winston.

Kerkham, Eleanor (2001) 'Pleading for the Body: Tamura Taijirō's 1947 Korean Comfort

174   *E. Kerkham*

Woman Story, *Biography of a Prostitute*', in Marlene Mayo and Thomas Rimer (eds.), *War, Occupation, and Creativity, Japan and East Asia, 1920–1960*, Honolulu: University of Hawai'i Press, 310–59.

Lee, Changsoo (1981) 'The Period of Repatriation, 1945–1949' and 'Koreans under SCAP: An Era of Unrest and Repression' in Changsoo Lee and George DeVos (eds.), *Koreans in Japan: Ethnic Conflict and Accommodation*, Berkeley: University of California Press, 58–90.

Mayo, Marlene (1991) 'Literary Reorientation in Occupied Japan: Incidents of Civil Censorship', in Ernestine Schlant and J. Thomas Rimer (eds.), *Legacies and Ambiguities: Postwar Fiction and Culture in West Germany and Japan*, Washington, DC and Baltimore: Woodrow Wilson Center Press and Johns Hopkins University Press, 135–61.

Mitchell, Richard (1976) *Thought Control in Prewar Japan*, Cornell, NY: Cornell University Press.

Mitchell, Richard (1983) *Censorship in Imperial Japan*, Princeton: Princeton University Press.

Mori, Keiyu (1972) 'Tamura Taijirō no nikutai no bungaku' (Tamura Taijirō's Literature of the Flesh), *Kokubungaku: kaishaku to kanshō* (Japanese Literature: Interpretation and Appreciation), 37(9): 163–4.

Morris-Suzuki, Tessa (2004) 'An Act Prejudicial to the Occupation Forces: Migration Controls and Korean Residents in Post-Surrender Japan', *Japanese Studies*, 24(1): 5–28.

National Archives II, College Park, MD, Record Group 331 (SCAP), Box 8634, folder 25, Box 8638, folder 11, and Box 8640, folder 4 for *Shunpuden* censorship documents; Box 5283, folder 68, for stage play adaptation of *Shunpuden* ('Spring Breeze').

Nihon Shōsetsu (Japanese Fiction) (1947) April/May issue, Tokyo: Taichi Shobō. Held in Gordon W. Prange Collection, College Park, Maryland.

Ōkubo, Tadashi (1959) 'The Literature of the Flesh: A Study of Taijirō Tamura's Thought', in Hidetoshi Katō (ed.), *Japanese Popular Culture: Studies in Mass Communication and Cultural Change Made at the Institute of the Science of Thought, Japan*, Rutland, VT: Charles E. Tuttle, 76–102.

Okuno, Takeo (1978) 'Hito to bungaku: Tamura Taijirō' (The Man and His Work: Tamura Taijirō), in *Tamura Taijirō, Kin Tatsuji, Ohara Tomie shū* (Works of Tamura Taijirō, Kin Tatsuji, and Ohara Tomie), *Chikuma gendai bungaku taikei* (Chikuma Modern Literature Series) 62, Tokyo: Chikuma Shobō, 495–504.

Onishi, Yasumitsu (2008) *Tamura Taijirō no sensō bungaku* (Tamura Taijirō's Wartime Literature), Tokyo: Kasama Shoin.

Roy, Denny (2009) *The Pacific War and Its Political Legacies*, Westport, CT and London: Praeger.

Rubin, Jay (1984) *Injurious to Public Morals: Writers and the Meiji State*, Seattle: University of Washington Press.

Rubin, Jay (1985) 'From Wholesomeness to Decadence: The Censorship of Literature under the Allied Occupation', *Journal of Japanese Studies*, 11(1): 71–103.

Shōwa War Literature Publication Committee (ed.) (1965) *Showa sensō bungaku zenshū: hateshinaki Chūgoku sensen* (Showa Period War Literature: The Endless Chinese Front), Tokyo: Shūeisha.

Slaymaker, Douglas (2004) *The Body in Postwar Japanese Fiction*, London and New York: Routledge Curzon.

Soh, Chunghee Sarah (2000) 'From Imperial Gifts to Sex Slaves: Theorizing Symbolic Representations of the "Comfort Women" ', *Social Science Japan Journal*, 3(1): 59–76.

Soh, Chunghee Sarah (2008) *The Comfort Women: Sexual Violence and Postcolonial Memory in Korea and Japan*, Chicago: University of Chicago Press.

Suzuki, Seijun (1965) *Shunpuden* (Story of a Prostitute *or* Joy Girls), Tokyo: Nikkatsu.

Takayama, Tsuyoshi (1948) *Sengo no bungaku* (Postwar Literature), Tokyo: Shigakusha. Partially translated into English by one K. Konishi as part of PPB records on current writers; see Record Group 331, Box 8593, National Archives II, College Park, Maryland.

Takemae, Eiji (2002) *Inside GHQ: The Allied Occupation of Japan and Its Legacy*, trans. Robert Ricketts and Sebastian Swann, New York and London: Continuum.

Takeuchi, Michiko (2010) '"Pan-Pan girls" Performing and Resisting Neocolonialism(s) in the Pacific Theater, U.S. Military Prostitution in Occupied Japan, 1945–52', in Maria Höhn and Seungsook Moon (eds.), *Over There: Living with the U.S. Military Empire from World War Two to the Present*, Durham and London: Duke University Press, 78–108.

Tamura, Taijirō (1947) *Shunpuden* (Biography of a Prostitute), Tokyo: Ginza Shuppansha.

Tamura, Taijirō (1948) *Tamura Taijirō senshū* (Selections from the Works of Tamura Taijirō), 2 vols., Tokyo: Kusano Shobō.

Tamura, Taijirō (1949) *Shunpuden* (Biography of a Prostitute), Tokyo: Yagumo Shobō.

Tamura, Taijirō (2005) *Tamura Taijirō senshū* (Selections from the Works of Tamura Taijirō), ed. Onishi Yasumitsu and Hata Masahiro, 5 vols., Tokyo: Nihon Tosho Sentaa.

Taniguchi, Senkichi (1950) *Akatsuki no dassō* (Escape at Dawn), Tokyo: Shin Tōhō.

Wagner, Edward W. (1951) *The Korean Minority in Japan, 1904–1950*, New York: Institute of Pacific Relations.

Winther-Tamaki, Bert (2003) 'Oil Painting in Postsurrender Japan: Reconstructing Subjectivity through Deformation of the Body', *Monumenta Nipponica*, 58(3): 347–96.

Yoshimi, Yoshiaki (2000) *Comfort Women: Sexual Slavery in the Japanese Military During World War II*, trans. Suzanne O'Brian, New York: Columbia University Press. Originally published as *Jūgun ianfu*, Tokyo: Iwanami Shoten [1995].

Youn, Myoung-sook (2008) 'Controversies Surrounding the Question of the Japanese Army's Comfort Stations and "Comfort Women"', in Tae-song Hyŏn (ed.), *The Historical Perceptions of Korea and Japan: Its Origins and Points of the Issues Concerning Dokdo-Takeshima, Yasukuni Shrine, Comfort Women, and Textbooks*, Paju Book City, Korea: Nanam Publishing House, 213–28.

10 Censoring imperial honorifics

A linguistic analysis of Occupation censorship in newspapers and literature

Noriko Akimoto Sugimori

Introduction

Most of today's Japanese daily newspapers use honorifics for members of the Japanese imperial family but not for dignitaries such as prime ministers and foreign royals. Although this may sound like a discriminatory language practice, compared with the use of imperial honorifics before and during World War II, it actually demonstrates the most significant change in the use of Japanese honorifics in the twentieth century (Nishida 1998: 372–81). A large part of the process of simplification took place during the Allied Occupation (1945–52). The famed literary critic Etō Jun (1994 [1989]) speculated that the Occupation administration's Civil Censorship Detachment (CCD), its Press, Pictorial, and Broadcast (PPB) Division more specifically, was responsible for this simplification, but no study has examined its influence in any depth. Therefore, this chapter compares articles about Emperor Hirohito and his family in the *Asahi*, a national newspaper, from 1945 to 1947, with the censor-reviewed (pre-publication) versions of those articles. The results confirm that the shifts in the newspaper's use of imperial honorifics were not attributable to PPB censorship, but rather to the independent decisions of *Asahi* journalists. The results also show that changes in language use were apparent between the censor-reviewed versions and their published counterparts. Data analyzed includes newspapers' in-house editorial policies, the censorship policies of PPB, and interviews conducted with PPB officials. However, the PPB did delete some imperial honorifics in literary works, such as novels. In consideration of these factors, this chapter also explores the reasons for these inconsistencies.

Honorifics and kanji in imperial Japan

In newspapers today, honorifics are often used to distinguish the actions of imperial family members from those of commoners. For example, when referring to the act of 'departure' performed by a commoner, newspapers use *shuppatsu-suru* (depart-do), a non-honorific plain verb, but when referring to the same act by a member of the Japanese imperial family, newspapers add an honorific to the verb, as in *shuppatsu-sare-ru* (depart-honorific) or *go-shuppatsu-ninaru*

Censoring imperial honorifics 177

(honorific-depart-become).[1] The use of these structures represents a drastic simplification from the complex imperial honorifics that had been used in newspapers from the late nineteenth century to January 1946.

The meaning and significance of imperial honorifics lies in the representation of the figure of the emperor in Japanese history. Leaders of the Meiji period (1868–1912) transformed the Japanese emperor from a remote figure to a central symbol imbued with a special mystique. In particular, the Meiji Constitution of 1890 fixed the emperor's status as absolute, sacred, and the very embodiment of the state, defining him as the commander-in-chief of the army and the navy. The Meiji leaders consecrated the emperor as a living divinity and the source of religious and political continuity with ancient times. From the Meiji period to the end of World War II, various linguistic devices were used to consecrate the emperor. The most well-known are imperial honorifics – special honorifics that were reserved for the emperor or god – written in kanji or Chinese characters. For example, for the 'departure' of the emperor himself, the imperial honorific *shutsugyo* was used. Usually the honorific prefix *o* or *go* is optional in common honorifics, but in some imperial honorifics the same kanji for *o* and *go* is pronounced as *gyo*, and it is a built-in component of the word.[2]

It should be noted that the use of imperial honorifics was not uniform in imperial Japan (1868–1945). In the years before the institutionalization of the emperor's power in the Meiji Constitution, newspapers also used honorifics when referring to elder statesmen (Watanabe 1986). The exclusive use of honorifics for Japanese imperial family members became legitimized in the process of Japan's move to become a nation-state with an absolute monarchy. During Japan's period of aggression in Asia, laws and regulations, such as *lèse-majesté*, were broadly applied to protect the emperor.[3] Criticism of the emperor or the national polity was forbidden. Honorifics were used to instill a sense of nationalism in Japanese society (Takiura 2005: 17–36). Using honorifics was propagated as virtuous, showing the Japanese people's traits of humility about themselves and respect for others, especially rulers, thereby maintaining social order. Imperial honorifics were also intended to be linguistic devices to make the emperor an extraordinary figure – and one worth dying for – in the minds of the people (Endō 2004). During wartime, soldiers were ordered to die for the emperor rather than to be captured. The Cabinet Information Bureau mobilized artists and literati, including tanka poets, to form several Patriotic Associations (Hōkoku Kai), whose activities included spreading tanka poems that glorified the emperor and the war (Uchino 1988: 92–133). Schoolchildren were also taught how to use hierarchical, complicated imperial honorifics.

However, the use of numerous kanji characters in newspapers created an obstacle to mass literacy. Therefore, the National Language Council (NLC) and its forerunners, the Japanese equivalent of Académie française, tried to limit the use of kanji from 1902 onward.[4] Daily newspapers also wanted to limit kanji in the interest of efficient typesetting. It was also believed that limiting kanji would make newspapers easier to read, thereby increasing circulation. During World War II, even the military put its own kanji limitation into practice. Prolonged

178   *N.A. Sugimori*

wars forced the military to enlist younger soldiers with poorer knowledge of kanji, and their unfamiliarity with kanji began to have a detrimental effect on Japan's war effort (Kurashima 2002: 35–6). In 1942, the NLC attempted to relax the use of 74 kanji about the Imperial Household, but failed due to right-wing opposition (Kai 2011: 29–37).

After Japan's defeat in August 1945, the Allied powers occupied the country. The Occupation's initial agenda was demilitarization and democratization. The Occupation authorities swiftly carried out many reforms, governing indirectly through the Japanese government and directly censoring the press. In January 1946, Emperor Hirohito renounced his claim to divinity, and in February, began making public tours to improve morale. The new constitution of 3 November 1946 guaranteed the nation's sovereignty and relegated the emperor to a strictly symbolic role. Amid drastic social change, the need for language reform was emphasized. The *Yomiuri hōchi* newspaper called for abolition of kanji to make Japan more democratic. The use of honorifics was also criticized as a remnant from feudal times. In the list of 1,850 kanji characters for general use that was notified by the Cabinet in November 1946 – the fewest number ever proposed – the NLC excluded most of the 74 kanji for the Imperial Household, which had been so categorized in 1942. Newspapers and government offices were advised to write using only these characters for general use.

Case study: the changing representation of Hirohito

Newspaper coverage of Emperor Hirohito (1901–89) seemingly captured the evolutionary change in his status. For example, on his birthday in April 1945, about three months before the war's end, major daily newspapers – the *Asahi*, the *Yomiuri hōchi*, the *Mainichi*, and *Nihon keizai* – published similarly long articles about him with a large photograph showing his visit to the Yasukuni Shrine.[5] After the war, the newspapers covered the emperor's birthday in various ways. In 1946, the *Asahi* published a small article marking the emperor's birth-day with no photo.[6] The *Yomiuri hōchi* and *Nihon keizai* did not mention the occasion. In 1947, the *Asahi* was the only national newspaper that published an article about his birthday.

Emperor Hirohito[7] remained on the throne through the Occupation, but during this time, newspapers simplified their use of imperial honorifics for him and his family. The reason for this change is still a matter of debate. The NLC stated that a basic understanding between the Imperial Household authorities and the press to use the highest forms of honorifics within the limits of words in common usage had been established in August 1947 (Monbushō 1952: 11). However, upon examining the Occupation's censorship policy, Etō Jun speculates that the PPB was responsible for this simplification (1994 [1989]: 347–66). However, historians caution that the existence of laws and regulations in Japan during the Occupation and the extent of their actual enforcement were not always the same (Dower 1999). Therefore, I compared articles about Emperor Hirohito and his family in the *Asahi* from 1945 to 1947, to the censor-reviewed (pre-publication) versions of those articles.[8] Because this study is concerned with references to the emperor as a person, I focused on articles describing the emperor's actions, excluding articles about the emperor system itself or the emperor's status under the new constitution, as detailed below.

Newspaper censorship from wartime to the Occupation

To understand accurately the simplification in the use of imperial honorifics in the early phase of the Occupation, one needs to understand the complexity in the use of imperial honorifics that had preceded them. According to Saegusa (1958: 3–15), long before World War II, Japanese newspapers had made sure that their coverage of the imperial family was extensive and dignified, regardless of the actual news value. Right-wing extremists would literally attack newspaper offices when they found things that they considered disrespectful, such as typographical errors in imperial honorifics.[9] Therefore, the *Asahi* tested prospective reporters on their knowledge of kanji characters used in imperial honorifics (Kumakura 1988: 17).

Japanese newspapers had many other restrictions as well (Kasza 1988: 121–231). In 1943, the Cabinet Information Bureau specified that the imperial family's photographs be printed on the right side of newspapers, above the fold. Newspaper reporters lacked direct access to the emperor, and were obliged to rely on what the Imperial Household Ministry dictated to them.[10] The Ministry prohibited newspapers from using other sources (Saegusa 1958: 3–15). From the 1930s onward, newspapers began to standardize the use of imperial honorifics by creating in-house style manuals (Sugimori 2010: 250–60). Using these style manuals, proofreaders checked the use of imperial honorifics in articles five times to ensure that their language was flawless (Saegusa 1958: 4). Further, newspaper photographers could only shoot from a distance of 15 or more meters from the imperial family, only at designated times, and then only after physical examinations and background checks (Saegusa 1958: 7–8).[11]

The Potsdam Declaration of 1945 stipulated that freedom of speech would be established in Japan, but what actually changed for Japanese newspapers was the source of censorship, which shifted from the Japanese government offices to the Allied Occupation, more specifically the Press, Pictorial and Broadcast (PPB) Division of the Civil Censorship Detachment (CCD). PPB decided what to delete in newspapers, and the Civil Information and Education (CI&E) Section also influenced newspapers in terms of what they should promote.[12] CCD censored movies, radio, telegraphs, personal letters, and published materials, including newspapers, magazines, and novels. The PPB's News Agency Section began its pre-publication censorship with five major Tokyo-based newspapers, including the *Asahi*, in October 1945 (Ariyama 1996: 219–23), but expanded its operation nationwide. Most newspapers' systems of pre-censorship (pre-publication censorship) were changed to post-censorship (post-publication censorship) in July 1948 (Yamamoto 1996: 311).

Although the censorship policy shifted in response to the world's changing political climate, the Press Code of September 1945, made up of ten articles, was

180   *N.A. Sugimori*

used as a reference throughout the period of censorship. Key logs were used to establish specific guidelines for deletions and suppressions. The Press Code expressed basic journalistic ideals and forbade falsities or destructive criticism regarding the Allied forces (SCAP 1945). Imperial honorifics were not mentioned in the Press Code. Newspapers were further instructed to publish articles without making censorship seem obvious. This policy was meant to ensure that the general reader would not know about the newspaper censorship.[13] The Press Code was the only document given to the press; the actual censorship standards or criteria were not given to them.

In actual censorship operations, Japanese-speaking PPB examiners were given a subject matter guide listing categories of themes that should not be made public (Yamamoto 2003: 3). The approximately 30 categories of deletions and suppressions included criticism of SCAP, the military tribunal, and Allied nations.[14] Among them, the categories directly related to the emperor seemed to be as follows:

17. <u>Divine Descent Nation Propaganda</u>: Propaganda which either directly or indirectly claims divine descent for either the Nation of Japan or the Emperor will fall into this category.

19. <u>Nationalistic Propaganda</u>: This will embrace all propaganda strictly nationalistic in nature, but will include militaristic, defense of war or divine descent nation propaganda.

(Press, Pictorial and Broadcast Division, 25 November 1946)

PPB censorship took the following paths.[15] A newspaper would be asked to submit two galley proofs or manuscripts to the PPB's News Agency Section. The proofs would be forwarded to Japanese-speaking examiners, who would scrutinize them according to the Press Code and key logs. Every examiner was authorized to approve publication. PPB press personnel had four options: 'to approve as written; to approve with major or minor deletions; to suppress entirely; or to hold for further consideration' (Spaulding 1988: 7). Only when a Japanese-speaking examiner found an objectionable item would he or she report it to the supervisor, who forwarded the material with English translation to the section head. Once a decision had been made on the item, censorship orders were marked on both pages of the proof, and comment sheets were made. Then, one of the two copies was returned to the newspaper. Major newspapers installed an exclusive, direct phone line from the PPB office to relay censorship decisions swiftly (Spaulding 1988: 8).

In those days, reporters would call in articles to the newspaper. About 40 liaisons were stationed in the *Asahi*'s headquarters in Tokyo, Osaka, and Kokura to receive phone calls about news around the nation, and the liaisons wrote down the article in shorthand to be transcribed later (Mori 1960: 174). It is worth noting that orthographies used in stenography are phonogramic (representing the sounds of language only). Therefore, the information regarding which character to use for transcription was not included, and it was left to the discretion of each transcriber to assign kanji characters or hiragana to the reading that he or she had heard. Because many kanji characters have the same sound and similar meaning, the transcriptions were often different from the original scripts. One may argue that the simplification of some imperial honorifics from kanji to hiragana may have occurred in this process. One may also argue that editors could have standardized the use of imperial honorifics in the articles, as they had done before and during World War II.

However, an unprecedented change within newspaper companies in the early Occupation might have interfered with any attempts at standardization. The Allied nations' investigation of war criminals led newspapers, including the *Asahi*, to reflect on their own responsibility for the war (Asahi 1995: 17, 43–51). As a result, in November 1945, responding to a growing demand by employees, 11 members of the *Asahi*'s administration, including the CEO, resigned in an unprecedented structural shakeup. The board of directors was elected by popular vote of the newspaper employees for the first time, and a newspaper labor union, one of the first such unions in Japan, was founded in the Tokyo headquarters, and expanded nationwide (Asahi 1995: 51–2).

Although some CI&E officials had initially supported the newspaper employees, they began to support the Japanese newspaper management, helping them to establish the Japan Newspaper Publishers and Editors Association (Bruno 1988). This Association then secured independent editorial rights (Nihon Shinbun Kyōkai 1948). While reporters could use their own words prior to 1948, since that time, newspaper management or selected editors-in-chief and directors have had the right to change reporters' wording.

The *Asahi*'s 1940 manual, which was full of details about imperial honorifics and was used through World War II, could not have been of much use after Emperor Hirohito's denial of his divinity in January 1946. The *Asahi*'s internal document dated 31 January 1946, which listed words to avoid in order to prevent a negative censorship decision, did not mention imperial honorifics. Although terminology research within the newspaper company began in late 1946 (Kai 2011: 123–47), the *Asahi*'s first style manual in the postwar period was not released until August 1947. A combination of these factors may have given newspaper reporters more freedom prior to 1948, allowing them to simplify imperial honorifics more easily.

Personal action in censorship: interviewing CCD officials

A search of all CCD documents housed at the National Archive II in College Park, Maryland, yielded no key logs regarding imperial honorifics. Thinking that such orders might have been given orally rather than in writing, I interviewed two PPB censors to learn more about the process. Robert Spaulding began his PPB career in October 1946, and became Chief of the Division as the first Head of Examination in the News Agency Section (Spaulding 1988: 7). Although his censorship work did not entirely overlap with the period under consideration in

182   *N.A. Sugimori*

this chapter, he answered my questions through correspondence and phone interviews. Regarding the Occupation's role in simplifying *keigo* (honorifics) for the imperial family members in Japanese newspapers, Spaulding wrote:

> I do not think Malloy or I ever gave the censors any list of 'prohibited expressions'. … We certainly never tried to suppress or change the use of *keigo*, and none of the Japanese or Eurasian censors ever asked me whether use of keigo was objectionable. … We thought that only Japanese should decide what changes, if any, to make in their language…
>
> (Spaulding, personal communication, 31 August 2002, italics in original)

To double-check his recollections, Spaulding also discussed my questions with William J. Chambliss, head of translation in the PPB News Agency Section from 1946 to 1947. Spaulding and Chambliss both recalled that the 'News Agency Section never instructed censors to delete or alter *keigo*. I don't think the idea even occurred to us. We had no desire or intent to change Nihongo (which we had spent so much time learning)' (Spaulding, personal communication, 31 August 2002, italics and brackets in the original).

In my telephone interview in 2006, Spaulding mentioned that nobody had reported to him about whether or not newspapers followed the censorship decisions. PPB, Spaulding said, paid particular attention to what was written in *Red Flag* (*Akahata*), the bulletin of the Japanese Communist Party, but not to what was written in other newspapers such as the *Asahi*. He also told me that it was indeed possible for newspapers to revise articles after censorship and that they could freely change the wording of parts that had not been deleted. Spaulding's recollections may show that the use of imperial honorifics declined because of the *Asahi*'s autonomous decisions.

I also interviewed Tanamachi Tomoya (1925–2010) in Tokyo in 2006. Tanamachi was hired by the Censorship Section of General Headquarters (GHQ)/ SCAP District III in Fukuoka (western Japan) in March 1946. He censored theatrical manuscripts. In October 1949, he retired as an assistant censor, the highest rank for Japanese in the PPB in Fukuoka. Although he was not in charge of newspaper censorship, he said the censorship standard was the same in all media types because it was highly unlikely that certain words were acceptable in one media and unacceptable in another. When I asked about imperial honorifics, he did not recollect any specific cases in his theatrical manuscript censorship work. I asked him what he would have done if he had found imperial honorifics in the materials he had to examine. He answered my question instantly, 'Of course, I would have deleted such words [imperial honorifics] because those words are militaristic. I wonder if you will be able to find such examples in other materials.'

As shown above, PPB officials' memories on the censorship treatment of honorifics differed greatly. Spaulding stressed his perspective as a learner of Japanese. But Japanese proficiencies among non-Japanese censors might have differed, and some non-Japanese censors with near-native fluency in Japanese

Censoring imperial honorifics 183

might have felt differently as well. In this sense, Tanamachi's comments are noteworthy for showing human subjectivity in censorship decisions. Even if censors were given themes to watch out for, the connection of a word and a theme depended on individual censors' subjectivity. Tanamachi would have deleted imperial honorifics, even if he were not ordered to do so, because he believed them to be militaristic. He also assumed that imperial honorifics would have been deleted in all media types, but I will demonstrate below that this was not the case.

Censor-reviewed and published *Asahi* articles on the imperial family

Whereas past studies on newspaper honorifics relied on published materials only, more recent studies have paid attention to the role of Occupation censorship in this process.[16] SCAP collected copies of various publications in Japan from 1945 to 1949, but the entire collection has not survived because many important censorship documents were discarded at the termination of CCD in October 1949 (Yamamoto 2003: 2). Even so, many of these censored publications are now housed in the Gordon W. Prange Collection of the University of Maryland Libraries. Among the 16,000 newspaper titles is the *Asahi*, the only national daily newspaper in which one can examine censor-reviewed versions from as early as 1945.

To understand how the simplification of imperial honorifics originated, I will compare censor-reviewed versions and published counterparts of the *Asahi* articles about the emperor and other imperial family members from November 1945 to April 1946.[17] A comparison of these published articles and their censor-reviewed counterparts will reveal whether or not these changes were brought about by the Occupation censorship. If the PPB censorship decreased the use of imperial honorifics, one should find traces of censorship, such as deletion marks by the censors in the imperial honorifics originally included in censor-reviewed versions. One should also find the published articles without those deleted honorifics.

Comparing censor-reviewed and published *Asahi* articles from the same region is desirable, but the *Asahi* in western Japan was the only censor-reviewed *Asahi* available in the Prange Collection, while the published *Asahi* available was from Tokyo. Therefore, I compared the published articles about the emperor in the Tokyo *Asahi* with the censor-reviewed versions in western Japan. Even after the inception of censorship in Tokyo, until sometime before 30 January 1946, it seems that the *Asahi* was able to send articles that had not passed the censorship process in Tokyo to Fukuoka and Osaka (Negi and Kotani 1995 [1946]: 28–30). In other words, after that time, the censor, who knew that the emperor-related articles from Tokyo had already been censored there, might have approved them without close examination. Therefore, both censor-reviewed articles about the emperor in western Japan and their published counterparts in Tokyo from as early as February 1946 onward may be identical, using the same imperial honorifics.

184   *N.A. Sugimori*

Overall, none of the *Asahi*'s censor-reviewed articles about the emperor and his family bore any traces of censorship such as the censor's handwritten comments or deletion marks. However, these articles are not identical. Surprisingly, in some cases, censor-reviewed articles actually had fewer imperial honorifics than did the published versions of the same articles. A published article of 14 November 1945 covered Emperor Hirohito's visit to the Ise Shrine to report the end of the war to his ancestors. The honorific *o/go* in kanji was used in all contexts in both versions. The honorific *sasu/tamau* (deign to do), which is high in level of deference, was used in almost all contexts. The almost exclusive use of kanji in *o/go* and imperial honorifics was also typical before and during World War II ('Ise', *Asahi shinbun*, 14 November 1945).

Although the emperor's 'Declaration of Humanity' on New Year's Day in 1946 might have been intended to change the people's perception of the emperor from a living divinity to a human being, the same highly deferential honorifics were still used for him after that. For example, the 13 January 1946 article described the emperor's solicitude for former soldiers ('Tenraku', *Asahi shinbun*, 13 January 1946). The censor-reviewed version mentions that former soldiers had trouble finding jobs and many had resorted to burglary. Emperor Hirohito became concerned and asked his officials to help them.

On the other hand, the use of imperial honorifics did not always mean praise for the emperor within the newspaper pages. For example, on the same page as this flattering article, and diagonally across from it, was a 'blasphemous' article that reported a Japanese Communist Party official's criticism of the emperor's concern for former soldiers, saying 'the fact that many former soldiers became criminals recently shows that the war of invasion (*shinryaku sensō*) trampled on young people's pure hearts', and 'the imperial solicitude is no use this late' ('Ōi', *Asahi shinbun*, 13 January 1946). Perhaps this was a rare case in which the *Asahi* ran an article blatantly critical of the emperor so close to a favorable article about him.

However, the article on the Communist party is not included on the same page of the censor-reviewed *Asahi*, and the article on the emperor's solicitude is longer than the published version as it incorporated added contents – namely, the newspaper's urging of the government to implement policies for economic stability and recovery and a quote from an anonymous former soldier. The content might have been added to Tokyo's original article before submitting for censor review at the western *Asahi* headquarters, because it is not evident whether Tokyo's original contained the added contents. This example shows that one cannot account for the difference between a censor-reviewed version and a published version solely from the censorship. Even after passing the censorship, negotiation and individual choices made by journalists themselves did change the contents of the articles.

In February 1946, the emperor began traveling around Japan. A 20 February 1946 article reported on his visit to Kanagawa, the first stop on his national tour. The article shows a dramatic increase in common honorifics. The use of the honorific *o/go* in hiragana increased, even though this sometimes resulted in ungrammatical sentences. In the following two examples, the position of *[*]* shows where the omission of an *o/go* honorific from *o/go*-verb-*ninaru* constructions makes the sentence grammatically incorrect:

1) '*Heika mo [*] naki ni natteiru no dewa nai ka*' (I wondered if His Majesty may be also crying)
2) '*[*] chikayori ni naru*' (comes closer)

('Fukkō jōkyō', *Asahi shinbun*, 20 February 1946)

A sharp decline in the use of imperial honorifics is also evident in the choice of verbs, as there was a dramatic increase in common honorifics such as *o/go*-verb-*ninaru* and verb-*rareru* structures. Considering that the imperial honorifics had been more frequent only about a month earlier, the increase in these common honorifics is remarkable.

Censor-reviewed and published articles about other members of the imperial family also showed inconsistencies. Furthermore, words with a negative meaning were revised to synonyms with a positive meaning. The 20 March 1946 issue covers Crown Prince Akihito's graduation from elementary school and entrance to junior high school. The censor-reviewed version referred to the education that Emperor Hirohito had received as *tokubetsu* (special), but the published version referred to it as *tokushu* (special). While both words carry the overall meaning of 'special', the nuance is different, and the censored version conveys a more positive connotation.

An article about Prince Mikasa commuting to Tokyo was published on the same page. In referring to princesses, the informal plural marker *tachi* was used (*hidenka-tachi* 'princess-plural') rather than the honorific *gata*. *Tachi* was in kanji in the censor-reviewed version, but it was in hiragana in the published version. The title 'Jostled in the crowd: Mikasanomiya's commute' with an instance of the honorific *go* in the censor-reviewed version was changed to 'Prince Mikasa in a crowded train' without honorifics. The published version contained two seemingly informal sentences for a mainstream paper like the *Asahi*, but those sentences were not included in the censor-reviewed version. The following are the sentences in question, and I have underlined the section added in the published version. In other words, the underlined parts were missing in the censor-reviewed version:

The degree of crowdedness in the Yokosuka Line during the rush hour is less unsatisfactory; Prince Mikasa was in the crowd.

I don't write here where in Shōnan his residence is located based on His Highness's request.

('Mikasa', *Asahi shinbun*, 20 March 1946, p. 3)

Both sentences include the journalist's perspective. A disclosure of Prince Mikasa's request suggests the journalist's closeness to the prince.

A distortion of Prince Mikasa's words in another article is also noteworthy. Observing several young princes studying for university entrance exams for their new lives, in the censor-reviewed article, Prince Mikasa mentioned, '...because it is an affectation for [imperial family members] of my [adult] age to enter university...' ('Shitsugyō', *Asahi shinbun Seibu-ban*, 6 April 1946); however, this quote in the published version was distorted to 'although [imperial family members] of my age also have motivation to study again as students if situations permit' ('Wakamiya,' *Asahi shinbun*, 6 April 1946), portraying Prince Mikasa as more forward-looking.

Another article from 6 April 1946 describes the struggles of younger members of the imperial family after the war. The headline '"Unemployed" Imperial Family' in the censor-reviewed version was changed to a more neutral 'Lives of the Imperial Family'. But the same headline referred to these imperial family members as *waka-miya-tachi* (young-prince-common plural), using the common plural *tachi*, not the deferential counterpart *gata*. The alteration of Prince Mikasa's words in this article is also noteworthy because his words are distorted. In the censor-reviewed article, Prince Mikasa criticized the preferential treatment of the imperial family members, saying they shouldn't be allowed to lounge around and do nothing. But in the published version, Prince Mikasa's complaint was reduced to the simpler description of an 'easy life'.

The 29th of April was Emperor Hirohito's birthday. A censor-reviewed version and its published version for the *Asahi* article marking his birthday had 13 differences that showed less deference in the published version than in the censor-reviewed one. In the censor-reviewed article, the honorific *sama* was used twice, one in Yoshinomiya-*sama* and the other in *san-naishinnō-sama* (the three princesses). The *sama* for Yoshinomiya, a prince, was intact, but the one for the three princesses was missing in the published article. Kanji was also changed to hiragana in three instances, all involving the honorific *o/go*. Both versions contained five contexts for the honorific prefix *o/go*, four in noun phrases and one in the *o/go*-verb-*ninaru* (honorific-verb-become) construction. Similarly, there were three instances in which one kanji was changed to different kanji with the same reading.[18] At the time the newspaper article in question was written, the national language reform of kanji limitation was to begin several months later. Considering these circumstances, one may wonder if these kanji substitutions indicate the *Asahi*'s preliminary experiments with the kanji limitation. However, all of the changes in these categories occurred among usable kanji characters. Furthermore, one change was made in an opposite direction: *hajimete* (for the first time) was changed from hiragana to include kanji.

The following is my translation of the 1947 article marking Emperor Hirohito's birthday, which is the shortest article marking his birthday in the postwar period:

> It is said that His Majesty the Emperor, who welcomes his forty-sixth birthday today the 29th, prays at the Three Shrines in the Imperial Court at nine in the morning, and holds the emperor's birthday celebration. Furthermore, at ten he receives congratulatory remarks from each imperial family member and others.

> ('Kyō', *Asahi shinbun*, 29 April 1947, p. 4)

The published article consists of only a paragraph describing birthday events for the emperor. However, the censor-reviewed version contained a second paragraph that did not appear in the published version: '[i]n addition, the GHQ has notified the Japanese government to the effect that one may raise the national flag'. This deletion of a GHQ notice has an important implication. Until the end of World War II, the rule was *shōsho hikkin* (once the emperor's words are given, one must listen to and carry out [the content of his words]). Stated differently, newspapers were obligated to print the emperor's words or orders regardless of how newsworthy they were. However, because the *Asahi* did not print the GHQ's notice, this deletion may imply the *Asahi*'s tacit resistance to the Occupation. The issue in which the article in question was printed was filled with information on the first popular election in Japan's history.[19] The journalists gave more space to the popular vote than to the emperor's birthday or the GHQ's 'trite' notice.

Changes from kanji to hiragana were also found in this article. The conjunction *nao* (furthermore), *gata* (deferential plural marker), and the *u* in *ukeru* (receive) were changed from kanji to hiragana. These changes were not imposed by the national language reform of kanji limitation.

In sum, as far as imperial family-related articles are concerned, none of the *Asahi* articles examined contained traces of censorship.[20] But censor-reviewed and published articles were different in many ways, especially in orthography, showing inconsistency in their levels of deference. Furthermore, innovative or ungrammatical expressions involving honorifics were also found. Although imperial honorifics were not censored in the *Asahi*, this situation was completely different in literature regarding the emperor.

Censoring imperial allusion in Japanese literature

Yokote (1995) lists specific examples of PPB censorship in 41 works of Japanese literature, illustrating which sections of the texts were deleted by the PPB censors for what reasons and listing the censor's comments on each literary work. Among works from the period of study (August 1945 to 29 April 1947), eight mention the emperor.

The first work is the proletarian poet Watanabe Junzō's *Reactionary Nature of the Tanka Poem Circles* (*Kadan no handōsei*) for the April 1946 issue of *The Freemen's Association* (*Jiyūkonwakai*). Criticizing the nationalistic tanka poem circles, Watanabe quoted six poets' tanka poems and the thoughts of three poets about tanka, all of which had been written in the early phase of the Pacific War. These poems glorified the emperor using imperial honorifics. For example, the translation on the comment sheet of one of the quoted poems, composed by Kitahara Hakushū, was, 'I glorify the illustrious virtue of His Majesty who wishes the whole world to be under one [the emperor's] roof' (Yokote 1995: 77). In this poem a variant of the wartime slogan *hakkō ichiu* (the whole world under one roof) was used. The seemingly archaic transliteration *aano shitaihe*, which no longer corresponded with the contemporary reading, was written at the side. The imperial honorific *mi-izu* (emperor's august grace) was also used. Shiga Mitsuko, the second poet Watanabe mentioned, wrote, 'To devote oneself to the Emperor is the eternally unchangeable belief of the Japanese race. This belief is at the same time the ideology of the tanka poet' (Yokote 1995: 78). All of these quotations from the poems and criticism were deleted as 'nationalistic religious propaganda' (Yokote 1995: 77). In December 1945, SCAP had issued the Shinto Directive, banning the use of *hakkō ichiu* in official documents; this example may show the expansion of the Directive's application.

The second work is Ara Masahito's *The Last Day* (*Shūmatsu no hi*) for the June 1946 issue of *Modern Literature* (*Kindai bungaku*). Several sections were deleted for 'disturbing public tranquility'. However, a section including *hakkō ichiu* was not deleted.

The third work is Arima Yoriyoshi's *Dear Father* (*Chichi yo*) for the July 1946 issue of *Salon* (*Saron*). The entire work was suppressed for being a 'key log violation defense of war criminal suspect'. Arima's essay contained the following: '...when thinking about the Imperial Household members his circumstances were immaterial; ... he was happy to think of himself as being a substitute for the Emperor' (Yokote 1995: 100). The Japanese original for 'a substitute' was *o-migawari*, with the honorific *o*.

The fourth work is Aoyama Rokurō's *Lecture on Man'yōshū azama-uta* (*Man'yōshū azumauta senshaku*), which was submitted to the PPB for publication in the October 1946 issue of *Fuji*, an ultranationalistic tanka magazine. It contains Aoyama's lecture and quotations of four tanka poems from *Man'yōshū*, a collection of poems from the eighth century. Three of the four poems were deleted. One of the deleted poems' translations on the comment sheet is 'From today on I'll sacrifice myself, For the sake of the Emperor as a safeguard against the enemy' (Yokote 1995: 41). The emperor in this poem ruled in ancient times and the poem does not contain imperial honorifics, but the poems, including this one, were deleted as 'nationalistic propaganda'.

The fifth work is the well-known novelist Nagai Kafū's *My Diary in 1941* (*Shōwa jūroku nen no nikki*), which was intended for publication in *New Life* (*Shinsei*). One sentence and two phrases were deleted for being 'militaristic' (Yokote 1995: 116). The deleted sections include the word *seidai* (the emperor's sacred time).

The sixth work is Tanaka Hidemitsu's *Voices of the People* (*Minshū no koe*) in *The Renovation* (*Kakushin*). This diary contained the words: 'but anyone who's really Japanese is mortified at the defeat and will persevere for two or three years holding the emperor as our center, and will take vengeance in the future' (Yokote 1995: 81). Because 'the emperor' was used in the object position of the sentence, verbal honorifics were not used. Several passages including this one were deleted for disturbing 'public tranquility'.

The seventh work is popular novelist Dazai Osamu's short story *Tokatonton* (*Tokatonton*), which was scheduled to appear in the January 1947 issue of *Gathering Images* (*Gunzō*). The following passage is a young officer's speech, delivered after hearing Emperor Hirohito's declaration to end the war on 15

August 1945. The portion in parentheses was deleted for being 'militaristic propaganda':

> (But this is only political. We soldiers must continue fighting to the best of our powers and in the end all of us should commit suicide to beg pardon of the Emperor. As I myself am already decided to do so, you must also willingly be prepared for it. All right?) That's all...
>
> (Yokote 1995: 48)

The section that was deleted contained humble honorifics 'to beg pardon of the Emperor'. Before this passage, the honorific *go* was used for the emperor's broadcast, as in *heika mizukara no go-hōsō* (His Majesty's own broadcast), but this honorific was not deleted.

The eighth work was written by Horiguchi Daigaku, a well-known poet and critic of French literature. His four poems of November 1946 were disapproved as 'propaganda', but the comment sheet was not specific about the type of propaganda that these poems contained (Yokote 1995: 26). Another poem contained the imperial honorific *ō-mi-gokoro* (the emperor's compassionate heart),[21] but the translation of this poem was lost in the briefer's summary translation. It is noteworthy that the imperial honorific *ō-mi-kokoro* passed the PPB's newspaper censorship in November 1945, yet it was deleted in Horiguchi's poem, implying the arbitrariness of the censorship operation.

Conclusions

Analysis of articles about Emperor Hirohito reveal that those published immediately after the war in late 1945 shared many features regarding the use of imperial honorifics with those before and during the war. Beginning with the 20 February 1946 article, which covered the emperor's national tour, the differences between the censor-reviewed articles and the published counterparts became more pronounced, and the use of imperial honorifics declined. In examinations of censor-reviewed versions of emperor-related newspaper articles, I found no traces of censorship of imperial honorifics. This result supports Robert Spaulding's memory that the PPB did not censor imperial honorifics. It also counters Etō's claim that imperial honorifics were simplified because of PPB censorship. Spaulding provided the perspective of a non-native speaker of Japanese who was in charge of censorship. However, it is premature to generalize that imperial honorifics were beyond the linguistic competence of non-native speaking censors because the Japanese proficiency of the censors might have varied.

Some questions regarding the extent of PPB censorship remain: Tanamachi Tomoya told me that he would have deleted imperial honorifics because these expressions seemed militaristic. PPB censors deleted some imperial honorifics in literary works. At the same time, these works, which showed an author's intense worship of the emperor(s) using various imperial honorifics, are different from

190   *N.A. Sugimori*

emperor-related newspaper articles, which employed commonly used imperial lexical items in a clichéd manner.

It seems to be common sense that the censors' perception of newspapers and literary works may have been different. On one hand, we can assume that newspapers are read and discarded within a single day. It is known that MacArthur as well as his supervisors at the Pentagon and the White House tried to ensure that the Allied Occupation of Japan appeared democratic; therefore, it was desirable for the Occupation censorship to allow major newspapers, such as the *Asahi*, to be published without disruption. In writing articles in a rushed manner, reporters tried to use imperial honorifics within the scope of those commonly used. On the other hand, readers typically keep books forever. Readers may enjoy the works over and over again, rereading stories and memorizing poems. These differences between genres in reader consumption might have made censors pay more attention to imperial honorifics in literary works.

Censor-reviewed newspaper articles and their published counterparts contained several differences that are unrelated to honorifics (such as the addition of a comma, and replacement of a kanji character with another kanji character with the same meaning). Such changes occurring mid-process show that the newspaper changed the wording after passing censorship, demonstrating the autonomy of the newspaper company.

The inconsistent use of imperial honorifics may also reflect the freedom of expression of individual reporters and editors. Kress (1989: 448) argues, 'It is unlikely, perhaps theoretically impossible, that any two language users will share the same positionings and hence the same coding orientation.' However, except for the occupation period after January 1946 (when the emperor denied his divinity), newspaper articles about the imperial family do not usually show these individual journalists' differences in coding orientations, probably because the newspapers' style manuals do not permit such differences. Therefore, these inconsistencies may show that individual reporters were free to write articles about the imperial family members and to experiment with the use of honorifics. They might also have been in a hurry or they were writing quickly, so they did not pay much attention to the inconsistencies, if they even noticed them.

Research pertaining to the process of newspaper publication has uncovered human agency that cannot be demonstrated by examining language policy or published articles only. Findings from this study have demonstrated that human subjectivity plays a much greater role in censorship decisions than was previously considered. For more accurate analysis, future research involving more newspapers and other reading materials, such as pamphlets and books, is desirable. CI&E's involvement in newspaper censorship should also be examined more deeply. Considering that newspapers serialize novels, it would be beneficial to examine honorific use in novels appearing in newspapers. Finally, links between language use in the new constitution of 1946 and the use of honorifics in newspapers should be examined, to discover whether public political discourse may have acted as another stimulus to change in the Occupation period.

Acknowledgments

The author thanks the Gordon W. Prange Collection of University of Maryland, the Harvard Yenching Library, and the National Archives II for data collection, as well as the Great Lakes College Association and the Northeast Council of the Association for Asian Studies for a research travel grant. She also thanks an anonymous reviewer and the following individuals: Mary Catherine O'Connor, John W. Dower, Sarah Frederick, Takahashi Hiroshi, Rachael Hutchinson, Denise Wyatt, and the University of Chicago East Asia Transregional Histories Workshop participants, especially Yamaguchi Noriko.

Notes

1 On degrees of deference in Japanese honorifics, see Kikuchi (1994: 116–20).
2 Writing systems used in modern Japanese include kanji along with the two basic syllabary scripts called hiragana and katakana. Hiragana and katakana are limited to 48 characters each and are phonograms standing for a speech sound, whereas the kanji in common use number 3,000 or more. Kanji do not stand for speech sounds but for ideas, and one kanji character may be read or pronounced in a number of different ways. The pronunciation of kanji thus requires more learning than hiragana or katakana, and it retains an elite aura (Kataoka 1997: 106).
3 Laws on *lèse-majesté* were originally enacted in 1880. The Peace Preservation Law of 1925 outlawed organizational activity aimed at altering the capitalist economic system or the (emperor-centered) national polity. This was broadened to prohibit free expressions about the imperial family members.
4 Proposals to abolish or limit the use of kanji were made from 1866, and the movement created a momentum to pursue the cause at a national level in 1902. The National Language Council (Kokugo shingikai) was established in 1934.
5 The Yasukuni Shrine is a Shinto shrine in Tokyo that commemorates the souls of fallen soldiers from modern wars. Titles of the newspapers translate roughly as the *Morning Sun, Yomiuri News, The Daily*, and *Japanese Finance*.
6 The 1945 article marking the emperor's birthday in the *Asahi* was in 4,644 character spaces, but the 1946 article was in 271 character spaces. For more quantitative analysis, see Sugimori and Hamada (2002), Sugimori (2008, 2010, 2011).
7 Emperor Hirohito reigned from 1926 to 1989, while the Occupation lasted from 1945 to 1952 on mainland Japan (1945–72 in Okinawa).
8 The *Asahi* is the national daily newspaper which has most frequently recorded the largest circulation in the twentieth century.
9 Well-known examples of right-wing extremists' physical violence against the *Asahi* in the prewar period include the White Rainbow Incident in 1918 and the February 26 Incident in 1936. See De Lange (1998: 144–5).
10 American journalists interviewed Emperor Hirohito for the first time on 25 September 1945. His first meeting with the Japanese press took place on 22 December 1945 (Takahashi 1988: 32–8, 390–4).
11 The prescribed distance to be kept from the emperor when taking photos seemed to shrink after 1945, but other forms of restrictions remained. For example, the media today can only use photos with the Imperial Household Agency's permission.
12 See Bruno (1988), Mayo (1991). For details about newspaper censorship by the Japanese government and the Allied powers in September 1945, see Ariyama (1996: 55–78, 150–97).
13 Although this entire censorship operation was later kept from the public, SCAP initially allowed newspapers to announce the operation (Ariyama 1996: 220).

192   *N.A. Sugimori*

14 Although the total number of categories of deletions and suppressions remained almost the same, the categories in key logs changed in number and themes as necessary.
15 For more details on this process, see Matsuura (1984), Spaulding (1988), Ariyama (1996).
16 Compare Takeuchi and Echizenya (1987) with Sugimori (2008, 2010, 2011).
17 Although CCD censorship began in Tokyo on 8 October 1945, the earliest newspaper data available in the Prange Collection begins with the *Asahi* in western Japan in November 1945.
18 Similar substitutions of kanji and hiragana were also found in provincial papers from this period (Sugimori 2008, 2010, 2011).
19 The right to vote had been given to men aged 25 and older in 1945. However, before the election, men and women 20 or older were granted the right to vote by Diet legislation in December 1945. As many as 39 female members of the House of Representatives were elected, a record that has not been broken.
20 Some articles, such as ones about atomic bombs, contained deletion marks by the censor on the same page.
21 *Ō-mi-gokoro* is derived from a sequential voicing, or the voicing of the word-initial consonant of the second word of the compounding as applied to *ō-mi-kokoro*.

References

Ariyama, Teruo (1996) *Senryōki media-shi kenkyū: jiyū to tōtsei 1945-nen* (Research on Media History During the Occupation: Freedom and Restriction, 1945), Tokyo: Kashiwa Shobō.
Asahi Shinbun Hyakunen-shi Henshū Iinkai (ed.) (1995) *Asahi Shinbun shashi Shōwa sengo-hen* (Asahi Shinbun's History: Postwar Showa), Tokyo: Asahi Shinbun.
Bruno, Nicholas J. (1988) *Major Daniel C. Imboden and Press Reform in Occupied Japan 1945–1952.* Unpublished Ph.D. thesis, University of Maryland.
De Lange, William (1998) *A History of Japanese Journalism: Japan's Press Club as the Last Obstacle to a Mature Press*, Richmond, Surrey: Japan Library.
Dower, John W. (1999) *Embracing Defeat: Japan in the Wake of World War II*, New York: Norton.
Endō, Orie (2004) 'Dai 2shō "tennō" ni kansuru yōgo' (Ch. 2: Terminology Regarding 'the Emperor'), in Endō Orie, Kimura Taku, Sakurai Takashi, Suzuki Chieko, Hayakawa Haruko, and Yasuda Toshiaki (eds.), *Sensōchū no hanashi kotoba – Radio drama daihon kara* (Spoken Language During the War – From Manuscripts of Radio Drama), Tokyo: Hitsuji Shobō, 65–81.
Etō, Jun (1994) [1989] *Tozasareta gengo kūkan: senryōgun no ken'etsu to sengo nihon* (Sealed Linguistic Space: The Allied Censorship and Postwar Japan), Tokyo: Bungei Shunjū.
Kai, Mutsurō (2011) *Shūsen chokugo no kokugo kokuji mondai* (Language and Orthography Problems in the Aftermath of World War II), Tokyo: Meiji Shoin.
Kasza, Gregory J. (1988) *The State and the Mass Media in Japan, 1918–1945*, Berkeley and Los Angeles: University of California Press.
Kataoka, Kuniyoshi (1997) 'Affect and Letter-writing: Unconventional Conventions in Casual Writing by Young Japanese Women', *Language and Society*, 26: 103–36.
Kikuchi, Yasuto (1994) *Keigo* (Honorifics), Tokyo: Kadokawa Shoten.
Kress, Gunther (1989) 'History and Language: Towards a Social Account of Linguistic Change', *Journal of Pragmatics*, 13: 445–66.

Kumakura, Masaya (1988) *Genron tōseika no kisha* (Reporters under Free Speech Restriction), Tokyo: Asahi Shinbun.

Kurashima, Nagamasa (2002) *Kokugo hyaku nen* (100 Years of Japanese), Tokyo: Shōgakkan.

Matsuura, Sōzō (1984) *Senchū senryōka no masukomi* (Mass Communication during the War and Occupation), Tokyo: Ōtsuki Shoten.

Mayo, Marlene J. (1991) 'Literary Reorientation in Occupied Japan: Incidents of Civil Censorship', in Ernestine Schlant and J. Thomas Rimer (eds.), *Legacies and Ambiguities: Postwar Fiction and Culture in West Germany and Japan*, Washington DC: Woodrow Wilson Center Press, 135–61.

Monbushō (1952) *Korekara no keigo* (Forthcoming Honorifics), Tokyo: Monbushō.

Mori, Kyōzō (1960) 'Nihongo no hyōkihō ni tsuite' (About the Japanese Writing System), in Ono Noboru (ed.), *Kokugo kaikaku ronsō* (Language Reform Debates), Tokyo: Kuorosio Shuppan, 172–8.

Negi, Tatsugorō and Kotani, Ichirō (1995) [1946] *Shagai hi: rengōgun shireibu no shinbun ken'etsu ni tsuite* (Confidential Memo: About GHQ's Newspaper Censorship), in Asahi Shinbun Hyakunen-shi Henshū Iinkai (ed.), *Asahi shinbun shashi Shōwa sengo-hen* (Asahi Shinbun's History: Postwar Showa), Tokyo: Asahi Shinbun.

Nihon Shinbun Kyōkai (1948) 'Henshū-ken seimei kaisetsu' (Explanation of the Japan Newspaper Publishers & Editors Association's Editorial Rights), *Shinbun kyōkai hō* (The Japan Newspaper Publishers & Editors Association News), 15 March.

Nishida, Naotoshi (1998) *Nipponjin no keigo seikatsu shi* (History of Honorifics in the Lives of Japanese People), Tokyo: Kanrin Shobō.

Press, Pictorial and Broadcast Division (PPB) (1946) 'Annex I to Monthly Report, A Brief Explanation of the Categories of Deletions and Suppressions', 25 November 1946, RG 331, Box 8658. National Archives II.

Saegusa, Shigeo (1958) *Genron shōwashi: Dan'atsu to teikō* (History of Speech in the Showa Period: Suppression and Resistance), Tokyo: Nihon Hyōronsha.

SCAP (1945) 'Memorandum for Imperial Japanese Government, Subject: Press Code for Japan', RG331, Box 5059. National Archives II.

Spaulding, Robert M. (1988) 'CCD Censorship of Japan's Daily Press', in Thomas W. Burkman (ed.), *The Occupation of Japan: Arts and Culture. The Proceedings of a Symposium at Norfolk, Virginia, 18–19 October 1984*, The General Douglas MacArthur Foundation, 1–18.

Spaulding, Robert M. (2002) *Discussion on CCD censorship* [Letter] (Personal Communication, 31 August).

Sugimori, Noriko Akimoto (2008) 'Senryō wa dono yō ni shinbun no tennō e no keigo o kansoka sasetaka: ken'etsumae to shuppango no kōshitsu kiji to kankeisha no intabyō no bunseki' (The Simplification of Imperial Honorifics during the Allied Occupation), *The Japanese Journal of Language in Society*, 11(1): 103–15.

Sugimori, Noriko Akimoto (2010) *Imperial Honorifics as an Index of Social Change in Modern Japan, 1872–2008*. Unpublished Ph.D. dissertation, Boston University.

Sugimori, Noriko Akimoto (2011) 'Shinbun no kōshitsu keigo kansoka eno senryō no eikyō: Kokugo shingikai, Kunaishō, CCD ken'etsu no hōshin to sono jissai' (How the Allied Occupation Influenced Simplification of Imperial Honorifics in Newspapers: Policy vs. Practice of the National Language Council, the Imperial Household Ministry, and CCD Censorship), *Intelligence*, 11: 120–8.

Sugimori, Noriko Akimoto and Hamada, Masako (2002) 'Discourse and Attitudes: Imperial Honorifics and the Open Society', in Ray T. Donahue (ed.), *Exploring*

194 *N.A. Sugimori*

Japaneseness: On Japanese Enactments of Culture and Consciousness (Civic Discourse for the Third Millennium), Westport, CN: Ablex (Greenwood), 105–19.

Takahashi, Hiroshi (1988) *Heika, otazune mōshiagemasu* (Your Majesty, I Have Some Questions), Tokyo: Bungei Shunjū.

Takeuchi, Toshio and Echizenya, Akiko (1987) 'Shinbun bunshō ni miru tokushu keigo (kōshitsu yōgo) no keisei' (Construction of Special Honorifics [Imperial Terminology] in Newspapers), *Nagoya daigaku sōgō gengo sentaa gengo bunkaronshū* (Nagoya University Language Center Bulletin of Language and Culture), 9(1): 1–14.

Takiura, Masato (2005) *Nihon no keigoron: Poraitonesu riron kara no saikentō* (Theories of Honorifics in Japan: Reexamination Through Politeness Theory), Tokyo: Taishūkan.

Uchino, Mitsuko (1988) *Tanka to tennōsei* (Tanka and the Emperor System), Nagoya: Fūbōsha.

Watanabe, Tomosuke (1986) 'Shinbun kiji ni okeru kōshitsu eno keigo hyōgen no rekishi to genjō' (History and Status Quo of Honorific Expressions for the Imperial Court in Newspaper Articles), in Kokuritsu kokugo kenkyūjo (ed.), *Shakai henka to keigo kōdōhyōjun* (Social Changes and Standards of Honorific Behavior in Japan), Tokyo: Kokuritsu Kokugo Kenkyūjo (National Language Research Institute), 32–48.

Yamamoto, Taketoshi (1996) *Senryōki media bunseki* (Analysis of the Media during the Occupation), Tokyo: Hōsei Daigaku Shuppan-kyoku.

Yamamoto, Taketoshi (2003) 'Senryōka no media ken'etsu' *to Prange bunko* (Media Censorship under the Occupation and the Prange Collection), *Bungaku*, 4(5): 2–10.

Yokote, Kazuhiko (1995) *'Hi'-senryōka no bungaku ni kansuru kisoteki kenkyū: shiryōhen* (Basic Research on Literature During the Occupation: Materials), Tokyo: Musashino Shobō.

Newspaper articles

'Fukkō jōkyō o goshinsatsu' (Emperor Observes Recovery Process), *Asahi shinbun* 20 February 1946: 2.

'Ise no jingū goshinpai' (Emperor's Prayer at the Ise Shrine), *Asahi shinbun*, 14 November 1945: 1.

'Kanagawa kenka goshinsatsu' (Emperor's Visit to Kanagawa), *Asahi shinbun*, 21 February 1946: 1.

'Kyō tenchōsetsu' (Today is the Emperor's Birthday), *Asahi shinbun*, 29 April 1946: 2.

'Kyō tenchōsetsu' (Today is the Emperor's Birthday), *Asahi shinbun*, 29 April 1947: 4.

'Kyōshutsu jōkyō o otazune' (Emperor Asks About Food Supply Conditions), *Asahi shinbun*, 2 March 1946: 2.

'Man'in densha ni Mikasanomiya' (Prince Mikasa in the Crowded Train), *Asahi shinbun*, 20 March 1946: 2.

'Ōi fukuin sha no nyūtō' (Many Former Soldiers Join the Communist Party), *Asahi shinbun*, 13 January 1946: 2.

'Shitsugyō jōtai no kōzokugata' ('Unemployed' Imperial Family Members), *Asahi shinbun Seibu-ban* (The Asahi, Western, censor-reviewed version), 6 April 1946: 2.

'Shotōka o gosotsugyō' (Crown Prince Graduates from Elementary School), *Asahi shinbun*, 20 March 1946: 2.

'Tenraku no fukuin gunjin o seijō fukaku goyūryo' (Emperor Worries about Fallen Ex-soldiers), *Asahi shinbun*, 13 January 1946: 2.

'Wakamiya tachi no hataraku ketsui: kōzokugata no okurashi' (Young Princes Decide to Work: Lives of Imperial Family Members), *Asahi shinbun*, 6 April 1946: 2.

11 'Art' il-legally defined?
A legal and art historical analysis of Akasegawa Genpei's Model Thousand-yen Note Incident

Yayoi Shionoiri

Introduction: can law adjudicate art?

Akasegawa Genpei (1937–) is now a member of the established Japanese cultural literati. Currently known mostly for his novels and essays, Akasegawa writes regular columns for newspapers and in 1981, even won the Akutagawa Prize, a prestigious literary prize awarded semi-annually. However, in the early 1960s, Akasegawa was still just another nameless member of Tokyo's avant-garde art community. During that time, Tokyo was a burgeoning hotbed of artistic activity. Attempting to challenge conventional definitions of art – which up to that point were mainly painting, drawing and sculpture – young artists were experimenting with alternative mediums and arguing for the elimination of distinct genres of artistic activity. These artists organized themselves into subcultural collectives, including the Neo-Dada Organizers and Hi-Red Center, the latter of which Akasegawa was a part.

Engaging the everyday world in what came to be referred to as the Direct Action (*chokusetsu kōdō*) mode, Akasegawa and his compatriots attempted to interject art as a form of live performance into everyday life.[1] Akasegawa argued that 'art' in the conventional sense required: a defined relation between the individual who is viewing and that which is viewed; and a conventional setting such as a museum or a gallery space (Akasegawa 1994: 12–13). In an attempt to break down barriers between the viewer and the object being viewed, the Tokyo avant-garde was interested in praxis that defined itself in opposition to this postulation of 'art'. Refusing to acknowledge conformity to convention, Akasegawa claimed that his actions were 'anti-art' (*han-geijutsu*), both criticizing the complacency pervading Japanese society through subtle but poignant performance, and acknowledging the necessity to define the work of avant-garde artists in the negative, as the mainstream reception of their work was, at times, mixed (Akasegawa and Matsuda 2001: 168).

While he may not have voluntarily sought the attention, Akasegawa succeeded in gaining long-lasting public exposure due to his involvement in what came to be known as the 'Model Thousand-yen Note Incident'. In this Incident, Akasegawa was charged in 1964 for the alleged contravention of the Act for the Regulation of Model Currency and Securities (Tsūka oyobi shōken mozō

196 *Y. Shionoiri*

torishimari-hō) of 1895 for his one-sided monochromatic thousand-yen note replicas. The relevant portions of this arcane law prohibit the manufacture or sale of items that have 'the misleading external appearance of currency' (Currency Act: Provision 1).[2] What ensued between 1965 and 1970 in Akasegawa's trial pitched his freedom of expression against legally prescribed standards of order.

In a series of insightful writings on Akasegawa and the Incident, Reiko Tomii argues that the Incident should be considered one of the first occasions whereby Japanese avant-garde artistic practice – which by definition is 'more often than not antagonistic to mainstream taste' and therefore, in some ways, limited in its very audience – was exposed to society at large (Tomii 2002: 142, 145). Tomii implies that Akasegawa's practice became coined as the 'Incident' at the point when the legal authorities became involved, arguing that the Incident is 'not an isolated object made by a solitary creator. ... While Akasegawa is its primary author, without whom the work would not have existed, the others played crucial roles, if only inadvertently, collaborating with him in its making' (Tomii 2002: 142–4, 145).

This chapter analyzes Akasegawa's navigation of a Japanese legal framework that attempted to censor his expression – both through his initial artistic output and in his active engagement with the court system. In deciding to engage with the legal framework, Akasegawa was forced to defend not only the legality of his actions but also the value of his artistic contributions to society. During the course of the Incident, Akasegawa's proactive engagement with the authorities who attempted to censor him may be read as a form of non-censorship, where he actively challenged the pre-existing legal framework to consider and decide on the validity of his artistic expression. Although Akasegawa did not succeed in convincing the courts, I shall argue that the Incident was successful when viewed through the lens of civil disobedience. In contrast to previous scholarship on the Incident by Tomii and others, I shall undertake an art historical and legal analysis, illuminating the Incident as a seminal example of an artist's personal attempt at negotiating an external apparatus of restraint on his freedom of expression.

Akasegawa's thousand-yen notes as *objet*: to be a *kakushin-han* or 'convinced criminal'

Akasegawa's artistic practice surrounding thousand-yen notes is multi-valenced. He not only produced 'models' that were printed and cut in the same manner as official currency, but also painstakingly copied the design of the thousand-yen note by hand in a mode that he referred to as 'superrealism'. Explaining the impetus for such detailed drawing, Akasegawa recalled his own frustration with the perceived lack of originality in his artistic practice prior to his thousand-yen notes (Akasegawa and Kikuhata 1987: 22); in earlier years, Akasegawa had pursued the creation of work using new media, but remained unable to convince even himself that he had succeeded in creating breakthrough work. Rejecting the possibility for true originality, he decided to pursue an entirely new direction in his *oeuvre*; on a quest to achieve a hand-drawn reproduction that was as close as possible to an original object, he chose the thousand-yen note as his target (Akasegawa and Kikuhata 1987: 22).[3]

Akasegawa started using the thousand-yen note in his *oeuvre* as early as 1963 (Akasegawa 1994: 86). The predominant design of the thousand-yen note in circulation at the time featured Prince Shōtoku (573–621), a regent that ruled during the Asuka period, with Hōryū-ji, a Buddhist temple in Nara, on the reverse.[4] A version of a blown-up rendition of the note in ink (90 cm × 180 cm), complete with the red seal visible on Japanese currency, entitled *The Morphology of Revenge (Look Well Before You Kill)* (*Fukushū no keitaigaku [Korosu mae ni aite o yoku miru]*, 1963), was submitted to the 15th Yomiuri Independent Exhibition in Tokyo, an exhibition that served as the breeding ground for contemporary art practice at that time (Nagoya City Art Museum 1995: 61–2) (Figure 11.1). While Akasegawa explained that he was merely attempting to undertake an act of copying that eliminated any evidence of the creator's hand of labor, he gave this work a title that ended up serving as a premonition for the development of further thousand-yen note works.

Akasegawa was also experimenting with what he felt was the 'next logical step' in the development of his thousand-yen note *oeuvre* (Akasegawa and Matsuda 2001: 134). Moving away from hand-drawn reproductions, Akasegawa outsourced the task of actual creation. No longer was Akasegawa pursuing the act of copying an object by hand in a mere attempt to transcribe the original; in his printed thousand-yen notes, Akasegawa was attempting to reproduce the design and look of currency, so much so that the reproduced version had the power to possibly overtake the original.

Around January 1963, Akasegawa had requested advice from a colleague in the printing industry to manufacture copper plates of a sheet of thousand-yen

Figure 11.1 Akasegawa Genpei, The Morphology of Revenge (Look Well Before You Kill) (*Fukushū no Keitaigaku (Korosu mae ni aite o yoku miru)*) , 1963. Ink on paper, 90 cm × 180 cm. Courtesy Nagoya City Art Museum.

notes. Akasegawa's friend brought Akasegawa's request to Itō Shizuka of Mie Printer who was willing to undertake the process of monochrome printing, but who declined to manufacture the copper plate. Akasegawa then requested another colleague to bring his request to another printer, Yasumasa Shigeru of Yasumasa Printer, who initially agreed to proceed with both the manufacturing of the copper plate and the monochrome printing of the notes. However, after the copper plate had been produced, Yasumasa halted the monochrome printing process, claiming that he was unable to accept the printing request. Akasegawa was given the copper plate of the notes, and took the copper plate back to Itō who proceeded with the monochrome printing of the notes (Akasegawa 1970: 186–8).

A total of 3,000 editions of Akasegawa's monochrome notes in various permutations were printed (Indictment, 1965, cited in Trial Reports: see 'Mokei' November 1966: 139). Some of these were used as an invitation to one of Akasegawa's exhibitions. Certain uncut sheets of these printed notes were used to wrap everyday objects, and still other uncut sheets were appended to panels and bolted down. Even though Akasegawa himself would not admit that he intended to carry out fraud by releasing his currency as an apparatus of economic exchange, Akasegawa certainly appeared to realize at the time that what he was doing might not be acceptable (Akasegawa 2009). In looking back on his actions, Akasegawa himself noted that while 'he never had any insidious intent', he sensed that having the notes printed up 'would be "bad", but everyone had a different idea of what was "bad"' (Akasegawa 2009).

Law and order: drama in the courtroom

On 1 November 1965 Akasegawa was indicted by the Tokyo District Prosecutors Office to the Tokyo District Court for alleged currency modeling (*mozō*).[5] What becomes immediately apparent from the language of the law is that a crime based on the currency modeling law does not require either the use of a non-currency item as currency, or the intent to pass off such object as currency. Therefore, one can violate the law without intent to defraud.[6]

In preparation for the court case, Akasegawa's colleagues formed the 'Sen-en Satsu Jiken Kondankai' (Council on the Thousand-yen Note Incident), an artist-driven organization that served as a bridge between Akasegawa's legal team and his colleagues.[7] In an attempt to provide evidence that what Akasegawa was doing was artistic, and therefore outside of the purview of legal analysis, the 'Kondankai' Council attempted to increase awareness regarding Akasegawa's case by publishing flyers and to raise funds to support Akasegawa's legal fees by undertaking sales of artwork contributed by its members.

The court proceedings provided an extended and unique opportunity for evidence prepared by the 'Kondankai' Council to be admitted. Over the course of several months in 1966, Akasegawa's defense counsel and witnesses were allowed to take over the courtroom, and turn this very site of propriety into a theatrical space of performance art. Nakanishi Natsuyuki's clothespins and other artists' raw materials were used to re-create the chaotic happenings that these artists had been undertaking in the streets of Tokyo around the time of the Yomiuri Independent Exhibitions. While the art of Akasegawa and his colleagues had previously been referred to as 'anti-art', in the courtroom, Akasegawa's defense counsel maintained that the happenings in the courtroom were 'art' in order to bolster the position that Akasegawa's artwork was outside the purview of legal judgment and should be protected. By turning part of the courtroom proceedings into a site for advanced art performance, Akasegawa and his colleagues were not only attempting to provide evidence for their legal argument but also capitalizing on the opportunity to further develop their art practice. Under the auspices of 'art', Akasegawa used the language of the law and the procedural tools of the legal framework successfully to stage a happening in the courtroom; by using the very tools of his opponent, Akasegawa highlighted the ludicrousness of the situation.

The spectra of the superreal

During the trial, Akasegawa also produced other forms of superreal *objets* in support of his argument that his printing of thousand-yen notes should not be considered illegal. Akasegawa amassed a large amount of ephemera that featured currency copies, calling it his *Collection of Currency Knock-offs* (*Shihei ruiji korekushon*, 1966) (Figure 11.2). Examples from this collection included play money from children's games, business cards from establishments that used currency as their logo, teacups with currency designs, and other parodic works featuring images of various individuals, in lieu of the figures printed on official

Figure 11.2 Akasegawa Genpei, Collection of Currency Knock-offs (*Shihei Ruiji Korekushon*), 1966. Mixed media, variable dimensions. Photograph courtesy Nagoya City Art Museum.

200   *Y. Shionoiri*

currency. All of these 'currency knock-offs' were not considered illegal pursuant to the currency modeling law under which Akasegawa was being tried, and he attempted to show that his work had a place along this spectrum of objects that resembled currency.

Furthermore, Akasegawa created a work entitled *Ambiguity Inspection Card* (*Magirawashisa kensa-hyō*, 1966), where a thousand-yen note was photocopied in various shades of darkness. Lettered in alphabetical order, like exhibits admitted as evidence, Akasegawa presented his results in chart form – from indiscernible black to indiscernible white, and shades of darkness in between, showing the thousand-yen note in various stages of photocopying. This work implied the existence of an ambiguity in the spectrum, between photocopying that does not yield a discernible trace of a thousand-yen note, and photocopying that does. Questioning the power of this trace element, Akasegawa implied that actions of photocopying currency should not lead to persecution, as the difference between the indiscernible black version and the indiscernible white version was merely the variation of lightness that existed in between.

Akasegawa as currency modeler: prosecution, defense and judgment

Using the plain language of the law, the prosecutors argued that Akasegawa violated the currency modeling law. Akasegawa had requested several printers to create the copper plates of the thousand-yen notes and had notes – that resembled currency – printed. Furthermore, some of the monochrome notes – originally printed up as sheets – were even cut-to-size. The prosecutors argued that at the moment when the notes were printed as a sheet of monochrome notes, Akasegawa and the printers who were prosecuted as co-conspirators, infringed the law (Nakahara 1967b: 60). The prosecutors downplayed the fact that Akasegawa did not have any intent to transgress the law and that the action took place without much planning or much parsing of intent (Akasegawa 2009).[8]

In response to the prosecution, Akasegawa's defense counsel, Sugimoto Shōjun of Miharabashi Law Firm – known for his representation of ideological defendants in public safety ordinance cases ('Mokei' December 1966: 65) – had no recourse but to argue that Akasegawa was creating art, and that such creativity should remain unfettered by the shackles of the legal framework. Sugimoto, together with poet and art critic Takiguchi Shūzō and art critic Nakahara Yūsuke – both of whom were appointed special defense counsel for Akasegawa – claimed that Akasegawa's work was critical to the development of advanced contemporary art in Japan and that his work should not, and could not, be tried by law. As an alternative, they argued that if Akasegawa's work was tried from a legal standpoint, the existing legal framework unconstitutionally restricted Akasegawa's freedom of expression.

In setting up a two-part argument, the defense first argued that Akasegawa's case should not be a mere question of whether his actions violated an outdated law. Discussing the development of contemporary art in Japan, the defense instructed the court that modern definitions of 'art' had expanded. Touching on the development of Western modern art, Takiguchi argued that Akasegawa's work should be contextually considered alongside Duchampian readymades and happenings by Japanese avant-garde groups such as Hi-Red Center (Trial Reports: see 'Mokei' November 1966: 146–9). Akasegawa's first line of defense rested on the assertion that art not only existed outside of the legal framework, but was superior to it; artistic trials therefore mistreated art by bringing it down to everyday dimensions (Nakahara 1967b: 63).[9]

The alternative legal argument by Sugimoto continued the exposition of this narrative. Unable to respond directly to the alleged infringement claim of the currency modeling law, Sugimoto argued for the protection of the artist's right to create. For example, Akasegawa's *Collection of Currency Knock-offs* was presented to the court as evidence that other objects – both artistic and commercial – that utilized currency did not infringe the currency modeling law. In setting up this spectrum of objects, the defense argued that Akasegawa's work should be included within this spectrum, and that Akasegawa's freedom of expression was unfairly restricted due to the application of the law to Akasegawa.

Despite the efforts of the defense, the Japanese courts found Akasegawa guilty of infringing the currency modeling law and sentenced Akasegawa to a suspended prison term of three months.[10] The court held that the moment when Akasegawa infringed the law was not when the notes were printed up as a large sheet, but when the individual notes were cut into the size of official currency. In its decision, it appears that the court was trying to find a moment closer in time to the moment of potential use of this *objet* as currency. The court also held that Akasegawa violated *lèse-majesté* (*fukeizai*), as he was found guilty of an attack on a custom held sacred by society.[11] The Tokyo District Court responded to Akasegawa's first line of defense by finding that Akasegawa's *objet* was scarce in 'artistic elements' (Recommended Sentence, 1966, cited in Nakahara 1967a: 14). While Akasegawa's *oeuvre* had been accepted as artistic happenings, 'such an evaluation was mere circumstance, after the crime had been committed' (Recommended Sentence, 1966, cited in Court Spectator Report: see 'Mokei' January 1967: 77). In response to the freedom of expression line of defense, the Tokyo District Court noted that the level of freedom of expression protected by the constitution was not unrestricted. The abuse of such protections was prohibited, and should be restricted for the sake of common welfare (District Court Opinion, 1967, cited in 'Mokei' September 1967: 75).

To summarize, the prosecution argued that Akasegawa's *objet* had artistic elements but should still be considered criminal activity. In response, the defense had very little recourse but to respond – within the existing legal framework – that Akasegawa's *objets* were artistic expression but not criminal activity. Due to the lack of available persuasive legal arguments that Akasegawa had in defending himself, Takiguchi claimed that Akasegawa's choice in going to trial already established 'a step towards concession' and that, by allowing himself to be tried by the legal system, Akasegawa had little recourse but to accept his

202 *Y. Shionoiri*

conviction (Akasegawa 1970: 160). Exploiting Akasegawa's lack of a strong legal defense, the Tokyo District Court, as well as the higher courts, found that Akasegawa's work was both artistic expression and criminal activity.

The intersection of law and art: punishment of a thought crime

On its face and unfortunately for Akasegawa, the Tokyo District Court's legal analysis was accurate. While arcane, the currency modeling law had not been repealed, and Akasegawa's actions firmly established the required elements to prove his infringement: the manufacture of an item that had the misleading external appearance of currency. The law, however, allowed the court to determine the degree to which an item looked like currency, in order for such item to have infringed the law. In its decision, the Tokyo District Court held that Akasegawa's work – when cut to the size of a thousand-yen note – had the misleading external appearance of currency, despite the fact that Akasegawa only printed one-sided, monochromatic replicas. In doing so, the court ensured that Akasegawa would be found guilty.

More significantly, however, the Tokyo District Court interpreted the currency modeling law to contain an element of intent on behalf of the object-maker. In other words, within the broad strokes of the law, the court evaluated the maliciousness of the action of the object-maker and determined that an object's misleading external appearance became more misleading, as the action of the object-maker was deemed to be more malicious. Underlying the court's decision, therefore, was the subtle implication that Akasegawa was being punished for his thoughts as an ideological deviant (Akasegawa and Kikuhata 1987: 29).

Through the trial, Akasegawa was in effect punished for his attempt to challenge societal standards through his work. In his own appeal to the Tokyo Supreme Court, Akasegawa admitted the danger that lurked in his work and was perceived by the courts. Akasegawa described his work as implicating a contestation of the concept that 'currency' – as both a self-sustaining concept and signifier for social order – was sacred and inviolable (Akasegawa's Appeal to the Tokyo Supreme Court, 1969, cited in Akasegawa 1970: 136–8). In Akasegawa's trials, the courts appear to have elided the concept of 'commonly accepted norms' (*shakai tsūnen*) as being applicable to Akasegawa's *objets*; according to the court, Akasegawa's work was both 'art' that existed outside of the realm of the everyday, yet retained elements in its external appearance that would mislead a third party to believe they were seeing official currency. In this way, the courts determined Akasegawa's guilty holding *a priori*, ensuring that the pre-existing legal framework could support its decision.

Real versus fake

Through his *objets*, Akasegawa was dangerous to state authority, as he challenged not just the currency modeling law, but also the concepts of the 'real', the 'pseudo-real' and the 'fake'. When Akasegawa first started creating work based on currency, he nicknamed his work 'fake thousand-yen notes' (*nise sen-en satsu*) for lack of a better term, while he claimed that he was 'in pursuit of the "real"' (Akasegawa 1970: 170, 172). In doing so, Akasegawa implied that it was possible to define an object as authentic or genuine through an examination of that which it is not. Arguing that in order for an object to become 'real', such an object necessitates the existence and validation of the 'pseudo-real', Akasegawa proved through his *objets* that the line between 'real' currency and 'non-real' currency is tenuous (Akasegawa 1970: 25). Just as much as a piece of artwork by a named artist increases in rarity and value due to the proliferation of mass-produced fakes that take after the style of the artist, Akasegawa's model thousand-yen notes are perhaps dangerous in their very embodiment of the 'pseudo-real'. Akasegawa's work was never meant to be used as 'real' currency, but as a model of the 'real' that served as a 'knothole to observe the battle between the real and the fake, and provided a key to its observation' (Akasegawa 1970: 32).

William Marotti (2001: 217) has argued that the forcible 'ascription of Akasegawa's activities into the delineated sphere [of] "art", drastically reduces the radical potential of his actions'. Marotti implies that the courts utilized the pre-existing legal framework to de-tooth the dangerous message inherent in Akasegawa's work (2001: 218).[12] If Akasegawa had intended to assert the fragility of accepted notions of orderly exchange by exposing the instability of currency as a concept, the courts attempted to reify Akasegawa's work as inapplicable to everyday life by proscribing Akasegawa's activities within the realm of 'art'.[13]

However, Akasegawa may have proven to be dangerous to state authority because his work investigated the relationship between the state and its people, using currency as his medium. Even if Akasegawa never had the intent to use his work as currency worth its value in the economic markets, his work implied that the intangible concept of currency and its exchange is built upon a tangible promise between the state and its people, based on the way people operate within that realm (Akasegawa 2005: 68). In identifying that the relationship between the 'real' and the 'pseudo-real' is one of mimesis, Akasegawa insinuated that the tangible promise between the state and its people can be disrupted. The better the quality of the model, the closer it becomes to the real; the best 'pseudo-real' currency will encompass the qualities of the 'real', so much so that it could pass for the 'real' thing and enter the economic market, cloaking itself in the value accorded to the 'real'.

Direct action

Attempting to put Direct Action into praxis whereby thought is linked to action in daily life, Akasegawa and his contemporaries took art outside of spaces conventionally devoted to 'art' and, instead, brought their activities to individuals going about their daily lives. All this was done in an attempt to raise pointed

204   *Y. Shionoiri*

questions about the nature of everyday society (Havens 2006: 149) – a goal that artists such as Akasegawa argued was neither artistic nor political, yet ended up producing work that encompassed elements of both.[14]

Taken to an extreme, Direct Action becomes strangely indistinguishable from any other action in everyday life. The inherent contradiction of the avant-garde undertaking that attempts to comment on reality becomes apparent as the art is 'no longer distinct from the praxis of life but wholly absorbed in it' (Bürger 1974: 50). Certain instances of Direct Action had a mixed reception: it appeared that fellow contemporaries appreciated the humor and irony with which many of these happenings were carried out, but that the general populace – by whom such Direct Action was intended to be seen – often expressed puzzlement at best, and disdain at worst.[15]

In the Incident, Akasegawa arguably engaged in the most extreme form of Direct Action because he attempted to effect change outside of the reified realm of 'art' – one of the very goals of Direct Action. When Akasegawa's work was initially released into the world, such work remained within the rarefied realm of Direct Action as an artistic happening. For example, in the hand-drawn work exhibited in the Yomiuri Independent Exhibition, the spectator was a visitor who chose to attend the exhibition; in the case of the invitation to Akasegawa's solo exhibition, the spectator was a selected recipient of the invitation. Therefore, Akasegawa's initial attempts at Direct Action had a limited self-selected audience to which the artist was communicating his message, many members of whom already considered themselves in alliance with the artist's position.

Relational negotiations

In comparison to the exhibitions, when Akasegawa's thousand-yen notes became the subject of a legal trial, and became the starting point from which the Incident arose, the work and the surrounding responses, reactions and discourses brought Akasegawa's Direct Action into even closer proximity to the everyday.[16] Bounded by the social apparatus that is the legal framework – a set of existing regulations by which individuals are expected to abide in modern society – Akasegawa's art and the presumptive intent behind his artistic practice were expected to pass muster against public notions of commonly accepted norms and the general public good. At the intersection of Akasegawa's practice and the social apparatus of the existing legal framework, therefore, Akasegawa ended up negotiating on several levels. First, he engaged the understanding of censorship, asking whether an object that was legally questionable in its existence in everyday life could still be considered art, and thus be excluded from the purview of the legal framework. Second, he challenged the impossibility of 'art' effecting social change.

As part of an unplanned – but highly memorable – strategy in the courtroom, Akasegawa's work was given broader public exposure. Indeed, without his interaction with the legal system and the opportunity for the public to read about the courtroom drama that ensued, Akasegawa would not otherwise have been able to transmit his message as effectively and as broadly. However, by choosing a legal argument that his work ought to be considered art and therefore subject to free speech protections, Akasegawa's strategy invalidated much of the pre-existing discourse that he and his colleagues had built around the concept of Direct Action. Moreover, the legal argument ended up proving unsuccessful for Akasegawa, as the court admitted that his work was art, but that his actions were nevertheless guilty of infringing the modeling laws.

The Model Thousand-yen Note Incident is one of the few instances in modern Japan where the courts attempted to elucidate the value of fine art. Unfortunately for Akasegawa, however, what becomes evident is that artistic practice – at least the version that Akasegawa practiced – does not intersect with the legal framework with positive results. That art historians, critics and cultural intelligentsia of the times attempted to prove that Akasegawa's work fitted under the definition of 'art' was irrelevant in the courts' evaluations of whether Akasegawa's actions were triable and whether he was guilty according to the law.

Tomii argues that Akasegawa's work became a fluid commentary on state authority and society through the involvement of the legal authorities and his compatriots. Tomii's reading, therefore, necessitates the various relational negotiations in order for Akasegawa's work to not only have discursive meaning, but also to exist as a work vis-à-vis society. However, my view is that the significance of Akasegawa's actions – whether defined externally as 'art', 'Direct Action' or otherwise – exists at the moment that Akasegawa began his practice of working with currency notes.[17]

The significance of Akasegawa's work and the ensuing Incident is not limited to the fact that he managed to have his artwork engage with the pre-existing legal framework with the assistance of his artistic compatriots, and at the assertion of state authority as represented by the courts, but also in his acknowledged challenge to make 'art' that attempts to effect social change. As such, the concept of civil disobedience might prove to be a more successful lens through which to interpret Akasegawa's work. First made popular by Thoreau's 1849 essay of the same name, civil disobedience is the active refusal to obey laws or governmental demands for the purpose of influencing legislation or policy. In seeking an active form of civil disobedience, protesters may choose to deliberately break certain laws in a non-violent manner.[18]

Akasegawa himself maintained that he did not initially intend for his artwork to expose the silent authority's power to regulate the quotidian life of middle-class Japanese (Akasegawa's Statement to the Tokyo District Court, 1966, cited in Akasegawa 1970: 109–10). However, by utilizing commonplace signifiers that simulated the 'real', and by transmitting his works into everyday life, Akasegawa placed himself in a situation where he ultimately became the torch-bearer for a viewpoint advocating the protection of freedom of expression. His actions – while deemed threatening enough to the authority of the state to be tried and found criminal – were never violent. Furthermore, the Incident certainly engendered more public exposure for the Tokyo avant-garde contemporary art movement; fellow artists, art historians, critics, gallery dealers, lawyers and educators were brought together under the auspices of the 'Kondankai' Council, to deliberate, discuss and formulate a viable argument in support of protecting an artist's right to freedom of expression.

As for the validity of Akasegawa's right to freedom of expression, his thousand-yen notes – in their various forms – appear to provide strong theoretical support for the idea that he should have the right, as an artist, to create work based on currency. Many of Akasegawa's works, such as the hand-drawn large-scale versions of the notes, are intricate and detailed works of labor that have merit in their technical execution. Still others, such as the mechanically reproduced currency sheets, are printed monochromatically and on one side of the sheet only, changing both the dimensions and the coloring of the reproduction. Moreover, and perhaps most significantly, Akasegawa neither intended for the currency to be released into the world of currency exchange, nor intended to carry out fraudulent acts in his challenge to protect his right to freedom of expression. Therefore, Akasegawa appears to be a perfect model candidate as the leader of a collective arguing against the censorship of protected expression in modern Japan.

Unfortunately, for our model candidate, Akasegawa was in the end unsuccessful in arguing that his form of expression should be protected by the law. From a purely legal perspective, the case law surrounding the Incident continued the precedent of allowing the juridical system to determine what would be acceptable activity within the bounds of the law. Furthermore, Akasegawa's line of legal defense – that his work should be defined as 'art' and therefore external to the application of the legal framework – ensured that his *objets* would be categorized with nomenclature that he himself had initially actively eschewed. Herein, therefore, lay the paradoxical position in which Akasegawa found himself. In negotiating the liminal boundary between the public and private space, the vanguard exists entirely outside of such discursive relationship, as 'vanguardism implies the existence of sovereign subjects whose superior social vision can penetrate illusions and perceive the people's "true" interests' (Deutsche 1996: 268). Yet, Akasegawa had to utilize the tools given to him within the legal framework in order to assert his stance. Akasegawa's non-censorship, especially during the trial, was itself a form of civil disobedience. Whether such a form of Direct Action is defined as 'art' still remains a poignant and open question.

Acknowledgments

A version of this essay was presented at the Association for Asian Studies annual meeting in March 2010, and the author would like to thank the conference participants for their comments. The author is indebted to Professors Matthew McKelway and Jonathan Reynolds for their thoughtful insights, to Professor Benjamin Mason Meier for his editorial assistance, and to Mr. Joe Takeba and Mr. Satoshi Yamada at the Nagoya City Art Museum and to Ms. Yumi Umemura at SCAI THE BATHHOUSE for their kind assistance throughout the image permissions process.

Notes

1 Akasegawa was a founding member of Hi-Red Center, an avant-garde collective operative in Tokyo during 1962–4, responsible for many happenings in the Direct Action mode. For example, on 26 and 27 January 1964, Hi-Red Center hosted the *Shelter Plan* event at the Imperial Hotel in Tokyo, whereby fellow artists, including Yoko Ono, were invited to visit a room rented by the group (Akasegawa 1994: 177–201). There, each participant's measurements were taken in various ways, with the intent to create customized boxes for each participant that would 'shelter' said participant. Similar to Andy Warhol's Factory – which was taking place contemporaneously in New York – Hi-Red Center brought together many avant-garde artists. However, Hi-Red Center prided itself on being rigidly formal and polite (*konsetsu teinei*) when attempting to engage the public, whereas Warhol's group became infamous for their drug-infused, sexually radical ways.

2 The Act for the Regulation of Model Currency and Securities (enacted 5 April 1895, Law No. 28), in effect as of Akasegawa's time, reads as follows:

(1) The manufacture or sale of items that have the misleading external appearance of currency, government-issued currency, bank notes, convertible bank notes, government bonds or local bonds is prohibited.
(2) Those who contravene the above provision shall be sentenced to a period of penal servitude that is at least one month and no more than three years.
(3) The items mentioned in Provision 1 shall either be destroyed by the police authorities or, pursuant to the Criminal Code, shall be impounded.

Unless noted otherwise, all translations are the author's own.

3 Akasegawa recalls that he was 'taken aback by the intensity of the [thousand-yen note] when seen as a phenomenon' (*genshō to shite mita kyōretsusa ni me o ubaware*), implying that at a certain moment in time, he became interested in the currency note as something other than a commonplace, quotidian object (Nagoya City Art Museum 1995: 102).

4 The thousand-yen note featuring Prince Shōtoku was initially issued on 7 January 1950 and suspended on 4 January 1965. Another thousand-yen note design featuring Itō Hirobumi was issued on 1 November 1963 after Akasegawa had already begun his thousand-yen note *oeuvre*.

5 See Sen-en Satsu Jiken Kondankai (1966). In comparison to the US court system, Japanese court documents are retained for far shorter periods, and documents from criminal cases are generally unavailable for public review. In a conversation with a representative from the Tokyo District Court in June 2009, I was informed that Akasegawa's case documents were not available for public review.

6 In comparison to the Japanese law, the US Counterfeit Detection Act of 1992 is much more narrowly tailored. The law permits color illustrations of US currency, provided that the reproduction is not the same size as the actual currency and is one-sided. Furthermore, photographic or other likenesses of US currency and foreign currency are permitted for any non-fraudulent purpose, provided that the items are reproduced in black and white and are not the size of the original currency being reproduced (The Counterfeit Detection Act of 1992, Public Law 102–550, in Section 411 of Title 31 of the Code of Federal Regulations).

7 The group included: Takiguchi Shūzō, Ishiko Junzō, Imaizumi Masahiko, Kawani Hiroshi, Sugimoto Shōjun, Tone Yasunao, Nakahara Yūsuke, Nakanishi Natsuyuki, Takamatsu Jiro, Hari-u Ichiro, Miki Tamon and Yoshida Yoshie.

8 It is clear that the Tokyo Metropolitan Police Department was sensitive about currency fraud. Around the time that Akasegawa was creating his work, the police were working on the infamous *Chi-37* case, an unsolved case where a total of 343 counterfeit notes were found throughout the nation between 1961 and 1963. Even before

Akasegawa was indicted, on 27 January 1964, the *Asahi* newspaper published an article falsely insinuating Akasegawa's possible involvement with the *Chi-37* case.

9 In its use of the term 'artistic trial' the defense did not distinguish the fact that previous postwar artistic trials in Japan were trials about alleged infringement by literary sources of obscenity laws and not about works of fine art. For a discussion of such precedents, see Marotti (2001: 215–17).

10 Akasegawa's defense was denied at all levels of the Japanese court system. The Tokyo District Court found Akasegawa guilty on 24 June 1967. Akasegawa's appeal to the Tokyo High Court was dismissed on 13 November 1968. The Tokyo Supreme Court then denied Akasegawa's appeal on 24 April 1970.

11 While entirely unrelated to the requirements of the Currency Act, Akasegawa was deemed to have offended the dignity of the imperial line by basing his artwork on the image of Prince Shōtoku. Significantly, *lèse-majesté* was deleted from the Criminal Code in 1947 and, therefore, it is likely that the courts intended to use the term in a more generic manner.

12 Marotti notes that an examination of the genesis of the Incident reveals 'provocative (but not atypical) critical, political impulses within a complex artist discourse' (2001: 212). While an analysis of the Incident *post-facto* may reveal the connection between political impulse and artistic practice, I would argue that the contextualization of the Incident – as it developed and progressed – was a significant external factor that crystallized the concepts underlying the Incident.

13 Implicit in the decision regarding Akasegawa's trial – in contrast to the obscenity cases – is the notion that certain works of art may be afforded the protections of freedom of expression. In a concurring opinion to Akasegawa's case, Justice Irokawa Kōtarō argues that art that was 'of a higher order' (*kōji de atte*) and had social value may be constitutionally protected (see Marotti 2001: 223). Of course, Akasegawa's work did not fall into this category according to the courts.

14 For example, in Akasegawa's memoir on the activities of Hi-Red Center, he noted that the group's activities were meant to be ambiguous, as it was trying 'as hard as possible not to make [the activities] seem artistic, [and] in order to achieve this, it had to make [the activities] appear to seem both political and apolitical, as well as commercial and non-commercial' (Akasegawa 1994: 104–5).

15 Akasegawa often self-deprecatingly referred to what he perceived to be the common response of Tokyo civilians to Hi-Red Center's antics: 'Don't know if this is supposed to be "avant-garde art" or what ... you can't help but wonder whether it's OK for such artist-types to remain in society's vest pocket when we're toiling away at our jobs' (Akasegawa 1994: 146).

16 Akasegawa succeeded in receiving more public exposure due to the Incident than he ever did prior to it. As the Incident progressed, the event received coverage in a number of art journals, including *Art Notebook* (*Bijutsu techō*), a monthly magazine that began publication in 1948 and currently has a circulation of approximately 60,000 a month. Perhaps due to the archaic legal rationale involved in indicting the artist, the mainstream media did not give the Incident widespread, sensationalist attention. However, in exchange for gaining a criminal record through the Incident, Akasegawa eventually gained widespread fame and arguably utilized his prominence to successfully catapult a writing career. He remains one of the most significant Japanese individuals in the letters today.

17 In conversations with the author, Jonathan Reynolds has insightfully commented on the possibility of there being multiple works within the Incident: the original production of Akasegawa's notes; and the court performance, neither of which preclude the other.

18 As a protest tactic, civil disobedience has been used in many well-documented movements, including those of Gandhi's campaigns for India's independence from the British Empire to the American civil rights movement.

References

Akasegawa, Genpei (1970) *Akasegawa Genpei no bunshō – objet o motta musansha* (The Writings of Akasegawa Genpei – Have-nots who Have Objects), Tokyo: Gendai Shichōsha.

Akasegawa, Genpei (1994) *Tokyo mikisā keikaku – Hi-Red Center chokusetsu kōdō no kiroku* (Tokyo Mixer Plan – Records of Hi Red Center's Direct Action), Tokyo: Chikuma Shobō.

Akasegawa, Genpei (2005) *Fushigi na Okane* (Strange Money), Mainichi Shinbunsha.

Akasegawa, Genpei (2009) (Conversation with author, 30 June).

Akasegawa, Genpei and Kikuhata, Mokuma (1987) '<Taidan> Aimai na umi no ue Akasegawa Genpei – Kikuhata Mokuma' (A Conversation between Akasegawa Genpei and Kikuhata Mokuma: Upon the Ambiguous Ocean), *Kikan* (14).

Akasegawa, Genpei and Matsuda, Tetsuo (2001) *Zenmen jikyō! Akasegawa Genpei* (A Fully Voluntary Confession! Akasegawa Genpei), Tokyo: Shōbunsha.

Bürger, Peter (1974) *Theory of the Avant-garde*, trans. from German by Michael Shaw, Minneapolis: University of Minnesota Press.

Deutsche, Rosalyn (1996) *Evictions: Art and Spatial Politics*, Cambridge: MIT Press.

Havens, Thomas R.H. (2006) *Radicals and Realists in the Japanese Nonverbal Arts: The Avant-Garde Rejection of Modernism*, Honolulu: University of Hawai'i Press.

Marotti, William (2001) 'Simulacra and Subversion in the Everyday: Akasegawa Genpei's 1000-yen Copy, Critical Art, and the State', *Postcolonial Studies*, 4(2): 211–39.

'Mokei sen-en satsu jiken de katsuyaku suru shunin bengoshi' (Lead Lawyer Active in Model Thousand-yen Note Incident), *Bijutsu techō* (Art Notebook), 276 (December 1966): 65.

'Mokei sen-en satsu jiken kōhan kiroku' (Model Thousand-yen Note Incident Trial Reports) (Indictment, Defendant Statement, Special Defense Counsel Statement, Defense Opening Remarks) (Trial Reports), *Bijutsu techō*, 274 (November 1966): 137–68.

'Mokei sen-en satsu jiken kōhan kiroku' (Model Thousand-yen Note Incident Trial Reports) (Tokyo District Court Opinion) (District Court Opinion), *Bijutsu techō*, 287 (September 1967): 71–6.

'Mokei sen-en satsu saiban bōchō-ki' ('Model Thousand-yen Note Incident Court Spectator Reports'), *Bijutsu techō*, 273 (October 1966): 74–5; 276 (December 1966): 64–5; 278 (January 1967): 76–7; 279 (February 1967): 72–3.

Nagoya City Art Museum (1995) *The Adventures of Akasegawa Genpei – Akasegawa Genpei no Bōken – Nōnai Resort Kaihatsu Daisakusen*, Nagoya: Nagoya City Art Museum.

Nakahara, Yūsuke (1967a) 'Hōritsu wa kannen ya kōsō o sabiki-uruka?' (Can Law Try Ideology or Structural Apparatus?), *Bijutsu Techō*, 281 (April 1967): 14–15.

Nakahara, Yūsuke (1967b) 'Mokei sen-en satsu jiken – geijutsu wa sabakare-uruka' (Model Thousand-yen Note Incident – Can Art Be Tried?), *Bijutsu techō*, 287 (September 1967): 59–70.

Sen-en Satsu Jiken Kondankai (Council on the Thousand-yen Note Incident) (ed.) (1966) 'Sen-en satsu jiken mokuroku' (Thousand-yen Note Incident Indices), 'Sen-en satsu saiban e – jiken no kei-i to appeal' (Towards the Thousand-yen Note Incident Trial – Leading up to the Incident and Appeal), and 'Sen-en satsu saiban e – butsu/hōtei/kō-i' (Towards the Thousand-yen Note Incident Trial – The Thing/The Courtroom/The Action).

The Counterfeit Detection Act of 1992, Public Law 102–550, in Section 411 of Title 31 of the Code of Federal Regulations.

Thoreau, Henry David (2001) [1849] 'Civil Disobedience', in *The Major Essays of Henry David Thoreau*, ed. Richard Dillman, Albany, NY: Whitston, 47–67.

Tomii, Reiko (2002) 'State v. (Anti-)Art: Model 1,000-yen Note Incident by Akasegawa Genpei and Company', *positions*, 10(1): 141–72.

Tsūka oyobi shōken mozō torishimari-hō (Act for the Regulation of Counterfeit Currency and Securities), 5 April 1895, Law No. 28.

12 Parodying the censor and censoring parody in modern Japan

Kirsten Cather

'Censorship' has long been something of a dirty word; calling someone a censor, an insult to their integrity and intelligence. The nature of censorship as an institution and the identity of the censor have changed considerably over time, but what has not changed, and has even achieved a degree of universality, is the charge that the censor is a backwards ignoramus. Or, to put it as bluntly as critics have, that the censor is 'either ignorant, imperious, and remisse, or basely pecuniary' (John Milton's 1644 *Aeropagitica*), a 'species of tittle-tattle, impertinence and malice' (Anglican Reverend Sydney Smith, writing in 1809), an 'unenlightened jackass' (Japanese playwright Kikuya Sakae, circa 1935), and 'a parasite, a pathogenic invader' (South African author J.M. Coetzee, writing in 1994).[1]

Underpinning the desire to demonize the censor with such vitriol lurks the notion that a break with censorship is essential to advancing civilization and art. The severity of censorship often serves as a benchmark for judging a nation's progress, or lack thereof. As Richard Burt has noted, 'distinctions between modernity and postmodernity have rested in large part on distinctions ... between early modern and modern modes of domination and between modern and postmodern forms' and 'censorship has been a key way of differentiating' among these (1994: xxi–xxii). As Sue Curry Jansen has pointed out, Freud somewhat counter-intuitively contended that 'it is a mark of the advance of civilization when men are no longer burned – merely their books', while eighteenth-century Enlightenment discourse celebrated the eradication of censorship as marking 'a decisive break with a superstitious, ignorant, and tyrannical past' (1988: 20, 4).

Such teleological models posit that censorship is eventually eradicated in modern liberal democracies. But as many scholars have noted, such claims draw artificial distinctions between periods to label one progressive and another repressive, and they fail to recognize that censorship endures, and is even a structuring component of all societies and discourse (Bourdieu 1999; Burt 1994; Fish 1994; Jansen 1988). If modernity was heralded by the ostensible disappearance of censorship, postmodernity is marked by an awareness that the censor never disappears entirely, but merely shape shifts, morphing from an overt externalized political or religious state authority in the older traditional model to a more diffuse and often internalized process. The rather vague term 'the new

212   *K. Cather*

censorship', coined in the wake of the US culture wars in the late 1980s, has come to refer to diverse forces, such as market capitalism, identity politics and interest groups on the left or right, that now enforce censorship in a more covert way (Burt 1994: xxv–xxvi, n1). With the advent of this 'new censorship', any neat alignment of the pro-censorship camp with reactionary state- or church-based authority, and the anti-censorship camp with liberal progressives no longer pertains. The censor is just as likely to be one's self as another.

This more fluid conception of how censorship operates and endures is clearly exemplified by the case of postwar Japan where the lines between old and new and between state and self-censorship have always been somewhat blurry. Japan has experienced a series of repeated revivals of state censorship, from the invisible political censorship conducted by the Occupation authorities to the moral censorship that continues to be conducted by the Japanese state even today.[2] Since the late 1980s and early 1990s, self-censorship (*jishuku*), a prominent feature of prewar and wartime publishing, has become entrenched with the systematic institution of voluntary self-censorship by publishers and broadcasters geared toward political correctness or, as it is pejoratively called in Japanese, 'word-hunting' (*kotoba-gari*).[3] Guided by in-house lists of taboo words (*kinkushū*) and suggested alternatives (*iikaeshū*), it resembles earlier self-censorship practices, but constitutes 'the new censorship' since political correctness and the economic logic of the market, not state politics, guide its practice.

Regardless of the fact that the old paradigms no longer hold (if they ever did), censorship continues to be vilified as a repressive pre- or anti-modern practice. The censor, however, also offers artists a powerful antagonist that can paradoxically stimulate the production of art. At the very least, as South African writer J.M. Coetzee puts it, 'the physical expulsion of the censor, vomited forth as a demon is, has a certain symbolic value for the writer' (1994: 10). Censorship has even been credited with inspiring a literary movement as in the case of modernism, which evolved amid a 'theater of censorship' with works by D.H. Lawrence and James Joyce becoming landmarks of both the new literary style and high-profile censorship battles in the West and in Japan.[4] As the theatrical analogy implies, censorship offers an ideal stage against which artists can define and debut their politics and their aesthetics.

In this chapter, I consider what happens when this struggle with the censor forms not just the background stage for the creation of art, but instead constitutes the art itself. What happens when the censor and the act of censorship *are* the artistic material, when the censor becomes the big bad wolf in one's fiction? What are the political and aesthetic effects of reflecting or reviving the censor in the medium of fiction, and what changes when works are produced in the 'old' versus 'new' eras of censorship? What can the presence of this censor-in-the-text tell us about the evolving relationship of censorship and art, or more broadly, of politics and aesthetics in modern Japan?

Below I trace the fictionalized representation of the censor in four Japanese works to suggest how the censor has figured in the cultural and political imagination in twentieth century Japan. Each work prominently features the encounter between artist and censor and was written by, or is about, artists who themselves experienced censorship in their careers: Iwasaki Akira's 1927 'Anthology of Love' ('Ai no ansorojii'), Tanizaki Jun'ichirō's 1921 short story, 'The Censor' ('Ken'etsukan'), the 2004 film *University of Laughs* (*Warai no daigaku*) directed by Hoshi Mamoru, and the 1987 short story 'The Dream Censor' ('Yume no ken'etsukan') by postmodern science fiction writer Tsutsui Yasutaka. In these examples, the figure of the censor changes over time from an evil antagonist who unsympathetically destroys art in the prewar examples to a benevolent and accomplished artist in his own right who helps to create art in the more recent works. On the one hand, the taming of the big bad wolf suggests the artist's sweet revenge on the censor, at least in the realm of fiction. On the other hand, it also suggests an acknowledgment of the productive possibilities of censorship and even a perversely nostalgic desire for its return.

Reflecting the censor in the 'old' era of censorship

First let us consider the case of artists who themselves were subjected to censorship: Iwasaki Akira and Tanizaki Jun'ichirō. Both depict the censor as the antithesis of the creative artist: an imperious boor ideally suited to being a government bureaucrat censor or *ken'etsukan*. For these two censored artists, the appeal of name-calling is somewhat obvious. What sweeter revenge than to tackle the censor on the artist's home turf by incorporating this inept bureaucrat into art and subjecting the censor to the rules of fiction just as the artist is subjected to those of the state? Based on the fact that neither story featuring the censor was itself censored, fiction seems to have provided both with a measure of protection in which they could publish critiques of the real-life censor with a degree of impunity. But what these two works and the subsequent fates of these artists demonstrate is that calling the censor out to play on the pages of one's writings was a tricky proposition not without its costs.

In writing the 1927 story 'Anthology of Love', Iwasaki was on new ground in two respects. First, he was not a literary author, but a Marxist film critic and filmmaker, a central member of the Proletarian Film League (Purokino) in the late 1920s until its dissolution by the government in the mid-1930s and the 'most intrepid' critic of the proposed 1939 Film Law (Eiga-hō).[5] Second, his story is set not in Japan but in Hollywood, featuring the chance reunion between a Pennsylvania state film censor named Leslie Howard and his old college friend Eddie Cleveland, an up-and-coming film director. Just as Iwasaki's non-fictional essays lodge a thinly veiled critique of domestic film censorship by criticizing the 1934 Nazi Film Law, this fictional story uses parodic transcontextualization, disguising a contemporary critique by world-shifting (*kakikae*), a common censorship-dodging strategy of Edo-period kabuki (Shively 1982). While this technique may have helped his story escape the notice of the domestic censors in 1927, it failed to sufficiently mask his critique in the non-fictional medium, and Iwasaki became the only film critic imprisoned by the thought police during the war from January 1940 through February 1941.

214   *K. Cather*

'Anthology of Love' consists almost exclusively of a one-sided monologue by the censor, a self-described 'talented graduate with a Classics degree' from G. University (Iwasaki 2004: 44). The director Eddie does not utter a single word throughout, replying audibly only through the censor, who echoes: 'What am I doing these days, you ask?', or 'Why, you ask?' (43, 48). Other than his many pseudo-scholarly and pompous digressions, the censor's monologue focuses on extolling his 'sacred occupation', which he at first coyly refuses to divulge, asking Eddie:

> Well, what do I look like? A county judge? A traveling medicine peddler? A university professor?... In a sense, I am a supporter of all of morality and its kind, a protector of noble pursuits, a patron of all authority.

When Eddie responds with his guess of 'Capitalist' (a jab that reflects Iwasaki's Marxist bent), the censor is compelled to produce his business card as proof of his occupation (44–5).

Describing the strict two-day employment exam, the censor unwittingly reveals his rather dubious qualifications and motivations. Two 'mental tests' evaluate if job candidates possess the required psychological traits for censors: 'absolute fidelity to all the beautiful, noble, good, and traditional things in this world and, conversely, a fine-tuned sense of disgust toward all the evil, ugly, and abominable things' (46). Passing the former exam was easy for the censor after studying a 365-day calendar of Christian proverbs. The latter exam, however, was where he truly excelled. In this test, subjects viewed the most tawdry censored film scenes with a 'precise Agitometer attached to their seats to record their psychological and biological states automatically at every moment during the screening in official percentages' (48). When he scores a perfect 100 percent excitability rating, his employment is secured.

The compilation of censored scenes used in the examination – dubbed *The Anthology of Love* – subsequently serves as a training exercise with a new edition screened every Monday morning to ensure the censors maintain the 'same degree of sensitivity as the most vulgar and lewd of the masses' (48). As his breathless description of the test film suggests, the censor has not lost his aptitude:

> Rudolph Valentino and Gloria Swanson kissing with lips glued fast and entwined like suckers,... a close-up of a dancing Joan Crawford's legs, Gilda Gray's hips shaking back and forth … just like a carnival of devils lacking any fear of God. – Embraces and kisses on chaise lounges – on beds, under the trees in gardens, on beaches – men and women, women and women, and women and men.
>
> (47)

Taking Eddie into his confidence, the censor reveals that the reason they cut so many scenes is in order to make this weekly *Anthology of Love* 'all the richer

Parody and the censor in modern Japan   215

and sweeter' (48), suggesting that censoring films is less in the name of 'public morals' than to create private smut. The story ends with the image of the censor rushing off a little too eagerly to catch the train so as not to miss a 'very important Monday morning meeting' (50).

The force and humor of Iwasaki's critique stems from his focus on the aroused censor lecturing about and reveling in the perks of his occupation – the titillating materials that the censors are privy to by virtue of their ostensible virtue. Like the real-life charges that such perks (and monetary bribes) offset their low salaries, or satirical depictions of the censor enjoying his job altogether too much, Iwasaki scathingly depicts the perfect censor as the very embodiment of the susceptible, immoral spectator whom he purports to protect.[6]

While the censor's tireless monologue reveals his imperious and impure nature, the artist's silence renders him impervious to the censor. In a reversal of the usual power dynamics, the censor in this story craves the attention and approval of the artist while the artist remains utterly immune to the censor. The censor conspicuously exclaims his old college buddy's name over ten times during their brief encounter, bidding him 'Eh, Eddie!' 'Listen here (*kikitamae*), Eddie!' and 'Look here (*mitamae*), Eddie!' His unsuccessful demands for the artist's attention are evident both from the escalating desperation of his summonses and from the artist's minimal and muted responses. Instead of an artist for whom 'the censor-figure is involuntarily incorporated into the interior, psychic life, bringing with it humiliation, self-disgust, and shame' (Coetzee 1994: 10), the censor here has fully internalized the corrupt spectator.

In sum, Iwasaki depicts the artist as triumphing over the censor-in-the-story by having the censor protest too much, while the artist never protests at all. To be sure, Iwasaki here points to the censor's destructive power to silence the artist. As the censor himself remarks, he has not seen Eddie for a long while during which time the director's career has taken off, but, as his last line 'Let's meet again somewhere soon' implies, he will not just disappear. But Iwasaki also suggests that silence can offer a powerful tool for the artist striving to resist the censor. Given that Iwasaki went on to become one of the 'most intrepid' critics of domestic, and later Occupation, censorship, he was surely not advocating that artists disengage from the political issue of censorship. Instead, his work suggests the artist's power to obliquely engage the censor in the artistic realm. For this very vocal critic of censorship in real life, muting the artist-self and turning up the volume on the censor in fiction offers a potent means to lambaste the censor in a politically charged, comedic and artistic way.

If Iwasaki's strategy was to subject the censor to performing a tireless monologue, Tanizaki's was to tango relentlessly with the censor. His October 1921 story 'The Censor' consists almost exclusively of the dialogue between a state police censor 'T' and a playwright 'K' embroiled in the negotiations characteristic of the prewar pre-publication consultation system (*naietsu*). The play in question, *First Love* (*Hatsukoi*), is based on Tanizaki's own play *The Age to Learn of Love* (*Koi wo shiru koro*), about a twelve-year-old boy from a wealthy family who willingly allows himself to be murdered by his 'first love', the family

216 *K. Cather*

maid, who then inherits all the family property. Although the script was published in May 1913, theater censors prohibited it from being staged. Fearing that his meta-fictional account of the play's censorship negotiations might cause a problem for any magazine, Tanizaki instead published the story in an anthology of his own works.

Like Iwasaki's story, this one also begins immediately with the censor, named T, launching into a monologue. But unlike Iwasaki's boorish censor, Tanizaki's appears to be the antithesis of the prototypical censor. He seems respectful and even reasonable to the artist and 'unlike the dreadfully arrogant, obstinate and intractable person he had expected'.[7] A gushing fan of the playwright, T (an initial that suggests the blurred identities of censor and artist) aspires to transcend his bureaucrat status and to achieve the lofty heights of artist. At first, the artist is silenced by the appearance of this obsequious and loquacious censor, 'at a loss for words' in the face of the censor's 'glib chatter' that goes on for sixteen lines (*TJZ* 7: 483). The writer-in-the-story (and the writer-of-the-story proper) are not, however, completely absent. Interspersed throughout the censor's opening monologue is the writer's own appraisal of the censor, which rapidly shifts from optimism to an awareness that the censor is a pretentious hypocrite who gloats over his familiarity with lofty English terms and literary insights (*TJZ* 7: 484, 486). In these moments, the censor-in-the-story is put in the ignominious position of becoming a fictional character subject to the narrator's judging eye and snide observations.

But with the exception of these few brief asides early on, any other narration is conspicuously absent until the closing paragraph. The negotiations soon shift to a fierce, protracted battle of wits and words with no introspection (or narration) in evidence, just a barrage of verbal volleys between censor and artist rendered in direct quotes. With only two exceptions, Tanizaki does not mark who the speaking subject is, further blurring the identities of the censor and artist. The silent observing artist-in-the-story gives way to an equally loquacious and smug artist who parries each and every of the censor's blows, and soon begins to return them with even greater vigor and rancor to the point that the censor himself is twice rendered speechless, blankly responding only '...' (*TJZ* 7: 505, 518).

Eventually, the writer K exposes the censor T's hypocrisy and vanity of presuming himself to be a bureaucrat-artiste when he advises the playwright to incorporate censorship-dodging strategies of dubious integrity and efficacy, such as substituting kidnap for murder so as 'to allow a bit of wiggle room' (*TJZ* 7: 496) and making the play appear to follow the cardinal principle of *kanzen chōaku*, or 'encouraging virtue and chastising vice'. The censor proposes equally dubious strategies for dealing with sexual expression:

> T: Problems arise in scene 3, where we find the following stage directions, and I quote: '*O-sai exits the bath, enters the living room, and seats herself in front of a mirror wearing nothing more than a long underkimono.*' Could you cut the line 'with nothing more than a long underkimono'?

K: Well, how about if I put another layer of kimono on top?

T: Hmm ... only one? How about two? The more the better, you know.

K: Fine, I'll deck her out in two more layers.

(Zheng 2008: 426)

In this passage, Tanizaki calls attention to the censored lines in his play by having them appear twice with emphatic diacritical 'ten ten ten' marks alongside. Tanizaki also exposes the censor's questionable moral integrity, invoking the familiar image of the aroused censor. In the most polite possible language, the playwright asks, 'If I may, a question. You continue to state that the play will arouse lustful desires, but how about you yourself? Do you find yourself aroused when you read the script?' (*TJZ* 7: 490).

While the censor is eventually revealed to be precisely the kind of bureaucratic stickler the writer had feared, the artist transforms from a cowed and pliable collaborator to a defiant resister. Taking his leave from the now 'silent and sullen' censor, he declares, ' "From now on, we will scorn you and treat you as the servile human being you are..." [and] with a faint smile around his eyes says quietly, "*Sayonara*" ' (*TJZ* 7: 518). In these last moments, the writer-in-the story vanquishes the censor by refusing to negotiate, instead resolving to accept an outright ban because 'at least that way its integrity as a work of art will survive intact – and minus your show of "respect" ' (Zheng 2008: 441). The censor resigns himself to the fact that 'my artistic conscience remains unsatisfied, but I have satisfied my conscience as a bureaucrat, and that is good enough because I am no artist' (*TJZ* 7: 515).

By ending this story with each party relegated back to their distinct spheres, Tanizaki points to the impossibility of a meeting of minds between the censor and artist that will allow either to retain their integrity. But Tanizaki's story itself recounts just such a meeting in painstaking and monotonous detail, becoming 'a lengthy and at times hair-splitting debate between writer and censor' (Tyler 2008: 423). Neither the censor nor the writer emerges from the debate unscathed. If the censor is forced to relinquish any pretense of being an artist, so is the artist. As he himself admits, 'A writer espousing the virtues of his own writings does not make for very interesting talk' (*TJZ* 7: 505).

What can we conclude about the efficacy of tackling the censor in fiction for these artists? Because of their many skirmishes with the state censors, both artists gained a reputation for anti-authoritarianism that would serve them well in the postwar climate. Fiction offered an ideal platform for lodging a pointed critique of the censorship they themselves faced, and the 'big bad censor' offered an eminently mockable antagonist over whom the earnest and innocent victim-artist could triumph, at least in the realm of fiction. Both stories testify to the ways that a writer could creatively transform the censor's destructive capacity into a productive one. Moreover, both stories managed to censure the censor while avoiding being censored themselves.[8] This represents a particularly remarkable feat both because the censor-in-the-text is depicted as such an irredeemable, unscrupulous fool and because the works reproduce precisely the objectionable material that the censor is intent on banning: the censor's litany of arousing scenes in 'Anthology of Love' and the morally ambiguous and sexually arousing lines of the play-within-the story in 'The Censor'. Both suggest the power of fiction, and particularly metafiction, to trump censorship.

For these artists, the 'symbolic value' of the 'physical expulsion of the censor, vomited forth as a demon' (to borrow Coetzee's phrasing) onto the page should not be underrated. Tanizaki's own trajectory from cowed conspirator to outspoken critic of censorship echoes the transformation of the writer-in-the-story in 'The Censor'. Whereas an earlier ban of a journal in 1916 because of one of his plays led him to respond with only a 'feeble attempt' of a rebuttal in which he even pled for a corollary pre-publication inspection system for literary works (Rubin 1984: 242), in 1921 he boldly published 'The Censor', using the ban of his 1913 play *An Age to Learn of Love* as material. In 1922, he protested bans on staging two of his other plays by publishing protest essays in two theater magazines.[9] These echo many of the points made in 'The Censor', including his charge that the censor's own 'obscene' imagination was working overtime and his defiant resolve to accept the censors' bans rather than submitting to their 'kindly' advice about artistic quality and 'wasting time visiting them over and over while they butcher what I've written' (*TJZ* 22: 136, 140). Together, 'The Censor' and these essays represent merciless critiques of the censor and admirable declarations of artistic autonomy and integrity.

Yet, by engaging this critique in the fictional medium, Tanizaki also unwittingly exposes the failures of the artist who engages in such polemics. As Coetzee notes in the preface to his own collection of essays on censorship, 'the polemics of writers against censors rarely do the profession credit' (1994: 8). Although it might seem unfair to evaluate Tanizaki's story on an aesthetic basis since it was produced under political pressure, the fact that it so closely echoes his non-fictional essays, with one sounding 'almost like a replay of the story "The Censor"' (Rubin 1984: 244), should give us pause. If we are considering what constitutes effective resistance for a writer facing censorship, I would argue that politics need to be subjected to aesthetics when articulated in the artistic realm, just as aesthetics are subjected to politics when they enter the political realm.

Successfully critiquing the censor in the fictional medium requires that the artist navigate the demands of politics and aesthetics, as the term '*reportage roman*' that Iwasaki used to describe his story 'Anthology of Love' suggests (Iwasaki 2004: 7–8). Ironically, the Marxist filmmaker Iwasaki succeeds by marshaling his literary powers and by remaining firmly planted in the realm of art even when advancing a political statement. In contrast, the literary artist Tanizaki falters when he so baldly and polemically advances the artist's politics in art. The 'seriocomic' tone of Tanizaki's writer-in-the-story (Tyler 2008: 423) might do better to yield to the fully comical, satiric tone of Iwasaki's censor-in-the-story. In other words, perhaps a good tactic for censuring the censor is sometimes self-censoring the artist.

Such self-censorship tactics were not without costs, however. In retrospect, Iwasaki expressed regret at mincing his words in his essays because he felt it had undermined his political integrity:

> At that time, in my heart I always said to myself, if I go this far it will be okay, if I write it this way it will be inside the bounds of safety; I had this kind of self-regulation and vigilance. My pen communicated it, and my writing started veiling the most fundamental things.
>
> (Nornes 2003: 128)

Nor did such a tactic improve his artistry; as one scholar has noted, Iwasaki's 1939 book 'reads as though the author cannot say exactly what he means' (ibid.). Nor did such self-censorship strategies, either veiled language or 'world-shifting', guarantee immunity from the censor, at least not by 1940 as evidenced by the fact that Iwasaki's non-fictional essays were what occasioned his arrest and imprisonment. In conclusion, although we should beware of overestimating the ability of art and artistry to trump censorship, we should note also the power of fiction and metafiction, particularly when it employs the protective veils of humor, parody and indirect language, to protect the political, personal and aesthetic integrity of the artist and the art.

Reviving the censor in the era of 'the new censorship'

Let us now consider examples that resurrect the censor in an era when prewar and wartime state censorship was long dead: Hoshi Mamoru's 2004 film *University of Laughs* and Tsutsui Yasutaka's 1987 short story 'The Dream Censor'. The film depicts the fictionalized negotiations between a real-life playwright and the wartime censors set in 1940. As a contemporary representation of wartime censorship, it offers a particularly useful example that suggests the imaginary place that the old form of censorship occupies in the era of the 'new' one. Postmodern science fiction writer Tsutsui's story offers a more complex example. The story explicitly addresses a timeless form of censorship identified by Freud back in the late nineteenth century – dream censorship. It also implicitly offers an analogy for 'the new censorship' as an exemplary form of the self-censorship that typifies this era. This analogy is particularly compelling when considered in conjunction with Tsutsui's much-publicized skirmish with computerised 'word-hunting' just a few years later.

When the idea was raised of making a film based on a 1997 play by Mitani Kōki that very much resembles Tanizaki's story 'The Censor', the filmmakers worried most about its artistic and economic appeal. Their concern was two-fold: first, that the play set in a single room and constituting solely of the negotiations between a governmental theater censor and playwright would not be conducive to the cinematic medium, and second, that the issue of censorship was not relevant for contemporary spectators. As one of the producers put it:

220   K. Cather

Before it screened, I was a bit worried about whether the rather plain set-up between playwright and censor would be well received by audiences. This work, after all, is not a story of people engaged in a battle over life and death. What if the audience decided, 'Well, if it's just a bit of censorship, he should just put up with it'?

(Hoshi 2004, DVD booklet essay by Ishihara Furu)[10]

Despite these initial concerns, the star-studded 2004 *University of Laughs* capitalized on the filmic medium and on censorship to great commercial and artistic acclaim, but not without some compromised ethics.[11]

Precisely what is ridiculed in Tanizaki's 1921 story – the artistic aspirations of the bureaucrat-censor and the possibility of a fruitful meeting of minds between artist and censor – is celebrated in the film. Pop-idol SMAP star Inagaki Gorō plays the part of the comic theater playwright Kikuya Sakae (1902–37) who worked for Enoken's Casino Folies in Asakusa in the early 1930s. The well-known actor (and coincidentally former government bureaucrat) Yakusho Kōji stars as the stern theater censor from the Police Public Safety department who has just returned from the Manchurian colonies in line with the government's renewed 'attention to cultural policies'. As he himself boasts, he is the perfect candidate for censoring comedy: he has never seen a light comedy, has never even told a joke or employed a pun, and, in fact, has 'never wholeheartedly laughed in his entire life'. Armed with these qualifications, he can, therefore, be merciless.

At first the interactions of the censor and playwright adhere to a stereotypical pattern – an interrogation drama set in a stark censorship bureau office in Fall 1940 pits the big bad censor, as mouthpiece of wartime propaganda, against the earnest comedic artist (Figure 12.1). This epic clash is signaled in the film's opening scenes that cross-cut between mismatched directional shots of the sterile bureaucrat ensconced in the uniform grays of the censors' offices and those of the plaid-suited, bow-tied playwright jauntily walking through the colorful, lively outdoor streets of Asakusa on his way to the meeting. Extreme low-angle shots of the towering menacing censor are juxtaposed with high-angle ones of the powerless artist to highlight their natural antagonism. The predictable nature of this encounter is signaled by the bored yawn of our proxy, an elderly policeman manning the interrogation room door. But over the course of a biblical seven days of meetings, the censor is transformed into a scrupulous and gifted co-director of the play and a lover of the arts.

In the film, the play under the censor's consideration is a parody of *Romeo and Juliet*, a point that is immediately obvious from its title: *The Great Tragedy of Juleo and Romiette*, a work in the vein of the code-switching gag-filled comedy of Asakusa for which Enoken and Kikuya were famous.[12] At first, the transposition of names stumps the bumbling censor, who asks the playwright: 'And what's this? This title. … Is "Juleo and Romiette" correct?' Then, referring to a notebook from his suit pocket, he earnestly informs the playwright, 'There was an English writer by the name "William Shakespeare". This Shakespeare

Figure 12.1 The Big Bad Censor versus the Beleaguered Artist in *University of Laughs.* ©2004 FUJI TELEVISION NETWORK, INC./TOHO Co., LTD./PARCO Co., LTD. All rights reserved.

222   *K. Cather*

wrote something called "Romeo and Juliet". Did you know that?' When told yes, he notes, 'I thought it was too close a resemblance to be a coincidence. Romeo and Juliet ... Juleo and Romiette. What is this about?' He is told, but far from reassured by the fact that the title is an intentional use of parody: 'It's what we call a "pun" (*mojiri*) ... or what's called "parody" over there'. When the censor objects to staging 'a barbarian love story' on 'the 2600th anniversary of Emperor Jinmu's accession', the playwright argues that Romeo and Juliet were actually Italians and that Italy is, after all, Japan's ally since the Tripartite Pact.

When faced with the censor's demands to replace the unacceptable Western source text and characters and to transpose the setting to Nippon, the playwright laments the censor's failure to understand the fundamentals of parody, complaining that 'the word play will all lose its meaning.... Won't you understand? Parody has its own rules!' But rather than capitulate to the censor's demands, the playwright responds to each challenge set by the censor with punning and parody as a counter-strategy. For example, when the censor insists that he include the patriotic lines 'for my country' (*okuni no tame*) no less than three times, the playwright incorporates a series of ingenious puns, for example transposing the letters of the word 'nation' so that the hero dies not for 'the state' (*okuni*) but for 'the steak' (*oniku*) his mother makes as his last meal. In fact, he revises the entire manuscript into a parody of a parody: Juleo and Romiette become none other than Kan'ichi and Omiya from Ozaki Kōyō's classic tale of ill-fated lovers *The Golden Demon* (*Konjiki yasha*, 1897–1903) and Friar Laurence becomes a Pure Land Buddhist priest.

Parody, as a 'coded discourse' to borrow Linda Hutcheon's broadest definition of the term (2000: 15), offers an ideal means for dodging censorship. The trick is to encode that meaning in such a way that renders it decodable by the audience but invisible to the censor. In this film, however, each and every use of parody as a censorship-dodging strategy is patiently explained to the dense bureaucrat. For example, when the censor first objects to the artificial transposition of only the setting and the characters without any plot changes, the playwright explains,

> Setting it in Japan has, conversely, made it funnier. The necessity of setting a play-within-a-play is clearer.... It's the humor of the double-layer. You laugh at the play and at the ensuing backstage chaos that arises out of forcibly setting the play in Japan. As a comedy, it has gotten much stronger. I wouldn't have thought of it without you.

What he does not note, but is obvious to the audience, is how the jagged edges that make apparent the censor's intervention in the play enhance not only the work's comedic and artistic value, but also its political potency.

Elucidating the charm and rules of parody to the humorless censor becomes the playwright's task and the film's source of humor. In the process, the censor is 'schooled' in both senses of the term, both mocked and educated in the eponymous University of Laughter. By the end, the censor emerges as a full-fledged

Parody and the censor in modern Japan   223

participant in the production, first as an actor rehearsing in the censor's office that is transformed into a theater stage (with the help of the cinematic medium), and finally as an editor and director par excellence whose revisions stem from his artistic, not bureaucratic, sense. As the playwright exclaims, 'I've never heard of a censor like this. It's not censorship. It's story editing!' His elevated status as co-director is not lost on the inept censor either, as evidenced when he becomes troubled by the unauthorized changes the playwright has made to his suggested edits:

> Is it me? This director *is* me.... Several things I said yesterday mysteriously appear. Page Three. 'If Churchill made soba, would you eat it?' You've changed 'sushi' into 'soba' but otherwise they're my words exactly!... Soba is weak. I want to you change it back to sushi.... That makes the director's point clearer.... Soba lacks the right feeling.

While the censor discovers his newfound artistic conscience, the playwright's own artistic integrity is questioned by his fellow troupe members who beat him for being 'a traitor, a stool pigeon, and a police lap dog'. But as the playwright ultimately reveals in a lengthy anti-censorship tirade, accommodating the censor's requests while making the play funnier was his 'own way of fighting against authority'. During the course of this almost three-minute monologue accompanied by melodramatic swelling music, the censor abruptly reverts to his stern bureaucrat's persona, a shift clearly signaled by the return of the extreme low-angled shot of his menacing, heavily shadowed figure.

This abrupt about-face on the censor's part reflects the artist's own transformation from a comic playwright to a humorless polemicist. Until this point, the playwright had succeeded in his mission by adhering to the letter of the censor's law while violating its spirit, deftly using the tools of his trade – slippery words – as his weapons. By laying bare his anti-authoritarianism in polemical and non-poetic language, the playwright forces the censor to reassert his own prescribed role as antagonist of art; the censor regretfully asks, 'Why speak of this to me? Absorbed in making this script, we forgot each other's places. I am the face of the authority that you despise.' This leads to the censor's final seemingly impossible request: write a comedy with no laughs. This challenge arrives on the same day as the playwright's draft notice from the army. With the playwright and censor safely returned to their proper spheres, censorship and the exigencies of war again spur both artistic potential and productivity: the artist's feats of wordplay reduce the censor to laughter no less than eighty-three times.

Once the censor finds out about the playwright's imminent deployment, their positions reverse one last time. Now the playwright voices the patriotic propaganda script while the censor employs the artist's own artistic pun to articulate antiwar ideology. When the playwright announces his intention to 'bravely go die for his nation', the censor reminds him: 'Don't say you will die for your country. Didn't you yourself write it? It's only worth dying for steak.' As the playwright walks off, left behind is the tearful and pitiable censor clutching the

224   *K. Cather*

playwright's precious manuscript as if it were a newborn and enjoining him, 'Come back safe!' His final line '*Daisuki nanda*!' (I love it/you!) offers a ringing declaration of love that can refer either to the script or to the playwright since the direct object is elided in the Japanese. As actor Inagaki remarked in an interview somewhat self-consciously, 'As we were making the film, I suddenly wondered: Is this a love story? Between two men? It's a strange way to put it, but...' (Hoshi 2004, 'Interviews', disc 2). If the film began as a parody of the stern interrogation drama, it ends as a parody of another genre entirely: a melodramatic romance about war-torn lovers with the censor transformed from big bad wolf to damsel-in-distress. The evolution from fearsome and ignorant militarist-bureaucrat into an art lover, and perhaps even the artist's lover, neatly encapsulates the trajectory that the figure of the Japanese censor has taken over time in the cultural imagination, from the era of the old censorship to the new one.

In Tsutsui's 1987 'The Dream Censor', the censor appears as a similarly beneficent presence, one that resides in the subconscious of a woman who is haunted by traumatic memories of her son's recent death caused by a bullying incident at his middle school.[13] The story's dream censor and his scribe are embodiments of Freud's theories of repression and the mechanism of dream censorship.[14] They also clearly resemble a writer-director and casting agent who scrutinize the elements that are to appear in their charge's dreams on what is called the 'dream stage' (*yume no butai*) complete with a stage door and curtain (Tsutsui 1994: 12). Their job is to ban or transform any potentially traumatic elements into innocuous ones with the help of stagehands and make-up and construction crews. Their transformations depend on precisely the kind of word play and world-shifting employed by real-life artists as censorship dodges in their art. For example, the censor deftly changes Osugi Daizo, the detested teacher whom the woman blames for overlooking her son's bullying, into her unlikable uncle Shima Daizo, while the bullies become a rotten ear of corn, recalling her own association after seeing the backs of their heads all lined up when seated at their desks (11, 13).

When, in the end of the dream, the son appears yet again, the censor is at his wit's end; as the scribe complains, they have 'exhausted their methods of substitution (*surikae*), abstraction (*shōchōka*) and paraphrase (*iikae*)' (16). Moreover, as the scribe reminds the censor, their job is not just to ensure a restful sleep, but also to relieve the dreamer's suffering as per items one and two of their mandate, which coincide precisely with Freud's own theories (Levine 1994: 190, n17). They decide to let him 'pass' (*tōsu*) for which the boy thanks them in the final lines of the story (18). This officially sanctioned return of the repressed in the woman's dreams courtesy of the kindly censor cum director suggests the disappearance of the explicit, external and harmful censorship of old and its replacement with one that is both internal and beneficial.

In both these recent works, the censor appears as a significantly less menacing figure than in the prewar examples: as co-director, lover or sleeping aid. Why this marked transformation of the censor-figure into an anodyne and even positive influence? Is it merely a reflection of the disappearance of overt state censorship in an increasingly unrestricted publishing realm? Or do the works perhaps exhibit a certain nostalgia for the censor in recognition of the paradox that censorship can be a productive force in the creation of art?

Tsutsui's case suggests just such a desire for the revival of the censor whose very antagonism can spur the artist to create. He originally published 'Dream Censor' in the *Mainichi* newspaper and subsequently an expanded version in a literary journal and short story anthology. In a postscript to the anthology, Tsutsui points to a very different kind of 'censorship' that constrained his creativity, explaining that 'because of newspaper page limit restrictions, it lacked sufficient explanation and so I extensively revised it' (Tsutsui 1994: 18). But Tsutsui also recognized the creative possibilities offered by such constraints. As he asked rhetorically when beginning serialization of his first newspaper novel, 'What is it that I can do *expressly because* it is a newspaper serialization novel with a daily limit of three manuscript pages?' (Gardner 2007: 85, italics in original).

In September 1993, Tsutsui became the target of PC 'word hunting' by the Japan Epilepsy Association (JEA) when his 1965 story 'Automatic Police' that includes an allegedly insensitive treatment of epilepsy was reprinted in a high school textbook.[15] This story describes a dystopic world in which robotic police regulate people's language, behaviors and even unconscious thoughts. Its plot anticipates by some thirty years the type of new censorship to which Tsutsui himself would be subjected: computerized 'word-hunting' guided by in-house publishers' lists. Tsutsui responded by dramatically issuing a 'breaking-of-the-brush declaration' (*danpitsu sengen*) that marked the beginning of a three-year writing strike.

As novelist Kobayashi Kyōji notes, rare is the writer, like Tsutsui, who voluntarily stops writing at their peak. Instead, it usually occurs among 'those who become unable to write, or for those whom societal conditions become such that they are disallowed to write' or, to put it another way, because of writer's block or 'real' censorship. In contrast, Tsutsui's self-imposed writing strike represents a 'fight with his own shadow, which for a writer will be that of his own making', and Tsutsui is a 'super veteran of fighting with his own creations' (Kobayashi 1994: 289, 290). Even Tsutsui joked that he could be accused of being a 'breaking-the-brush profiteer' for publishing bestselling essays on the incident, which also spurred his transformation from 'the representative metafictionist' into the 'exemplary cyber-fictionist' with his founding of JALInet, the 'first literary server in Japan' (JALInet 2010). Far from being the end of his writing career, his print media strike 'only increased Tsutsui's "bandwidth" on multiple media channels' (Gardner 2007: 94).

It seems that censorship has become a highly marketable commodity. *University of Laughs* similarly capitalized on the economic and aesthetic potential of marketing censorship, billing the film as a stark 'battle between the censor, the man who hates laughter, and the comic playwright, the man who loves laughter' set 'during an era when laughter was taboo' (Hoshi 2004: 'Previews', disc 2). Like Tsutsui, the filmmakers stressed how they too were circumscribed by

226 *K. Cather*

constraints faced in production: '90% set in a single room. Can it possibly stand as a film?... Only two performers, one set!' (Hoshi 2004: 'Television Commercials', disc 2). The deluxe DVD set even comes with a set of censor stamps that attest to the kitschy appeal of censorship today. The figure of the censor in these recent works suggests less the existence of any moral, political or market censorship than the economic appeal of resurrecting and marketing the censor in the era of 'the new censorship'.

The pleasures and politics of parodying the censor

What, then, has changed in the era of the new censorship where page restrictions and constraints related to one's chosen source text loom in place of any state censor? What is the political significance of parodying the censor, or of the genre of parody at all? Bakhtin dismisses the role of parody in modern-day democracies, claiming that without repression, it lacks political efficacy: he writes, 'in modern times the functions of parody are narrow and unproductive. Parody has grown sickly.... We live, write and speak today in a world of free and democratized language' (see Hutcheon 2000: 70). Disputing this, Hutcheon advocates parody as an effective response to 'linguistic reification caused by bourgeois neocapitalism' in an era where language has been 'totally bureaucratized' (2000: 71).

In Japan's era of old censorship, parody worked because it effectively laid bare the political impetus behind a work's creation. Such is the case with Iwasaki's story, and especially with Tanizaki's 'The Censor' as well as the play-within-the-film in *University of Laughs*. As metafictional works, these last two possess an added pedagogical function as primers that reveal the jagged edges of parody as a censorship dodge. While this had political potential for readers in the 1920s and for the audience-in-the-film circa 1940, what potential did it hold for the audience of the film proper in 2004? If Enoken's prewar parodies were effective because 'their audience would both recognize the allusions and appreciate the fact that censorship both necessitated such parody and lent it a critical edge' (Silverberg 2006: 239), then what is the critical edge for twenty-first century film audiences? If, as Bakhtin suggests, the pleasure and politics of parody go hand-in-hand with censorship, then perhaps only by reviving the figure of the censor can parody regain its former appeal. After all, to understand and appreciate parody requires knowledge of not just the parodied text, but also of the political context of censorship that necessitates such a parody. That today's audience is unfamiliar with these codes is suggested by the information supplied in the DVD booklet of *University of Laughs*. A list of unfamiliar terms defines everything from the classic literary characters Kan'ichi and Omiya to the term for 'the censor' (*ken'etsukan*) at the head of the list. Parody is seemingly as obsolete as the censor.

The politics of reviving and romanticizing the censor is a particularly pressing ethical question in the case of the film because it is based on the life of playwright Kikuya Sakae, who died at the age of thirty-five on the battlefields of China in 1937, three years before the film is set. As the DVD pamphlet notes without a hint of irony, 'Unfortunately (*zannen nagara*), it seems that the real Kikuya was unable to encounter a censor like the one in the movie.' Rewriting the censor from – to borrow Kikuya's own words – 'unenlightened jackasses who dare to mess with my work' (Hoshi 2004, DVD booklet essay by Yagi Kentarō), into a veritable lover of the arts, risks trivializing the role that real-life censors had in supporting the wartime propaganda machine that sent so many young men to their early deaths.

In Tsutsui's case, where is the critical edge for which this postmodernist is famous? His self-imposed writing strike hyperbolically equates the new and old kinds of censorship, a stance that 'implicitly discounts the rather significant difference between going to the gulag for saying something subversive and not getting an NEA grant...' (Burt 1994: xiii). After the incident, author Ōe Kenzaburō (whose own son suffers from epilepsy) criticized his friend Tsutsui's antics by asserting that 'an artist's job is to create new expressions if there are limits on words in society' (Kajuen 2007). In other words, he suggested that Tsutsui should have employed censorship-dodging tools that can enrich rather than impoverish art, just like the dreamer in his story.

As Freud, Tsutsui's own muse, suggested, censorship can be beneficial both to the psyche of the dreamer and to the creation of art:

> All dreamers are equally insufferably witty, and they need to be because they are under pressure and the direct route is barred to them.... The stricter the censorship, the more far-reaching will be the disguise and the more ingenious too may be the means employed for putting the reader on the scent of the true meaning.
>
> (Levine 1994: 168, 174)

Freud warned against imagining his ' "dream censor" (*Traumzensor*) as a severe little manikin or a spirit living in a closet in the brain and there discharging his office' (Levine 1994: 172). When artists are faced with 'linguistic reification' caused by either 'state censors in a period of national emergency' or by 'bourgeois neocapitalism', their most effective response is perhaps not parody, and certainly not polemics, but instead artistry. When faced with the fixity of language demanded either by the wartime state military censor or by the new censor's computerized lists, the artist's best tactic seems to be to create their own words as per their job description, as Ōe suggests. As the four works analyzed above demonstrate, maintaining some antagonism between censor and artist was critical to retaining political and aesthetic integrity. But when taking on the censor as one's antagonist, one must also not forget to capitalize on their potential role as muse.

Notes

1 Milton (1874: 29), Smith (1852: 289), Yagi (2004: n.p.), Coetzee (1994: 10).
2 For more on postwar youth protection agencies and legislation, see Leheny (2006); on postwar obscenity trials of literature, film and comic books, see Cather (2012).

228   *K. Cather*

3 For information on postwar self-censorship practices by publishers, broadcasters and the mass media, see Gottlieb (2006), Havens (1998) and Sterngold (1994).

4 See Parkes (1996) on European literary modernism and censorship; for the Japanese case, see Tyler (2008: 398–400). Although Britain's censorship trial of *Lady Chatterley's Lover* in 1960 became a landmark of decensorship (the eradication of censorship laws) there, in Japan, the high-profile Chatterley trials from 1950–57 instead marked a renewed beginning (Cather 2012).

5 High (2003: 71); Iwamoto (1987: 134). On Iwasaki and Japanese wartime censorship, see High (2003: 70–6, 324–9), Makino (2001: 32–5) and Nornes (2003: 19–47, 125–30). On Iwasaki and Occupation censorship, see Hirano (1992) and Iwasaki (1975).

6 Such charges have plagued prewar, Occupation and postwar film censors (Hirano 1992: 101; Sakata 1977: 215). For satirical cartoons of the censor, see www.cartoonstock.com/cartoonview.asp?catref=shr0295 and www.cartoonstock.com/cartoonview.asp?catref=njun407 (both last accessed 30 August 2012).

7 *Tanizaki Jun'ichirō zenshū* (Complete Works) 7.483; hereafter referred to as *TJZ*. Translations are my own except for the indicated two passages, which rely on the felicitous phrasing of Guohe Zheng's complete translation in Tyler (2008: 424–44).

8 The suspicious timing of bans on Tanizaki's plays in 1922 suggests they were a form of retaliation for his metafictional attack in 'The Censor', but it is impossible to know for certain, especially since by this time, Tanizaki was already something of a 'marked man' with '[f]our bans in close succession in 1916 … surely a record of some sort' (Rubin 1984: 139). On Tanizaki's skirmishes with the Japanese censors, see *TJZ* 22: 135–41, 142–4 and Rubin (1984: 135–41, 235–45).

9 These two essays were 'The Ban of *The Eternal Idol*' (*Eien no gūzō no jyōen kinshi*), originally published in September 1922 in *Theater Illustrated* (*Engeki gahō*), and 'Some Requests Regarding the Censorship of Scripts' (*Kyakuhon ken'etsu ni tsuite no chūmon*) in the September 1922 issue of *New Performance* (*Shin engei*) (see *TJZ* 22: 142–4, 135–41).

10 See also the essay by director Hoshi Mamoru in the DVD booklet (Hoshi 2004) and the director's commentary accompanying the film.

11 In 2005, the film gained a nomination for best screenplay and best actor from the Japanese Academy and a win for Yakusho Kōji as best actor at the Yokohama Film Festival.

12 On Kikuya Sakae's career, see Kita no kai (1992). On Enoken's code-switching gags, see Silverberg (2006: 235–52).

13 Tsutsui (1994: 8–18). All translations of the story are my own.

14 Freud (1989: 161–72). On Freud's theories of dream censorship, see Levine (1994: 168–91).

15 For a detailed account of JEA's objections to Tsutsui's 'Automatic Police' (*Mujin keisatsu*), see Gardner (2007: 91–6).

References

Bourdieu, Pierre (1999) 'Censorship and the Imposition of Form', in John Thompson (ed.), *Language and Symbolic Power*, Cambridge: Harvard University Press, 137–62.

Burt, Richard (1994) 'Introduction: The "New" Censorship', in Richard Burt (ed.), *The Administration of Aesthetics: Censorship, Political Criticism, and the Public Sphere*, Minneapolis: University of Minnesota Press, xi–xxix.

Cather, Kirsten (2012) *The Art of Censorship in Postwar Japan*, Honolulu: University of Hawai'i Press.

Coetzee, J.M. (1994) *Giving Offense: Essays on Censorship*, Chicago: University of Chicago Press.

Parody and the censor in modern Japan 229

Fish, Stanley Eugene (1994) *There's No Such Thing as Free Speech, and It's a Good Thing, Too*, New York: Oxford University Press.

Freud, Sigmund (1989) 'On Dreams', in Peter Gay (ed.), *The Freud Reader*, New York: W.W. Norton & Company, 61–72.

Gardner, William O. (2007) 'Tsutsui Yasutaka and the Multimedia Performance of Authorship', in Christopher Bolton, Istvan Csicsery-Ronay, Jr. and Takayuki Tatsumi (eds.), *Robot Ghosts and Wired Dreams: Japanese Science Fiction from Origins to Anime*, Minneapolis: University of Minnesota Press, 83–98.

Gottlieb, Nanette (2006) Review of *'Okama' wa sabetsu ka: 'Shūkan kinyōbi' no 'sabetsu hyōgen' jiken* (Does 'okama' have discriminatory connotations? The 'discriminating expression' case in the weekly magazine *Shūkan kinyōbi*), *Intersections: Gender, History and Culture in the Asian Context*, 12 (January 2006). http://intersections.anu. edu.au/issue12/gotlieb_review.html. Last modified by Carolyn Brewer (editor), 18 March 2008. Last accessed 20 August 2012.

Havens, Thomas R.H. (1998) 'Media Self-Censorship and the Good Society in Japan', in Kawahara Hiroshi (ed.), *Landscape and Water Vein of the Japanese Mind*, Tokyo: Perikansha, 801–34.

High, Peter B. (2003) *The Imperial Screen: Japanese Film Culture in the Fifteen Years' War, 1931–1945*, Madison: The University of Wisconsin Press.

Hirano, Kyoko (1992) *Mr. Smith Goes to Tokyo: Japanese Cinema under the American Occupation, 1945–1952*, Washington: Smithsonian Institute Press.

Hoshi, Mamoru (2004) (dir.) *Warai no daigaku (University of Laughs) Special Edition* DVD Set, Tōhō Studio, 2 discs and booklet, 121 min.

Hutcheon, Linda (2000) *A Theory of Parody: The Teachings of Twentieth-Century Art Forms*, Urbana: University of Illinois Press.

Iwamoto, Kenji (1987) 'Film Criticism and the Study of Cinema in Japan: A Historical Survey', *Iconics*, 1: 129–46.

Iwasaki, Akira (1975) *Senryō sareta sukurīn* (The Occupied Screen), Tokyo: Shin Nihon Shuppansha.

Iwasaki, Akira (2004) 'Ai no ansorojii' (Anthology of Love), in Makino Mamoru (ed.), *Nihon eiga ron gensetsu taikei* (A Collection of Japanese Film Debate and Discourse), vol. 11, Tokyo: Yumani Shobō, 43–50.

JALInet (2010) 'Japanese Literature Net', www.jali.or.jp/tti/index.htm. Last accessed 1 July 2010.

Jansen, Sue Curry (1988) *Censorship: The Knot that Binds Power and Knowledge*, New York: Oxford University Press.

Kajuen, Keiei (2007) No. 75 Posting on 'Kure Tomofusa: Ōe Kenzaburō no "Okinawa nōto"' Thread, posted on 1 December at 4:56 p.m. on Ni-chan. http://mimizun.com/ log/2ch/news/1196449051/. Last accessed 12 January 2012.

Kita no kai (ed.) (1992) *Enoken o sasaeta Showa no modanizumu Kikuya Sakae* (Kikuya Sakae: the man who supported Enoken's Showa modernism), Aomori: Kita no Machisha, 1992.

Kobayashi, Kyōji (1994) 'Kaisetsu' (Afterword), in Tsutsui Yasutaka, *Yoru no konto fuyu no konto* (Nighttime and Wintertime Short Stories), Tokyo: Shinchōsha, 287–93.

Leheny, David Richard (2006) *Think Global, Fear Local: Sex, Violence, and Anxiety in Contemporary Japan*, Ithaca: Cornell University Press.

Levine, Michael G. (1994) 'Freud and the Scene of Censorship', in Richard Burt (ed.) *The Administration of Aesthetics: Censorship, Political Criticism, and the Public Sphere*, Minneapolis: University of Minnesota Press, 168–91.

230   *K. Cather*

Makino, Mamoru (2001) 'Rethinking the Emergence of the Proletarian Film League of Japan (Prokino)', trans. Abé Mark Nornes, in Aaron Gerow and Abe Mark Nornes (eds.), *In Praise of Film Studies: Essays in Honor of Makino Mamoru*, Victoria, BC: Trafford; Yokohama: Kinema Club, 15–45.

Milton, John (1874) [1644] *Aeropagitica*, in John Wesley Hales (ed.), *Aeropagitica: A Speech of Mr. John Milton for the Liberty of Unlicenc'd Printing, to the Parlament of England*, Oxford: Clarendon Press, 1–58.

Nornes, Abé Markus (2003) *Japanese Documentary: The Meiji Era through Hiroshima*, Minneapolis: University of Minnesota Press.

Parkes, Adam (1996) *Modernism and the Theater of Censorship*, New York: Oxford University Press.

Rubin, Jay (1984) *Injurious to Public Morals: Writers and the Meiji State*, Seattle: University of Washington Press.

Sakata, Ei'ichi (1977) *Waga Eirin jidai* (My Era at Eirin), Tokyo: Kyōritsu Tsūshinsha.

Shively, Donald H. (1982) 'Tokugawa Plays on Forbidden Topics', in James R. Brandon (ed.), *Chūshingura: Studies in Kabuki and the Puppet Theater*, Honolulu: University of Hawai'i Press, 23–57.

Silverberg, Miriam Rom (2006) *Erotic Grotesque Nonsense: The Mass Culture of Japanese Modern Times*, Berkeley: University of California Press.

Smith, Sydney (1852) [1809] 'Proceedings for the Society of the Suppression of Vice' in *The Works of the Rev. Sydney Smith*, Philadelphia: A. Hart, late Carey and Hart, 287–92.

Sterngold, James (1994) 'Ideas & Trends; Fear of Phrases', *New York Times*, 18 December. www.nytimes.com/1994/12/18/weekinreview/ideas-trends-fear-of-phrases.html. Last accessed 8 August 2008.

Tanizaki, Jun'ichirō (1966–1970) *Tanizaki Jun'ichirō zenshū* (Complete Works), 28 vols., Tokyo: Chūō Kōron.

Tsutsui, Yasutaka (1994) 'Yume no ken'etsukan' (The Dream Censor) in *Yoru no konto' fuyu no konto* (Nighttime and Wintertime Short Stories), Tokyo: Shinchōsha, 8–18.

Tyler, William J. (2008) 'Part Four: *Modanizumu* in Politics', in William J. Tyler (ed.) *Modanizumu: Modernist Fiction from Japan 1913–1938*, Honolulu: University of Hawai'i Press, 397–405.

Yagi, Kentarō (2004) 'Tsubaki Hajime no moderu – Kikuya Sakae ni tsuite' (The Model for Tsubaki Hajime: Kikuya Sakae) in DVD booklet for *Warai no daigaku* (University of Laughs) *Special Edition* DVD set, Tokyo: Tōhō Studios.

Zheng, Guohe (trans.) (2008) 'The Censor', in William J. Tyler (ed.), *Modanizumu: Modernist Fiction from Japan 1913–1938*, Honolulu: University of Hawai'i Press, 424–44.

Index

Page numbers in **bold** denote figures.

Abe, Jirō 47

Abe, Takeshi 120, 121, 123

Act for the Regulation of Model Currency and Securities 195–6, 207n2, 208n11

actors *see* kabuki: actors

adventure stories 48, 50, 75

Akasegawa, Genpei 10; *Ambiguity Inspection Card* 200; and 'anti-art' 195, 199; artistic process 196–8; career 195, 208n16; *Collection of Currency Knock-offs* **199**, 199–200, 201; and Hi-Red Center 195, 201, 208n14; as ideological deviant 202–3; and 'Model Thousand-yen Note Incident' 10, 195–206; *The Morphology of Revenge (Look Well Before You Kill)* 197, **197**; trial 196, 198–202, 204–6, 208n9, n10

Akiyama, Kiyoshi 117–18

Akutagawa Prize 195

Alcock, Rutherford 16

Allies: and 'Reverse Course' 145; use of term 149n2; versus Japan 118–19, 140, 143

America 77, 85; booksellers in 37; censorship in 51; in novels 46, 79

Americanism 36, 70n2

anarchism 95–6, 97; in novels 47; renunciation of 117

Andō, Minoru 69

Antiquarian Society 25

anti-war feeling 52, 54n23, 123, 124–6; lack of 113

Aoyama, Rokurō 188

Ara, Masahito 44, 188

Arima, Yoriyoshi 188

art: definition of 195, 201, 205, 206; exhibitions 197, 198, 204; versus legal system 198–203, 204–6; performance art 198–9; and praxis 195, 203–4; real versus fake 202–3; and social change 204–6; versus state 13; the 'superreal' 196, 199–200; value of 196, 203, 208n13

Article 29 5

artist: and censorship 5, 10; choices made by 2; compromise 8, 75, 136; responsibility of 2–3; versus state 1–2, 35, 124, 198–203, 204–6, 217–24

artistic freedom 2, 7, 8, 10, 218–19; *see also* free speech

artistic work 2, 8; in manuscript form 3; stages of 11

Arts Market 40–1, **41**, 43, 48, 52

Asahi newspaper 9, 60, 67, 178, 180–1, 182, 190, 191n8, n9; comparing versions of 183–7, 189–90; and imperial honorifics 176, 179, 181, 182, 183–7; kanji limitation 186–7; pre-publication censorship 179; and resistance 187; style manual 181; stenography 180–1; war complicity 181

Asia 7, 77, 88; Japan leading 78, 82, 86; in novels 161; in poetry 118, 125, 127

atomic bomb 8, 134, 146, 192n20

audience 2, 141, 147, 148, 204, 226; age of 2, 5; choices made by 2; decoding parody 222; and fourth wall 142–3, 144; responsibility of 2–3, 67; and taste 66; in theater 13, 16, 24–5, 29, 31n6

avant-garde art 195, 196–9, 203–4, 205–6; Japan and America 207n1; reactions to 204, 208n15

avant-garde poetry 117, 122

Ayukawa, Nobuo 121

232   Index

Azuma, Tairiku: *see* Umehara, Hokumei

bakufu 1, 3, 4, 14, 19–20; critique of 25
ballet 16
banned books 40, 45–6, 96, **106**, **107**,
    108–9n1; confiscation of 96, 97, 104,
    108; destruction of 35, 104, 108; genres
    51; handling 93, 95, 96–7, 99, 101–3,
    105–8; protective custody 99–100, **100**,
    103, 104–5; in special collections 102–3
bans 4, 5, 7, 11; of books 35, 36, 40, 45–6,
    47, 51, 93, 96; of films 8, 146, 151n25;
    of kabuki 21, 28–9; of magazines 40–1,
    42, 80; of popular music 60–2, 71n5, n9
Beautiful Voyage 74, 75; plot 78–9;
    illustrations for 80–2, **81**, **87**
Beautiful Voyage, the Sequel 83, 84–8
The Beckoning Spirit and the Scout 48–50
benshi 5
Biography of a Prostitute 9; book version
    167–9; censorship procedure **154**,
    156–67, **160**; plot 155; production of
    153; prologue **154**, 157, 161, 163,
    167–8, 169; reprints and adaptations
    168, 172n19
black market 134, 143
Boccaccio, Giovanni 38, 41; *Decameron*
    38–9, 40
Buddhism 222; in poetry 127–9
Bulwer-Lytton, Edward 26
Bunka-Bunsei era 14
bunmei kaika 18, 20, 27, 31n10
bunraku 8

Cabinet Information Bureau 6, 71n16,
    85–6, 177, 179; stages of formation 6
café culture 36, 58, 154
capitalism 46, 212, 214
Capra, Frank 149n1; *It's A Wonderful Life*
    133
CCD (Civil Censorship Detachment)
    Section 8–9, 69, 145, 146, 148, 151n25,
    153, 156, 165–7, 192n17; and
    Biography of a Prostitute 156–67;
    dissolution 9, 183; and imperial
    honorifics 176; role of 134, 145, 179;
    see also PPB
censor 3, 5, 11, 62–4, 135–6, 139, 148,
    170; critique of 213–19; as cultural
    critic 64–8; dual role of 8, 36–7; as
    inspiration 212, 227; and modernism 36;
    as obsolete 226; power of 35, 36;
    representation of 10, 41, 211, 212–19,
    220–4, **221**; as sexist 170; and

subjectivity 145, 170, 181–3, 190;
    working conditions 145–6, 156
censorship: academic models of 1–2, 5,
    148–9, 151n27, 211–12; as analogy 212;
    and artist's reputation 10, 125, 217, 225;
    benefits of 5, 7, 35, 39–40, 42–3, 136,
    204–5, 208n16, 212–13, 217, 225, 227;
    categories for 35, 36–7, 165–7, 192n14;
    change over time 1, 211; 'classical'
    model 1–2, 10; as commodity 225–6;
    and complexity 3, 4, 9–10, 11, 58, 134,
    147–9, 153, 170; and context 9–10, 11,
    134–5, 143, 144–9; continuities in 1, 3,
    4, 5, 9, 68–9, 211; critique of 213–19;
    definition 1–2; dual nature of 7, 8, 36–7,
    38, 94, 134, 148; and financial loss 3, 4,
    7, 63; as guidance 79–80; as human
    process 2, 4, 11, 64–6, 68, 144–6, 149,
    170, 190; informal methods 3, 5, 6, 9,
    62–4; interwar 6; motivation for 113; as
    negative 1, 211–12; and negotiation 1,
    3, 93, 102–5, 108, 149, 204–6; nostalgia
    for 213, 225; old versus new 10,
    211–12, 219, 224–5, 226–7; and
    patronage 27–8; and state power 1, 4,
    51, 70; and subjectivity 1, 2, 9, 65,
    71n7, 145, 182–3, 189–90; as top-down
    suppression 1, 2, 3, 4, 11, 35–6, 37; and
    teleological models 211–12; visibility of
    6–7, 8, 134
censorship avoidance: in kabuki 14, 22–4,
    27, 213; parody of 216–17, 224; in
    poetry 124; pseudonym 42; strategies
    for 217–19, 222–3, 226; by Umehara
    Hokumei 40–2; world-shifting 213, 219,
    224; see also self-censorship
censorship laws: Film Law 7, 213; Libel
    Law 21, 24; Peace Preservation Law 5,
    93, 97, 109n6, 191n3; Press Law (1875)
    21; Press Regulations (1883) 4;
    Prohibition of Heterodoxy 3; Public
    Gatherings Ordinance 28; Public Peace
    Police Law 62; Publication Law (1875)
    21, 60–1, 62; SCAP Press Code 133–4,
    139, 140, 141, 145, 153, 159, 166,
    179–80; Three Guidance Edicts 18–19
censorship methods 35, **156**; bans 4, 5, 7,
    8, 10, 11, 21, 28–9, 60–2, 80; cuts 7, 10;
    deletions 5, 10, 114, 187; pencil marks
    80, 139, **154**, **160**; warnings 5, 80; *see
    also fuseji, kondan, naietsu*
censorship regulations 2, 3–9; application
    of 2, 5, 8; artist's knowledge of 2, 38,
    136; enforcement of 2, 3, 4, 8, 178;

Index 233

internalization of 8, 69; limitations of 46; and logistics 2, 4, 69, 145–6; in Meiji period 4–5, 13–14, 16, 17–20, 28–9; in Occupation 8–9, 112–14, 133–4, 140, 141, 144–6, 153, 170, 179–80; on the press 4–5, 21, 60–2, 85–6, 133–4, 179–80; on films 5, 7, 133–4, 140, 141, 144–6, 213; on theater 14–15, 19–20, 28–9; Shōwa period 6–10, 58, 61–8, 79–80; Taishō period 5–6, 35; Tokugawa period 3–4, 13–15; wartime 6–7, 85–6; working around 2, 3, 5, 8, 14, 22–4, 38–9, 40–2, 93, 136, 139, 142–3; *see also* kabuki censorship, Occupation censorship, wartime censorship
Censorship Weekly 100
Central Review 113–14
Chambliss, William J. 182
children's literature 7, 76–7, 83, 84, 89n13
China 80, 84, 98; compositions from 77; in kabuki 25; in literature 49; in song 64; war against 6, 36, 48–50, 61–2, 63, 66, 78, 153, 154–5, 158
Chinese language 83
chōnin 13–14, 30
Christianity 3, 79, 85, 214
church 2, 79, 212
Chūshingura 23
CI&E (Civil Information and Education) Section 8–9, 146, 148, 168, 179, 181, 190; role of 133–4; film guidance 135, 136–8
civil disobedience 196, 205–6, 208n18
class 36, 44, 153; and fetishism 46, 54n18; in literature 48–50; middle class 44, 50, 58, 205; in Tokugawa period 14, 29; upper-class 39; working class 44, 77; see also proletariat
Coetzee, J.M. 212
Cold War 44
colonialism 77–8, 83–8, 89n16
Comintern Theses 36
comfort women 155, 157–8, 161, 165–9, 171n10, 173n40; and public discourse 9, 170; as 'prostitutes' 155, 161–2, 163, 165–9; research on 169; terms for 172n19
Committee on Film Control 7
Communism 6, 8, 9, 36, 53n4, 95–6, 97, 101, 116, 118, 135, 145, 146, 154, 182; Japanese Communist Party 182, 184
Complete Works of Marx and Engels 50
complicity 2, 3, 5, 6, 35, 38, 44–5, 47–50

composition movement 7, 76–8; and colonialism 78, 83–5, 86; *Collection of Model Compositions* 77; and composition delegation 86, **87**; *Composition Classroom* 77
confiscation 11, 35, 93, 96, 97, 104, 151n25
Confucianism 14, 15, 23
Consitution (1890) 5, 177
Constitution (1946) 178, 190
constitutional law 10, 200, 201
copyright violation 114
counter-discourse 1, 134–5, 139–43, 147–9
courts 10; see also trials
creativity 8, 135, 138–9, 142; and reform 27; suppression of 1, 136
critique: of censor 213–19; of government 4, 14, 25, 137, 213; of imperial system 5–6, 7 177; of *kokutai* 6, 7; of Occupation 113, 134, 139–43, 145, 148, 180
cultural critics 2, 7, 64–8, 69, 70
currency 1000 yen note 197, 207n4; counterfeiting 207n6, 207–8n8; currency modeling law 195–6, 198, 200–2, 205, 207n2, n6, 208n11; models of 196–200, 201, 202, 205–6; printing 197–8

Daiei studios 7, 150n11
Dazai, Osamu 169, 188–9
Decameron 38–9, 40
democracy 211, 226
democratic values 8, 114–15, 137–8, 146, 178
democratization films 137; and Kurosawa Akira 10, 137–9, 144, 146–7
Department of Religious Affairs 18, 20, 31n11
detective fiction 48, 50, 51
Direct Action 10, 195, 203–4, 205, 206; and Hi-Red Center 207n1; reception 204
discourse 2–3, 7, 10, 35, 190; and censorship 147–9, 170, 211; on censorship 2; and comfort women 9, 170; mainstream versus margins 1, 35; on music 60, 64–8
disturbing the peace 5, 21, 28, 60, 188
Dower, John 9, 138, 142
Drama Reform Society 29–30
dramatic performance 1, 8; see also bunraku, kabuki, Nō
Dutch learning 3

234 *Index*

editors 2, 4, 6, 80; and *fuseji* 5; independence of 9, 181, 190; as middlemen 2; as negotiators 8; and self-censorship 113–14, 120, 121

Edo period 3, 13, 90n18; see also Tokugawa period

Edogawa, Ranpo 51

education 2, 7, 79–80, 177; for disabled 79; for girls 76; and kabuki 17, 20; and libraries 94, 95; in Manchukuo 83–4; and music 60; and newspapers 31n7; and pan- Asianism 74, 78, 83–5

Education Ministry 6, 8, 60, 109n7; Committee of Popular Culture 60; and libraries 94, 95, 96, 97, 98, 103, 104, 108; officials 96

educators 79–80, 82, 88; and popular music 60; in Manchukuo 83–4, 85

Eguchi, Kan 52

Eirin 9

emperor 6, 9, 19, 94, 109n2, 222; anti-emperor views 101, 120, 184; and colonialism 158–9; as divine 177, 178, 180, 184, 190; imperial decree 4; imperial palace 86; and literature 187–9; representation 6, 9, 20, 146, 150n13, 177, 183–7, 208n11; and SCAP 146; tours by 184–5; viewing kabuki 30

Emperor Hirohito 176, 178–9, 181, 184, 188–9, 191n7, n10; reportage of birthday 186–7, 191n6

Engels, Friedrich 103, 105

English language 141–2, 150n18, n19, 216; and censorship 145, 156, 180

Enlightenment 211

Enoken (Enomoto Ken'ichi) 220

erotic literature 3, 6, 35, 36, 37–8, 50; in America 37; and genre 44–5, 50–1; in libraries 94, 101, 102; and proletarian literature 37, 50–2

eroticism 36, 62

ethics 8, 76

Etō, Jun 9, 176, 189

etsuran kinshi 42, 101, 105, **107**

family state 6

fascism 8, 112, 129n2, 138, 146

February 26 Incident 102, 109n8, 191n9

feudalism 8, 144, 146, 150n6, 178

Fielding, W.H. 164–5, 166, 172n29

Fifteen Years' War 115

film 1, 5, 7, 8, 58; categories of 145; and CCD 8, 145–6, 179; and CI&E 8, 137–9, 140, 144–5; criticism of 60; cuts

to 7, 141; destruction of 146, 151n25; film critics 68; Film Law 7, 213; forced revision 7; foreign films 7; import and export 7, 145; and locations 138; pre-screening 5; proletarian 5, 138, 213; and propaganda 7, 63, 134, 146, 150n9; ratings system 5; regulations on 7, 133–4, 140, 141, 144–6, 213; scripts 7, 145, 135

Film Ethics Regulation Control Committee *see* Eirin

film studios 2, 7, 135, 150n13

filmmakers 7, 136, 137, 144, 149, 213

fines 3, 35, 36, 42, 53n9

Foucault, Michel 52, 151n27

fraternization 134, 165

free speech 1, 2, 5, 21, 136, 137, 138, 145, 179, 196, 200, 201, 204–6

Freedom and Popular Rights Movement 21, 28

Freud, Sigmund 219, 224, 227

Friedrich, Ernst 51–2

Fuji 188

Fujiyama, Ichirō 65

Fukiya, Kōji 83, **87**, 90n24

Fukuchi, Gen'ichirō (Ōchi) 19, 22, 24, 26, 28, 31n7

Fukuzawa, Yukichi 93

fuseji 5, 6–7, 11, 38, 48

gangsters 134, 143

Gathering Images 188

gender relations 44, 153

genres: art 195; literature 44, 53n14; songs 58

Gercke, George 150n14; 'Mr Garky' 139

Germany 51–2, 82

Gertzman, Jay 37, 39, 45

girls: and language 76; in literature 75, 76; magazines for 75–6; and nationalism 80–2, 88; as *shōjo* 80–2, 88; and war 81–2

Girls' Club 89n3

Girls' Friend 7, 78, **81**, **87**, 89n3; and censorship 80; Children's Culture Award 86; and Kawabata Yasunari 74–6, 77, 84, 86–8; and nationalism 7, 80–3, 84–8; and *shōjo* 80–2, 88; transformation 75, 80–2, 86–7

Great Japan Film Association 7

Great Kantō Earthquake 36, 58, 59; and reconstruction 64

Griffis, William Elliot 16

Groening, Victor 162–3, 164, 167, 172n31

Index 235

Grotesque 41, 42, 52
grotesque literature 37, 45–7, 51–2, 54n17

Hagiwara, Tatsuo 99–100
Hakubunkan 106–7
Hanada, Kiyoteru 117–18
Haraszti, Miklós 1–2, 5, 8
harmful to public 5, 60–1, 93–5
Hashiba, Hideyoshi 18
Hatanaka, Shigeo 113–14
Hatsuyama, Shigeru 81–2, **81**
Hayashi, Fumiko 74, 75, 80, 88n1, 90n27, 169; 'Frozen Land' 80
Hayashi, Fusao 52, 169
Heian period 90n18
Hi-Red Center 195, 201, 207n1, 208n14, n15
High Treason Incident 95–6
Hino, Ashihei 84
Hirano, Ken 44, 116
Hirano, Kyoko 135, 137, 139, 147
Hiroshima 8, 134
Hisaita, Eijirō 137–8, 146; and *Morning of the Osone Family* 138, 146
Historical Research Society 25
Hollywood 213
home front 61, 66, 82
Home Ministry 4, 5, 6, 21, 93, 96–7; archives 51, 54n20, 61, 80; Bureau of Reconstruction 64; Cabinet Information Bureau 6, 71n16, 85–6, 177, 179; Censorship Division 80; and children's magazines 79–80; Criminal Affairs Bureau 63, 64; dismantling of 58, 69; and film 7; formation of 21; and libraries 8, 94–5, 96, 98, 102, 104, 108; Police Bureau Censorship Division 5, 6; and records 58, 60–2, 63, 69; revising Publication Law 60–1
Hong Kong 118
Horiguchi, Daigaku 189
Hoshi, Mamoru 213, 219
House, Edward 17
human rights 170, 171n10
Hyakunin isshu 49
hypocrisy 8, 117, 216

Ichikawa, Danjurō VII 15
Ichikawa, Danjurō IX 20, 24, 25–6, 28; and kabuki reform 25–6, 27
Ichimura-za 23
ideologues 2–3, 7
ideology 3, 4, 6, 7, 95–6, 97; democratic 8, 113, 137; fascist 8, 112, 129n2, 146;

left-wing 36, 38, 44, 48, 95–7, 98–9, 101–3, 105; nationalist 47, 78, 85, 159; proletarian 44–5, 48, 52; right-wing 98, 109n6, 178, 179, 191n9; shifts in 9, 115; Shintō 16; and writing 48, 74–5, 112–13
Ihara, Usaburō 153, **154**, 169, 171n4
Imai, Tadashi 146; *People's Enemy* 146
imperial family 176, 178, 179, 183, 188, 190, 191n3; Crown Prince Akihito 185; Imperial Household Agency 191n11; Imperial Household Ministry 179; photographing 179; Prince Mikasa 185–6; representation of 183–7
imperial honorifics 9, 128; censorship of 181–3, 187–90; decline in 184–5, 189; in literature 176, 187–90; as militaristic 182–3, 189; in newspapers 176–8, 179, 182–7, 189–90; and Press Code 180; simplification 176–9, 181–2, 183, 189
imperial system: abolishing 6; critique of 5–6; praise for 128
imprisonment *see* prison
in-house rules 4, 176, 212, 225
Inagaki, Gorō 220, 224
Inoue, Kaoru 15, 19, 22, 29, 30, 32n24
interrogation 6, 220, 224
'invisibility rule' 9, 134, 141–2, 143, 180, 191n13, 212
Iraq 112
Ise Shrine 184
Itagaki, Taisuke 19
Italy 39, 222
Itami, Mansaku 150n10
Itō, Hirobumi 15, 19, 22, 27, 29
Itō, Sei 43; trial 10
Iwakura Mission 19, 22, 24, 93–4
Iwakura, Tomomi 15, 19
Iwasaki, Akira 213–15, 218, 226; 'Anthology of Love' 213–15, 218; imprisonment 213, 219; self-censorship 219

Japan: defeat in war 44, 69, 115, 120, 138, 143, 178, 188; as leader of Asia 77–8, 82, 84–6; move to war 35, 36; overseas image of 7, 16–17; surrender 112; as victorious 118–19, 127; war with China 6, 36, 48–50, 61–2, 63, 66, 88–9n1; versus West 15, 32n24, 79, 82, 85, 118–19; as Yamato 118
Japan Association of Music Culture 68–9, 71n15

236 *Index*

Japan Association of Phonograph Record Culture (JAPRC) 68–9, 71n16; renaming 71n19
Japan Epilepsy Association 225
Japanese army 155, 157, 158–9, 163, 164, 165
Japanese censorship: versus Allied censorship 179; versus other countries 10, 36, 51; research on 2, 10–11, 13
Japanese Communist Party 182, 184
Japanese Fiction 153, 155, 167, 170n3
Japanese language: and censors **156**, 181–3, 189; changes in 176–8, 181, 184–5; and colonialism 83–6, 87–8; honorifics 191n1; kanji 177–8, 179, 181, 186–7, 190, 191n4, 192n18; National Language Council 177–8, 191n4; puns in 222; and stenography 180–1; writing systems 191n2; *see also* imperial honorifics
Japanese music 59, 70n2; see also popular songs
The Japanese Tragedy 9, 146
Japanese values 77–8, 80–2, 85–6, 87–8, 90n18, 114–15, 138, 144, 177, 188
jazz 59, 65, 70n2
Jitsugyō no Nihonsha 75, 80
journalism 1, 2, 180–1
journalists 2, 190; access to emperor 179, 185, 191n10–11; independence of 9, 176, 180–1, 184, 190; in kabuki 23; kanji knowledge 179; and negotiation 184; and self-censorship 112
Joyce, James 212
Justice Ministry 6; Thought Section 6
Juvenile Club 114

kabuki 5; actors 14–15, 16, 18, 19, 20, 24, 27, 28, 32n14; attitudes towards 13, 18, 26, 29, 30; audience 16, 17, 24–5, 29, 31n6, 31–2n13; banishment of 15; development 13; as educational 17–18, 20, 29; false names in 14, 18, 20, 21, 23, 24, 27, 31n9; film adaptations 135–6; and modernity 22–3, 29–30; origins 13–14; social status of 13–14, 16, 20, 29, 31; text versus performance 13; viewed by Westerners 15–16, 17; as useful 18; as vulgar 13, 14, 16, 27
kabuki censorship 5, 8, 13–14, 23–4, 30–1; Meiji edicts 16, 17–20, 21, 28–9; Tempō reforms 14–15; and Western historians 13
kabuki plays 15, 22, 23, 24, 25, 26, 32n21

Kamei, Fumio 9, 146; *Between War and Peace* 146; *The Japanese Tragedy* 9, 146
Kaneko, Mitsuharu 124–6
Kaneko, Yōbun 52
Kansei reforms 3
kanzen chōaku 15, 19–20, 25, 26, 216
Karafuto 77
Kasza, Gregory 2, 4
Kataoka, Teppei 88n1
Katō, Ken'ichi 114
Katsutarō 65
Kawabata, Yasunari 7; adopted daughter 76; *Beautiful Voyage* 74, 75, 78–9, 80–2; *Beautiful Voyage, the Sequel* 83, 84–8; 'Book of Manchukuo' 84, 90n26; and 'children's sentiment' 7, 76–7, 86; 'On Compositions' 77; and compromise 75, 82–3, 84, 86–8; depiction of girls 76, 89n9; as editor 77, 90n30; *Flower Diary* 74; and 'girls' culture' 7, 75, 88; and *Girls' Friend* 74–6, 77, 84, 86–8; *The Izu Dancer* 76, 89n11; *Maiden's Harbor* 74, 75; in Manchukuo 83–4; on Manchuria 74; as mentor 76; reception 74–5, 76; self-censorship 80; *Snow Country* 74; stance toward war 74–5, 77–8, 82–3, 84–8; 'Thoughts through Books' 76; utopian vision 77, 78
Kawakami, Hajime 103
Kawatake, Mokuami 24, 25, 32n19
Keene, Donald 77–8, 113, 118, 120
Keio University 101, 102, 103, 105–6
Keller, Helen 78–9, 90n19
key logs 180, 181, 192n14
Kikuchi, Kan 74, 88n1
Kikuya, Sakae 220, 226–7
Kinoshita, Keisuke 146; *Morning of the Osone Family* 146
Kishida, Kunio 88n1
Kita, Ikki 102
Kitahara, Hakushū 187
Kitasono, Katue 114
Kobayashi, Hideo 90n18, 116
Kobayashi, Kyōji 225
Kobayashi, Takiji 43, 44, 47; *Lifetime Party Member* 44
Koga, Masao 59, 70n2; *koga merodii* 59
Kojima, Masajirō 88n1
kokutai 6, 7, 20
Komatsubara, Eitarō 95
Kōmyōji, Saburō 26
kondan 62–4, 71n10
'Kondankai' Council 198, 206, 207n7

Index 237

Korea 71n9, 77, 100
Korean-Japanese relations 170
Korean language 83
'Korean problem' 166–7, 173n35
Korean women 153, 155–6, 165, 169;
  erasure of 153, 161–2, 167–70; and
  Tamura Taijirō 157, 161; versus
  Japanese women 161–2, 167–8
Koreans: in Japan 172n29; racism towards
  9
Kōtoku, Shūsui 95; *Essence of Socialism*
  95
Kume, Masao 88n1
Kunzman, Richard 164–5, 172n30
Kurosawa, Akira 7–8; aims 136, 138; and
  American censors 139; career 8, 135–6,
  150n7, n8; and CI&E 135, 136–9, 168;
  and compliance 135, 136–9; and
  Escape at Dawn 168; as humanist 133,
  134, 147; idea of 'self' 138–9; and
  Japanese censors 135–6; *Men Who
  Tread on the Tiger's Tail* 135–6, 146,
  150n6; *The Most Beautiful* 136, 146;
  *No Regrets for Our Youth see No
  Regrets for Our Youth*; One *Wonderful
  Sunday see One Wonderful Sunday*;
  Rashomon 143; *Sanshiro Sugata I* and
  II 136, 146; as subversive 134, 148;
  track record 134–5; war complicity
  136, 150n10; wartime films 136, 146,
  150n9
Kuroshima, Denji 44, 52
Kusuda, Kiyoshi 146; *as Long as I Live*
  146
Kwantung army 83, 84
kyōgen 19

Ladies Review 121
Lady Chatterly's Lover 10, 228n4
Lawrence, D.H. 10, 212
leftism 36, 38, 44, 48, 95–7, 98–9, 101–3,
  105
leftists 5–6, 95–6, 97, 137; and *New
  Japanese Literature* 115–16
legal system 196; versus art 198–203,
  204–6; challenges to 196; and freedom
  of expression 196, 200, 201, 204–6;
  Japan versus America 207n5, n6; and
  societal norms 204
Lenin, Vladimir 103, 105
lèse-majesté 177, 191n3, 201, 208n11
libel 4; Libel Law 21, 24
librarians 8; and banned books 93, 96–7,
  98, 99–100, 101–3, 104–8; as

negotiators 93, 102–4, 108; reactions to
  censorship 97, 102–4
libraries 8, 42; academic libraries 94,
  101–4, 105, 106; access to books 94,
  101–2, 103–4, 105–8; British Library
  93–4; Fukagawa Library 99, **100**, 101,
  104; Hibiya Library 99, 105;
  Hitotsubashi University Library 106,
  107; Imperial Library 93, 95, 96,
  99–100, 103, 104; informants in 101;
  Ishikawa Prefectural Library 101;
  Kōfūkai Library 104–5; National Diet
  Library 94–5, 105; Osaka Municipal
  Library 104; Prange Collection 166,
  183, 192n17; private libraries 94, 96,
  99; public libraries 93–5, 99, 106–7;
  role of 94, 95; Sankō Library 106–7,
  107; Shinshū Kamisato Library 98–9;
  Suragadai Library 99; Tokyo Library
  94–5; Tokyo Metropolitan Library 101,
  105
licensing: for *benshi* 5; in film industry 7;
  for newspapers 21; in theaters 18, 19,
  24, 31n12
Literary World 84
literature 1, 6, 7, 187–9, 190; adventure
  stories 48, 50, 75; detective fiction 48,
  50, 51; mystery fiction 48, 51; and
  propaganda 7, 85–8, 112, 165; *see also*
  banned books, poetry, proletarian
  literature

MacArthur, General Douglas 136, 149n2,
  190
Maedakō, Hiroichirō 52
magazines 4, 58, 79–80, 85–6, 115–16,
  133, 138, 145, 179; erotic 50; for girls
  75–6, 84–5, 88; and illustrations 80–2;
  and roundtables 65, 67–8; and
  subscribers 42
mainstream 1, 6, 10, 19, 20, 37, 39, 44, 49,
  147–8; and art 195, 196; and girls'
  magazines 74–5; and margins 1, 35, 37,
  39–40; and subversion 49; working
  outside 38
Malaya 118, 119
Manchukuo 80, 83–4; compositions from
  77; definition 89n16; and Japanese
  language 83–5; as utopia 80, 83; *see
  also* Manchuria
Manchuria 220; definition 89n16;
  Kawabata's view of 74; literature from
  83; South Manchurian Railways 86; *see
  also* Manchukuo

238 *Index*

Manchurian Incident 35, 36
Man'yōshū 188
manzai 62, 71n9
Marco Polo Bridge Incident 61
Maruya, Yoshizō 63–4
Marx, Karl 103, 105
Marxism 48, 49, 50, 52, 213, 218
Matsuda, Michiyuki 25, 27
Matsudaira, Sadanobu 3
Matsumoto, Jun 24
Matsuzaki, Keiji 138
McCarthyism 53n4
media 1, 2, 7, 9, 11, 58, 62, 63, 64, 65, 69,
   70, 75, 88, **101**, 112, 133, 134, 170, 182,
   183, 196, 208n16, 225
Meiji period 1, 4–5, 13; and modernity
   15–16
Meiji policy 4–5, 30, 31n1; on kabuki 13,
   16, 17–20, 28–9, 30–1; legacy of 2, 4,
   31; and modernization 13, 15–16, 22;
   shifts in 13; versus Tokugawa policy 4,
   5, 19
Meiji Restoration 13, 15, 16, 66
Meiji statesmen 15, 16, 24, 26; and
   newspapers 17; and Shintomi-za 27–8;
   travel to West 16, 19, 22, 24
Meiji University 99, 101, 116
militaristic works 8, 187–9; concealment
   of 116–18; and film 8, 134, 137, 146,
   151n25; in *Girls' Friend* 86–7; by
   Miyoshi Tatsuji 118–20; and postwar
   anthologies 8, 112–13, 120, 121, 122,
   125; and Tamura Taijirō 159, 164; by
   Takahashi Shinkichi 127–8; by Tsuboi
   Shigeji 121–4
military rule 1, 6, 135
Minister of Education 42
missionaries 3
Mitchell, Richard 2, 4
Mito, Komon 24
Miyamoto, Saburō 81–2
Miyatake, Gaikotsu 42
Miyazawa, Jūichi 69
Miyoshi, Tatsuji 8, 117, 118–20, 124;
   News of Victory Has Come 118–19
Model Thousand-yen Note Incident 10,
   195–206; as Direct Action 204, 205;
   significance of 205–6
Modern Literature 116, 188
modernism 36–7, 44, 45, 212
morals 21, 23, 35, 45–6, 47, 212, 214–15,
   217; and books 93, 95, 96, 97–8; and
   kabuki 17–18, 19; and popular songs
   60–1, 62

Morita, Kan'ya XII 24, 26, 27, 33
Morita, Tama 77
Morita-za 22, 23, 24–5
Morning of the Osone Family 138, 146,
   150n12
Morse, Edward 16
Motoori, Norinaga 78
Murata, Masao 123
Murayama, Tomoyoshi 52
Murayama-za 23
Murder Incorporated 45–7, 49
Mushakōji, Saneatsu 169
Music World 65, 68
mystery fiction 48, 51

NHK 71n5
Nagai, Kafū 2, 43, 188
Nagasaki 8, 134
naietsu 63, 71n11, 215
Nakahara, Jun'ichi 75, 80–2, 89n6, n7,
   90n31; and *shōjo* image 80–1, **81**
Nakahara, Yūsuke 200, 207n7
Nakamura-za 22
Nakanishi, Natsuyuki 198, 207n7
Nakano, Shigeharu 44, 116, 122
Nakata, Kunizō 101
Nakayama, Shimpei 59, 68, 70n2, 71n5;
   shimpei-bushi 59
Nanking 6, 128
nation-state 6; *see also kokutai*
national emergency 63, 66, 67, 97, 227
national security 104–5
nationalism 47, 48–50, 61, 81, 122, 136,
   180; and honorifics 177, 187–8; and
   Kawabata Yasunari 77–8, 84–8; and
   Kurosawa Akira 146–7; and *Yamato-
   gokoro* 78, 85–6, 90n18; *see also*
   patriotic literature, militaristic works
naturalism 95
Nazism 119, 213
negotation 219–24; censor and artist 1,
   139, 196, 215–17, 219–24; librarians
   and police 93, 102–5, 108; by journalists
   184; sites of 14; state and intellectuals
   58; systems of 3, 5, 6, 11, 62–4, 93, 149,
   204–6
Neo-Dada Organizers 195
New Japanese Literature 115–18
New Life (Shin-seikatsu) 116
New Life (Shinsei) 188
New Women's Garden 77, 80, 87, 89n15
New Youth 39, 42, 44
News of Victory Has Come 118–19
newspapers 4, 40; and Akasegawa Gempei

195; attacks on 179, 191n9; censorship of 61, 133, 145, 179–81, 182–7, 189–90; editorials 17–18; Japan Newspaper Publishers and Editors Association 181; and Kawabata Yasunari 83; and labor unions 181; linguistic changes in 9, 176–8; and literature 190; *Mainichi* 178; *Nihon Keizai* 178; page limitations 225; role of 17; and serialized novels 190; *Yomiuri hōchi* 178; *see also Asahi* newspaper
Nichiei studios 9
Nietzsche, Friedrich 47
nihilism 47, 66
Nikkatsu studios 71n5
nikutai bungaku 171n14, 15, 155–6
Nippon 86, 222
Niwa, Fumio 169
Nō 8, 19, 135–6
Noguchi, Yonejirō 116
noir fiction 51
non-censorship 134–5, 143, 196, 206, 213; significance of 9–10, 11, 47, 147–9
No Regrets for Our Youth: and CI&E guidelines 135–9; as collaboration 138; making of 137–9; as pro-democratic 133, 137–9, 146; reception 10, 139, 147; screening of 139; and Takigawa Incident 109n7, 137
Nosaka, Akiyuki 42

obscenity 35, 36, 47; and parody 216–17, 218; and sedition 35, 36–7; trials 208n9, n13
Occupation 1, 58, 191n7; aims 144, 178; agrarian reform 137; as 'American' or 'Allied' 149n2; as discursive structure 148–9; in film 139–42, 144; and invisibility 9, 134, 141–2, 143, 180; and 'Korean problem' 166–7; as liberal 9, 138, 190; paradox of 9; Reverse Course 145; *see also* SCAP
Occupation censorship 4, 8–9, 112, 124, 153, **154**, **156**, **160**, 156–67, 170, 212; aims of 8, 144–5, 165, 170; and atomic bomb 8; and English language 141–2; and film 133–4; and imperial honorifics 9, 176, 178, 181–90; and Japanese militarism 134, 137, 140; shifts in 9, 179; transitions in 145, 148; *see also* CCD, CI&E, PPB
Oda, Nobunaga 18
Odagiri, Hideo 115–16, 122
Ōe, Kenzaburō 227

Office of Shintō Worship 15, 31n11
Ogawa, Chikagorō 7, 10, 69, 70; aims of 58; career 64–5, 69; as cultural critic 64–8; on 'Don't You Forget Me' 61; *Popular Songs and Social Currents* 66
Ogawa, Mimei 79–80
Okamoto, Jun 117–18
Okinawa 191n7
Ōkubo, Toshimichi 21, 24
Ōkuma, Shigenobu 15, 19, 30
One Wonderful Sunday 7; as counter-discourse 134, 135, 139–43; flouting regulations 134, 140; making of 135, 139; *mise-en-scène* 140–2; music 142–3; narrative mode 139–40; and *No Regrets for Our Youth* 133, 135, 137, 146–7; versus other films 146–7; as pro-democratic 135, 144; as problematization film 144, 147; reception 133–5, 147; sound 142; story 133, 149n1
Ono, Yoko 207n1
Onoe, Kikugorō V 25, 28
opera 16
Ōsugi, Sakae 103
Otobe, Senzaburō 98
Ōtsuka, Kinnosuke 103–4
Ōya, Sōichi 84
Oyama, Hisajirō 10
Ozaki, Hotsumi 137
Ozaki, Kōyō 222; *The Golden Demon* 222, 226
Ozaki, Shirō 88n1

Pacific War 36, 42, 71n16, 78, 113, 115, 118–19, 140, 153, 187
pan-Asianism 74, 78, 83–5, 87
pariah capitalism 37–8, 39
parody 10, 213, 216–17, 224; definition 222; political significance 226–7; of *Romeo and Juliet* 220, 222
patriotic literature 112; poetry 8, 114–15, 118–24, 127–8; rewriting of 116–18, 121–3; and romanticism 117; and shame 114–15, 120; in various countries 115
Patriotic Writers' Association 123, 177
patronage 5; of kabuki 27–8, 31; of newspapers 17
Peace Preservation Law 5, 93, 97, 109n6, 191n3
Pearl Harbor 118–19
Pen corps 74, 88–9n1
Perry, Commodore Matthew 23
personal relationships 5, 6, 24, 27–8, 31, 42

240 *Index*

Perverse Matters 40, 42, 51; and anti-war
feeling 52
Philippines 118
The Pickled-Overnight Revolutionary 48,
49
poetry 8, 49–50, 112–29; avant-garde 117,
122; Four Seasons School 117; haiku
112; *shi* 112; proletarian 117; tanka 112,
119, 187–8
police 8, 95–6, 97; and confiscations 11;
and counterfeiting 207–8n8; and *fuseji*
5; increased power of 98; and libraries
93, 97, 99–101, 102–3, 104–5, 108;
Military Police (*kempeitai*) 93, 104,
105; Police Department 28; Special
Higher Police (*tokkō*) 93, 97, 102–3,
105; and theaters 25, 28; *see also*
thought police
political correctness 212
political meetings 5, 28
politicians 2, 15; see also Meiji statesmen
politics: and aesthetics 115, 212, 218, 227;
and reading 126, 129; and sex 36, 37,
43, 45, 52
popular culture 58–60; and the state 58, 68
popular songs 1, 7, 58, 59–60, 71n9; 'The
Apple Song' 142; characteristics 65–6;
'China Nights' 64, 67; criticism of 60,
67, 69; 'Don't You Forget Me' 61–2,
63, 65; *enka* 70n2; *hayariuta* 59;
'Hidden Tears' 65; *koga merodii* 59;
'Longing for You' 60, 70n2; as
propaganda 63, 66; public and private
66–7; *ryūkōka* 59–60, 70n2; *shimpei-
bushi* 59; singers 65; *Songs and Social
Currents* 66
pornography 14, 38, 45, 53n4
post-publication inspection: books 3, 4,
8–9; film 7, 9, 145
postmodernity 211
postwar: meaning of 141, 143; struggle
134, 139–43, 144, 147, 155
Potsdam Declaration 137, 179
PPB (Press, Pictorial and Broadcast)
Division 134, 145–6, 148, 149n3, 153,
156, 156–67, 168, 170n2, 176, 178, 179;
different units in 167; and literary works
187–9; News Agency Section 179–80,
181–3
Prange Collection 166, 183, 192n17
pre-publication inspection: books 3, 4, 5,
8–9, 85–6; dramatic performance 8, 18,
215–16; films 7, 145; newspapers 179;
radio 8; records 61, 63, 69

press regulations *see* censorship
regulations: on the press
prison 3, 4, 6, 35, 42, 103, 201, 213, 219
prison editors 4
problematization film 144, 147
Proletarian Film League 5, 213
proletarian literature 6, 35, 36, 37, 44–5,
48, 50, 52; poetry movement 117;
stereotypes of 53n14
proletariat 36, 43, 44, 48; as subaltern
53n12
propaganda 6, 7, 15–16, 36, 85, 180,
188–9, 227; and art 171n4; and film 7,
63, 134, 146, 150n9; and literature 7,
85–8, 112, 165; and magazines 82–3;
and newspapers 17; and popular songs
7, 63, 66
prostitution 13, 14, 16; in novels 46,
167–8, 170–1n3; *see also* comfort
women: as 'prostitutes'
pseudonym 42; *see also* kabuki: false
names in
Public Gatherings Ordinance 28
public order 4, 5, 28, 35, 60–1, 62, 85
publishers 2, 3, 4, 6, 35; in America 37;
and *fuseji* 5; guilds 3–4; and informal
censorship 5, 80; as middlemen 2; and
new censorship 212; responsibility of 2,
3
publishing boom 6, 35, 38
punishment 3, 6, 21; and courts 10;
increasingly severe 35
purges 101, 114

racism 170; anti-Chinese 159, 165; anti-
Japanese 101; anti-Korean 9, 157–9,
163, 165, 166, 168; and colonialism 85
radicality 6, 15, 37–8, 43–4, 47, 49, 203;
of Drama Reform Society 29–30; of
ero-guro- puro 37; of sexual expression
42, 50
radio 2, 8, 58, 71n5, 133, 145, 179;
criticism of 60; and Kawabata Yasunari
83
rakugo 62
ratings boards 2
recanting *see tenkō*
Reconstruction 113
record censorship 58, 60–4, 65–9, 70, 145;
legacy of 70
record companies 58–60, 61, 62–4, 68–9;
Columbia Records 59, 63; Deutsche
Gramophone 59; Japan Phonograph
Company 59; Japan Polydor 59; Polydor

Index 241

59; and propaganda 63; Victor 59, 61, 70–1n5
Record Production Standard Committee 69
records 58; banned 60–2; list of approved 60; production process 63–4, 70n1
Red Bird 76
Red Flag 182
Red Flag Incident 95
reform: versus self-censorship 26–7; of theater 22, 24–6, 29–30
reformers 5, 25–6, 29–30
The Renovation 188
resistance 1, 35, 87–8, 136, 149, 215, 217, 223; faked 122; to Occupation 187; to war 117, 123, 124–6
retrospective censorship 4, 8, 96, 97, 145
Reverse Course 145
rhetoric of failure 47
rising sun flag 50
Rokumeikan 28, 30
romanticism 117
Rubin, Jay 2, 5, 9, 113, 138
Russian Revolution 36, 38, 46
Russo-Japanese War 95

'S' relationship 75, 79, 89n5
Saigō, Takamori 19
Saijō, Yaso 71n5, 75, 116
Saitō, Mokichi 116
Sakaguchi, Ango 153, 171n5, n14
Sakai, Toshihiko 99
Sakuramoto, Tomio 114, 115, 120, 121, 125–6
Salon 188
samurai 14, 15, 16, 23, 39
Sanjō, Sanemori 26
Saruwaka-machi 15, 16, 17, 24, 25
satire 3
Satō, Haruo 88n1, 116
Satō, Tadao 140, 142
Sawamura-za 23
scandals 3, 14, 30
SCAP (Supreme Commander for the Allied Powers) 8, 135, 137, 145, 147, 183, 187; changing aims of 145, 146, 165–7; definitions of 149n2; and emperor 146; Press Code 133–4, 139, 140, 141, 145, 153, 159, 166, 179–80
schools 2, 95, 96
Schubert, Franz: *Unfinished Symphony* 142–3, 151n22
scripts: film 7, 135, 136, 137, 150n9, 168, 173n37; kabuki 18, 20, 21, 28; plays 216; radio 8; translation of 145

sedition 35, 36–7, 38, 93; and obscenity 35, 36–7
Segawa, Jokō III 15
self-censorship 1, 2, 3, 4, 9, 212; definitions of 26–7, 112; in film 136, 143; and *fuseji* 6–7; and ideology 112–13; and journals 113; in kabuki 20, 21, 26–7; in literature 80, 155, 167, 218–19; motivation for 1, 112–15, 129; and new censorship 219; in poetry 8, 112–29; and publishers' guilds 3–4; versus reform 26–7; and war guilt 8, 114–15, 120; as widespread 121
Self-Help 32n17; adaptations of 23
self-regulation 68–9, 71n18
senkyōshi 16, 18–19
sexuality: expression of 42, 45; in film 5; of girls 80; in postwar literature 153, 156
Shakespeare, William 220, 222
Shanghai 39, 47, 53n6, 101
Shibusawa, Eiichi 15, 19, 22, 28, 29
Shiga, Mitsuko 188
Shillony, Ben-Ami 113, 114
Shimazaki, Tōson 43, 77
Shintō 15, 127–9, 191n5; Shinto Directive 188
Shintomi-za 24–6, 28, 29, 30; and Meiji elite 27–8; style 27
Shioiri, Kamesuke 67–8
Shōchiku studios 7, 150n11
shogun 3, 20
Shōji, Tarō 65
shōjo 80–2, 88
Shōtoku, Prince 62, 197, 208n11
Shōwa period 1, 6–10
Singapore 118, 127
Smiles, Samuel 23; *Self Help* 23
social unrest 14
Socialism 53n4, 95–6, 145, 154
Socialist works 8, 95–6; *Essence of Socialism* 95
Socialists 6, 95–6, 97
Society for the Promotion of Science and Technology 42
soldiers 90n22, 101, 153, 178, 191n5; American 64, 145, 165; crimes committed by 113, 169, 184; and emperor 184; in film 134, 143, 144; in literature 48–50, 54n21, 123, 155, 157, 158–9, 161–2, 164, 167–8, 188–9
Sonobe, Saburō 68, 71n14, n15
Sovietism 36–7
Spaulding, Robert 181–2, 189

242 *Index*

Spivak, Gayatri Chakravorty 53n12
Stalin, Joseph 105; *Collected Works of Stalin* 105, **106**
stamp 3, 5, 105, 106, **107**, 226; figurative 148
state: versus art 13; versus artist 1–2, 35, 124, 198–203, 204–6, 217–24; choices made by 2; and film production 7; and new censorship 212; and popular culture 58, 68, 70; power of 1–2, 4, 51, 70; responsibility of 2–3
Story Club 39, 42, 48, 49
subjectivity 136; in censorship process 1, 2, 9, 65, 71n7, 145, 182–3, 189–90
subversion 6, 8, 21, 30; and complicity 38, 45, 49; and counter-discourse 147–9; fear of 36
Suematsu, Kenchō 29
Sugimoto, Shōjun 200–1, 207n7
Sugiyama, Heisuke 67, 88n1
surveillance 2, 35, 97, 101, 103–4
suspension of publication 4, 81
Suzuki, Miekichi 76
Suzuki, Seijun 168, 173n38
Suzuki, Tomi 2

Tachibana, Takahiro 36, 68
Taishō democracy 36
Taishō period 1, 5–6
Taishō policy 5–6, 35
Taiwan 71n9, 77
Takahashi, Ryūji 114, 115
Takahashi, Shinkichi 127–9; *Kirishima* 127; *Pilgrimages to Shrines* 127–8
Takami, Jun 169
Takamura, Kōtarō 114, 116, 118, 119, 120, 124
Takarazuka theater 75, 80
Takebashi Incident 43, 53n11
Takeda, Rintarō 52
Takigawa, Yukitoki 109n7, 137
Takigawa Incident 101, 109n7, 137
Takiguchi, Shūzō 200–1, 207n7
Tamura Taijirō: *Biography of a Prostitute see Biography of a Prostitute*; career 153–6, 168–9, 170; critical reception 156, 169–70; *Devil of the Flesh* 154–5, 171n8, n9; *Gate to the Flesh* 154–5, 171n8; later fiction 168–9; *Locusts* 168–9, 173n39; and *nikutai bungaku* 155–6; repatriation 153, 154, 167; as soldier 153, 154
Tanabe, Hisao 60
Tanaka, Hidemitsu 188

Tanamichi, Tomoya 182–3, 189
Taniguchi, Senkichi 168
Tanizaki Jun'ichirō 43, 213, 215–17, 218; *The Age to Learn of Love* 215, 218; 'The Censor' 213, 215–17, 218, 219, 220, 226, 228n8; essays 218, 228n9
tax: on theaters 19; on records 59
Tayama, Katai 43
Tempō reforms 14–15, 31n4
tenkō 6, 47–8, 53n4, 116, 120
theater: censorship of 13–14, 17–20, 31n2, 133, 182, 216, 219–24; as education 17; *jidaimono* 14; *katsurekigeki* 25, 30; as political 30; and popular culture 60; reform of 22, 24–6, 29–30; *sewamono* 14, 25, 27; as unique 13; in West 16; *zangirimono* 25, 27, 30
Thoreau, Henry David 2, 205
thought control 7
thought guidance 6, 94, 95, 97, 98
thought police 42, 93, 97, 102–3, 105, 114, 213
Three Guidance Edicts 18–19
three ROs 37
three Ss 37, 53n2
Tōhō studios 7, 135, 137, 150n9; Scenario Review Committee 135
Tokugawa period 1, 3–4, 10
Tokugawa policy 3–4; on kabuki 13–15; legacy of 3, 10
Tokugawa, Yoshimune 3
Tokyo 5, 24, 28, 60, 154–5; art community 195, 199, 207n1; bombing of 105, 114, 134, 140, 141; and earthquake 58, 64; in film 134; libraries 94–5, 99, 100, 101, 102, 104, 105, 106; lifestyle 58; in literature 78–9; Metropolitan Government 99; and newspaper censorship 180, 183, 184; postwar ruins 114, 134, 140, 143, 154, 155; publishing world 51; reception of *One Wonderful Sunday* 142–3, 147; Tokyo District Court 198, 201–2, 208n10; Tokyo High Court 208n10; Tokyo Supreme Court 202, 208n10
Tokyo War Crimes Trials 169
Tomii, Reiko 196, 205
torture 6, 35
Toyoda, Masako 77; *Composition Classroom* 77
trials: of Akasegawa Gempei 196, 198–202, 204–6, 208n9, n10; artist's use of 10, 195, 198–9, 204–5; High Treason Trial 96

Tsuboi, Hideto 120, 121
Tsuboi, Shigeji 8, 52, 117, 120–4; *Fruit* 122; 'A Poem Admonishing Myself' 123; 'A Poem Dedicated to an Iron Kettle' 121–3; *War Eye* 122
Tsubota, Jōji 80
Tsuruoka, Yoshihisa 120, 121
Tsutsui, Yasutaka 213, 219, 225; 'Automatic Police' 225; 'The Dream Censor' 213, 219, 224–5; writing strike 225, 227

Uchiyama, Motoi 80–1, 89n6
Ueno, Chizuko 42, 51
Umehara, Hokumei 6, 35; anti-war views 54n23; avoiding censorship 40–2; as 'Azuma Tairiku' 42, 48; *The Beckoning Spirit and the Scout* 48–50; *A Complete History of Modern Social Trends* 42; cultural award 39; death 42; and the *Decameron* 38–9; early life 39; exile 39, 47; manipulating censorship 38–9, 40, 42–3; *Murder Incorporated* 45–7; *The Pickled-Overnight Revolutionary* 48, 49; reception 42–3, 45; and *Through the Russian Revolution* 40; as translator 38, 40; various jobs 42; wartime writing 48
Unequal Treaties 22, 32n15, 32n24
Unfinished Symphony 142–3, 151n22
University of Laughs 10, 213, 219–24, **221**, 225–6, 228n11; cinematography 220; source text 219

violence: and activism 95, 191n9; in film 5; representation of 35, 50–2

war: cost of 51–2, 153; depiction in film 134, 168; depiction in literature 48–50, 54n24, 155, 158–64, 165; as sacred 81–3; slogans 82
war complicity 47–8, 74; and Kawabata Yasunari 74–5, 82–3, 84–8; and Kurosawa Akira 136; and newspapers 181; and postwar literature 114–18, 121–3
war crime 153, 169, 181, 188
war guilt 8, 114–18
war memory 121
war stories 75
Warhol, Andy 207n1

wartime censorship 4, 6–7, 61–4, 65–8, 69, 71n16, 79–80, 85–6, 113–14, 135–6
wartime writing 48, 48–52, 74–5, 82–3, 84–8, 88–9n1, 90n31, 112–29; censorship of 187–9; literary merit of 113, 115
Watanabe, Hamako 61, 64, 65
Watanabe, Junzō 187–8
Western art 201
Western films 133, 214
Western ideas 3, 16, 28, 29, 79, 93–4
Western music 59, 65, 70n4, 142–3; bans of 71n16; imports of 59
Western theater 22, 26, 27, 29
Westerners 26, 28; attending kabuki 16–17
Wheeler, F.L. 36, 52n1
White Rainbow Incident 191n9
Williams, Albert Rhys 40; *Through the Russian Revolution* 40
word-hunting 212, 219, 225
writing process 2, 129; and ideology 48

Yakusho, Kōji 220, 228n11
Yamamoto, Kajirō 135; *Horses* 135
Yamamoto, Satsuo 146
Yamamoto, Yūzō 79
Yamanaka, Minetarō 75
Yamane, Ginji 68, 71n14
Yamato 118
yamato-gokoro 78, 85–6, 90n18
Yamato race 78
Yasukuni Shrine 42, 62, 86, 191n5; emperor's visit 178
Yoda, Gakkai 25, 27, 32n20
Yokomitsu, Riichi 171n3
Yomiuri Independent Exhibition 197, 199, 204
Yoshida, Shin 67
Yoshikawa, Eiji 53n10, 54n17, 74, 88n1
Yoshimoto, Akimitsu 67, 71n20
Yoshimoto, Takaaki 116–18, 119, 121–3
Yoshiya, Nobuko 74, 75, 88n1, 89n4, 90n22
young girls' army 153, 157, 167, 170, 172n19
young men's associations 93, 97, 98; and red cells 98

Zahn, Robert 162–3, 164, 166

Taylor & Francis

eBooks
FOR LIBRARIES

ORDER YOUR FREE 30 DAY INSTITUTIONAL TRIAL TODAY!

Over 23,000 eBook titles in the Humanities, Social Sciences, STM and Law from some of the world's leading imprints.

Choose from a range of subject packages or create your own!

- ▶ Free MARC records
- ▶ COUNTER-compliant usage statistics
- ▶ Flexible purchase and pricing options

- ▶ Off-site, anytime access via Athens or referring URL
- ▶ Print or copy pages or chapters
- ▶ Full content search
- ▶ Bookmark, highlight and annotate text
- ▶ Access to thousands of pages of quality research at the click of a button

For more information, pricing enquiries or to order a free trial, contact your local online sales team.

UK and Rest of World: **online.sales@tandf.co.uk**

US, Canada and Latin America:
e-reference@taylorandfrancis.com

www.ebooksubscriptions.com

A flexible and dynamic resource for teaching, learning and research.